Universities
in the
Western World

Published in cooperation with

, The International Council on the Future
of the University
745 Fifth Avenue, New York
New York 10022

This book, which was made possible by a grant from the National Endowment for the Humanities, is the first in a series of publications which the ICFU is planning as part of its effort to explore the international dimensions of higher education. The International Council on the Future of the University is an organization of scholars from fifteen countries who are concerned with examining current problems and future possibilities for universities in modern industrialized countries.

Universities

in the

Western World

Edited by Paul Seabury

THE FREE PRESS
A Division of Macmillan Publishing Co., Inc.
NEW YORK
Collier Macmillan Publishers
LONDON

The Free Press
A Division of Macmillan Publishing Co., Inc.
866 Third Avenue, New York, N.Y. 10022

Collier Macmillan Canada, Ltd.

Library of Congress Catalog Card Number: 75–5235

Printed in the United States of America

printing number

1   2   3   4   5   6   7   8   9   10

Acknowledgment is made for use of the following material:

Hans Daalder, "The Dutch Universities between the 'New Democracy' and the 'New Management'," *Minerva*, Vol. 12, No. 2 (1974), reprinted by permission. *See p. 195.*

Charles Frankel, "Reflections on a Worn Out Model," *Daedalus*, Journal of the American Academy of Arts and Sciences, Boston, Massachusetts. *American Higher Education: Toward an Uncertain Future*, Vol. 1, Fall 1974, reprinted by permission. *See p. 279.*

Edward Shils, "The Academic Ethos Under Strain," *Minerva*, Vol. 13, No. 1 (1975), reprinted by permission. *See p. 16.*

Table 1, "Free University of Berlin Faculty Voting," adapted from Jürgen Domes and Armin Paul Frank, "Problems and Prospects of the Berlin Free University," *Minerva*, Vol. 13, No. 2 (1975). *See p. 136.*

Contents

Preface

In 1970, after half a decade of major university upheavals in Europe and America, a small group of scholars meeting in Norwich, England, established what was first known as the International Committee on the University Emergency; subsequently its name was changed to the International Council on the Future of the University. It was enlarged to include 150 members, drawn from Western European, North American, Japanese, and Australian universities. Those who founded ICUE shared a common concern that recent events had gravely threatened the freedom of learning and scholarship. The most conspicuous threat to such freedom was that universities would become political battlegrounds; that political forces would gain control, transforming them into ideological engines of doctrinal conformity; and that countervailing political forces might take reprisal by bulldozing the walls of learning to impose different conformist controls upon them. With politicization came also threats to the quality of scholarship and excellence, with the risk that major Western centers of learning would be irreparably gutted and leveled.

In recognizing such dangers, the original founders of the ICUE also recognized the concerns of an international community of scholars in the Western world, which would collectively be impoverished were any of its national components permanently debased. A major role which the International Council on the Future of the University has chosen today is that of alerting the academic community to new developments in any of its parts which portend major changes elsewhere; also it has chosen to serve as a permanent forum in which scholars might address their colleagues on philosophical aspects of higher education and learning.

In October 1973, the ICUE convened its first major conference of scholars in Venice, addressing the theme of the future of the university. Attended by more than 200 distinguished academic figures, its proceedings evoked widespread attention in both Europe and America.

The essays in this book (aside from two subsequent additions) originated as conference papers presented in Venice. In editing these, I have again been struck with the remarkable degree of commonality of issues and problems which cut across national and even continental divides. But it is the exposition of specific tendencies in national universities which gives this volume its greatest immediate value. Since the Venice conference occurred considerably after the militance and chaos of the 1960s had subsided, it afforded its participants a chance to assess the tendencies in their profession with an eye towards the future, not merely toward the urgencies of the present.

On behalf of the Board of Trustees of The International Council on the Future of the University, I wish to convey our appreciation to the several foundations which provided support for the conference. These include The Andrew W. Mellon Foundation and the Stiftung Volkswagenwerk which provided grants as well as the Cini Foundation which hosted the conference. We also wish to thank the National Endowment for the Humanities for providing funds enabling this book to be prepared.

In the preparation of this volume, I wish to single out particularly for special gratitude several collaborators who helped consummate it: Mr. Nicholas Farnham, director of the International Council on the Future of the University, whose work in planning the conference was indispensable to its success and to the appearance of this book; my wife, Marie-Anne Seabury, for her steady editorial hand and eye in preparing the final version; and Florence Myer, for her indefatigable and meticulous preparation of our final copy.

As editor, I wish to express the deep sense of grief shared by all of the steering committee of our international council at the untimely death of our colleague Alexander Bickel, whose essay appears in this volume. His magisterial qualities as constitutional lawyer reflect an abiding commitment to the highest ideals of scholarship in a free society, and to the necessary social conditions for their perpetuation.

PAUL SEABURY

Introduction

The world of scholarship and learning should be unitary. But the universities dedicated to it are not. In the Western world, universities have originated and matured according to unique circumstances of time and place. The individual form and content have depended greatly upon the special ways in which each related to its surrounding society.

Yet certain common qualities distinguish them from all other social institutions, including other educational institutions. They are centers of *higher* learning; their central functions purport to be the exclusive transmission of such learning and the advancement of knowledge. This unique character gives rise to an intrinsic dualism: they contain those who temporarily attend them in order to learn, and those who are in them vocationally in order to transmit and to advance learning. Students and faculty are thus their essential corporate components; and it is in the nature of the university that the two differ greatly in their relation to it. An indispensable social role of the university is to make possible a steady passage of students through it. As pilgrims, they traverse the uplands of learning and knowledge, in transit to careers and occupations beyond, in society at large. The university not only affords them temporary and intense exposure to higher and to specialized knowledge; it also finally certifies and attests to their acquired competence. The act of certification is not merely (as some would have it) the conferral of a privilege, or a "status ticket." It is also a signal of accomplishment and competence, so that extrauniversity institutions may later judge of known, acquired skills and manifested merits. Passage through the university confers upon them the rights of transit. To speak of the *status* of students then, in a strict sense, is absurd, for being a student means a through passage on the route to ultimate destinations. All who have completed this journey once were, if briefly, university students; this, *in order to* become something else.

In this respect, the transitory role of students in a university differs from that of its more permanent corporate body, the faculty. The profession of higher learning is an occupational one, as are all other professions. The special rights, privileges, and obligations of students and faculty arise from their differing activities. In Germany, the freedoms accruing to each have come to be known as *Lern freiheit* for students and *Lehr freiheit* for professional scholars. While each must be regarded as indispensable in its own way, the two are not the same, nor can they be regarded as equal. The activity and the justification of learning presume a condition of inequality which, for a student, is a transient but necessary way station. For the faculty, it is a permanent and necessary characteristic of the vocation itself.

A decade ago a book about higher education in Western societies would not have commenced with such basic, even banal, observations, nor subsequently highlighted them, as the following essays by an international group of scholars now do. Commotions and upheavals which commenced in the mid-1960s have served to elevate these commonplace questions to positions of fundamental importance.

There has always been an inevitable tension between the claims and pretensions of higher education, the demands and expectations of the state, and the influences of and tendencies of society in general. Although universities require minimal conditions of autonomy in order to perform their unique responsibilities, they cannot in fact be insulated from society, or from the state, which since the nineteenth century has been their principal benefactor in both Europe and North America. The history of American higher education, for example, suffices to show the continuing interplay and friction between the autonomy of higher learning and the pragmatic demands originating outside the university, insistent that the university take up tasks deemed beneficial, either to society at large, or to important sectors of society.

The acceptance of such tasks by universities poses acute dilemmas time and again. The "free" advancement of learning and scholarship requires the encouragement of both intellectual spontaneity and inner-directedness in research and scholarship. But the expectation that the university justify itself by accepting social responsibilities, however defined, places limits upon such free play of the intellect and the autonomous work instinct. This has notably been true, for more than a century, in the experience of great state universities in the United States. Their vigor and dynamism, as well as the strong public support afforded them, can be attributed to their responsiveness to demands of a democratic society that they educate the meritorious and qualified sons and daughters of all strata of society. However imperfectly American universities have fulfilled this task in the past, the American pretension to do so came to prove highly infectious elsewhere. This democratic example and ideal for higher education is today generally accepted in most advanced Western societies as a responsibility of both university and government.

However complex the reasons for widespread university unrest, commotion, and violence in recent years, clearly these troubles have been directly related to authentic, if often hypocritical, demands that universities actively and positively respond to asserted needs of society at large. They have been particularly connected to strong, emotive demands for equality and equalization within the university. In a sense there is nothing novel in this—at least in America. What *has* been novel is both the extraordinary intensity of such demands and the fact that these have arisen for the most part from *within* the university. The secular university, which now commands unheard-of prestige among Western institutions, became the principal focal point for reformist zeal in the 1960s. The university has been designated, in some quarters, not so much as an *agency* of such reform as its principal locus and instigator.

There is a certain paradox entailed in this, in that simultaneously universities have also become more dependent than ever on the benign support of the state. As Clark Kerr has warned, universities—including even private ones—have become "public utilities." It would now be difficult to see how this could be otherwise, given the willingness of taxpayers and legislators to fuel the resources of universities. This has not been done simply to reward and honor higher learning for its demonstrated accomplishments. It has been done as part of a mutual understanding that universities perform certain assigned and accepted tasks. Included chiefly among these has been that of educating large, even vast, numbers of students. Nevertheless, the fact remains that the quest for the zealous university, with all that this may imply for the future of *higher* education, entails a self-arrogated role to the university ultimately incompatible with its principle tasks of learning. In a secular age, the social gospel movement poses as grave a threat to the unique functions of advanced learning as in an earlier era a similar movement posed a threat to the central, abiding role of the church. In each instance, an institution risks the loss, and betrayal, of its central essential function and justification, as it shifts its attention to other purposes. If fundamental misunderstandings spread, both within and outside, about the mission of the university, its essential nature could be wholly debased.

Universities
in the
Western World

PART 1
UNIVERSAL PERSPECTIVES

The Aims of Education and the Proper Standards of the University

Alexander M. Bickel

ALL OF US must bear wounds inflicted by life in the universities of the Western world during the decade of the 1960s. So do our institutions. Some of our wounds are grave, some less so. None I believe were superficial, though few if any were fatal, perhaps because in so many instances they were self-inflicted, or at least inflicted upon us as consenting adults.

But we need not commiserate with each other. And we must not celebrate the peace—at any rate, the external peace—that in this new decade has descended on many of our institutions. The words emergency and crisis still fit prevailing conditions, even if often in less obvious ways than before. It behooves us, therefore, to reexamine what Justice Holmes used to call our "can't helps," the very foundations of our conduct. For they have been questioned, radically and violently, and we shall not solve our crisis, indeed we shall not survive it, unless we can answer for them.

With good cause, but not without difficulty, our societies have by and large been persuaded to the belief that knowledge and insight, like art, are the products of independent minds following each its own bent, and will not often be attained otherwise. That is why we value the freedom of qualified men and women to pursue self-directed work. Universities are places where professionals of many disciplines can follow lines of inquiry determined by themselves, individually and collegially, and not dictated by anyone else, on either ideological or practical grounds.

Not all universities, and certainly not all colleges, pretend to be such places, and different sorts of institutions—research institutes and "think tanks" of one and another variety—can be. But only in a university can inquiry and teaching constitute one creative whole, so that the knowledge and insight of the scholar and the methods by which he gained them are shared with the student; so that students may be the scholar's company, nourishing him, giving as well as taking—in a word, collaborating. To this end, teachers must be free to teach—as free in their teaching as in their scholarship—and the enterprise must be judged by professional criteria and none other. The twin freedoms of inquiry and of teaching are best secured by faculty self-rule in matters of appointments, curriculum, and academic standards.

No one will claim that the ideal university exists, or that all members of all faculties are intent on independent intellectual labors. But we will make no closer approach to the ideal by compromising it. We will collect no more of the kind of people the ideal calls for, and allow no more of them to function as they should, if we let avowedly nonprofessional and nonintellectual criteria play a role in their recruitment, or in prescribing their activities.

To be sure, the young as well as society at large have their own perceptions—which may not coincide with a faculty's intellectual interests—of the skills the young should be trained in, and of the information that should be transmitted to them. Academic freedom is limited, as the universities pay their way by meeting the felt needs of their clients, which change over time. Society has an instrument at its disposal for bringing its needs home to the university. It is the market, inside the university and out, and over time it is quite effective in the aggregate. Students vote with their feet, choosing the university they prefer and then, within it, accepting or rejecting parts of the elective curriculum; their parents vote with their pocketbooks. The curriculum of every university is witness to that.

Nevertheless, like many other institutions, universities are seen to be sluggish in times of rapid change. One way to counteract sluggishness is to engage students in the professional decision-making process by putting them on committees, and giving them access to some, though not to all, faculty deliberations. Students are that part of the larger society which is most easily accessible to the university, and they are, in a sense and for a brief time, most immediately concerned, even if they are by no means alone in their concern.

But the university as practical servant of the society can all too readily swallow up the university as haven of independent inquiry; and it would do so, to the ultimate detriment, of course, of the society itself, if students were given a decisive voice in setting the curriculum, or otherwise directing the intellectual life of the university, just as if alumni, or government, or churches, or labor unions, or business, or professional associations were given such a voice.

The disruptive tactics of some students have at times amounted to the assumption of control in faculty decision making, and they are not to be tolerated for this fundamental reason, as well as for other more obvious ones. But whatever the tactics of students, even if they are entirely civil, and however embarrassingly unfashionable it may be to insist on power and privilege, administrators and faculties should realize that inroads on the autonomy of the latter are inroads on academic freedom; abandonment of faculty control, or any part of it, over appointments, curriculum, and academic standards is the abandonment of the ends of the university.

But the ends of the university, we have been told by those who have questioned the foundations of our conduct, and the methods and structures designed to attain the ends of the university—all are political. And politically, we were told, our ends and our methods are wrong, or at least unacceptable or undesirable. Hence a different set of political objectives and means must—by means themselves political—be substituted for those we have avowed and practiced. This charge against the university and this effort to transform it require close analysis.

There is an extended sense of the term in which, it may be admitted, the university is politically involved. We are committed to freedom of inquiry, to the method of reason, however fallible. We are agnostic, and we are neutral to a degree. Now, from certain vantage points, reason, agnosticism, neutrality can be seen as a political position. To the activist—of the left or of the right—intent on the attainment of immediate social ends, which he conceives as moral imperatives, the activist who will say, "no thought without action," we appear politically committed to the other side, to a position which at the very least allows the commitments of the activist to be questioned. Ours is a position that is likely in practice to result in an attitude of gradualism as compared to one of absolute activism. We are committed, in short, to thought without action, and to thought which may oppose action. It had as well be conceded that a neutrality proceeding from such a commitment has practical political consequences, and that it can, therefore, in a sense be viewed as constituting a political position. Not for nothing did Hermann Goering say: "When I hear the word culture, I reach for my gun." A brilliant young leftist radical writer in the United States a few years ago put it his own way. Morality, he said (and he could as well have added reason, too), is what comes out of the barrel of a gun.

There is an analogy between the agnosticism and neutrality of the university and the agnosticism and neutrality of the free, secular public school in the United States and elsewhere. The public school does not appear neutral to people who believe that primary education ought to have a moral content, and who are certain that the revealed truth of religion describes the proper moral content that primary education ought to have.

There is an analogy as well to courts of law and to the attitudes of some radicals toward them. Again we have an institution the essence of which is a lack of political involvement—neutrality. Yet the essence of the institution is also the deepest sort of commitment to the judicial process and to the process of law—deliberate, gradual, consensual, responsive ultimately to majorities but not to plebiscites, and limited as to means. This is a commitment to one political position as opposed to another.

The analogy to courts suggests also that, somewhat like courts, universities and professional and scholarly organizations are institutions of the existing order. They are special institutions with special functions. Their particular functions include questioning their own premises and those of other institutions and of the society itself, and entertaining ideas subversive of the society. But nonetheless these are institutions of the existing order, supported by it. There is necessarily an implicit bias towards the society's basic presuppositions, an implicit allegiance to the minimal principles and structures that tend towards preservation of the society in recognizable form.

This is a political bias, even if it consists of no more than a presumption in favor of no more than the ideals professed by the existing order. The bias is of course clearer with courts than with universities and like institutions. Judges do not take an oath to humanity at large, or to follow their own consciences; they take an oath to support the law, and in our country the Constitution of the United States, which has some political meaning. Universities are not as explicitly committed, and certainly private universities are not. But I indicated earlier that their freedom to pursue their own ends without prior commitment is limited by the market—the existing, if evolving, market—inside the university and outside it. I said it earlier to suggest that those who demand change and response and adjustment to their felt needs on the part of the university will ultimately and gradually, if there are enough of them, and if they can sustain their desires, have their way in some measure. I make the point now that if we look at the university as of any moment, as of this moment, we find it dependent on the society that harbors it.

It is difficult to imagine that public or even private funds do not come to universities on the tacit assumption of some sort of vague institutional allegiance to the regime. There can be and there most often has been absolutely unlimited freedom of inquiry and freedom of radical opinion within such a vague assumption of institutional acceptance of the legitimacy of the regime—and there is freedom to rest and support private institutions on the contrary assumption. But it is difficult to accept that the major institutions which require substantial support from the society can realistically be viewed as not resting on an assumption of generalized allegiance to it.

Political involvement in these extended senses of the terms is as defensible as it is ineluctable. And it is fully consistent with freedom of inquiry, and with the absence of political involvement in other, more specific senses. Of course, the specific sort of political involvement has also been known to occur in some institutions, particularlly in public ones, but that is no good reason for urging it on other institutions now.

What has more recently been asked of universities is a measure of ideological, policy commitment, an active engagement with immediate social and economic problems, to be manifested by espousing, and by putting institutional resources into effectuating, specific cures for the ills of society, by undertaking institutional commitments to specific policies and their practical implementation. This is quite something else again.

A variety of consequences and problems may be foreseen. If a man joins a legislature or a court, he expects to—and it is expected that he will—take individual positions which are clearly distinguished from institutional positions. His votes are recorded and publicized, and he is nowhere identified automatically with the positions of his institution. University populations, student, faculty and other, are so large, however, that it is impossible to expect individual positions to be adequately maintainable as separate from institutional ones. It is difficult to see how an economist— not necessarily the famous man, just an economist—who thinks minimum wage laws are foolish and bad can maintain his identity in an institution that favors minimum wage laws, or how a non-Marxist can maintain his identity in a Marxist institution. The upshot must be that faculty and students and others will sort themselves out among various institutions on political grounds, and that the institutions will become monolithic. The consequences for free inquiry and for the exchange of ideas are obvious. Everyone will be preaching to the converted. Solidarity rather than diversity will be at a premium.

Moreover, an institution politically involved in the sense that it has a commitment to one or another political end will hardly avoid committing its resources to that end. Its resources are largely human, and the institution will try to induce and finally to force its members to devote themselves to the attainment of the end to which the institution is committed. That is the death not merely of diversity and exchange of ideas, but of free inquiry altogether. It need not follow, some will say, and some departments of learning (classics?) will not be touched (if allowed to survive) but, in the last analysis, what else can be intended by demands for political involvement, and even if not intended, how can it be avoided? If an institution has a political objective, how can it not mobilize itself to attain it, and if it bends its efforts to that end, how will it regard the shirker or oppositionist in its midst and on its payroll?

The prospect, however, is not only of the loss of diversity and of the imposition of severe limits on free inquiry. The prospect is a good deal worse even than that. It is of the loss of intellectual quality, and ultimately of content. Institutions that serve political ends will use effectiveness in the service of those ends as a standard for judging members. They will begin by diluting and end by abandoning intellectual standards. Not only faculty but student recruitment would be inevitably affected. Four years ago, Tillman Durdin reported from Hong Kong in the *New York Times* (September 25, 1970) on the reopening—after years of cultural revolution —of Chinese universities:

> The admission process . . . of the universities [has] been radically revised according to directives of Mao Tse-tung, putting class background ahead of academic achievement. . . . Students were selected as meritorious workers, soldiers and peasants after repeated discussion among the masses.

Many of those selected . . . have meager intellectual qualifications but rate highly in proletarian credentials.

Last summer Mr. Durdin and a visiting Australian-American academic, Professor Ross Terrill, reported some backsliding in Chinese universities. But it was mostly covert, and it was only backsliding. Here and there, college entrance examinations covering intellectual subject matter had re-appeared. Not under their proper and despised name, however. They were called, with touching disingenuousness, "investigations of cultural knowledge," and if an applicant was rejected because he had failed the "investigation," the university had to explain and justify the rejection—which, says Professor Terrill, makes it hard (*New York Times*, August 13, 1973).

Without suggesting too close an analogy to the Chinese experience, this is the logical place to note that American universities have been sub-jected—and many have in varying measures succumbed—to political pres-sures for the dilution and even abandonment of intellectual standards in the recruitment of faculty and students from certain minority groups, including women, who are assuredly no minority in the population at large. Now the problem is complex. The groups in question have certainly been disadvantaged in the past, and an effort to recruit them and open opportunities to them is called for. Moreover, our admissions tests are—sometimes and to a degree—not tests of capacity only, not even sure in-dicators of performance in the university environment, but, in the words of the Chinese euphemism, "investigations of cultural knowledge." They are, I mean to say, sometimes and to a degree class bound, and framed not in terms of the culture in a large sense but in terms of the culture of a given dominant group. To the extent that this is true, they test not merely for capacity but for a given background which may not be relevant to capacity, and candidates may fail them not because they lack relevant capacity, but because they lack irrelevant background. To the extent that this is true, we are under an obligation in the universities, as best we know how (and we do not know how very well), to try to test for true capacity when we deal with members of groups which have not in the past had full access to the dominant culture. We must not forget that culture in a larger sense is what we aim to transmit and what our students must work and achieve in, but we should try to transcend parochial standards within the culture and seek, uncover, and give a fair chance to true capacity.

We in the United States have not done this very well, and have often yielded instead to pressures to simply relax our standards—not to seek in different and more suitable ways to assess capacity that goes undetected by our usual tests, but to apply our usual tests and lower the standard of performance in deference to race or sex. And this—a political concession—is wrong.

The dilution of standards in the university as a whole, administrators and faculties have told themselves, is not serious if the number of those recruited as faculty and students is kept low in proportion to total numbers. The solution, in other words, is the quota, the *numerus clausus*, by whatever name it may be called, or by whatever euphemism disguised. But the cost to the university and to the society is serious. There is a cost in loss of efficiency and productivity—in the university immediately and in business and the professions later on—from which no one benefits. And there is a cost in injustice. For a quota is a two-edged device. For everyone it includes, it excludes someone else, and we are not wise enough to administer the exclusions justly, even assuming the justice and wisdom of our inclusions, which I do not. Standards and their impersonal application —free of group as well as personal prejudices—guard us against our inevitable tendency towards injustice, I would say our human appetite for injustice, well meaning and no less than ill intentioned. Man is born to injustice in another sense, no doubt, divine injustice, the injustice of unequally distributed endowments. I think the teaching of our tradition is that the only way to avoid adding the crueler injustice of man himself to that of the cosmos is to accept the latter in its irreducible form. Especially since it is just to all men to enrich the material and spiritual life of all, and only human capacity can do that.

I come to another cost of politicizing the university—by pressing on it commitments and missions. I approach this point with caution because the university is not a church. Its members are no priesthood, they are not even any sort of political elite whose judgment on affairs is particularly acute and worth heeding. On the whole, I think the contrary is true. John Roche, exhibiting his Irish wit, has said that the average university faculty is not fit to organize a two-car funeral, and I think that is true. And yet, though not priests or philosopher-kings, scholars often bring a valuable detachment to affairs. There is all too little in the way of information and opinion entering the universe of political discourse with the credit that attaches to disinterestedness. Much of what there is comes from academic and professional persons, whose credentials are certified by universities or other professional and scholarly organizations, known to be certified in accordance with neutral standards, rather than under the influence of political objectives. Persons so certified then speak with a certain moral authority, and inject into the political process something that it has difficulty generating itself—dispassionate, informed, disinterested judgment, which looks beyond the interests and objectives immediately engaged in the debate on any given issue. If the accrediting institutions, so to call them, themselves become politically engaged, their accreditation loses its value, and society will be the poorer. Disinterested judgment may still be exercised by scholars and the like, but it will have lost much of its moral authority and much of its credit.

It is as if people were to assume that judges decide on the basis of personal predilection, class interest, or political affiliation. No one of course can step altogether out of himself but there is a category of men, including judges, who make the effort, to whom we assign the role of making the effort. There have always been those who have maintained that the whole thing is a sham, that nobody really plays any such role. If that were so, it would be as well to be candid about it. For those who believe that the whole thing is a sham, political involvement on the part of universities and like organizations constitutes being candid. But in truth the role can be played and is a valuable one and, if that is so, then political involvement on the part of universities and like organizations constitutes a wanton abandonment of it.

Such consequences, to be sure, do not come about all at once. Probably nothing fundamental occurs if a university board of trustees or a university faculty votes by a preponderant majority to commit itself to one or another political cause. The effect is cumulative. The consequences follow over time from many actions in the aggregate. Hence it has been urged that a faculty or a board of trustees of the annual meeting of a professional association can permit itself to vote on a critical issue of fundamental moral importance, an issue of the sort that does not arise every other day—for example, in the United States, the Vietnam War. Yet, while issues of seemingly fundamental moral importance do not arise every other day for everyone, they arise every day for someone, and these days for increasing numbers of people. And it will have to be a majority each time which decides the jurisdictional issue, so to speak, as well as the substantive one —which decides both whether a given issue is of such fundamental moral importance as to call for taking a position, and what that position should be.

One may concede that, within the confines of any given culture, some rare ultimate issues would be almost universally viewed as highly exceptional and of overriding moral significance. Even then, however, one is entitled to ask what would be gained by taking an institutional position as opposed to the quite customary taking of individual positions in large groups, which often constitute the overwhelming majority of institutional membership. All the institution can do that individuals cannot is in some sense to put its function on the line, to close its doors, or something of the sort, or else, over the longer run, commit its resources. But is enough gained by that? The point is that if exceptions are conceded for institutional political involvement on certain issues of the greatest magnitude, the danger of sliding into a continuous course of political involvement on all sorts of issues is all too great.

The Scranton Commission, appointed by President Nixon in 1970 to study the causes of student unrest, enjoined universities to "remain politically neutral, except in those rare cases in which their own integrity, educational purpose or preservation are at stake." It is not altogether clear what this means, but perhaps it brings us back to the notion that universities are after all committed to a set of basic values and processes, and when those values and processes are in question, they should act in their defense. The commitment, among other things, is to political neutrality. The Scranton Commission was saying that political involvement is justified only when necessary to resist such pressures from outside. And this is the sort of political involvement that the German universities in the 1930s failed to undertake. They did not resist being pushed into political involvement; that was their sin. We have been urged to sin in quite the opposite direction, and will hopefully resist.

Freedom and Equality in the Universities

Søren Egerod

FREEDOM AND EQUALITY—*liberté et égalité*—do we agree what they mean?

Intellectual, personal, and economic freedoms, and freedom from evil, are semantically related but not necessarily interdependent concepts. Equal rights, equal opportunity, equal results are not the same. Equal input does not guarantee equal output. Leveling and regimentation are negative sides of equality and do not follow from all definitions of equality.

It has been known since the French Revolution that freedom and equality can be abused to suppress each other. Fraternity is the forgotten mediator. Freedom and equality must, by explicit political action, be delimited in relation to each other.

Traditionally, academic freedom has been primarily the right of the teacher to present his views without interference or fear of persecution from inside or outside the university. But freedom within the university also involves the right of the scholar to control his research and publish his results, as well as freedom for scholarly bodies or the institution as such to publish opinions and criticism, even of the state, and even if the state is its sponsor. Academic freedom for students, though equally important, has not been stressed as much as for teachers.

Academic freedom is not a special privilege in a society in which individual and personal freedom is otherwise not suppressed; but its curtailment is a specific act of discrimination against one sector of society.

The demands raised in the name of equality in different universities and societies have been of a very uneven nature: equal influence of all academic personnel (teachers, researchers, students) on all academic matters; equal influence of all academic personnel on all university matters, whether academic or nonacademic; equal influence of all university personnel, whether academic or nonacademic, on all university matters; equal access of all persons to university studies irrespective of academic and nonacademic factors; equal rights of all persons to continue such studies for the prescribed number of years irrespective of measurable academic achievements; equal rights of all persons leaving the university to employment, irrespective of academic achievements; equal rights of all persons to teach in the universities irrespective of nonacademic factors and irrespective of academic achievements.

12

Traditionally, in the university context, freedom has been stressed above equality. False concepts of equality have deemphasized freedom. Most places have conceded to some of the demands outlined above, a few to all of them. This power struggle is counterproductive. Those who feel they are controlled want to control. A permanent crisis has been built into many university constitutions.

In the political university, teaching, research, and appointments have become "unfree." Studying is defined as political action. But Marxism cannot monopolize progress. Collective efforts have been stressed in study and research in the name of teamwork spirit, efficiency, and unselfishness. In case after case the individual has found himself intellectually and politically in a position of inequality.

The lower standard and the decrease in scholarly results are a consequence not only of the time-consuming bureaucracy of the divided university, but also of the direct control exercised by pressure groups mutually. Research projects have suffered most, but teaching programs are affected too. The universities have already lost much of their institutional freedom and self-government. In some cases state interference has been clearly necessary; in others the crisis provided a convenient excuse for interference.

Many danger signs can already be seen heralding a fascist reaction to the university with its unresolved internal struggles and its one-sided politicization.

In the demands for change there has been such a mixture of causes and motives involved that it has been very difficult for the general public to form any opinion as to right and wrong, but increased awareness of social injustice and abuse of freedom in other sectors of society explains a certain initial prejudice against the institutions of learning. Reasonable and unreasonable claims have come from students, teachers, and politicians alike, and action has been taken by some of them as well as by professional revolutionaries and paid troublemakers. No clear definition of equality has emerged.

What should be done about it?

The university cannot go it alone. Even if adherents to free teaching and research within the university should regain some of their lost influence this will in most countries not be enough to reverse the trend. Society has to be convinced of the validity of these goals before the totalitarian trends can be halted, let alone reversed. The university must not turn its back on positive change in society and must not lose all initiative in bringing about such change.

Society demands that more people must be educated. If the university fails to grasp the importance of this demand, initiative and funding will be removed from the university. The dispensing of facts is no longer the most important part of teaching. Academic methodology and a creative and visionary outlook are the goals of education. Therefore, a narrow job orientation in the old European style no longer suffices. The creation of an academic proletariat must be avoided.

A narrow view of relevance of studies has played into the hands of those who want to curtail free teaching and research. There are no short-cuts to the gaining of knowledge; results of scholarship dealing with remote times and peoples throw light on human psychology, the ultimate motivations of man, the history of mankind. A general education in less job-oriented programs and in smaller schools will in itself help to instill feelings of relevance and combat the dropout psychology, which is but another side of the same crisis.

Just as society must solve the problem of the dehumanized bigness of factories and housing units, the universities must reverse the trend and move away from multiversities to manageable schools with a place for the individual.

Universities and scholars must give up outdated privileges and false symbols, but stand firm on essentials. Standards must be maintained, and the individual must not be downgraded. A totalitarian point of view is neither a necessary nor an adequate solution to the crisis.

From a global viewpoint the pedagogical reforms move in all directions—towards greater rigidity of teaching in some places, towards general relaxation of rules and regulations in others. This is not necessarily a part of the university crisis. But the tendency to separate teaching from research and to create special research academies outside of the university is a last-ditch defense of research against control of nonresearchers and nonacademics. The lifeline from research to teaching must not be cut.

Total freedom is utopian, just as total equality is utopian. The concept of one-man-one-vote does not work in the university. There must be some consideration of competence. Scholars must be responsible for continuity in their fields of competence. Numbers must not negate all consideration of skill. The acquisition of competence and the stress on quality is what the university is all about.

There can, however, be some expansion of freedom, and there can be some expansion of equality. Academic freedom should be available to all members of the academic community, including students, at all levels. Some instances of abuse are no argument against such freedom; this is the calculated risk of remaining free, and not only in the university. Increased influence of all university people, academic and nonacademic, on their own work and within their own sphere of competence is a natural development. One-sided yielding of power to academic or non-academic personnel on matters totally outside their competence is a simple instance of thwarted political pressure, and perversion of the democratic process.

Society must create the kind of university it needs, and must itself live up to the standards of the university it creates. Universities are a good index of national health, and what is good for the university is good for the nation.

The Academic Ethos Under Strain

Edward Shils

I

THE DECADE before World War II began was a very hard time for universities. The worldwide economic depression affected universities as it had all other institutions. In Great Britain, perhaps least injured, universities did not recruit many young members to their teaching staffs, though already established teachers were not loosened from their moorings. A small number became Communists or supporters of communism, but they did not attempt to impel universities towards their own political objectives. Under the dominion of an ungenerous ministerial bureaucracy, French universities carried on in a humdrum way. Graduates were finding jobs hard to get, and teachers were becoming somewhat more radical politically. Nonetheless, French academics retained their traditional view that teaching was a chore, supervising dissertations was ordinary, and that best of all was to do scientific or scholarly research. In the United States universities were more sorely affected. Salaries were reduced; there were few new appointments; and in the middle of the depression the student body contracted slightly. But there were no novel conceptions of the academic calling: it was, as in the past, a life to be spent among books or in scientific laboratories and among young students. The radicalism of a few younger teachers in New York, Wisconsin, and California did not attenuate devotion to learning in the sense which that idea had acquired in the course of the movement from the study of the Bible to the study of history and nature.

In Germany universities were struck by a catastrophe. A large proportion of the teaching staff was dismissed on ethnic grounds; the student body declined from 124,500 in 1931 to 85,000 in 1935. New appointments were made in the light of political and ethnic criteria and many teachers trumpeted Nazi phrases which were the antithesis of scholarship and which flattered the prejudices of their politicized students. Non-Nazis who survived this carried on silently in an atmosphere in which Nazi leaders did not conceal their animosity towards the universities. In Italy (where universities had already been afflicted by the requirement of the oath of loyalty to the Fascist regime at the end of the 1920s) the depression and the racial laws of 1938 had effects resembling those in Germany; distinguished scholars, both young ones and those already established, had to go into exile. Some time-servers were appointed; others just carried on. (Yet in Rome, in the 1920s and until 1938, physics had an extraordinarily fruitful existence.) Spanish universities had been lagging far behind Great Britain, Germany, and France for some time; the Civil War set them still further back—disrupting studies, driving many teachers into exile, and depressing the mood of those who survived. Spain became even more of an academic backwater than it had been before, and the morale of its academics declined accordingly.

The war years accentuated the trend of the depression. In all the combatant countries, conscription of young men reduced student bodies drastically. Teaching staffs, already attenuated by the financial stringency of the 1930s, were now depleted by the demands of military and civilian governmental service. Buildings deteriorated; in Germany, and to a lesser extent in Great Britain, many were destroyed by enemy military action.

Nonetheless, powerful academic traditions in Great Britain and the United States showed great hardiness. The universities remained productive centers of scientific and scholarly knowledge during war years, just as they had during the depression. The natural sciences (with modest needs for physical equipment) had flourished even during the depression. The United States had already advanced to become an important center in the natural and social sciences in the 1920s; the increment of displaced Germans and Italians, together with the active part played by private philanthropic foundations, led to a further access of creative power and brought the United States into the front rank of these sciences by the time that country entered the war. World War II, although it deprived scientists of the students, brought them an unprecedented material prosperity and increased their confidence in the profession to which they had committed themselves. The sciences prospered intellectually, although for a time in secrecy.

In the humanistic and social science subjects, the tradition of nineteenth-century humanistic erudition prevailed. Research was still largely conducted in the style of a handicraft, and it could be under conditions of relative adversity, as long as there was a will to do it. It was done by scholars who had been appointed as university teachers, and the additional sums needed for such research were not large. To the extent that humanistic scholars were not drawn into the service of the war (and although they, too, lost their students) they continued to work in a number of countries. In the occupied countries, material hardship and Nazi oppression placed a great strain on scholarship—some great scholars were killed in concentration camps or were executed by German soldiers, or they were arrested—but it was not extinguished. In the Axis countries, the brutal repressiveness of the regimes joined the material hardship of life in rendering scholarship more difficult. But there, too, it flickered on faintly and it proved more difficult to revive in more favorable times.

Valuable work was done in sociology, political science, economics, and anthropology in the United States and Great Britain during the depression. Historiography flourished in these countries, too, and especially also in France and the Netherlands. The war gave much encouragement to the social scientists of the United States and Great Britain. Many were able to do research of a sort which would have been out of the question in the preceding decade, and many ideas germinated in governmental and military service to flourish in the open after the war.

II

Universities were generally esteemed during both depression and wartime in the United States and Great Britain, as well as in the smaller democratic countries of Western Europe. They were considered to be among the important institutions of their respective societies, as were the church, the army, the higher civil service, the judiciary, and private business enterprise. They were regarded as being approximately of the same order of merit, but no more so.

The respect which the universities received was accorded to them on the grounds of their dispassionate concern for truth, the contribution which they made to national well-being by training young persons for the practice of important learned professions, and their scientific and scholarly accomplishments in behalf of their respective national societies. Even before the war Western countries saw universities as sources of the kind of knowledge which improved the life of man by protecting his health and improving his standard of living through the increase of the productivity of industry and agriculture. In wartime, their capacity to contribute to military technology made them even more appreciated. This was especially so in the United States where the state universities and engineering schools traditionally had been expected to concern themselves with matters of immediate practical importance.

In the United States, there was an approximate consensus between the expectations of the more serious parts of the lay public—state legislators interested in higher education, members of the classes whence came the private patrons of higher education, more serious publicists—and the beliefs of academics about what academic life should be about. The situation was similar in Great Britain, although there was less concern with the immediate services which universities could provide for industry and government. Even the experiences of World War II did not fundamentally change these attitudes in the laity or in the academic profession.

In France, in the quarter century which followed the end of World War II, the universities were viewed grudgingly by civil servants and legislators. Little seems to have been expected of them except that they should qualify young persons for the professions and for the middle ranks of the civil service. Academics had a correspondingly unexalted conception of their role. The intellectual traditions of the *Collège de France*, the *Ecole normale*, the *Ecole pratique des hautes études*, and the Sorbonne carried with them a sense of obligation to live up to the highest standards in research and in advanced teaching. Generally, in the Western countries, the tasks of teaching were taken as an inevitable and unquestionable part of the profession of learning. Special attention was given to training postgraduate students and those in certain professional schools.

In Germany the twelve years of Nazi rule shook the self-esteem of the universities very badly. The Nazi government, unlike previous German governments, did not take universities seriously. Although many German university teachers had welcomed the Nazis after hating the republican regime, the Nazis did not reward them. They appointed unworthy men of no scholarly or scientific accomplishments to leading positions. The decent Germans who remained in German universities were humiliated by their own acquiescence and by the indignities represented by Nazi appointees and policies. These good men in a wicked state did not lose their love of learning, but they felt ashamed of themselves as Germans and as once proud professors. They had no sense of affinity with their students who were by and large permeated by the anti-intellectual outlook of national socialism. They saw no *Nachwuchs* in sight.

In Western countries which did not live under totalitarian or authoritarian rule, it was generally thought that the high status of the members of universities entitled them to freedom to pursue truth in accordance with the rules and traditions of their various disciplines and institutions; indeed, freedom was deemed to be integral to the effective performance of their calling. It was also thought that they should also enjoy the same freedom of political action which was the right of citizens in a liberal and democratic society; in most Western countries it was generally believed that even the radical political views of a university teacher, as long as they did not intrude into his teaching, should not affect his appointment or promotion.

Academics were jealous of their rights, but they were not often courageous in defending the rights or academic freedom of their colleagues who had been deprived of them. The academic profession in Great Britain was probably not only the freest from external intrusion, but it was probably also the freest from internal restrictions on the application of strictly intellectual and academic criteria in appointments. In Germany, where the literature on academic freedom was greatest in quantity and elaboration and where there was great insistence by members of the academic profession that once habilitated or appointed they must be free of external intervention, academics also were not very zealous in defending the rights of those whose freedom was in fact infringed upon.[1]

---

[1] See Max Weber, *On Universities: The Power of the State and the Dignity of the Academic Calling in Imperial Germany* (Chicago: University of Chicago Press, 1974).

In Germany before 1918, unlike Great Britain, Sweden, France, and Italy, it was rare for socialists to obtain university appointments. Within these restrictions those who were appointed enjoyed, and were aware that they enjoyed, the prerogative of *Lehrfreiheit*. Despite some striking infringements on academic freedom, as in the Gumbel case in Heidelberg,[2] the Lessing case in Hannover,[3] and a number of others,[4] in which the academic profession and not government was at fault, there was a general observance of the standard during the Weimar Republic. Affronts against academic freedom in the Weimar period arose mainly from teaching staffs which gave preeminence to political and ethnic criteria of assessment on these and other occasions. Even the reactionary professors who mourned for the Wilhelmian Reich and who hated the liberal, democratic republic, were staunch in their devotion to the older idea of the professorially ruled university. Indeed, one of their (unjust) charges against the republic was that the new regime was destroying the old university and degrading its dignity. Nonetheless, the academic ethos was weakened by the political, partisan, and ethnic shift of many German scholars and scientists. As soon as the National Socialists acceded to power, this traditional standard was replaced by one which was practically its diametrical opposite, a replacement which was, moreover, appreciated widely in the German academic community. As in Germany, in Italy the fascist government replaced a regime which showed a very high degree of respect for academic freedom by one which, as the years passed, came closer and closer to the practices of National Socialist Germany. Even before the alliance with Nazi Germany, Carlo and Nello Rosselli were persecuted—they were later murdered. Gaetano Solvemini and Giuseppi Borgese were forced to retire from Italian academic life. An oath of allegiance to fascism was required to which many yielded unwillingly and many others eagerly.

In the United States academic freedom, particularly in major private universities, was generally very far reaching and respected in the 1930s and during the war. Nonetheless, even in some of the most distinguished state universities the principle of freedom of university teachers in their civil role was, on various occasions, under assault from state legislatures and from civic bodies, as well as from influential—especially wealthy—individuals. Within universities which were from time to time afflicted there was no doubt that such political intrusions were wrong and there was much resentment. On the whole, however, during this period academic freedom and the freedom of

[2] E. J. Gumbel was a statistician who published several important works on political violence; as a result, he was persecuted by nationalistic colleagues and students and censured by the philosophical faculty of the university. He was later dismissed.

[3] Theodor Lessing was a teacher of philosophy at the Technical College of Hannover. He wrote disparagingly of Field Marshal Hindenburg and was transferred to a research post in consequence of the protests of nationalistic students.

[4] These included the censure by the academic senate of George Friedrich Nicolas, a pacifist who was assistant professor of medicine in Berlin, and Hermann Kantorowicz, an eminent teacher of law in Freiburg who criticized the tradition of Bismarck.

the university teacher, as a citizen outside the academic sphere, increased: some of this improvement may be attributed to the complex combination of an enhancement of public esteem for the academic profession and the correspondingly heightened self-esteem which was engendered by its considerable accomplishments since the beginning of the century.

In Switzerland and in Scandinavia and the Low Countries academic freedom was very seldom infringed. University teachers were respected; they were enabled to go about their business with practically negligible external interference, within the framework of their own charters, or of charters which, although laid down for them by the state, recognized the autonomy of the university in governing itself and the academic freedom of its members to teach and do research according to their best lights. The high status of the university teacher was acknowledged by the lay public and taken for granted by academics. In France, too, despite the high degree of centralization of governmental control, the academic and civil freedom of university teachers was firmly established and immune from questioning.

In all the Western countries (excluding the totalitarian and authoritarian countries) there was never any doubt within the universities about the definition of the fundamental and permanent tasks of universities and the obligations of academics. It was to teach the best that was known as a result of dispassionate and zealous study and to pursue new truths in the most scrupulous manner. By doing so, university teachers believed that they had a vital role in national life. This view was shared by influential parts of the public at large; it was recognized that they enriched the national culture, contributed to national prestige, supplied trained young persons to the professions, and supplied knowledge which improved health and wealth. To teach in a university or college was thought by those who did it to be following an honorable and esteemed career. To attend a university was thought by many of the students to be a privilege for relatively small groups of young men and even smaller groups of young women.

Before the war universities were not in the center of intense public attention, but were left largely to themselves to get on with their academic tasks of teaching, training, and research. An important discovery by a university scientist or a rare incident of political commotion might gain attention in the press of any of the Western countries. Athletic contests in the United States, much less frequently in Great Britain, and practically never in the rest of Europe, called the attention of the wider public to the existence of universities. In America a book like Upton Sinclair's *The Goose Step*, which challenged the legitimacy of the universities and of the academic profession, was a phenomenon. It was written by an "outsider" who had no contact with universities. Thorstein Veblen's *The Higher Learning in America*, scathing though it was, did not depart from the widely accepted standard of what a university should be, namely, an institution of science and scholarship. There was, indeed, much criticism of universities, but most of it was intended to bring them closer to the ideal.

III

There were many changes after World War II. First of all, there was the enormous swelling of the size of the student body once the young men were released from military service. The accumulated "deficit" of the war was being made up, and much more. The provision of grants to demobilized soldiers not only aided those who would have gone to university had they not been called up; they also made university attendance possible for young men who would otherwise have been socially or financially unable to do so.

Teaching staffs of universities also expanded markedly, particularly at lower levels of the hierarchy. After the fall in the rate of recruitment during the depression and its virtual practical cessation during the war, there had to be a rapid expansion to meet teaching requirements.

Continental universities responded more slowly than the Anglo-American universities. In Germany candidates for recruitment were simply not available, and teaching staffs were further shrunken by the exclusion of those who had been the most arrant Nazis. Few refugee scholars and scientists returned. Some very old men who had retired early in the Nazi period were recalled to service. The traditional system of large lecture audiences continued; professors simply increased the number of those who attended professorial lectures. Seminars became extremely large. Still, universities on the continent did move very slowly to expand their *Mittelbau*. This expansion was much disliked by many older academics who thought it was disastrous to the old pattern of the university. *Habilitation* in Germany and *agrégation* in France restricted recruitment. But there, too, staffs had to expand. New recruits were usually appointed from the generation which had been trained in the overcrowded and undertaught generation of the period when professorial lectures had become a travesty of higher education.

British and American universities moved more swiftly, with the larger American institutions resorting also to creating or enlarging a stratum of "teaching assistants." The greatest expansion in Great Britain occurred only in the 1960s with the realization of the proposals of the Committee on Higher Education under the chairmanship of Lord Robbins. British universities thus were able to draw on the products of the more moderate expansion which began in 1945, but there, too, they began to press against the outer limits of the well qualified and deeply devoted.

One consequence of the expansion—in whatever stage in the quarter of a century in which it occurred—was the encroachment on teaching staffs of secondary schools. Not only were persons who otherwise might have become sound secondary school teachers drawn into university teaching, but there were also transfers of already practicing secondary school teachers. This little-noticed and insufficiently documented phenomenon, which had been going on in the United States for a much longer period, has not only lowered the quality of secondary education in most countries, but it has also had a serious effect on the conception of the tasks of universities. The more poorly prepared are the secondary school leavers who come up to universities, the more the tasks of the universities have to diverge from the traditional ones. Latterly in the United States, where "open admission" has been instituted, a certain amount of the required teaching has been not only elementary, it has had to be remedial as well. This has meant recruiting teachers to do this kind of teaching, onerous but akin to academic traditions. This has also meant that the intellectual seriousness of the academic staff has been affected.

Higher education was ceasing to be regarded as a privilege: it was beginning to be seen as a right of which all young persons should seek to avail themselves. Governments in most Western countries which desired or accepted this expansion of numbers now became much more munificent towards higher education than they had ever been before. They began, in varying degrees, to provide funds to construct buildings, to found new universities, and to establish new libraries and new teaching posts.

IV

Governments, impressed by the accomplishments of research in various fields emphasized during the war, turned their attention to policies which would maintain a high standard and large volume of civil and military research. They became concerned lest there might not be sufficient "scientific manpower" to meet the diverse needs of societies aiming to promote national military strength and prestige and the health and economic welfare of the people. This naturally implied support for the study and teaching of scientific subjects in universities—one of the main sources of the series of decisions whereby higher education in the United States, for example, came to depend increasingly on the federal government for financial support. The same thing came about but somewhat differently in the United Kingdom; there modern universities had come to depend on the central government for the support of their teaching and training activities as well, even before World War II. In Western Germany and Canada—where like the United States the federal system had previously denied the central government a dominant position in higher education—central governmental support began to take place also until this pattern spread throughout the world. Training scientists and technologists was not the only objective of the policy of this mode of support for higher education, but its effect was to involve universities much more closely with central governments than had been true before.

Governments also began to spend much more money directly on

research itself, both through a great increase in their own departmental research activities and by supporting independent research institutions: the institutions maintained through the *Max Planck Gesellschaft*, the *Conseil national de recherche scientifique*, the Medical Research Council, and so on. Governments made contracts with private bodies such as business firms and research institutes; this was especially common in the United States. They also did so through grants to and contracts with universities. Such activities increased the demand for research workers and thereby enabled universities to train more graduate students and also to employ more persons to do research. As a result, the scientific faculties of universities thrived as never before. One consequence was that scientists became less centered on their universities, which became conveniences to house their research projects and administer funds which they had obtained on their own initiative. The university as a community, already weakened by specialization and by the growth and size of its constituents' departments, lost in coherence.

This development in governmental policies for the promotion of science was part of a movement of ideas that included the idea of "science-based industry" which ripened into that of a "science-based society." Universities naturally appeared to be the devices by which such a society would be created and maintained. The idea of a science-based society rested in part on the expectation that great numbers of occupations formerly carried on on a strictly empirical basis (and which were therefore to be learned by experience and apprenticeship rather than by academic study) did in fact, or soon would, require academic qualifications. Although this view had been canvased by various visionary writers of the present century, such as H. G. Wells, Thorstein Veblen, and J. D. Bernal, it gained wide acceptance first in the United States after 1945, and from there returned to Europe where it had been born. In a very modest way it was espoused in the United Kingdom, reaching a high point of public enthusiasm in Mr. Harold Wilson's Labour government of 1964 when C. P. Snow was its prophet. It came later to France and Western Germany. In this, as in other respects, the Organization for Economic Cooperation and Development (OECD) served as an amplifier for the scientific outlook and for adaptation of the universities to its exigencies. It did so through a large number of publications and conferences and particularly through the conferences of ministers of education and science of the states which were members.

If the traditional manual occupations were on the verge of disappearance —the proportion of the gainfully occupied in the primary and secondary occupations had been declining steadily while their output was increasing no less steadily[5]—then the future of society appeared to depend on higher

---

[5] These trends had been observed by German writers as early as the first decade of the century; they were again taken up in the 1920s by various German writers on the "white-collar worker." Just before World War II, Colin Clark's great book, *The Conditions of Economic Progress*, gave it the imprimatur of a daringly imaginative econo-

education for administrative services and professional and quasi-professional occupations. Since industry, transportation, and commerce increasingly depended on research, they would necessarily need institutions which did such work and which trained young researchers; both such activities demand outside support in order to increase the study of science at universities. Only in this way could "highly qualified manpower" be obtained to meet society's need for more productive technology.

There had always been a tendency towards this kind of scientism in the United States where many "newer professions" such as social work, city planning, library administration, and so on, with only a slight scientific or scholarly content, have sought to increase their prestige through the prescription of courses of study under the auspices of universities.[6] Abraham Flexner had already noted this feature of American universities at the end of the 1920s. The trend of opinion which was so marked in the United States in the late 1940s was only an extension of the older view of the desirability of a marked practical intention in university education. University administrators, especially in the United States, took like ducks to water to this appreciation of universities and to the endless horizons of opportunity which it seemed to offer.

A new branch of journalism, to which many university teachers contributed, arose; it was concerned with science policy and higher educational policy. Journals like the *Times Higher Education Supplement*, the *Chronicle of Higher Education, Change*, the *New Scientist, Atomes* (later *Recherche*), were full of articles about the "new challenges" to higher education. Newspapers like *Le Monde*, the *New York Times*, the *Guardian* (once the *Manchester Guardian*, of lamented memory), *Die Zeit*, and so on, added their powerful voices to the promulgation of the new tasks of the universities. Foundation officials, the officials of professional associations, particularly those concerned with educational administration, and the practitioners of the new journalistic specialization, all proclaimed the new task of the university. In doing so, they produced a chorus of criticism of the universities as they had been.

---

mist. Since that time many writers have rung changes in the tune. The numerous names, "postindustrial society," "information society," "techtronic society," "science-based society," "automated society," and so on, all testify with varying degrees of learning and sophistication to the common belief that the future belongs to science and technology. These ideas go back at least as far as Saint-Simon in some respects and to Francis Bacon's fantasy of the House of Solomon. In the postwar period they were put forward in the Steelman report in the United States and in the Barlow report in Great Britain, both of which stressed the urgent need for the production of scientific manpower by the universities. These reports did not go as far as the later prophets of "high-level manpower," but they were steps in that direction. All these prophetic writings were eagerly welcomed by the spokesmen for economic growth and the reshaping of universities to the "needs" of the science-based society, which is as yet still awaiting its birth, although it is being announced by many self-appointed midwives.

[6] See Nathan Glazer, "Schools of the Minor Professions," *Minerva*, XII, no. 3 (July 1974).

V

Ever since the nineteenth century there had been a demand—especially in the United States—that universities should cease to be "ivory towers" and contribute directly to the well-being of their societies. After World War II this demand was echoed in Europe. It coincided with the expansion of the student bodies. Clearly, not all students were to become university teachers or pure scientists, teachers in *lycées* or *Gymnasia* or grammar schools, or lawyers or physicians or higher civil servants, nor would they enter into business firms owned by their relatives. They would have to enter occupations for which a university education qualified them, but these occupations might not be those for which universities had educated and trained their students in the earlier decades of the century. Furthermore, many of these students had no strong intellectual interests in the traditional sense. The traditional education in the sciences, mathematics, classics, modern languages, history, and economics was not for them. In the light of all these considerations, the conclusion was drawn that universities must be more "practical," less "idealistic," less "remote" from the realities of contemporary life.

As far as numbers alone were concerned, the transition from "elite" to "mass" higher education was, of course, a step toward realizing the ideal of equality of opportunity. It awoke populistic sentiments which had been strong in America ever since the Jacksonian revolution but rare in Europe.

The upsurge of "anti-elitism" of the latter 1960s naturally found the traditional university a fitting object for its critical attitude. Politicians who in most countries had not taken much interest in universities responded sympathetically to these programs for making universities useful to "the people." Resurgent populism in the United States and a more newly born populism in Europe helped greatly in heightening the demand that the universities adapt themselves to the practical requirements of the new science-based "postindustrial" society.[7]

The "cognitive expansion" of the postwar period—long in gestation—has resulted in cognitive idolatry. The juggernaut of cognitive expansion would, in this view, go on steadily rendering obsolete all old beliefs, old practices, old institutions. The solution to this particular problem seems to have been discovered in "recurrent" or "lifelong" education. Human beings must recurrently "retool" themselves, discarding old knowledge and replacing it with new knowledge. Universities exist not merely to provide training for new occupations or professions, but according to this view must go on retraining and retraining the already trained.

As the cult of the degree replaced the "cult of success" and pushed aside

---

[7] It is now called "the information society" in Japan, which refuses to be behind in these matters.

the traditional principle of "each in his own stratum," it began to become apparent to the reformers of universities that the acquisition of a university degree by a person from a family in which no one had ever been at a university meant ascent in the social hierarchy of status and income. But neither in the United States nor in Europe had this led to demands to change the substance of what was taught in universities or in the intellectual qualifications for admission to them. The "transition to mass higher education" and the attendant (perhaps consequent) anti-elitism have led to a demand that universities go much further in offering opportunities for substantial social ascent, that in fact they should promote substantive social equality or be condemned as "elitist." Although European universities have been less subjected to this demand than those in the United States, it has begun to crop up there too.

Universities had never before been regarded as devices for establishing equality of status. Even in countries like the United States, with the most open access to universities, only an approximation was sought to equality of opportunity to make entrance into universities available to larger numbers of young persons than was true in Europe. Equality of opportunity only— not equality of status—was demanded by the critics of inequality of modern Western societies. "Universal higher education," or the substantive equality of status which would flow from it, was not dreamed of, however. The university's task was to educate and train those who came to it for education and training and to discover new truths; if it had anything to do with changing society, it was only through the knowledge it offered. There was no idea, furthermore, that as a result of university education the degree of substantive equality in society would be increased, since only a small proportion of the relevant age groups could ever receive higher education. At most, equality of opportunity could cause rewards to be more justly distributed, that is, to be distributed proportionately to natural endowment and exertion in the exercise of that endowment.

It could not have been otherwise where the opportunities to enter the university seemed inevitably to be very narrowly restricted. It would have been deemed preposterous before World War II to believe in the possibility of universal higher education. After the war, the idea has nonetheless made steady progress, even though the reality—less in the United States, however, than in Europe—has lagged far behind. The notion that everyone should go to university has slowly taken hold as a criterion for assessing the adequacy of a country's higher educational system. Although there is in fact little chance that universal higher education will be realized in the present century —if ever—the standard or ideal of universal higher education has become one additional platform of the argument against the universities as they stand.

There is no evidence that this particular argument is widely shared; but it is heard among disgruntled radicals on the staffs of universities and among some of the "higher educational publicists"; in a more amorphous form, it penetrates into the minds of those who are already ill at ease about the elitist character of universities.

VI

In the minds of some persons, universities (especially in the United States) have become vehicles of a new utopianism in which equality of status is only one part. It is not a revolutionary utopianism; it is a progressivistic, rationalistic, scientistic utopianism in which the ideal of a fully gratified society is conceived of as a result of the application of scientific knowledge. Despite recent setbacks (fuel shortages, environmental pollution, economic problems), there are still persons who believe that the ideal can be realized if only enough higher education is provided. Recently one American university president, attempting to overcome pessimism in administrators about the future demand for higher education, said: "The [political and educational] leaders must decide what kind of society we want and how much higher education will be needed to build that society." [8]

One current of this utopianism—found within universities as well as in an energetically asserted public opinion outside them—believes that it is not a universally solvent knowledge alone which should be provided by the universities, but other kinds of gratification as well. The older tradition that the higher educational system should form character has been transformed into the demand that university education should make its beneficiaries creative. This has two subsidiary aspects. One is that universities should become places where training in the arts—plastic, literary, and representational—should be given. Thus universities must have schools of drama, painting, sculpture; of novel and poetry writing; and of musical composition and performance. American universities had already begun to take in writers-in-residence, musicians-in-residence, painters-in-residence, composers-in-residence, after the end of World War II. Even in the 1950s one could get a Ph.D. at a prominent American university by submitting a novel. Teaching "creative writing" became common in departments of English—alongside the teaching of elementary composition!

Once such "creativity" had obtained a foothold, thanks to the zeal of university authorities to be all things to all men, the demand was extended to persons, regardless of whether they produced works or not. This demand for universal creativity requires that the universities modify their aims and methods so that all students can realize the potential originality which is believed to reside in all human beings. It has become taken for granted that an objective of undergraduate education should be the student's discovery of

---

[8] Report of a talk by President Howard Bowen, Claremont University Center, in *Chronicle of Higher Education*, VIII, no. 32 (May 13, 1974), 4.

his "true self," his "identity." In the 1950s in the United States it became fashionable to speak about an "identity crisis" among young persons, postulating an essential core in every human being which was suppressed or disordered by the pressure of institutions; it became therefore a task of undergraduate education to let the student discover and bring to expression this essence of his being. "Doing your own thing" was a colloquial way of formulating the end state of this process of uncovering the suppressed self and giving it expression. "Experimental colleges," student-designed courses, courses taught by students and examined by students, have found a place in certain parts of the American higher educational system. The power of tradition and the resistance of governmental bureaucracy have prevented such manifestations in Great Britain and on the continent, although similar demands can now be heard.

The demand for "relevance" is an amalgam of many conflicting demands which are directed towards universities—for practical service, for training for numerous "minor professions," for contemporaneity of subject matter, for exciting, gratifying, and developing the personality. They are very different from each other and some of them are incompatible with each other; each has its supporters. Of course they have not had their own way, but they do have some effect on opinion in the universities.

In addition to all this, there has been another fashionable demand made on universities—although it seems to have abated somewhat recently. It is that they become centers of criticism. It is not just the old demand that students be taught to think independently, to scrutinize discriminatingly the tradition which they inherit, to seek evidence rather than to accept dogmatically asserted propositions from their teachers or their textbooks. What is demanded now is much more. The ideas of "thinking independently" and "thinking critically" came for a time to mean thinking *hostilely* about contemporary society. The "status quo" having become morally abhorrent, it is asserted that the task of teachers and students and of the university as a corporate whole is to set its face against present-day society and to criticize it relentlessly. In Western Germany and in France, this point of view is now well established in certain universities, especially in the social sciences. Even in Great Britain this view has its followers, mainly in social science departments. This is a radical extension and application of the more general belief that the universities should be at least "abreast of the times" and, even better, should meet the "needs" of the society of the future.

To attain these grand ends, universities must change; they must innovate, innovate, and innovate again. To become innovators they must outgrow their attachment to old tasks, to old learning, to old beliefs, and to old ways of doing things. They must reorganize themselves internally so to transcend the confining boundaries of disciplines. In some circles, within as well as outside the universities, it is thought that the failures of universities to solve the problems of society and to arouse the creativity which lies dormant in their students arise from the inherited constriction of departmental boundaries. The resolution of "ecological" problems (transportation, drug addiction, criminality, unhappiness and mental disorder, conflict, poverty, divorce, boredom, etc.) rests on the utopian belief that a synthesis of the knowledge contained in a plurality of (at present separated) disciplines can "solve" the problems of contemporary society. Hence, new "problem-oriented" courses of study must be devised with new syllabi and new methods of teaching.

Thus the university must go beyond its "ivy-covered walls," into the streets, into workshops, and into offices. It must bring the streets and workshops into itself. It must bring together "work and study." It must recognize that "learning and living" must be seen as one.

One current of this movement is the "comprehensive university," the *Gesamthochschule.* American state universities and the "multiversity" have already reached this goal. The universities of California and Michigan are *Gesamthochschulen.* In Germany it is still being striven for; in Great Britain the criticism of the "binary system" represents a similar tendency. The examples of Berkeley and Ann Arbor show that this aspiration is not necessarily injurious to the higher intellectual functions of a university. Still, the movement in its most recent form, such as the terminological leveling of university education to "tertiary education" or "postsecondary education," shows an animus against the distinctive features of the university as a place for the training, refinement, and disciplining of higher intellectual powers of young persons and for their exercise of those powers in the discovery of new truths.

The upshot of all these demands is that the universities must recognize that they have many "constituencies" to serve—all at the same time and in the same place. The entire program is rarely put forward in all its elaborations. Bits and parts are variously demanded by various reformers, but they all fit into a single and consistent pattern. Some variants are more progressivistic; others, closely akin to them, are more radical or revolutionary. Radicals and revolutionaries, much as they dislike the existing society, are as insistent as moderate progressivists that universities must serve society immediately and directly. It is not society as it is now constituted, or the institutions which are the centers of this society, which they must serve. From these they must isolate themselves—except of course that they must continue to receive financial support from the condemned society. They must associate themselves with "people" who are the bearers and harbingers of a new and better society and they must serve their interests. The natural sciences must become "people sciences," the social sciences must cease to be the instruments of an internal and external "colonialism"; they must forswear "spying" on the poor at the behest of their paymasters. They must become a "true learning community" where students and teachers abolish arbitrary differences and boundaries between themselves in order to bring into being "participatory democracy," which will be a prototype of the future of the entire society. This is a theme common to the new radicalism and no

Western country has a monopoly. The publications of Suhrkamp in Germany and the Penguin Education series in Great Britain keep those countries abreast of the United States and France. Such radical criticism is not an affair of "outsiders." A great deal of it originates from within their universities, from their teaching staffs.

The clearly visible success of this campaign of radical reform are relatively few; yet this is not a measure of its influence. Much of it appears in convocation day addresses, in speeches before professional associations, and in the popular literature of university reform. It has never taken a palpable hold in the daily life of any worthwhile American university, although there are places where some of the demands have been granted an officially acknowledged realization. It does, however, form an element in the atmosphere in which universities have been living in the United States. Naturally, such reforms have not made much progress in British universities, despite a handful of vigorous spokesmen there. In France, although it is more the stock-in-trade of radical students and the teachers who make common cause with them, real advances have been made. Universities there have been made into spurious "communities" by the system of tripartite governments in which the various "constituencies" are given a role as well as a voice. In German universities tripartite government (*Drittelparität*) has become a reality, to their great loss as institutions of teaching, training, and research. They are less communities than they ever were, even in the time of the now hated "*Ordinarienuniversität.*" In Denmark and Holland similar things have happened. But the effect of all these demands is not to be looked for in substantial institutional modifications. Their more serious effect is to be found in the disordering of the academic ethos, in the conception of what a university ought to be and what its members owe to it and hence to each other.

VII

Never before has so much been demanded of universities and never have they been under such scrutiny and publicity. It could scarcely be otherwise when such unprecedentedly large sums of public money are given to them; when so many persons aspire to, and do in fact, for the most part, enter them as students; and when there is so much sensitivity to and discussion of the problems and needs of contemporary society, and so much animosity against the existing society and its authorities.

Contemporary culture inherits a powerful and triumphant tradition of "cognitive expansion." The idiom of the "breakthrough"—the idiom of tank warfare—in the cognitive sphere has become an essential part of the contemporary vocabulary. Scientific progress has supported and drawn support from a scientistic outlook which has placed systematic empirical knowledge of the universe, the earth, and all its inhabitants from viruses to man at the forefront of the objects it prizes. The rationalistic, hedonistic, individualistic progressivism which has been expanding since the seventeenth century has peaked since World War II. The close association between science and the universities has made universities into the bearers and agents of these grandiose hopes.

Little is now expected of the churches; armies are no longer the glory of the nation; the family has been shorn of its responsibilities. Trade unions never carried the hopes of any but a few syndicalists that they would become harbingers of a new social order of which they would be the center. Business firms are likewise in the shadow. The older pride of businessmen in the firms which they had built through their own exertions has yielded to an eagerness for wealth and an indifference to the moral dignity of the institutions through which they gain that wealth. Where else then can a beleaguered and demanding humanity turn for its redemption except to education? Of the entire educational system, universities are the pinnacle which alone holds out the promise of the redemption which mankind seeks in an inchoate, inarticulate way.

There is public ambivalence about universities. On the whole they are greatly esteemed for what is believed to be their practical value and, in part, as places where there is disinterested submission to a transcendent ideal. There is a real respect for truth in society and for those who devote themselves to it dispassionately, although not all parts of society are equally respectful.

Universities are the objects of all sorts of contradictory sentiments. They are nowadays disliked for being "elitist," although they are supported because they are, in fact, elitist, training as they do young persons who become well paid and influential lawyers, civil servants, journalists, business managers, and even politicians, as well as physicians and engineers who are also well paid and sometimes influential. They are also disapproved of because many of their students, at least over the past ten years, have behaved atrociously and have not been censured or punished for doing so. Again, universities are disapproved of because there is some sympathy with the criticisms of radical students.

Opinion about universities outside them is complicated and heterogeneous. It is ambivalent. In the present and recent situations those who, from the outside, press upon universities to reform themselves or to be reformed, stress their practical value if they are sympathetic, and express traditional animosities if they are unsympathetic. Within the universities, where every increment to revenue is welcomed, it seems most feasible to address the utilitarian, practical, and nationalistic interest in the universities. It is difficult for modern intellectuals, even those who are far from radical and who do not hate their own society, to believe that their fellow countrymen, and especially the powerful who dispose over great wealth—their own

or the taxpayers'—can have reverence for the disinterested pursuit of knowledge. This very much affects the university teacher's conception of his
obligations. Devotion to the academic ethos is rendered insecure by this
complex situation in public opinion.

All this attention and criticism is something new in the history of universities in most Western countries during the past hundred years—except,
of course, for their maltreatment at the hands of Nazis and fascists. University teachers believed themselves to be part of the center of their societies
—even in the United States. There were conflicts within universities about
courses of study, about the relative dignity of various subjects, about the
creation of new chairs and the filling of old ones, but there was no challenge
to the idea that universities—at least as far as the teachings were concerned
—existed for the cultivation and advancement of higher learning. All else
flowed from that. Training for the professions, and even practical service,
derived equally from the character of universities as institutions devoted to
the disinterested and disciplined pursuit of understanding. This was taken
for granted and not much discussed. When reformers wished to change universities, they did so in the belief that their reforms would bring them closer
to this ideal.

All the more recent attention, when it has been favorable, has made for
unthinking pride and ambition. When it has been negative, it has made for
a shakening of self-confidence and a weakened fidelity.

VIII

Those who shoulder the task of conducting the affairs of universities—
teaching, research, administration, procurement of funds, admission and
examination of students, maintenance of buildings and all sorts of equipment, acquisition and care of books and manuscripts and much else—have
to face in many directions simultaneously. Besides these internal matters,
they must also attend to expectations directed towards them from outside by
their various "constituencies" in order to assure the continued flow of necessary financial resources and societal support. They must recruit new members
at all levels and assimilate them—into the culture of the university in
general, and into that of the particular university of which they are members.
They must make decisions regarding whom to admit, appoint, promote, dismiss. They must educate and train a wide variety of students. They must
allocate their resources among many conflicting demands within the university. They must strive against dispersive forces to maintain the corporate
integrity of the institution. They must govern themselves in a way which
permits needed decisions to be made, which does justice and gives consideration to the diversity of interests of the various sectors and strata of the
university's membership. They must also maintain and extend the favor of

their patrons and please them by their readiness to serve interests which are not necessarily the interests of the university.

This has all become much more difficult in recent times. Even if all else had remained constant, the greatly increased size of the student body has meant larger teaching staffs. The larger the numbers, the greater the diversity of interests, concerns, and tastes which must be reconciled, contained, and assimilated with the traditions of the university. Increasing numbers have brought into the universities types of students from strata of societies whose cultural outlook differs markedly from those of earlier generations.

Many of the students have been carried along by a wave of unthinking assumptions, in the generalized expectation that a university education is mandatory before beginning life in a profession and a career, and thus have found themselves in university without having thought much about why they should be there: many have been perplexed, recalcitrant, and dissatisfied. The university has turned out to be not what they wanted, even though they had had no clear notion previously of what that might be. In various types or groups of students, reluctance and being ill at ease have been symptoms commonly observed within the university community but less noticeable in a university of five or ten thousand students; in a university twice as large they are more noticeable, more self-reinforcing, more demanding of attention and influence, and much more difficult to assimilate.

Growth in numbers alone would have demanded an increase in the size of the administration of universities. But the number of things to be done by administration has also increased. The standards of amenity have risen and more provision must now be made for student health and psychiatric and counseling services; the great increase in the number and proportion of students who cannot pay their own fees means that more scholarships must be provided, more contacts with external bodies which support students maintained, more facilities for student borrowing created. In the United States the recent insistence on increasing the proportion of "minority" students (blacks, "Spanish-surnamed Americans," American Indians, etc.) who attend universities has resulted in a draft of students whose culture differs markedly from that of former student generations; many have had inadequate secondary school education and require "remedial instruction." This calls for more staff, and more staff requires more money, more accommodations, and more paperwork. Each sector of these auxiliary staffs acquires a momentum of its own; each develops its own "professional culture," as sociologists would say. Each thinks it needs more colleagues and more office staff to do the same thing as they themselves are doing.

Teaching staffs have increased. They have needed more space. They have been more actively engaged in more connections with the outside world: they have applied for more research grants and fellowships than their predecessors of forty years ago because along with the increased importance attributed to universities have come more opportunities and more pressure to do such research. Staff members go to more conferences and write more papers, research and publication having become a means of self-legitimation of teachers (even in colleges which traditionally concentrated on teaching undergraduates). There has been more contact with colleagues in other universities within their own countries and abroad. The universities of the United States and Great Britain have gone further to meet these needs; France and Italy have done least.

Research has become more expensive in all countries. In the natural sciences, the scale of equipment has become much greater; more assistants, graduate and postdoctoral fellows, and technicians have been needed to use and maintain it—as well as to manufacture some of it. In the social sciences, research projects have become more numerous and more expensive, especially with the wide use of sample surveys and computers. Large grants from governmental and private bodies have consequently become necessary. The National Science Foundation, the National Institute of Mental Health in the United States, the Social Science Research Council in Great Britain, the *Conseil national de recherche scientifique* in France, and numerous private foundations have tried to fill these demands. Individual scientists became a little more independent of the rest of the university and more concerned about their projects and their research assistants. As a result, they became less attached by sentiment to the university as a whole and had less sense of responsibility for it. They also tended to become more distant from the administration of the university and even came to look upon it as an antagonist.

In humanistic subjects, previously, as in the social sciences, research had been a "one-man affair," or the affair of a teacher and graduate students paid for by a very small grant of a few hundred dollars from an internal university research fund or an academy. Now grants have come to be sought from private foundations or governmental institutions such as the National Endowment for the Humanities, with an attendant pyramiding in the amount of administration and paperwork in the offices of deans and of vice-presidents. Parkinson's law operates here as well as in the Admiralty. Moreover, custodial staffs and security departments ("campus police") have become larger since there has been more to clean, and more to watch, especially in the larger universities and those in large cities. Security departments have had to be enlarged to supplement the regular police. This has been especially true of the American urban universities. Parenthetically, all this has meant more money for wages and "fringe benefits" and more administrators with larger budgets to administer them.

"Development offices" in American universities have become large-scale enterprises with their own culture and momentum. Even in Europe, where governments provide most of the funds for higher education and where private foundations and individual patrons have been less forth-coming, financial administrations of universities have also grown along with the belief that a stronger and larger administrative hand is needed in European universities. The recent decision of the University of London to have a permanent vice-chancellor, the decision of Oxford in the past decade to have the vice-chancellor serve a four- rather than a two-year term, and decisions in the same direction in France and Western Germany are evidence of the increase in administrative tasks.

Where the university administration is prominent and strong, there is a tendency for the academic staff to become alienated, to make a stronger distinction between "we" and "they," and thus for universities to become less unitary. Even within departments the increase in size of staffs has led to a situation in which older teachers scarcely know their younger colleagues.

The academic staffs of American universities, by and large, have been very serious about their work. They have certainly been conscientious and scrupulously devoted to their research, to teaching and supervising grad-uate students and training students for the professions. Generally, despite what has been said, they have also been painstaking in the teaching of undergraduates, especially in smaller colleges where traditionally there have been no graduate students and relatively little concern with intensive research. In British universities, teachers have been even more painstaking in teaching undergraduates, as graduate students have been thought to be more capable of looking after themselves intellectually. The tradition of concern by teachers for students has been weaker in Italian and French universities. German universities were in between. The principle of in loco parentis did not obtain on the continent, but in practice it operated in seminars and in institutes where a student who worked under a professor received close supervision. The expansion of numbers and the radical politicization of students in certain faculties have both weakened this relationship.

On the whole, thanks to competition from government, quasi-governmental and private research organizations, and private business, university teachers are paid relatively well. In impoverished small colleges in the United States this is not so, but in major private universities, in the municipal college systems of large cities, and in the state universities of prosperous states, salaries are equivalent to those of moderately success-ful businessmen. The situation has not been very different in Europe. This has been a marked change from the situation which prevailed before World War II.

In the great period of expansion in the quarter century which followed the war, departments and faculties went on growing in all Western countries. Each member could lecture on whatever subject interested him most; he could pick and choose among the research students whom he would supervise. If an American university teacher wanted an interesting colleague from another university, and if he could persuade his departmental colleagues to agree, that colleague could be appointed. Research grants from government and from the private foundations helped greatly in this. Each member of a department could do pretty much as he pleased. In Great Britain, France, Western Germany, the older tradition of one professor for each major subject has given way to something like the American pattern of several professors in fields which attract many students. In these countries, too, departments have become larger, more diverse in their interests, and less solitary and submissive to the authority of the head of the department.

Generally speaking, in most of the period after World War II, the prestige of university teachers and especially of professors was high, and their confidence in themselves, their intellectual powers, and their subjects was great. The pride of a continental professor was legendary, and among American academics during this period modesty of aspiration was not a universally practiced or admired virtue. This was a source of great accomplishments, but it is also one of the sources of present discontent.

There is still a great deal of money available for research in the United States and Great Britain, in France and Western Germany, but also there is a sense of constriction. Graduate fellowships are in shorter supply than they were in a number of fields, and dramatic gestures of the United States government (such as abolition of the post of president's scientific advisor; repeated insistence that research should be "related to national needs"; the "crash" program in cancer research, with its implied criticism of the National Institutes of Health; the Mansfield amendment, which prohibited expenditures by the Department of Defense on research not clearly related to military problems) have made many American academic scientists feel they live now in a hostile society. British scientists too have felt that they are more straitened now than they were before.

Actually, the difference today is not large when compared with the period of expansion; and the contrast to the period of indifference which always prevailed before World War II remains great. Still, it is not seen that way: most contemporary academics do not remember that earlier period, and they have only the universal laudation which prevailed until relatively few years ago as a standard of what scientists may regard as their proper due. Their sense of buoyancy is somewhat deflated. Less melodramatically the same thing is seen in Great Britain where the displacement of the Dainton report by the Rothschild report represented a similar development. In Western Germany professors are a beleaguered class, not because of the niggardliness of governments, but because the university laws have greatly restricted their powers; in France the situation is very similar, even though teachers do not have such a hard time from their radical students as do many of their German colleagues.

Not all of this collapse of buoyancy can be attributed to difficulties in obtaining research funds. Many scientists have come to realize that (after the savage attacks on American scientists for being connected with the government which was conducting the war in Vietnam—even though not very many scientists were directly connected with the conduct of the war —and for their vaguely conceived connection with the technology of motor cars, strip mining, and industrial effluvia—again, though very few scientists have been connected with these particular activities) they do not have the world at their feet as they had it only ten years before. In Great Britain, as well as in the United States, scientists feel also an atmosphere of constriction which affects universities beyond the scientific departments. They see, too, that graduate students whom they trained for the doctorate have not been able to find appointments at the same high level of opportunity and remuneration which the immediately anterior generation had expected. All this has made for a certain despondency of spirit; it has also made some scientists (who feel less appreciated) more skeptical about the value of what they are doing.

The same sense of constriction also affects the social sciences and humanities departments although they, too, have not been suffering from a severe diminution of research funds. (The humanities departments in American universities are indeed rather better off now since establishment of the National Endowment for the Humanities, and the situation is not too different in most other Western countries.) The social scientists in nearly all these countries have felt the sting of the student rebellion and the rancorous and irrational criticism of the social sciences by radical sociologists, political scientists, and anthropologists. It was in social science departments that the student disorders had—and, in some, still do have— their greatest activity. There is very little intellectual substance to the criticisms which the radical students make of their social science teachers, but social scientists—except for economists—have felt their sting nonetheless. The currency of this critique of disinterested research and denial of the worth and even possibility of objectivity among members of the social science professions has made social scientists who do not share those beliefs more uncertain of the value of their intellectual activity.

The culmination in the United States of two great bursts of productivity in the study of political development and in construction of general sociological theory coincided with the outcrop of radical vituperation. Perhaps social scientists in these fields who are the most progressivist liberals feel sufficient affinity to some of those radical aspirations for them to take such criticisms more to heart than their intellectual insubstantiality merits. But, justifiably or not, many social scientists have fallen into a state of dismay and diminished self-confidence about their own powers about which they were so overwhelmingly optimistic only about ten years ago.

What I have said refers mainly to senior members of faculties and to those with permanent tenure. It applies rather differently to junior members of academic staffs. For one thing, their economic position was not so favorable as that of their elders. In the younger generation, two factors have coincided to justify a considerable degree of unease. For one thing, in the period of expansion many appointments of quite young men were made to full professorships. This meant that faculties and departments acquired a disproportion of persons on permanent tenure, at rather high salaries and with a long period of service ahead of them. The United States, Great Britain, Canada, and France all suffer from this situation. In Western Germany university teaching staffs have continued to expand so this particular problem is not yet acutely felt. The expansion could not have continued at the rate at which it went from the early 1950s until nearly the end of the 1960s, and the recruitment of new members of departments was bound to have slowed down. Still, these young persons who were at university in those expansive years anticipated that they, too, would benefit from the continuous widening of opportunities. Now, however, because some American and English universities are even reducing their staffs by not replacing retiring and deceased senior members, chances for advancement and permanent appointment of the younger group have been pushed backward.

In addition to this, the drive in the United States for "equal opportunity" of blacks and women has made a difference. Departments for a time leaned over backwards to appoint blacks, even some below standard quality; this caused the preponderantly white graduate student body—whenever they thought about the justice of the procedure—to see a further restriction of their field of opportunities. After a time the movement to appoint blacks lost its momentum. This afforded no respite. The "women's liberation" movement—far more persistent, energetic, and resourceful than the blacks, and perhaps with better grounds, as far as quality of achievement and capacity for future achievement were concerned—came next onto the horizon and darkened the air around the young men with recently received doctorates. This affects all fields.

The disaffection of some of the younger members of the academic profession in the universities of most Western countries is of course not a monopoly of this generation, nor is it expressed only in a loss of buoyancy. It is expressed also in a disparagement of academic work and ideological radicalism. American academics in all fields outside business studies, medicine, law, and economics have tended for many years to be progressivistic in the special American way. The radicalism which was interwoven with the student agitation of the second half of the 1960s was an abrupt extension of this progressivistic outlook. The younger generation of teachers—teaching assistants (TAs) and teaching fellows, as they are variously called; instructors and assistant professors—were close to the

agitating students in age and in cultural outlook and also they sympathized with student demands for equality in the exercise of authority in
the university. Many of them shared the "Vietnik" culture; they were
sensitive to the actuality of the war in Southeast Asia and had little sympathy with the centers of American society. For all these reasons, the younger
generation of academics, including many of the blacks and women whose
appointments have cut into the prospects of the young white male
academics, have a sense of bitterness and even resentment against universities as they are, and against their own branch of the academic profession.
Many of them deny its validity. Insofar as they are victims of the recent
campaign—which many of them join—against the standard of objectivity
in science and in scholarship, they feel that they have been launched on
a vain enterprise, which, quite apart from its personal frustrations, its
practical disadvantages, is itself very problematic. If they are radicals then
they are actively aggressive, although this has gone down pronouncedly
in the past few years. In some universities, they favor the formation of
trade unions of university teachers; in others, they form part of the radical
bloc who support radical student initiatives and join camarillas against
"the administration." Where they gain permanent tenure, these younger
academics seek to further the appointment and promotion of those who
share their political outlook. In general, they are the carriers of the
politicization of the university and regard the academic ethos as having
nothing to do with them.

The situation is little different in European universities. In Western
Germany the denial of objectivity, the conviction that politics is the "be-
all and end-all" of academic life, has gone much further than it has in the
United States. There "assistants" are far more radical than professors,
often in fact allied with radical students and at war with the professors.
This is especially so in the popular social science fields, but it is prominent
in the humanistic disciplines as well. Objectivity as a guiding standard in
the assessment of scientific and scholarly beliefs is denied. In appointments,
thanks to their cooperation with radical student representatives, young
assistants are much more active in bringing onto the teaching staff politically sympathetic persons with little regard to their qualifications. In
fact, in some German universities the deterioration has gone so far that
scarcely any academic ethos remains into which new appointees can be
assimilated. The groups of radical students are more entrenched and
supply a powerful reinforcement for their radical teachers.

In France the assistants, in a terribly difficult situation with little hope
for promotion, are very disaffected. Their Italian counterparts seem to have
the same problem.

Though Great Britain is the least afflicted by the alienation of the
younger generation from the academic ethos, there do exist pockets of
radicalism in teaching staffs. Very few, however, go as far as their fellow

believers on the continent, in cooperating with or in encouraging their radical students. A more sedate radicalism has a longer tradition in British universities; when the situation in the universities is calm, radical staff members usually behave in a conventional academic manner—at least by comparison with the conduct of academic radicals in Western Germany and the United States. In Britain, too, the disaffection is most pronounced in the social sciences, especially in sociology.

Except for several West German universities, radical teachers in practically all universities form a quite small minority, but one which sometimes wields a disproportionate influence, because there are so many other dissatisfactions among those who do not share the radical ideology. In this period, when so many spirits are in the slough of despond, bits of their ideology find occasional resonances, even if not a large and continuous following. The radicalism of students and teachers in Western universities is not confined to a radical antagonism against the existing society. It is directed as much against the universities. They share the view, which prevailed in the great period of expansion, that the universities are integral to the operation and growth of their societies; radicals hate the society, therefore they hate the universities which serve these societies. Their more-or-less Marxist ideology furnishes them with an elaborate criticism of the entire cognitive enterprise of modern culture, and it renders them alien to the academic ethos which postulates the appreciation of the disinterested cultivation and pursuit of knowledge.

The radical disturbances have affected the mood and the quality of performance of the universities. For one large cohort of students there were several years when classes were frequently suspended or boycotted and minds were more generally unsettled. Students of that generation can look back on the exhilarating experiences of occupying buildings and wasting much time. The enthusiasm of those years has largely gone from student bodies. Some professors in the more affected West German universities declare that it is still impossible to teach effectively under the conditions which prevail;[9] this probably does not apply equally in all faculties or disciplines, even in the more troubled universities. In French universities the reorganization which followed enactment of the *loi d'orientation* has still not been completed, and at least some professors have quietly withdrawn from teaching in the first two cycles, confining themselves to work with more advanced earnest students in the third cycle. Italian students seem to be still in a state of turbulence. In the United States, although the angry enthusiasm has gone, its recession has left considerable stains on certain departments, even in outstanding universities. The coherence of academic staffs, already damaged by the increase

---

[9] See, for example, "The Resignation of Professor G. N. Knauer from the Free University of Berlin," *Minerva*, XII, no. 4 (October 1974), Reports and Documents.

in size, the self-centeredness of many individual members, the attraction of external interests and possibilities, has been further impaired by the memory of conflicts of the time of the student disturbances.

Even more important is the change in the conception of what education in a university might be. Whereas long years of immobility have left Italian university teachers cynical about change—short of that brought about by revolution—changes beckon to American university teachers as ever present possibilities. "Innovation" had permeated the atmosphere before the disturbances; the disturbances made some of the innovations come about. There are in the United States many colleges whose student initiate and conduct courses of study, set and mark their own examinations. Even in Great Britain there have been innovations in examination procedures with little to recommend them except that they were vigorously proposed by some students and supported by others. Examination assessment is said to have become less scrupulous in many Western countries; it is also said that political considerations enter into that assessment. Certainly there is more preoccupation with political views of colleagues, and more political factionalism in universities.

Although the turbulent students of that generation have presumably developed somewhat more civil attitudes, their teachers (those who took sides in the conflict) remain members of the universities. Cleavages within whole faculties and particular departments still persist and find new issues on which to be sustained. Those who sympathized with the radical students remain bitter against colleagues who opposed them. The wavering of university administrative officers left both radicals and moderates with discontents which persist, and actually are aggravated by the ending of the period of expansion.

The ethos of academic life had already been under strain before the students ran amok. Universities had become too dispersed in their activities, so eager were they to satisfy the many demands made on them and to seize all the opportunities which were offered. They tried to do too many peripheral things and they forgot some of the central things. Above all, they forgot that even though universities are not their own justification, institutional coherence is crucial to accomplishment of the teaching, training, and research which justify the very existence of universities.

IX

Against this background—great expectations on the outside, great and conflicting demands and some uncertainty on the inside—it is appropriate to ask what universities should do in these times which seem unprecedentedly difficult for them. There is no doubt that genuine difficulties exist and that they are those arising simply from the inflation which raises all their costs, causes hardship, and necessitates renunciations. The internal coherence of universities has already been damaged by the availability of large sums of outside money for research projects for which the university was little more than the physical site; it has been even more damaged by the divisiveness precipitated and aggravated by the student agitations, and by the strain on the younger academics.

The simplest fact is that the universities (above all in the United States) have allowed themselves to be seduced by affluence in the first two decades following World War II. There was little that they could do to resist the growth in size, and they should not have done so, even if they had been able. But they should have insisted that universities be given the means and the time to figure out how to provide for the expanding numbers. They should have insisted on being allowed to obtain the kinds of teachers they needed rather than to be forced to take whatever they could find. This would have been difficult because politicians would not have been sympathetic. It was impossible to expand the staff with sufficient rapidity and to assimilate it sufficiently into the state of mind in which it would take seriously the tasks of the university. This occurred not only at the lower levels of the staff but also at the higher levels where there were many permanent appointments of persons not of high intellectual quality. The universities were partly responsible for the rapid expansion; they welcomed it partly out of the morally good reason that it represented an extension of the equality of opportunity, partly for the much poorer reason that it flattered their vanity and brought previously unheard of affluence. Teachers and administrators were both swept along by the belief in education as a universal solvent. Most went along, in differing degrees of activity and passivity, with the idea of a science-based society in some of its most extreme forms.

Certain things cannot be changed. The numbers attending universities will never go back to what they were. Nonetheless, it is likely that, quite apart from some fluctuations in applications for admission in consequence of fluctuation in birth rates twenty or so years earlier, there will be a little less eagerness to attend university than there has been. The wide experience and availability of university attendance might make it appear as less of a privilege and more young persons might decide not to seek admission. This is especially likely to be true as the student's responsibility for bearing some of the cost is enlarged. The availability of other paths in life, and of university education at a later stage, might also help to reduce the pressure of numbers.

It is also likely that governments will continue to expect universities to do certain kinds of research and to train young persons for careers in research to a far greater extent than before World War II; this will provide an assurance to the universities that they will not be forced into attrition.

At the same time, university teachers must set their faces against accepting proposals from governments and foundations, which have some merit and which will for a time give them additional financial resources, but which will after five years leave them to support these schemes from other sources of funds. Such arrangements cause excessively rapid expansion in certain fields and when they end, leave many persons trained and specialized to work in them bereft of equally remunerative employment. This counsel is especially relevant in the United States where "bright ideas," "crash" programs, and "innovations" are much favored. Bodies external to universities often will support innovations but they will not support them past the first stages. Now some of these innovations are worth adopting when there is a substantial body of sound scholarly or scientific knowledge on which to build in order to attain some desired practical or technological goal. If it does not, universities have only burdened themselves with added staff and institutional arrangements which are alien to their primary tasks.

It is hard to resist these temptations of often attractive projects and funds. They appear to contribute to the public good, enabling the universities to do their public duty and also bringing them esteem for having done so.

The issue of innovation is one of the most serious of all those with which universities must deal. I have no doubt that great mischief is done in the name of innovation, as in the past great harm has been done by invoking the sacredness of tradition. Universities exist to promote important discoveries in science and scholarship and to teach and train students in the substance and spirit of the best of these newest and older discoveries. In that sense, universities are "about" innovation. But innovation nowadays has come to be very indiscriminately used, and very indiscriminately sought. Just as being "innovative" is one of the most laudatory adjectives in the vocabularly of the publicists of university affairs, so anything new, however trivial and however superficial its novelty, is welcomed. Universities should be on their guard against their own *faiblesse* for innovation which joins transient publicity and short-lived support.

There are certainly some innovations which universities ought to make in their courses of study. New "majors" or "special subjects" (sometimes calling for a new department or committee) should be available to students as soon as they can be taught and supervised at a high standard. Universities should not resist such a development if there are good intellectual or professional arguments for it, and able scholars or scientists who will take the administrative responsibility. But to rush into a new "interdisciplinary" arrangement just because there is money to pay for it brings trouble in its train.

The duty of universities, in the United States at least, is to get rid of some of the institutional encumbrances acquired during the period of expansion. Indeed, one benefit of more limited resources is that universities might be forced to discontinue certain activities which they should not be carrying on. The universities must find a means of declaring that they cannot do all the things which society needs to have done.

The myth of the university as redeemer will die hard. It is painful for human beings in their present state of mind to believe that some problems are insoluble now, perhaps forever, and that we do not know how to solve them. It seems inhumane to tell this to those who suffer from these problems; it may seem unduly defeatist to say in advance that a problem cannot be solved when in the past some problems thought to be unanswerable turned out to be solvable through improved knowledge and administrative procedures, as well as by more generous political attitudes.

It is also terribly difficult to decide in advance whether a problem is soluble. Certainly it is important for universities to render unto Caesar what is Caesar's, not only because Caesar is powerful and wealthy but also because they owe something to him and to the society of which they are equally members. But it is also necessary not to promise all things to Caesar and his society, because in the end there will be disillusion and distrust. If it becomes fixed in public opinion that academics will promise anything if money is provided for it, and are then unable to deliver the promised solution, universities will reap a crop of resentment—and deservedly so. The position of universities in public opinion is one of their greatest problems. The good opinion of the public and of politicians cannot be neglected, but universities will fare better in public and political opinion if they do what is right, rather than being blown about by every breeze of policy and opinion.

Universities must be jealous of their reputation for honesty and disinterestedness, which is in danger. Intemperate partisanship on the part of individual scientists and scholars, and corporate declaration of partisan attitudes by universities, can do harm both to the public image of the universities and to the individual academic's conception of the true calling of the university. It alienates those who have an equal and opposite partisanship and discredits academics and universities among those who are not partisan. This honesty and objectivity also is extremely hard to maintain in our politicized Western societies, especially when it is generally believed that there is little that governments, if they are so minded, cannot accomplish. It is especially difficult when the social sciences are so much looked to, when social scientists (quite justly) are so concerned with public issues and so often involved—as advisers of various levels of government and as beneficiaries of their financial bounty.

Disengagement from political partisanship is difficult for those who find activist partisanship often stimulating and sometimes accompanied by an intellectual elan which generates interesting ideas and worthwhile research. Subservient partisanship also seems to be rewarding. It was one of the vices of the German universities in their greatest age, though covered up by great intellectual accomplishments; but it brought a bitter harvest, especially in the lean times when the German universities seemed to lose their creative intellectual powers. It is one of the reasons for the revenge taken in recent years by politicians against universities in Western Germany. Partisanship is a threat to universities, both externally and internally. Universities must become more centripetal. I do not mean by this, as I have said before, that they must cut themselves off from society and disregard their obligations to it. On the contrary, one of their main obligations is that each of them should *be* a university. I mean that the university must not be simply an assemblage of diverse and separate activities of research and teaching. It must be an institution in which such activities are carried on; the fact that they are carried on in the same institutions makes a tremendous difference to each of these activities, however separate they seem to be from each other. Thus a teacher must not only perform his obligations of teaching, training, and research, but must also fulfill his obligations to his university and to the idea of the university. This is what I mean when I say that the observance of the academic ethos is a necessary condition for the fulfillment by the universities of their obligations.

The disaggregation of universities and the decomposition of the academic ethos are a menace to universities as they become larger, richer, and more specialized and as their members regard them only as administrative conveniences for their own particular interests. The academic ethos is weakened by other factors, too, such as administrative arbitrariness and the individual's parochial and self-interested conception of his tasks.

The academic ethos and academic citizenship—focused on the university as a corporate cultivation of important truths in the various disciplines, among them, and in the long-term service of society and cilivization—are the decisive factors in determining the fate of the universities. All those strains and distractions of busyness, and the desire to please one's patrons by flattering subservience and large promises—of self-advancement and radical partisanship; and of all the burdens of large numbers and insufficient resources—are significant because they weaken the academic ethos.

A few years ago Lord Ashby wrote a moving paper on "A Hippocratic Oath for Academics." [10] We all have some traces of the academic ethos in our consciences, which have been formed and nurtured by our own training and long experience in universities and by the academic traditions which we inherit. It is that element which we must affirm and strengthen.

[10] "A Hippocratic Oath for the Academic Profession," *Minerva*, VII, no. 1 (January 1969), Reports and Documents, 64–66.

The Educational Class

Ralf Dahrendorf

WE MUST ALL share a concern for maintaining conditions under which noble and enlightened scholarship can flourish at a pace which inspires the advancement of knowledge as well as the progress of free societies. Thus I am honored to be regarded as a member of the scientific community after all these years in the wilderness officiating over only that part of research, science, and education in Europe which is in the charge of the European Community.

Perhaps my perspective is distorted—indeed, distant in its own way—but it is certainly less pessimistic than that of many contemporary scholars, even though I do not share the ironic optimism of those who claim an academic victory for a new old-regime.

Moreover, I have read some interesting views on scholarship and politics with which I naturally do not agree, much as distinguished scholar-ex-politicians may be right in their comments on ex-scholar-politicians and their dilemma. I, for one, continue to think that this question of values and science is the one point where Max Weber exaggerated the Protestant ethic.

The greatest embarrassment from which I suffer is that I have little, if any, knowledge of universities today. Indeed, I am tempted to call this paper "The University Seen from Outside." Thus I have to start not with observations about the present, but with memories of the past. Just over ten years ago, the German Science Council (*Wissenschaftsrat*) invited an ad hoc group to reflect on the need for and, if this was demonstrated, the shape of new universities. Our reflections turned around two major issues. One of these was social (although we were inclined to tackle it from a statistical rather than a sociopolitical angle): the observed and, even more, the anticipated increase in student numbers—thus, the challenge of mass higher education long known in the United States of America. New universities would be needed to take care of more students, "relief universities" (*Entlastungsuniversitäten*), as we called them at the time. They have, in fact, sprung up in large numbers all over Europe: Bochum, and Guildford, and Paris II, Paris III, Paris IV, Paris V, Paris VI, and so on. The other issue, or perhaps motive, was methodological, thus classical, at least for those reared in the Humboldt tradition. We felt that

47

not only the medieval, but equally the nineteenth-century European university was unable to provide the conditions under which science and scholarship in some of the most promising areas at the frontiers of knowledge could flourish. This was due partly, so we felt, to a traditional faculty structure which grouped disciplines in such a way that the study of animal behavior or of human language or of the economics of education could not easily find their place. It was due partly to an organization of teaching and research which gave little incentive to cooperation across the borders of disciplines, or indeed to a problem-oriented development of knowledge. It was due in part to rigidities in the hierarchical structures of universities in which a quasi-feudal status of the professor prevented many junior members of the staff from playing their part fully.

There were other considerations, but these were some of the elements which went into foundation of "reform universities" such as the University of Constance in Germany. When the first professors were appointed in the spring of 1966, they were expected to keep the report of the founding fathers under their pillows at night. In the memorable, enlightened, and rewarding discussions among these founding fathers, the word "student" was rarely mentioned. I remember one session in which we decided that it might be a good idea to have two student representatives on the senate; but our real concern in this respect was with the assistants, by contrast to whom we regarded students as a passing and perhaps ultimately accidental ingredient of the university which we were creating. There was also little concern with the justification for having the luxury of a small, research-oriented university at a time of rapidly growing demand for mass higher education; we took it for granted that multiplicity was the salt of a free society. Moreover, and perhaps more surprisingly in view of the composition of the founders' committee, while we devoted much thought to quality, and to the need for national and international links to insure the highest possible quality of research and of teaching, we thought little of the place of the university in the social and political universe of the day. Probably, most of us were guided by the idea that standards of scholarship must not be confused with those of political relevance, and that the extramural commitments of individuals would in any event guarantee a link which at least some of us regarded as desirable.

I have no reason to believe that either our motives or our substantive reflections at the time were wrong. But it is clear today that they were at least in part irrelevant for the developments which went on around us and of which universities are necessarily a part. By the time the University of Constance had lived through its first quinquennium, "reform" no longer meant scholarly cooperation across the boundaries of discipline and rank but, rather, student participation and the politicization of science. The University of Constance in fact agreed on a pattern of internal organization which would have given considerable power to active students, but which also foresaw a balance of groups that might have become a model for others. The donquichotterie of individuals, the belated political intransigence of government agencies, and the notorious tenuousness of compromise agreements within universities have since led the University of Constance through a series of crises and a long period in which a government plenipotentiary had to take charge of running it. Today many in Constance, as elsewhere, are thinking of peace and quiet rather than reform of any kind.

Perhaps I should add at this point—and before I go on to look at some of the reasons and consequences of such developments—that I do not intend to add my voice to the choir of those who deplore the development I have sketched. I regard such tears about lost causes as not only pointless but shortsighted and rather irrelevant. Those who try to brace themselves against the stream of events may, if they are lucky, manage to hold on to their branch of plank and scream, but the sight is not very impressive and does not change either the speed or the direction of the stream. This is not an argument for soft-center liberalism, for an attitude of acquiescence, of happily swimming along in the stream wherever it takes one. But it is an argument for taking a close look at the direction of things and the forces behind them, and then finding ways of influencing them—of learning to swim in the right direction even in a rapidly moving stream, of using appropriate means to correct banks and bed of the river, in the light of convictions oriented towards a real future and not a bygone past.

But let me return for a moment to the analysis of the situation. The changing meaning of the word reform reflects a number of possibly interrelated developments. In some countries the crisis of authority evidently affected far more than just the junior staff. Universities were not made—or so it came to appear—for those who came to them with considerable and clearly legitimate expectations; students did not have a firm and recognized place in them. Here I am not—or at least not only—referring to the composition of decision-making bodies. Rather, I am thinking of the fact that teaching occupied a clearly secondary place in the minds of many university "teachers." They looked upon themselves as scholars working at the frontiers of knowledge; and the frivolous remark reported by one of the eminent professors at my old alma mater, Tübingen, "Term is beginning, our enemies are coming back" (made, to be sure, long before the so-called "troubles"), had a more serious background to it. There is a sense in which universities in some countries underwent what might be called a sectoral revolution, an internal upheaval aiming at a total reversal of power. And, much as one may disapprove and as revolutionaries themselves are bound to be disenchanted before long, it has never helped anybody to disapprove of revolutions.

Here internal developments within universities are linked with wider concerns of people in the developed world today. As part of the new and understandable desire to improve not only the material conditions of life but also its quality, there is a widespread demand for participation in running one's affairs. I understand such participatory demands to be genuine and not necessarily related to any purpose beyond participation itself—that is, an end in itself. This is why counterarguments in terms of efficiency (of industrial enterprises, for example) or of intrinsic and irremovable inequalities which make full participation impossible (between teachers and pupils, for example) are simultaneously correct and beside the point. To me, as a sociologist, it seems obvious that total participation means total immobility and is thus exactly as dangerous, as injurious, to a society which is trying to increase the life chances of individuals as is the immobility of authoritarian rule. But, unless we realize that the demand for participation in all walks of modern life is part of a major turn from quantitative chances of life—that is, from those capable of expression in money terms—to those which are not, we shall fail to come to grips with the problems around us.

The significance of participation is accentuated by an even more serious development in modern societies which directly involves institutions of higher learning. More and more people spend a considerable amount of their adult life in universities, polytechnics, and the like as students, assistants, teachers. Many others work in schools, in adult education, in training establishments of one kind or another. The educational world may be definable by its transitional and temporary character, at least for pupils and students, but it has acquired an order of magnitude and an order of significance for those in it which makes it a major and a peculiar social force. I do not want to give figures which I cannot substantiate, but I think teachers and students together are beginning to be something resembling a social class—a social force, in any case—which brings its own interests and conceptions to bear on the political debate of developed and developing countries. These conceptions, as is true for all classes, derive from the positions of those who hold them: a profound aversion to things economic, barely camouflaged by a so-called neo-Marxism which is actually a kind of political antieconomy, a romantic ideology of a world without the occupational rat race, without commerce and industry, without conveyor belts and advertisements; a world in which a notion of emancipation plays an important part in itself educational, that is, in which power is replaced by educated dialogue, an antirepresentative, almost syndicalist element which serves to safeguard the *Freiraum* (the protected social space of universities) from the influence of general political authorities, including democratic parliaments; a demand for security, a status similar to that of those relics of the feudal world, the fully protected *Beamte* (civil servants), which permits the unworried enjoyment of an emancipated existence. The new ideology has often been described, usually in either cynical or naïve terms. My point here is that it should not be confused with anything called Marxism or socialism in the past, both of which were in fact the ideologies of the natural opponents of the educational class, that is, the industrial class; nor should it be underestimated. The educational class, if that is what it is, is only beginning its historical course. It adds important and necessary elements to societies which were overdetermined by the values of the industrial sector. Also, however, it tends to place universities and educational institutions generally into a peculiar and new position of conflict with other institutions of our societies; it gives them a partisan position rather than one in which all particular approaches have their place.

This is obviously a very simplified and almost irresponsibly general presentation that stops far short of an analysis. Much differentiation is needed to describe the diversity of factual developments, which above all would have to be national. There are factual differences between countries which play an important part; obviously, the force of the educational class is different in a country where young people leave universities at the age of twenty-one from one in which most of them stay on until they are twenty-five or even twenty-eight. There are also differences in national traditions so far as the relative importance of teaching and research is concerned; those universities which remained medieval throughout were and are much more student oriented than those which underwent Humboldt's process of modernization. National traditions are reflected also in the forms in which new conflicts are expressed; it is discouraging to see how historical propensities to violence, intolerance, indeed inhumanity, return in some places. Thus the generalizations of the sociologist must be taken with more than a grain of salt. They may point, nevertheless, to tendencies which are present in many universities.

Such tendencies have a number of significant consequences, of which I want to mention two sets before I come to some more practical considerations. There is first the transformation of universities themselves. Inevitably, certain traditional structures and styles in which the authority of teachers was taken for granted will give way to those more strenuous conditions under which authority has to be rejustified day by day. Beyond that, it seems to me that an increasing emphasis on teaching, and a corresponding detraction from research, is already taking place at least in those countries which have not preserved patterns. Furthermore, the chances of nonpolitical scholarship are being reduced; there is pressure to force every scholar to justify what he is doing in terms extraneous to scholarship itself. Above all, many accepted and established rules and structures of universities have fallen into a state of flux without the appearance of new structures which would obviously take the place of the old. I know that it is a serious and (for some) discouraging statement to make, but I believe that despite appearances it is vain to expect universities to settle down in the foreseeable future to the quietness of a barely changed equilibrium. This is a period—not, incidentally, the first of its kind—in which universities are somewhat uncomfortable institutions.

The political counterpart of such internal developments is above all a change in the attitude of important social groups and of parliamentary majorities. Universities, for a long time the darling of conservative groups, for a much shorter time the instrument of social reformers to promote full citizenship, are now seen as a threat by conservatives and reformers alike. Paradoxically, this change of mood will, in budget terms, hit scientific research more than scholarships for students or salaries for teachers; spending for individuals seems an acquired right in the organized bureaucratic society of today whereas expenditure for ventures seems expendable. In some countries today it would already be possible to mobilize the industrial class against the educational class, that is, workers and employers against students and teachers. At the same time, there are temporary citizens protesting the construction of a nuclear power station, indeed, alliances—between students and workers revolting against their unions or between students and the advocates of community politics—which indicate the new political relevance of the university world. Progressive liberal and socialist parties everywhere are trying to cope with the new conflict between industrial and educational groups. In whatever manner, the university of today and tomorrow is present in the marketplace and is part of the political game.

In looking at these and other consequences of recent developments affecting universities or originating from them, no doubt everybody will draw his own conclusions. So far as I am concerned, I find some of these changes necessary and deeply justified; although it has become almost trivial to say so, many people have not fully departed from the comforts of protected authority often uncovered by achievement. Some other changes may not seem equally justified; indeed, they are incapable of any assessment in terms of their justification, for they are above all unavoidable. The acceptance of a civil right for an education necessarily creates a large group, perhaps a class, of educators and students; whoever wishes it away wishes away the advantages of modernity along with the unavoidable price to be paid for it. I am convinced that a modern society of educated citizens is a necessary condition for giving greater opportunities to the greatest number. There are also changes which are unfortunate, in part regrettable and dangerous. Among these I count the tendency toward uniformity in academic matters. From the foregoing assessment, certain conclusions stand out. Let me mention four—different in kind, but born out of the same desire to promote universities in our world—which are both rich and subtle in their offerings and relevant for the real issues of our time:

First, some of the important rules of civilized life under conditions of freedom are as valid today as they were at any time. Their reassertion, without hysteria, but also without ambiguity, is particularly useful at a time of dramatic changes. One of these rules, the most elementary of civilized life, is the inviolability of the person. This may be a time in which many obsolete structures have to be dissolved in order to make room for new human possibilities; but there remain structures without which all progress becomes impossible. Protection from violence is one of them. Another rule, possibly the most elementary of life in freedom, is freedom of speech. It implies freedom of opinion, of belief, of expression; it implies also that no one opinion must be dogmatized whether in the form of pseudorevolutionary graffiti on the walls or in that of forbidden views in the classroom.

I am not unaware of the fact that these rules, while clear and simple in theory, are often hard to establish in practice. A great deal of nonsense has been said in these years about "psychological violence," both by students who resent their own inability to put up a convincing case against arguments of their teachers, and by teachers who lose all nerve if faced with an unruly class. There is such a thing as psychological terror, to be sure, but in our societies it is much more rare than either side claims. Similarly, there are difficult discussions of the meaning of freedom of speech. Does freedom of speech imply that whenever one opinion is expressed an opposing one must be presented at the same time and to the same audience? I think not. Freedom of speech is a process; it is realized by the presentation of opposing views over time and, incidentally, after due examination of views previously expressed. But here, too, we need to think about applications of rules as much as about the rules themselves.

To leave no doubt, let me add that the rules in question are those at the base of free societies. They cannot be sustained or abandoned in any single institution within societies. It is for maintenance of such rules that we have set up generalized institutions, including courts of law and bodies whose task it is to enforce that law. University autonomy is important, but in the hierarchy of values it is clearly second to the more elementary rules to which I have referred. Those who are responsible for universities are thus for their part responsible also for maintaining freedom of speech and the inviolability of the person.

Second, one of the important political tasks today in the realms relevant to universities is to develop a multiplicity of institutions in the field of science and education. Whatever the justification of educational expansion—internal university reform, a greater emphasis on teaching, a more political quality of university life—it cannot and does not follow that all academic institutions should be alike. I am not unaware of the fact that egalitarian movements—and egalitarianism is both a root and an interest of the educational class—have an intrinsic tendency to create equality by abolishing what appears to be privilege rather than by making apparent privilege gradually possible for all. But, apart from the ideological problem and the pressure by some, there is no reason to believe that a variegated system of science and higher education would fail to satisfy the demands of the many.

Multiplicity can take many forms. There is a peculiar charm to some of the great American universities with their mélange of ingredients ranging from pure research institutes to girls' colleges and from hotel management centers to graduate schools of political science. There is less charm but similar appropriateness to systems in which public and private institutions, teaching and research establishments, small and large, open and closed, limited and comprehensive universities compete. This is a time in the fields of university education and scientific research in which we shall want to see a thousand flowers bloom rather than reduce our gardens to a single lawn, however well kept and weatherproof it may be. May I just make clear at this point that this was my view also with respect to my former charge as commissioner of the European communities responsible for research, science, and education. In promoting the establishment of a European Science Foundation, I deliberately abstained from organizing "from above" a unified framework for fundamental research. Our own Joint Research Center and, in another way, the European University Institute in Florence should be effective competitors; two further flowers in the garden of science, rather than seeds of a new monopolistic claim. Mutual recognition of diplomas must mean convertibility of achievements for the individual, and not the harmonization of educational systems which are different (at least in part) for good reasons and whose differences offer scope for further developments. Indeed, let me add that had fate, or whatever else determines a man's political opportunities, led me into a position of responsibility for the universities of the federal republic, I would have examined the question very carefully to see whether there is anything to be gained from federal legislation when it is obvious that this has an inherent tendency towards unification rather than multiplicity.

Third, the new political quality of the educational world is a process which warrants reflection and perhaps also, at an early date, action. In part, the emergence of an educational class is an inevitable consequence of the expansion of higher education. To some extent, however, it results from a certain conception of higher education, and perhaps of education generally. Public general education started as a relatively brief period of preparation for life in society and, more specifically, for the basic and specific requirements of occupations. Throughout the expansion of education, the character of the educational process as one of limited preparation remained an undisputed assumption. Even the merry students of the 1900s knew, while they pretended to enjoy their beer parties, that the bittersweet life would end soon and give way to more serious things. But today education has expanded to such a degree, and takes up such a large part of many people's lives, that this sense of the preparatory and transitional—and with it the necessary orientation towards and contact with other walks of life—is lost. At the same time, the occupational world itself has developed in such a way that a once-for-all education becomes increasingly useless. Unless people remain intellectually capable and economically able to renew their knowledge in the light of experience, they lose both occupational opportunities and the ability to give meaning to their leisure time.

All this is commonplace, and so is the inference which I want to draw from it: recurrent education, involving a new relation between educational and practical experiences, is the greatest single task ahead of us in that borderline area between educational and social policy. Drawing this conclusion, however, and acting upon it seem to be two very different things. I think the time has come to examine much more seriously proposals for shortening undergraduate courses of study, introducing an obligatory period of practical experience for all boys and girls, extending systems of educational leave from jobs, restructuring tertiary education so as to cope with adults returning from employment for limited periods of time, and so on. There are beginnings, but only beginnings—among them the interesting venture of the open university in Britain. We shall have to move much more quickly.

I am not unaware that the development of recurrent education is politically controversial. There are those who fear that this is a left-wing invention to expose even more people to the control of Marxist ideologists. I can only register such fears with a mixture of surprise and anger: surprise at the lack of confidence of some of the more conservative groups in our ability to cope with the problems of modern societies, anger at the readiness to dismiss on narrow party grounds one of the great social opportunities for many people. My own feeling is, on the contrary, that redefining the relation between education and application—in this sense, theory and practice—may well be the most important single task ahead of us if we want to break out of the unhappy dialectic of authoritarianism and revolution in our universities. This leads me, fourth and finally, to a point about which I feel strongly. I feel entitled to make it now that it is more than gratuitous advice from somebody who speaks from the sheltered rostrum of political office. I think the attitude of many of those responsible for our universities towards the developments at which I could but hint in this selection is regrettable. And, in saying this, I am referring to those who wallow in self-pity as much as to those who sail happily along with a wind they know is blowing in the wrong direction and those whose imagination ranges no further than to a nostalgic revival of the past. Let me be more specific and, instead of engaging in a polemic which in itself yields little for the solution of the problem, make a positive case; but let me do so with a slight *Verfremdungseffekt* and use a metaphor.

I am a liberal in the European political sense. European liberals in the past were not easily inclined to advocate policies which involved intervention in the process of a market economy based on private property. Policies, say, of income redistribution or of codetermination were abhorred as such. Now it is evident that these and similar social problems are the very issues which determine the political process today, at least in Europe, so that liberals were faced with a difficult set of options. My own party in Germany, I believe, has become a model of one kind of choice which I happen to think is right. We have accepted the fact that the issues of the day are defined in a way which makes irrelevant some of the specific tenets of classical liberalism; but we have insisted on policies which make codetermination, or the redistribution of incomes by systems of sharing the increments of productive capital, real for individuals rather than for collectivities. We have, in other words, applied the basic values of a society of free men able to help themselves and stand on their own feet to new problems in new ways. In the process we have lost some old members who have left the party and are since looking in vain for a vehicle for their mournful and self-pitying apocalyptic emotions. We have lost others who have formulated a rigid counterposition, formed their own party, and engaged in a continuous battle against everything modern in liberalism. Their party is not very successful; it needs the help of other parties far removed from the original values even of the liberal dissenters. Indeed, it has become a pathetic representation of a declining group which has actively defined itself out of the mainstream of social and political development. There are, of course, those also within the renewed Liberal party who want to make the painful process of accepting new factual developments the basis of a policy of continuous adaptation—opportunists who are more interested in being with it than in being liberal. I do not want to claim that the attempt to combine traditional values with contemporary relevance has been fully successful or is even complete. But I think there is a lesson to be learned from this process for the attitudes of those responsible for universities today.

There is no way back to the old university which existed before mass education, participatory demands, and the emergence of an educational class; the attempt to reestablish it in the form of a few remote monasteries carries little conviction as an example for others (even if I do not doubt its legitimacy in a free society), especially those of subtle and enlightened scholarship in favor of a university which becomes the bridgehead of a newly emerging class. Between these two extremes, however, there is an open field of practical actions which can and must be taken: actions of reform within universities and within the educational systems; actions of safeguarding rules and values indispensable to the progress of knowledge and of our social and political order as well. These must not—and cannot effectively—be tackled in a defensive manner. A university defense organization will not only of necessity find itself outside the mainstream of development, an ineffective advocate of declining groups; it is also bound to find itself in a kind of political company which will defeat its motives purely by association. One of the things learned in politics is that it is not enough to say the right things—one has to say them in the right place, at the right time, and in the right company. An active reformist attitude is as necessary today as ever. It is the company of those prepared to engage on this uncomfortable course which needs to be developed nationally, and above all internationally, and it is their support which I seek.

The Governance of the Universities

Zelman Cowen

A WRITER on university governance is well aware at the outset that, in addressing an international readership, he can write with particular knowledge and modest confidence of his own system and structure, knowing that university systems of governance differ significantly from country to country, and within countries. Historically, the role of the state and state administration in at least some European university systems differs from their role in the United Kingdom, the United States, and in my country, Australia. Even within a particular country there may be significant differences. For example, in the United Kingdom, the Oxford–Cambridge system of governance differs significantly from that of the "civic" universities such as Manchester, Leeds, Birmingham, in that in the latter there is a significant role for lay participation which does not exist (and historically has not existed) in the distinctively collegial government of the ancient foundations. In the United States an extensive and diverse private university and college system operates alongside a state or public university system. In both types of institution there is an involvement of lay participation in governance, but the sources of support for and the relationship to government of the various groups of institutions have historically been different. In recent years the expansion in terms of role, numbers, and activities and the attendant cost burdens have meant that the private institutions have become increasingly reliant on funds derived from public sources and as some public institutions have increased in reputation and eminence they have attracted a significant measure of private endowment; earlier distinctions to some extent tend to blur.

At the same time, particularly in recent years, when the university in many parts of the world has been wracked by "crisis"—perhaps crisis with changing emphasis—the problems of governance have exhibited a more general character. It is true that not much attention was paid to questions of governance in the discussion of university matters until the events and pressures of the sixties forced upon us consideration of a wide range of problems intimately linked with issues of governance. The recently published report of the Carnegie Commission on Higher Education on *Governance of Higher Education* (1973) made this point in saying that, on the surface at least, for some two decades after the end of World War II there was consensus on governance. If one rereads the Robbins report, one of the historic postwar documents on university developments in the United Kingdom, it is readily apparent that, though written and published as late as the early 1960s, it is a "before the deluge" statement, at least in respect of many issues which came to be—or to appear to be—of urgent importance only a few years later. This point was made in the course of discussion on the governance of higher education at the recent quinquennial conference of the Association of Commonwealth Universities. There it was pointed out that the Robbins report assumed the continuance of a predominantly professorial role—using the word "professorial" in the technical British sense as applying to the senior echelon of academic persons, collectively embodied in the senate or professorial board—in the academic governance of the university. Moreover, there is little in that report which has to do with the role of the student in university governance. In the early 1960s, in a pervasive sense, he was *in statu pupillari* and while, even earlier, some attention had been drawn to the desirability of consultation with students, and in some instances there was modest student representation on university boards, the general proposition remained true.

A few years later, questions directly related to university governance faced us urgently; in 1970 Clark Kerr—one among many to use the word, and one who had had personal and bitter experience of the change in the university situation—wrote of crisis in university governance, specifically in the context of the United States, but also, by implication, more generally. Students, he said, were the new men of power. He drew attention also to the changing attitudes of university teachers and to the new problems which their demands and their developing patterns of association and combination presented for the university. In an excellent analysis of the Columbia (New York) crisis of 1968, Walter Metzger pointed out that older unchallenged structures of university government proved themselves to be manifestly incapable of dealing with massive and unanticipated pressures and threats, and that this pointed to the need for devising structures which would anticipate rather than trail events. The Carnegie commission, in its statement on governance to which I have already referred, observed that while the immediate crisis pressures of the late sixties and early seventies appeared to be abated, there was an urgent need to come to grips with problems of governance: it said that we might well look forward to a period of continuing conflict and tension with universities and institutions of higher education, that while the great issues of a few years before had focused on the student role, the major problems of the seventies might be concerned primarily with the role of the "faculty," using that word to encompass the whole academic body of teachers and instructors. The Carnegie commission report also discussed at length the relationship of the university with government; in a world in which higher education loomed much larger as a matter of public concern and regulation. Such matters are certainly germane to any discussion of the governance of higher education.

The point is that many of these problems, although they arise within university systems which exhibit differing historical characteristics, are common. If one reads Henri Janne's comprehensive statement on the *Universities and the Needs of Contemporary Society* (1970), a report to the International Association of Universities which takes into account issues which appear important to universities in many countries at varying stages of development; if we consider a range of reports such as the perceptive Hart *Report of the Committee on Relations with Junior Members* (1969), which considered particular issues in Oxford University; and the already mentioned recent Carnegie commission report on *Governance of Higher Education* (to instance a very few among a *copia* of reports relating to universities in many countries); as one reads the multitude of books, essays, symposia, and discussions on themes bearing on higher education which have appeared during or in the wake of the events of these last few years, it becomes readily apparent that many problems of university governance have significant common elements. In the first place, it is clear that the apparent consensus on matters of governance of only a few years past has disappeared. In the midst of such growth in higher education, why the apparent consensus lasted so long is perhaps the question we should ask. It has been suggested, in an American context, that the underlying consensus was not around any *specific* set of academic values but, rather, around a set of values that were seen as justifying the coexistence of quite diverse educational enterprises. These were the distinguishing values of what we have come to call the "multiversity": general acceptance and tolerance of the broadest range of functions and services; and a very flexible set of governmental values which were (or were thought to be) educationally neutral, not interfering with any educational programs, and providing a very substantial measure of autonomy for organizational elements, chiefly departments, but also including research centers, schools, colleges, and so forth. The whole was tied together by a complex set of procedures, which were both collegial and bureaucratic, but which appeared to achieve the required degree of coordination of a wide range of diverse activities and people and maintained the necessary control over expenditures and records while preserving for the teaching and research units a very high degree of freedom and autonomy. While these procedures were very often irritating, cumbersome, slow, and defective in many respects, nonetheless they gained the acquiescence of most of the participants in the institutions and (what is also of major importance) the basic assumption was that the procedures themselves could be modified by regular and generally accepted procedures.

In the scope of a short discussion of an enormously wide-ranging topic, it is not possible to explore what has elsewhere been explored at exhaustive and exhausting length, the reasons why this is no longer so. In the latter sixties particularly, universities experienced corrosive forms of ideological controversy which made their work often very difficult, sometimes impossible. As Martin Trow says, "It [made] the ordinary compromises of organizational administration impermissible as unprincipled and corrupt and most of all it [was] charged with a kind of moral passion that makes any tactics seem to be justified by the virtuous end." That was written in 1970 in bad times, and it may well be that the bitterness and the urgency do not seem so apparent at this point in time. But the underlying problems of governance remain and have, so far as I am capable of knowing, a broadly universal character. How is the university to be governed *within*, that is to say internally? What is the role of president, rector, or vice-chancellor, or a board of governors which may include a substantial lay element? What is the role of the faculty and of the varying elements and levels within the faculty? What is the role of the student in university governance? What are the roles *inter se*? In exploring the role of the student there are issues which go to his place as participant or as consultant, the definition of his role *in statu pupillari*, the function and ambit of university discipline, and who should be involved in the administration of a disciplinary system. These are all issues which are the common concern of those of us who make our lives in universities, whether as administrators or as teachers and all of them go to questions of university governance. They cannot be sensibly discussed, of course, without some definition of the role and activities of the university. As we explore the problems of governance, in the light of the issues which have led to the crisis in the university in so many places, we must keep in mind Stanley Hoffman's point that "while 'who governs' may well be one of the key questions of politics, 'what for' is the other one. The wrong 'who' cannot reach the right 'what' and, depending on the what, the right who will not be the same." Put another way, the proposition must be that governance should be, must be, related to a proper consideration of functions; this in turn means that the search for fixed, universal formulas may be the quest for fools' gold. While any general examination of university governance will consider problems of broad and far-reaching concern to institutions of higher education everywhere (so far as I know), a useful examination of the problems must be responsive to the historic and specific situations and problems which arise in particular contexts.

I have dealt thus far—and I shall return to the theme of the problems of governance of the university *within*—with the relationship of the university estates; I have referred also to the relationship of the university to the wider community and government. The capacity of the university (viewed as a corporate entity) to govern itself depends obviously upon the constraints which the wider community imposes upon it—and the fact is that university autonomy is under serious challenge. The Carnegie commission report, in a study of American problems, devotes a very good chapter to issues which bear upon autonomy and university independence and implications for academic freedom. Autonomy is a word which has very different meaning in differing university contexts. In the American, the British, the Australian contexts, it is seen as very important. While it does not mean precisely the same thing as academic freedom (which is a cherished claim for universities at large), institutional autonomy is seen in these countries as serving broadly the ends of academic freedom. I was struck, however, in participating in a recent seminar on problems of higher education with a group of European colleges, by their reaction to my discussion of autonomy. In some historic European university contexts it was observed that autonomy might be seen as the enemy of academic freedom—viewed at least from the standpoint of the university body as a whole, and particularly from the standpoint of the junior teaching staff. The imposition by state law of the *Drittelparität* was seen as a challenge at least to the abuses, but fundamentally to the structure, of the German *Ordinarienuniversität*, and as an act of state policy to assure shared authority and privileges and participation in a *Gruppenuniversität*. It was seen as a protection of the interests of more junior academic staff. I shall return to this point later.

To come generally to the issue of the relationship of the university to the state, the fact is that the freedom of the university from external control has declined significantly since World War II, particularly in recent years. In some important senses, autonomy in the fullest sense has never been asserted; many charters and constitutive acts of universities in my country and elsewhere depend upon state law and, while one may and does question particular exercises of state law, the broad power of the state in this area is not ultimately questioned. Moreover, as the Carnegie commission pointed out, while autonomy is much demanded in principle, much of higher education is actually trying to escape as fast as it can from the remaining provinces of full financial autonomy. Universities want more public financial support and must in consequence accept some dependence. The public financial commitment to higher education bears decisively on issues of autonomy; but, as well as this, public concern with universities and higher education is voiced as never before, and this has attracted attention to issues bearing on university governance. As Clark Kerr has said, higher education has become everybody's business; the campus is no longer on the hill with the aristocracy but in the valley with the people. There are many more young people attending universities and associated institutions. Higher education has assumed an increasingly important role in placing people in the occupational structure and thus in determining their adult class positions and life chances. In industrial societies, in particular—and the United States is a conspicuous but not an exclusive example—there is a growing feeling that there is a legitimate claim on the part of a very wide range of people to the benefits of a higher education, no longer the exclusive preserve of a narrow class which possesses understanding of the higher culture.

Higher education, then, is seen as assuming a public-utility status, subject to regulation in the name of the public interest. One of the important issues to be explored in any comprehensive examination of university governance is the definition of the elements of essential independence for universities and associated institutions. The use of the words "associated institutions" draws attention to the growth of *systems* of higher education, to the proliferation of diverse institutions serving a wide variety of purposes. In Australia, alongside the traditional system of state universities (which have themselves multiplied), there has developed a structure of colleges of advanced education responding to a somewhat uncertainly articulated philosophy of distinctively vocational emphasis, and a body of specialized institutions such as teachers' colleges. All depend very heavily upon state support. Up to this point public resource allocation has been made by government on the basis of recommendations by separate authorities (that is, separate for universities and other institutions). However, with increasing claims on the public purse in areas of education extending beyond the post-secondary, and with increasing claims extending far beyond those of the education sector, the time cannot be far distant when (for fiscal reasons, at least) governmental oversight over the structure as a whole will become tighter and increasingly specific. The implications of all of this for institutional independence, for the claim of universities and other institutions of higher education to govern themselves, become readily apparent. To this may be added the impact of events in recent years: publics which foot the bill have witnessed with no great relish the development of dissent and disruption on university campuses and have seen the development of life styles which are nonconformist and unpalatable to public opinion. The Carnegie commission speaks in the context of governance of a "crisis over independence," while pointing out that one has to view institutional autonomy coolly and with an awareness that in places where it is more freely available it has at times been poorly used, in that it has at times aped and copied and has failed to seize the initiative to experiment and diversify. The commission argues, however, that the interests of the university as an intellectual institution are served by an ample measure of independence. It makes the point very effectively that governance can be profoundly affected to the extent to which public authority intrudes into the affairs of institutions primarily in the interests of systematization, but, it may also be, for broader political purposes. One proposal of the commission, in the specific American context, is that the American Council on Education establish a commission on institutional independence to be concerned with policies affecting independence and with the degree of adherence to them. Once again this may be affected by particular American contexts and by some governmental intrusions and pressures perceived to be unwarranted, but it is an interesting proposition to explore in a wider context. At the same time, no one with a proper view of the purpose of higher education should question the commission's proposition that "the purpose of public support for higher education . . . is not to aid faculty members or administrators to serve their own self-interests when these depart from socially useful functions. The higher education community earns independence by what it does in the public interest, not by what it does for itself alone or by what it demands for itself alone. It has no inherent right, regardless of its conduct, to support an independence." Such propositions need to be fleshed out; but I have no doubt that the general proposition is sound.

In dealing with constraints imposed by public authority on the university's power and scope of authority to govern itself, it is necessary to have regard to the limiting operation of the law generally. In recent years, particularly, the courts have intruded into the university domain, in holding that particular acts may not be lawful. This results to some extent from particular national or state constitutional provisions, not least those of a "bill of rights" character; and, to some extent, they are applications of common law principles as understood and enunciated in particular systems. In the context of British systems the intrusion is not dramatic. It is good that judges have stated firmly that the campus is subject to the general law of the land. I cannot boast any certain knowledge of all systems and I understand also that, according to views held in some places, there is some distinctive freedom from the general law, some operative principle of asylum within the physical area of the campus. While public authority may take the view that it is the course of wisdom not too readily to intrude into the domestic affairs and authority of the campus, it is utterly unacceptable to me that the campus should claim any special privilege of immunity. Indeed the rule of law, which university people should cherish, asserts that the university and members of the university can claim no such immunity.

Having said so much, it is clear that the law does impose some fetters on the power of university authority. In the United States we have seen this as an outcome of doctrines of due process and the equal protection of the law, in such contexts as admission policies, differential fee-charging policies, and procedures relating to staff contracts and to hearings affecting student and staff discipline and tenure. In British systems the principle of *audi alteram partem* (the right in substance to a fair hearing) has been asserted in particular contexts affecting university matters.

One of the most interesting legal decisions affecting university governance has been the recent German constitutional court's decision on the constitutionality of the Lower Saxony state law imposing upon the university the obligation to observe the governmental requirements of the *Drittelparität* in university operations. The implication of the decision is, if I understand it correctly, that such a requirement would, in the context of teaching and research anyway, be inconsistent with the fundamental law of the Federal German Republic, whether it was imposed by state or (as here) by university law. I have not yet had an opportunity to read the court opinion *in extenso* and I acknowledge the courtesy of Professor Edward Shils in making available his extended note on the case in the winter, 1973, issue of *Minerva*. The *Drittelparität* was a legislative assault on the *Ordinarien-*

universität; it called for the participation of a variety of elements, a broad range of academic staff, students, and nonacademic staff, in the various decisional and governmental processes of the university including the scope, ambit, and operations of teaching and research. The court said this contravened the clause in the fundamental law of the federal republic which assures freedom of teaching and research; while allowing state law (and by implication university law) some latitude in imposing governmental rules on the university, it was said that the law was unconstitutional in that, in this form, it did not accord to those distinctively concerned the necessary measure of voice and control over teaching and research programs and policies.

I turn now to other questions bearing upon university governance. It has been well said that no clear theory about governance within institutions is generally accepted as a basis for formulating policy. As the campus has grown in size and complexity, as its demands for resources have grown, as it has come to occupy a more significant place in the eyes of the community (for reasons I developed earlier in discussing questions of autonomy and independence), questions of efficiency, expressed in administrative and managerial terms, have been raised. The model of the corporate structure has been discussed. As to this, it is readily apparent that the corporate analogy has very marked limits. The university, as Clark Kerr has said, concentrates on inputs not outputs; corporate performance, on the other hand, is concerned with outputs, with value added to inputs. Indeed, much of the input and output of universities consists of people rather than things and this may produce an organizational consequence, alien to corporate and bureaucratic concepts alike, of the desirability of a considerable degree of decentralization to give the greatest scope to pupil-teacher relations. There is little in the university to compare with the corporation's "mission-defining force of profits"; in the corporation this calls for a particular coordinated and hierarchical form of organization. There are many other areas of comparison which lead to the conclusion that ideas drawn from business and public administration alike have only a limited application to the university. Yet, clearly, some aspects of university governance and administration do lend themselves to good corporate experience and practice. Various examples come to mind: the construction and operation of buildings (though in the field of operation there are some qualifications); purchasing supplies; selection, retention, training, and promotion of significant sectors of staff who are unquestionably described as employees; investment of funds; designation of some control centers; the use of cost accounting—in these and other areas there is a strong reason for applying business measures of administration and governance. In a field central to the academic purpose, research, there is much value in the analysis of research projects—and, in particular, the acceptance and operation of such projects—for a more hardheaded business analysis of their overhead costs.

The corporate analogy is, then, relevant to some degree in university government and administration. In some respects consumer analogies apply; while some would argue that the producer-consumer analogy is inappropriate to the university model, the fact must remain that as a matter of resource allocation no university can design its offerings without regard to student enrollments. No rhetoric can deprive of validity the proposition that a system of university governance which does not take account of consumer analogies in this regard is unsatisfactory and will inevitably distort the operations of the institutions.

What has emerged as a matter of major concern in the last decade has been the issue of faculty and student participation in the governance of the university. This was central to the crisis period of the late sixties when, it was said, students became the new men of power. Whereas earlier they had asked for more freedom for themselves, they now sought to reduce the established authority of others. Within the faculty—the academic body, a substantial segment of which has won for itself the entrenched privilege of tenure—there have been significant developments. Vast growth and accretion of resources have inevitably damaged if not destroyed, collegiality; the very fact of size, the specialization of discipline, the thinning of common knowledge, all have had a major impact. Often, staff identification has been with disciplines rather than with institutions; faculty have seen themselves as physicists or economists in a wider world of physicists or economists transcending the individual university. Many have built up for themselves independent baronies in their relations with foundations, institutes, and governments; this has made for formidable distortions in budgets and overall university planning as well as for general cohesiveness. As Stanley Hoffman has put it, this has turned many academics away from the university, made them over into men of affairs and entrepreneurs for whom the university is merely a base, a part-time employer, and a focus of partial allegiance. This is no rhetoric, as those of us responsible for university administration know only too well. There is, furthermore, the schism (not diminishing, by any means) between junior and senior staff—described by one able American president at the recent quinquennial conference of the Association of Commonwealth Universities as one of the major problems in universities today. The junior staff member, without tenure, without the perquisites and outside interests and commitments of his senior colleagues, not infrequently identifies himself with students vis-à-vis senior faculty and administration. There is, too—and this is of growing concern for a complex of reasons which bear upon university governance—the development of industrial action, of unionization of university staff, which poses a variety of problems. It gives rise to tensions in the claims of staff members vis-à-vis the institution with which they are bargaining. On the one hand, in analogies to a political community, they claim the right of participation in the collegial process of self-determination of the operations and activities of the university; on the other and simultaneously, they take up an adversary position to the institution or at least to some part of it in their industrial claims whether these are given a narrow or an extended ambit. How consistency may be maintained in these positions is not readily explained and in terms of university governance it presents a formidable set of problems. I return to this later.

At this point I would like to offer some general observations about students as members of the university. Earlier, I said that when the Robbins report appeared in the early sixties there was little consideration of the political, governmental role of students in the university. In general, the description of the student *in statu pupillari* was not much questioned, or very precisely analyzed. The functions of governance assigned to students related to student representative councils, and from time to time the operation of unions, campus papers, and the like. The major issues of dispute were freedom from irritating dormitory-related house rules. Discipline still meant a mass of regulations, little analyzed and little challenged, save in these dormitory rule areas, and the definition of the role of the university *in loco parentis* was of comparatively little concern to anyone defining the role of discipline. In the sixties, in the context of university discipline, this changed profoundly, with respect both to the scope and legitimacy of university discipline and to the definition and constitution of the disciplinary authority. Once again, this is familiar ground to many who have been in the battle. There have been many discussions and pronouncements on *in loco parentis* questions and it is clearly stated in the Hart report on relations with junior members (the Oxford reports of 1969) that, having regard to its strict Latin context, it was implausible to maintain that the university occupied in this respect any role precisely comparable with that which a parent maintains over his child. There was, however, a broader meaning assigned to *in loco parentis*, in that the university did assume a paternalistic posture in its disciplinary codes, and in their operation.

It is this paternalistic posture which has been under insistent challenge; many universities and reports have asserted that it is no part of the role of the contemporary university. Only a few years ago, a University of Toronto report stated formally that

> the doctrine of *in loco parentis* would make the university responsible for the moral and social behavior of students. We reject the application of *in loco parentis* at this university. There is an important communication problem in respect to *in loco parentis*. It is desirable that the parents and guardians of students of the university be informed that if this doctrine ever were in force, such is no longer the case. The university assumes its students are sufficiently mature that they should make their own decisions concerning moral and social behavior.

A similar proposition was empathically stated by the Ontario Commission in its *Report on Post Secondary Education in Ontario*, published in 1972. "The time has come for all vestiges of *in loco parentis* or guardianship rules to be abolished." Lord Devlin said pretty much the same thing in his *Report on the Sit-In in February 1972 and Its Consequences* (a report relating to Cambridge University), published in early 1973. While I believe that universities have complex responsibilities for their students, and that university teachers should properly be exemplars in a broad sense, I agree.

This carries with it consequences with regard to the definition of university discipline. This merits discussion because it concerns a very controversial area of university governance. Whatever happened in the past, university discipline should be concerned (putting aside the necessity to regulate such things as motor cars on the campus) with fitness to remain a member of the university society. University discipline is not concerned with general criminal behavior which is a matter for the civil authority; it should not seek to protect the student from the criminal consequences of what he has done. The offenses with which the university is exclusively concerned are those which go to the fitness to remain a member of the society. There are obvious examples: disruption of university activities, exemplified in sit-ins and, in a particularly ugly form, in denying to speakers who hold unpalatable views the right to be heard or to move unimpeded within the university. A number have experienced this; and, particularly in the life of a university, it is among the vilest of offences against the university code. The disciplinary inquiry, therefore, is concerned with the question whether to exclude the transgressor from the society. If a lesser punishment of temporary suspension or fine is imposed, the reason is quite simply that the offense is not of sufficient magnitude to warrant permanent exclusion, though it partakes of the character of a university offense and cannot be disregarded. The sooner discipline is seen in this light, the sooner we shall approach a clear and rational approach to this aspect of university governance. There are cases which are uncertain; the Hart report debates some of these and I myself had to grapple with a complex set of issues in 1970, but the principle is clear. As the Oxford report rightly said, "Punishments are not to be multiplied beyond necessity." Once this is seen, the often heard arguments about double jeopardy resolve themselves. That argument goes this way: no person should be punished twice for the same offense. Therefore, if a person is punished by the criminal courts for a particular act, the university should take no further action against him. It is a nonsense argument: the very fact of a criminal conviction for an act of a particular character may be the very best evidence and reason for excluding him from the university because he is unfit to remain a member of the society. It does not mean of course that certain criminal acts, punished in the courts, properly justify the university in excluding the student. There are very good and sound analogies drawn from the practice of professional bodies which expel persons from a profession, following the commission of a criminal act punished by criminal conviction.

I believe, furthermore, that university discipline defined in this way is an area in which students of the university should properly be involved in judicialized proceedings. There are differing views and practices on this matter, and I have been involved in remaking the discipline laws of two

Australian universities. In my present university, the disciplinary body concerned with more serious offenses has equal staff and student representation and while there have been problems (going to the form of appointment of the students) I believe it is soundly based. Students have a real concern with the fitness of others to continue as members of the society; they bring to their consideration a careful—indeed, it may be a severe—judgment. I believe, without developing the point at great length, that there is a substantial student representation on tribunals concerned with the discipline of the university.

I turn now to other points with regard to university governance. There has been much discussion about the role of lay persons in that governance. In a number of countries—in the United States, in many universities in the United Kingdom, and in my own country—university acts and charters accord a significant role to lay representation on governing bodies. There are varying historic reasons; public concern with the institution is reflected in the desirability of involving persons who do not spend their daily lives in the university. The Carnegie report on the *Governance of Higher Education* devotes considerable attention to this aspect; it concludes (in my view, rightly) that lay participation well serves the interest of the university. It subjects this proposition to qualification in terms that it is undesirable to import politically elected officials as ex officio members of governing bodies and the reasons are plain: it sees a board with lay representation as holding the "trust," as serving as two-way communication—interpreting the community to the university, and university to community. It sees a board with substantial lay representation as a supervisor, as assuming basic responsibility for the financial welfare of the campus, as a final arbiter of internal disputes involving various elements within the university. It is well put by the Carnegie commission in terms that such a board "acts as a 'buffer' between society and the campus resisting improper external interference and introducing a necessary contact with the changing realities of the surrounding society; it is the principal gatekeeper for the campus." Of course in times of acute pressure, such as we have witnessed in recent years, things may go bad. Martin Trow, reviewing the difficulties and problems confronting the University of California in the sixties, observed that under heavy pressures the Board of Regents—so far from serving its buffer functions—wilted under a diversity of pressures and, instead of defending the university to its external publics, began to function as a conduit of popular sentiment and pressure on the university; this placed all the functions of the university in grave jeopardy. Yet, as Clark Kerr, himself a victim of this, says—the properly constituted lay board serves the university well as an instrument of governance, though its role often needs clarification, particularly in determining how best it may review performance. Moreover, its membership needs scrutiny, particularly in determining how members may best be chosen to assure an understanding of the devotion to the institution in its myriad aspects.

Lay involvement in governance is not universal, but one of the issues most broadly and intensively debated during the crisis of the latter sixties has been the involvement of the university community—teachers and students—in governing the university. The claims of the senior professoriate to a special role was challenged by more junior staff; students have laid claim to participate in university government at many levels. In its most extreme form, the claim has been made that the university should be seen as a political democracy, and governed on a one-man-one-vote basis. Just as the corporate analogy is of limited validity in relation to the university, so too is this one. The reasons were well and explicitly stated by the Hart Committee:

> A University has as its distinctive purpose the advancement of knowledge and teaching conceived not as the mere transmission of knowledge but as the development of powers of criticism and judgment and the adjustment of the vitalizing interplay between research and teaching. In our view, no theory of legal and political rights for the conduct of society as a whole, not even democratic theory, is transferable to the government of these distinctively academic activities. Since these are the distinctive purposes to be pursued it is, we believe, plain that teachers equipped by skill, knowledge and experience, training and professional association with a university should have final authority as to the manner in which they are pursued. We think that the contrary view can be held by those who ignore the complexity of the truth and the extent to which its attainment is dependent on experience, accumulated knowledge and organization.

The analogy to democratic political society breaks down in many respects. Political society does not operate as a participatory democracy of the whole; that is too absurd to contemplate. The way democracy works in political society, with party systems and diverse forms of executive government, seems scarcely relevant to the situation of the university; and within political society specialized adjudicative and other complex functions are discharged by persons and bodies who are not themselves chosen by democratic processes. Also, while the very size, complexity, and diversity of function of a political society makes participatory democracy of the whole impossible, it is also unworkable and undesirable within the university for the reasons adumbrated in the Hart report and for other reasons as well. Participatory democracy simply does not achieve the expression of the philosopher's general will. It opens the door to crude majoritarianism; if not that, it leaves open the door to manipulation by a determined and comparatively small group who will stay while others have wearied and gone off to work which they see as more rewarding and more relevant to their role with the university. The costs of "voice" in time and energy are demonstrably high—as those who have experience of committee systems within universities know full well. Many, faced with the price of involvement in university governance, turn away from it. It is not only students who, offered the choice of participation and membership of university bodies, respond with limited enthusiasm; it is also true for faculty who often prefer the ancient academic ways to the not infrequently dreary and time-consuming tasks of governance. In the context of large-scale universities deliberative bodies, it is well to heed the views of the Carnegie commission which cautions against hasty consideration of "community councils" or "university-wide senates," whether of an advisory or a legislative type. The experience to date of such bodies yields quite mixed results: at times contributing to the solution of problems, and at times detracting from solution. The commission, on the basis of American experience, urges that where such councils are created it is best that they have only advisory authority.

The arguments advanced so far do not lead to a rejection *in globo* of participation by elements of the university community in governance. Indeed the Hart Committee, from whose report I have quoted, argued in favor of substantial *student* participation and consultation in various areas of university operation in Oxford.

I shall come back shortly to the question of student participation. I wish to say something first about faculty participation. Academic participation in university governance, of course, is not "new wine." What is newer is the increasing demand for this to be spread more widely. While the system of faculty governance most familiar to me was not devised in the shape of the German *Ordinarienuniversität*, the role of the full professor was very important and, as the Robbins report of the early sixties made clear, there was a special role in university governance for senior academics both collectively in academic senates and as department heads. This has come under increasing challenge; it has been successfully argued that the base of university academic senates should be broadened to include a much wider range of academic grades; within the departments consultation by the head of department with members of the department may be and is prescribed by university law; and departmental headships, on a rotating and short-term basis, are open to academics of more junior rank. What is now opening up, as I said earlier, is a demand on the part of untenured junior academic staff for a greater voice, as well as for better conditions of appointment, and this may become one of the difficult issues of the seventies. The Carnegie commission says that the seventies may well be "the decade of the faculty" and that the locus of activism is shifting from students to faculty. One of the significant developments now unfolding is the growth of unionism and collective bargaining. This has developed most rapidly in the United States where it is at its strongest in community colleges, and specialized bodies such as teachers' colleges, rather than in established universities. The growth of collective bargaining and the extension of the ambit of the bargain poses some very important questions. Hitherto, the faculty has been pressing for a collegial view of the university, for comanagement of the institution in areas of academic concern—curriculum, research, selection and promotion of colleagues, admissions, selection of academic administrators, and determination of grades and degrees. Where the ambit of the collective bargain is broad, it would seem that a position inconsistent with the claim to codetermination is asserted: that the postures of the parties specifically oppose management to the managed.

The development of collective bargaining has other implications for university governance. Since the claims inevitably have a major fiscal aspect, the paymaster is involved. The consequence is that in negotiations government becomes an important party at the table; this may have a significant, and it could be an increasing and enduring, impact on campus autonomy. Furthermore, students have shown an increasing concern with collective bargaining between faculty and university. One of the significant recent developments, with the lowering of the voting age, has been the growth of the student political lobby. A recent press report referred to the student lobby in California as voicing to government its opposition to the collective bargaining stance of the faculty on the ground that the student body had a legitimate interest in the outcome and saw itself as frozen out by a collective bargaining process between faculty and university administration. The Carnegie commission, in its thoughtful review of developments in collective bargaining, observes that it may tend to supplant codetermination in an irreversible process. The commission expresses concern at the wider orbit of collective bargaining which extends over a broad range of academic affairs and does not confine itself to economic benefits. It counsels restraint and calls for study of the implications; it urges that collective bargaining, to the extent to which it enters higher education, should not become the new system of governance. It advocates this in the interests of preserving strong faculty influence over academic affairs and of retaining a reasonable degree of independence from external control for institutions of higher education.

Much has been written and spoken about student participation in university governance. It was one of the great issues of the latter sixties. Earlier than that, in the mid-fifties a conference of European rectors and vice-chancellors of European universities had recommended that students should be consulted and accorded some measure of initiative in all questions relating to their welfare and social life within the university, and had expressed the hope that academic authorities (whose right it was to make decisions about the curriculum) should seek ways of making it possible for students to make known their point of view on these matters. Little more than a decade later, the joint statement of the United Kingdom Vice-Chancellors and Principals and the National Union of Students committed the heads of institutions of higher learning to take into account students' views on curriculum, courses, teaching methods, and major organizational matters affecting the planning and development of the university, while reserving the power of decision to the statutorily responsible bodies. Also it committed the signatories to take into account the view of students on the general principles involved in decisions regarding appointments and promotions, admissions and assessment, though it was agreed that student membership on bodies concerned with such matters was inappropriate.

That students in the sixties should have pressed for a larger voice in university affairs is not surprising, looking at the massive increases in their numbers, at the shifting interests of faculty, and at the growing complexity of universities. Generally, there has been a significant growth of political concern and involvement on the part of students, accentuated by the operations of the media. Moreover, as already pointed out, the political processes have worked to give them a voting voice at an earlier age in general political affairs; this inevitably affects their stance in relation to university matters. To what extent their role should be that of participation in the work of university at various levels, and to what extent the role should be consultation without direct participation has also been much debated—I draw attention, for example, to the debate between Lord Ashby and Dr. Anderson on the one side and Edward Shils on the other in the pages of *Minerva* in 1970—but there is certainly no disagreement on the claim to appropriate consultation. Students have rejected, and have persuaded universities to cast aside, older notions of *in statu pupillari*; it is not surprising that they should have carried the argument over into broader areas of university governance. It has been fairly said that older notions assigned responsibility to student government only for trifles and left matters which most affected their lives as students to be dealt with without student consultation and participation. There are important questions to be explored: What are the appropriate areas for participation and consultation? What is the educational value of student participation? How does participation and consultation impact upon effective university government? What areas of governance should be reserved to the faculty in the sense that (while there may readily be consultation on principle) decision must ultimately be reserved to the faculty because of the distinctive purposes of the university? The Cambridge report of Lord Devlin observed that "student participation is new wine and it would be unsafe to receive it in the firm conviction that the old bottles will do." There is general sympathy now, I believe, for the proposition that students should have a voice in areas of governance where they have a substantial interest, adequate competence, and where they are willing to assume the responsibilities of participation. Whether the particular formula be that of consultation or participation, whether representation or consultation be at the departmental, faculty, or university-wide level, there is obvious good sense in the proposition that students can inform the decision-making agencies in the university about their experiences and desires; they can contribute advice and judgment and give support to innovation. There are many questions which have been discussed so many times: what should be the appropriate constituencies from which to draw student representatives, what should be the procedures devised to assure that they contribute freely to discussion and not under mandate from their constituencies? I believe that the conclusion of the Carnegie commission on this point is sound when it says that "students should be involved in governance to the extent—which in some areas can be significant—that they contribute to the quality of decisions and to the overall performance of the campus. . . . Students should now be incorporated more fully into the on-going decision-making process on campus within the limits of their interest and competence." This does not answer the question when, where, how, with precision because, I suspect, there are no general, universal answers. We do well to heed the statement of Clark Kerr in his discussion of problems of governance and functions, that area by area, the central questions should be: Who has an interest in the problem? Who has competence to deal with it? The test should be performance and this practical, pragmatic approach can lead to a whole series of agreements, area by area, at any moment of time.

One final point may be made which emerges from the experience of those who have major responsibilities in universities. This is the importance of providing for effective communication throughout the campus of decisions, actions, of what is going on. The capacity for misunderstanding, misinterpretation, and, in the hands of those who wish to have it so, falsification, is well-nigh unlimited. The Assembly on University Goals and Governance of the American Academy of Arts and Sciences has said rightly that, if the internal and external constituencies of a college or university are to be kept properly informed, effective use of the written word is required. Colleges and universities should have regular publications reporting on a wide variety of specifications taken by various groups with responsibility for governance in the institution. The importance in facilitating the good and effective governance of universities is great.

Such an essay as this is inevitably selective in its discussion of aspects of university governance. It has omitted much, and space has allowed only posing questions which do not and perhaps cannot yield precise answers. It has perhaps given special emphasis to problems which appear most relevant to the author, having regard to his particular university context, but it is hoped that it will open up debate on a range of topics bearing on university governance.

The University's Autonomy versus Social Priorities

Richard Lowenthal

THERE IS A COMMON CONVICTION that the values of the university as we have known it are threatened in our time—and threatened by forces more general and more lasting than the particular forms of interference which each of us may have experienced, whether by student radicals or by dilettante politicians. In fact, the university faces a profound dilemma—between the inherent needs of the republic of scholars and the requirements of contemporary industrial societies. That dilemma has found expression in wide disagreements, not only in public opinion at large but also among university teachers themselves.

The challenge to the university is directly linked to its partial change of functions. At its core there remains what may be termed its "classical" function: the education of future scholars and scientists. There is still an overwhelming weight of argument favoring the view that this should be done in universities based on the unity of teaching and research. Also, the "modern" function of education for practical professions requiring scientific knowledge and skills, existing for centuries with regard to the study of medicine and the law, has expanded immensely both by the development of new professional fields and by the growth of numbers in the old fields. But here we find much disagreement on whether this function should continue to be performed in universities proper or in separate "educational institutes" and, if within the universities, whether the mass of professional students and their problems can be accommodated in the framework of traditional university constitutions. It is indeed primarily from this side that the public demand for university reform has arisen in some countries. Finally, there is least agreement on another function that used to be fulfilled by the universities of the past—the education of homogeneous social and political elites by imparting to them a common sense of values, largely on the basis of humanistic studies: must this function inevitably disappear with the transition from the old "elite university" to the egalitarian "mass university," or must it rather be transformed into a new kind of "civic" education so as to strengthen a wider sense of common values needed for the cohesion of any civilized society?

I propose to deal with three controversial issues concerning the place of the university in contemporary society: first, with the importance and the limits of the university's autonomy and with the institutional consequences of its social obligations; second, with the relation between the independent pursuit of truth and the political duties of scholar and student as citizens; third, with the reasons for or against continuing to combine in a single institution the various functions here discussed. In other words, I shall deal with the range and limit of the university's autonomy, with the value and limits of its political neutrality, and with the case for maintaining its unity.

I

1. I shall start from the statement that what I have called the core or classifical function of the university, the education of future scholars and scientists, offers also the core of the case for its autonomy. To formulate it in the terms of Professor Alexander Bickel's paper, "faculty self-rule" is indispensable for the continuation of scholarship—for the selection, education, recognition, and appointment of future scholars and scientists— and with it, for the preservation of the standards and the development of the methods of teaching and research. (I shall explain presently why I have omitted the word "curriculum" from the list of issues mentioned by Professor Bickel.) Autonomy of the qualified members of the university in these minimum essentials is crucial not only for assuring the quality of teaching and research in the university itself, but for the continuation of an open and dynamic society. For, along with separation of secular from spiritual rule and the growth of self-governing and self-defending cities, the autonomous universities of the West ever since the Middle Ages have been among the specific institutions responsible for the unique dynamism of Western society: it was the scope they gave for individual, critical thought and its communication that helped to produce the characteristic Western pattern of multiple, unplanned, and gradually accelerating change that has transformed first the West and then the world. Today, as in the past, the dynamism of an open society depends to a vital extent on the assured freedom of scholars to develop their thought in a community of mutual criticism and common standards. Only a university based on "faculty self-rule" can preserve that.

2. But the case for full autonomy of the universities is by no means equally obvious with regard to the "modern" function of education, in which requirements for diplomas opening the entrance into various practical professions, and for courses of study leading up to them have to be decided upon. Faculty self-rule in decisions on the curriculum is a self-

evident principle with respect to the education of future scholars and scientists. But the masses of future lawyers and physicians, schoolteachers and social workers, engineers and business economists, civil servants and market analysts—and many others who go to the university to qualify for their jobs—need in part a different course of study from the future academics; and present academics are not necessarily the best or the only judges of what they require. What these students must learn in order to perform their function in society is not an exclusive concern of the university—it cannot, therefore, be treated purely as its internal affair. Hence it is sensible that examination requirements for diplomas leading into such professions, and the general framework for courses of study preparing for them, should be settled jointly by representatives of public authorities responsible for higher education, of professional organizations concerned (including those of their future public or private employers), and by the experts within universities.

I know that many objections may be raised to that view. It is argued, for instance, that society's view of just what it requires from its professionals is often uncertain and ever changing. Indeed, it is inevitable in rapidly changing conditions. But that does not make the universities better judges of society's requirements—on the contrary, it demands their flexible adjustment to changing needs. Another argument for leaving that adjustment to autonomous decision inside the university is that, over time, the necessary corrections will be assured by the pressure of "the market": students in a particular field will flock to those universities that present attractive programs and whose alumni succeed in professional life. That road may indeed have proved less slow than it sounds in the United States, with the intense competition among widely different types of public and private universities. But in Western Europe, which has almost exclusively state universities, based in some countries on highly centralized systems, the market has made very little impact on a quasi-monopolistic university structure—with the result that reforms for practical-oriented courses of study have made little or no progress unless imposed from outside. In some countries where traditional autonomy was transferred by legislation from faculties to "democratized" university organs with strong student participation, the sluggishness of tradition-bound faculties has been merely replaced by the obstruction of radical student representatives to any reform that could serve the interests of the wicked "late-capitalist" society.

Of course, universities should remain autonomous with regard to *methods* of teaching as well as to concrete shaping of curricula in the field of professional study courses. But the basic requirements for entry into the professions outside the universities can be effectively settled only in cooperation with qualified representatives of the polity in general, and with the professional groups concerned in particular.

3. There is, however, one direction in which the influence of "market

demand" tends to become so strong that faculty self-rule needs strengthening against it—its impact on the subjects as distinct from the methods of research. Modern research in both the natural and the social sciences has come to be recognized as a "revolutionary productive force"—the Marxist term is indeed appropriate here, for science has long been changing the conditions of living for all of us. The result of this dependence of society on the progress of research has been a rising demand for research and its results from both government and industry; much of this is directed to the universities, influencing the size and distribution of their research budgets and with it the proportions in which different university departments develop at any given time. Obviously, this financial pull is not only an effective, but also a reasonable and legitimate, mechanism for bringing social priorities to bear on autonomous decisions of universities, but only with limits that may be summarized in four conditions.

The first such condition is that privately financed projects, often stimulated by the expectation of profit from particular discoveries, should not divert the university scientist from those public duties in teaching and research which must have first call on his time: the university is both obliged and entitled to insure that he give priority to its teaching program and to public research requirements over the demands of private industry.

The second condition is that application-oriented research (whether financed from public or private funds) should not be allowed to restrict the time and resources needed for basic research. This is recognized in principle by all public research institutions and many big firms, and is much facilitated by grants from independent foundations. But generally speaking, a university must have sufficient funds under its own control to distribute according to the faculty's independent judgment for initiating projects of basic research, free from application-oriented pressure.

Third, the same kind of safeguard is needed, particularly in the social sciences, to protect the necessary critical detachment of the scholar from shallow conformity with the given institutions of his society. Critical detachment is not, of course, the same as irresponsible disregard for society; still less should it be confused with doctrinaire commitment to a total attack on existing society. It means simply that research must be sufficiently independent to be free to criticize, to see where new social problems arise, and to pursue them without fear or favor, without ideological bias towards some preconceived "final solution" or apologetic bias towards things as they are. Now the anticonformist, doctrinaire bias has lately found its advocates among radical student representatives in a number of universities; however, the conformist, apologetic bias may easily arise where research projects offered from outside are passively accepted, and even more where government or public opinion attempt to impose a kind of tutelage on research to keep it "innocuous." I understand from American friends that in some places university bylaws have recently been instituted which require preliminary examination by a board to see whether projected research could hurt the image and interests of any social group. Obviously, there is no social research worth the name that could not hurt the image and interests of some social group. Hence if you establish a tutelage to prevent that, you prevent social research altogether. So in this field a fully autonomous faculty using the plurality of sources available for financing independent research offers the most favorable framework.

A final condition is that a university must be free, and should be determined, to reject projects for "secret" research, whether the secrecy stems from commercial or from military reasons: however legitimate such a project may be in the particular case, its secrecy is incompatible with the unity of research and teaching and with the principle of the public verification of methods and results. Hence it should find its place in other institutions than universities.

4. Let me conclude this brief treatment of the value and limits of university autonomy by mentioning an issue in which the threat to freedom of research arises primarily from inside a number of universities: the issue of banning "destructive" or "inhuman" research. It is obvious that many scientific discoveries and technological inventions may be applied for destructive and inhuman purposes. Moreover, we may well be on the threshold of many other discoveries with such a potential—apart from weapons research, one need only think of "confession drugs," of mind-changing drugs, or of methods of influencing the biological inheritance of man. The "new left" advocates of university politicization have proposed to use "student power" to prevent the abuse of such discoveries by stopping in good time those dangerous directions of research. In fact, there can be no doubt that the ambivalent potential for good and evil of many discoveries poses a moral problem both for the individual scholar and for society, and it is at least conceivable that sometimes the balance of argument might favor the suppression of a invention as the safest course; but the question remains who has a legitimate right to decide that.

It seems to me that it would be fatal to leave this decision to the autonomous organs of the university, and of a democratized university at that. This would amount to turning the university from an institution protecting the freedom of inquiry into an institution exerting censorship against its own members in the name of the supposed higher interests of society—and that without a legitimate democratic mandate from society. Clearly, a scientist making a potentially destructive discovery has the moral duty to inform society of the possible consequences, and the moral right to stop working on it if his conscience tells him so. Clearly, too, the political organs of society, once so informed, have the right either to ban continued work on the pending invention or to ask the inventor to cooperate in developing adequate methods of controlling it. But the university has no democratic mandate to take this kind of decision autonomously upon itself. Its duty is to protect its members' freedom to work or not to work on a particular line of research, not to act as thought police. Only the organs of the democratic state have the right, and the responsibility, to decide on the social priorities.

II

Let me turn now to the meaning of "political neutrality" for the university. Under the impression of the recent student revolt, many university teachers have rushed to the defense of their institutions against an imposed "politicization." What they oppose, and rightly, is the attempt to alienate universities from the pursuit of truth and turn them into bastions of a single, militant ideology. Such commitment to an ideological dogma is incompatible with the spirit of free inquiry. It should be equally obvious that no university is entitled to pronounce on the political questions of the day on behalf of its members on the basis of majority decisions. Nobody who joins a university, whether teacher or student, does so in order to espouse the views of a particular political grouping, or intends to empower his colleagues to speak in his name on current political issues. In that sense, the university as an institution must be neutral between the political parties and on the various issues disputed in a democratic community at any given moment, both in order to respect the freedom of opinion of each of its members and in order to preserve its own primary commitment to the unbiased search for truth and to the principle of tolerance.

But there is one "political" issue on which, in my opinion, no university can be neutral—and that is the defense of the fundamentals of a free society, of the principles of political freedom and tolerance themselves. I have stated before that the Western university has been one of the basic institutions which made the growth of an open and dynamic society possible in the West. It is equally true that the university has flourished only as an increasingly open society enabled it to emancipate itself both from dogmatic shackles and from the interference of authoritarian governments, as its freedom of inquiry became respected and protected by a general framework of liberal institutions. Thus there is a historic and logical link between freedom of science and learning and the other basic freedoms of an open society. On these grounds, one who has taught many years at a university that arose through an exodus of students and scholars from the territory controlled by an illiberal government may be permitted to qualify the view that a university must be politically neutral to preserve its standards, and to assert that in defending the foundations of its own existence the university necessarily defends the basic principles of a free society. With regard to these principles, the university cannot be neutral—it is committed. Hence it is both entitled and obliged to pass them on in its teaching.

It follows that education for freedom is a third, inescapable function of the university. From its own point of view, this is a requirement of self-preservation. From the point of view of society, it is an essential part of the political socialization of students as young citizens just entering adult life. From the students' point of view, it responds to their need for a concept of their own role in polity and society—a concept transcending their special field of study and integrating it into a broader social philosophy. In the elite universities of the past, the goal of educating the student as a citizen and potential leader was taken for granted as the rationale for the importance of nonspecialized, "humanistic" studies for all. In the new, egalitarian mass universities with their infinite professional diversification and specialization, the belief in the value of a broad, humanistic culture has frequently gone down along with its limitation to elites of birth and property, with no new integrating idea to take its place. The student revolt with its attacks on the "idiotism" of the specialist and its quest for "relevance" was in part a response to that situation. It is time for the defenders of freedom of inquiry to recognize that they cannot afford to leave the demand for the broader social meaning behind specialized professional studies to be answered only by the doctrinaire enemies of the open society. They must see that the opening of the minds for the humanistic belief in the autonomy of the reasoning individual, and for an understanding of the institutional safeguards protecting that autonomy in a free society, is as vital a task for the mass universities of the democratic age as it was for the elite universities of the past.

That does not mean, of course, that the university should in its turn attempt to "indoctrinate" the young by an affirmation of existing Western society as the best of all possible worlds; that would be incompatible with the spirit of free inquiry, and it would also be self-defeating. For the basic value shared by the university and modern Western society is the idea of freedom, including in particular freedom and tolerance for a plurality of views—and you cannot indoctrinate for pluralism. Rather, I believe that it is the task of the university both to supply students with a basic understanding of the institutions of a free society and to give them time and opportunity to get acquainted with various, contradictory views about that society, with their philosophical background, and with their implications for their own special field. What may be termed "civic education for liberty" in that sense is something radically different from indoctrination for conformity. At the same time, it is something far more positive than the mere "education for criticism" that is sometimes proposed in its stead—and criticism must become empty (and indeed destructive) in the absence of positive standards.

It may be objected that today's university teachers, selected largely on the basis of their specialist competence, are hardly qualified for this kind of educational task. The failure of most of the German academic community to resist the early impact of the Nazi movement, let alone the perversion of university teaching by the Third Reich, is often quoted in illustration. More recently the majority of professors in Germany, and not only there, have been only too happy to "get out of politics" and to withdraw from its conflicts and challenges into the single-minded, not to say blinkered, pursuit of their special studies—until politics returned to their ivory tower with a vengeance in the shape of student disturbances which shook them rudely out of their idyllic existence. But if it is true that our overspecialized universities have frequently failed in the broader task of educating for liberty, and have had to pay a heavy price for that failure, the lesson surely must be not that the problem can safely be ignored or its solution be abandoned as hopeless, but that the educators must be educated. In other words, we cannot hope to overcome the crisis of the university without becoming, in our daily work as well as in our fundamental convictions, dedicated and conscious defenders of the libertarian, humanistic principles on which that institution is founded: that is precisely why I am raising the question here and now.

To sum up, I reject the view that the remedy for the present crisis of the university would be to "keep politics out of it." On the contrary, I plead for *bringing politics in as a subject accessible to all students*, whatever their special field, and for showing them how it can be discussed in an "academic" way, that is, in a spirit of rational argument and mutual tolerance. It is not a keen and even passionate interest in politics, nor a conscientious sense of social responsibility, that endangers the peace and detachment of the republic of scholars; it is the attempt to conduct a political struggle for its control in the name of a single, militant ideology, often facilitated by the lack of preparedness on the part of those who ought to defend it.

III

There remains the question of whether the different functions of the contemporary university which we have analytically separated here should continue to be performed in practice by a single institution. At first sight, the idea of reserving the "true" universities exclusively for the education of scholars and scientists and leaving preparation of the masses for the professions to a different kind of vocational institute may seem tempting for the creative scholar. It appears to promise him a new kind of elite university, conceived for an elite not of birth and property but for one marked by the breadth and depth of its intellectual interest, in which an elite of professors would dedicate itself to the delights of true academic education while their less outstanding or less lucky colleagues would groan under a routinized teaching load next door. Moreover, such an elite university could continue also to enjoy its full traditional autonomy, since the modern need for limiting that autonomy has sprung, according to our above argument, from society's legitimate concern with the requirements of training for the practical professions.

The temptation is increased by the familiar problems and frictions of the modern mass university—its endless administrative complications, its jealousies between academic teachers of very different breadth and originality, its struggles for the division of time between advanced and elementary teaching and between teaching and research. Nevertheless, I believe that the temptation should be resisted, and on several grounds. One is the need not to foreclose the student's chances of development too early; one who has engaged in limited professional studies may at any point discover his interest in and gift for original research, and should be free to change the orientation of his studies accordingly without necessarily changing the institution. Another is the need to maintain the quality of the professional studies themselves. The future physician, schoolteacher, and so on, should have the chance during his studies to come into contact with the scholarly vanguard of his field and not be abandoned to routine and mediocrity. It is not too high a price for these advantages if some share of the burden of elementary mass teaching is imposed on the truly creative scholars.

But the strongest (and, in my view, decisive) argument for maintaining the unity of the university arises from what I have termed its third function—that of giving all students access to a "humanistic" and civic education for liberty. I put the term humanistic in quotes because in common usage it is still largely tied to the medium of the Latin and Greek languages—and, while I am convinced of the usefulness of this medium, I do not regard it as indispensable for teaching the humane values of the Western tradition. What I have in mind is, rather, that civic or political education in the narrower sense of an understanding of the institutional framework and functioning of a free society should be put in a broader philosophical and historical context, that each student should have a chance to become conscious of the nature of rational thought and the heritage of the human struggle for liberty. But if this is a necessary, formative element for *all* students, for the mass of professional students no less than for the future scholars and scientists, then they should have time and opportunity to acquire it together, in a framework that corresponds to their equality as citizens rather than to the different orientations of their future careers.

The institutional form for this humanistic and civic education may have to vary according to the different traditions of our countries—in particular, to the differences of their school systems. In France the last year of the secondary school offers a great deal in this direction, and, until recently, so did a first "propaedeutic" year at the university, thus permitting a stern concentration on specialized knowledge in the following years. In the United States college begins at an earlier age and devotes a great deal of its effort to nonspecialized tasks, including much general knowledge along with the formative studies with which I am here concerned. In the German Federal Republic, the question of how far the secondary school should lead—whether or not it should include a "Kollegstufe"—is in flux, and there is danger that some of the young will not acquire the needed humane and civic education either at school or at the university. But whatever the national situation of the educational institutions, it seems to me vital that the university should offer time and scope, before and besides all professional specialization, for acquiring or expanding a broad civic education for liberty.

In conclusion, I should like to take up the formula used by Dr. Halsey, who treated the ideas of freedom, equality, and fraternity as different aspects of the university education of our time. I believe that education for freedom cannot be confined to an elite of scholars; that therefore this elite will have to put up with the pressures of a mass university founded on equality of chances; and that it is our common task to develop, in such a complicated and heterogeneous university, the mutual understanding that will enable us to maintain a spirit of fraternity.

Mutations: Religio-Political Crisis and the Collapse of Puritanism and Humanism

David Martin

IN THIS ESSAY I am concerned with the nature of the student movement and wish to deal in particular with the political attitudes of that movement by referring to the religious aspect. If we want to understand why it is that student attitudes are only marginally political, then one must look at them as a form of religiosity. The modern Brethren of the Free Spirit—virtuosi of ecstacy and experiential freedom—necessarily reject the contingent, pragmatic, constricting, disciplined character of political action.

To set out the religious aspect involves attention to the theme of secularization and to what has happened to two key elements in the ideological underpinning of the university: humanism (both as a life style and as a rationalistic approach to religion) and the Protestant ethic. I will be concerned with how humanism came to be stigmatized as irrelevant and elitist, and how the Protestant ethic came to be linked with the evils of industrial society and the misuse of science.

There are two points which I want to make at the outset in order to make clearer the intellectual strategy I am employing. The first is that I cannot hope to deal with the whole of what is called the student movement, since it extends across a very wide variety of societies with very different systems of higher education and different types of social problems. I shall be concerned with very broad developments as I have experienced them in an Anglo-American setting. This means that I am describing and criticizing trends in affluent, democratic, Protestant societies. Clearly, to the extent that student movements operate in societies which are neither affluent nor Protestant nor democratic, my analysis would have to be modified very considerably. In Italy, for example, an interest in magic would be seen as a phenomenon of the extreme right, not the extreme left.

Historical Background

So far as historical background is concerned, the principal difference between Protestant and Catholic societies is the degree to which intellectuals

85

in the latter have been anticlerical and opposed to the political power of a monolithic ecclesiastical institution. In Protestant societies there is no historical background of an anticlerical (or, indeed, of a Marxist) intelligentsia. So far as Britain is concerned, there was some intellectual commitment to a rationalism in the mid-nineteenth century, an interest in socialist ideas from the 1880s onward, and an element of Marxism during the crisis of the 1930s. But, on the whole, the dominant style even among left-wing intellectuals has been one concerned with the gradual elimination of social evils and the extension of personal liberties. The dominant theme has been the peace issue, and on this issue collaboration between nonreligious and believing intellectuals has been particularly easy. Both have respected what they believed to be the benign figure of a liberal-socialist Jesus and have assumed that the New Testament is a pacifist manifesto about building "Jerusalem in England's green and pleasant land." And one has to remember that the religion which they espoused was not usually conceived by them in terms of a strong institution, but rather as a set of images, visions, and ideals. If they rejected the institution of the church, it was often more a rejection of the public school chapel than the Church of England itself. Even institutional religion presented no special dividing line among intellectuals: after all, nonconformist churches had always tended to espouse the peace issue and the Catholic party in the Church of England was notorious for its vigorous socialist wing. In any event, the Church of England as a whole was not so strong as to make the issue of institutional religion a major focus of attention. So the position of intellectuals vis-à-vis religion is easily summarized: adhesion or lack of it to the institutional church was not a major dividing line and along the poorly defined margins of belief, half belief, and nonbelief there was a general reverence for a liberal-socialist Jesus and the progressive tenets embodied in the Gospels. All instructed intellectuals knew that Jesus was against war and riches, and if for some of them he happened to be God as well that only showed how right they were to agree with him.

Now I think it is probably true to say that this complex of attitudes lasted until the end of the 1960s. The last major expression of such attitudes in England was the movement to ban the atom bomb: the Campaign for Nuclear Disarmament. In this campaign the usual elements of the "responsible," liberal-minded middle class were well to the fore and made their usual point: Britain must set a moral example to the world. In other words, the progressive and educated section of the middle class once more showed a characteristic concern for a moral issue focused on foreign policy. To that extent their attitudes were a final expression of Britain's imperial past, when British policy might have had an important influence on the world. But bringing up the rear behind the representatives of the middle class conscience was the shape of things to come. The "ban-the-bomb" marches were a kind of gypsy caravanserai in which the mobile, relaxed style of a new youth culture was clearly evident. The newspapers took special care to focus on the bizarre tail of long-haired troubadours who made up a substantial part of the marchers. Among these troubadours the overlap between student culture and the culture of pop music was particularly clear. It is not my object to go into this increasing symbiosis between the student way of life and pop music; it has been adequately analyzed elsewhere. Suffice to say that after the failure of the ban-the-bomb movement the troubadours gradually took over from the "responsible" educated middle class and began to adopt an expressionistic, vitalist, semimystical style. This style became more and more opposed to education, more especially the values of science and rationality. It posed the subjective person against the objectivist world of science and against the objective organization of society, identifying science as part of the social and political establishment.

This is the point at which I must introduce the second point, designed to clarify the intellectual strategy behind my statements. This revulsion against science can be seen as a crucial element in the development of the intelligentsia vis-à-vis religion and the "secularization process," so called. Up to the 1950s the liberal, progressive middle class had contained certain secular elements, even though religion was not a crucial issue. After all, this element of the middle class adopted a ratonalistic approach to social problems: it desired better social engineering. It contributed to better knowledge about society: the London School of Economics was one of its achievements. It might be further argued (though it is a matter of definition and debate) that to concentrate on the ethical aspects of the New Testament and to make religion a set of cultural ideals rather than an institutional and dogmatic loyalty was a move towards secularity. Certainly, this section of the middle class tended to be moralistic rather than ritualistic and to combine a rationalist liberalism with a secularized puritanism. On these criteria one might say that important elements in the progressive middle class were semisecularized.

But I have already mentioned the socialist emphasis in the Anglo-Catholic wing of the Church of England. In the figure of some like William Morris this overlapped an anarchistic, utopian strain of socialism, concerned to recover the right relation of the arts to society. It tapped the alienation of the artistic intelligentsia from a capitalistic society whose main criterion of worth appeared to be utility. It linked with the feeling of those who felt engulfed by vast centralizing bureaucracies and who were anxious to maintain local customs and to regain the elan of life in small communities. For these people, science was often regarded as an ally of the puritan ethic and a major component in an ugly industrial civilization indifferent to life and beauty. For people who saw the puritan ethic in this light Catholic civilization seemed more integral, more rooted in genuine community, more conducive to art and beauty. Thus science, puritanism, industrial society, and utilitarian ugliness became linked together as mutually supporting evils. For some middle-class people their rejection of these evils took the form of conversion to Catholicism; for others it spawned a philosophy of art for the sake of art. The sensations of beauty supplanted the imperatives of morality. Both Catholicism and aestheticism were influential in the 1890s and they were augmented by a margin of western mysticism.

It was *this* strain of progressive feeling which lay behind the appearance of a new youth culture in the wake of the ban-the-bomb marches. This culture was anarchic, morally deviant and experimental, aesthetically exploratory, mystical. In the 1890s, of course, this deviant style was confined to a relatively small section of society. But in the situation which arose after World War II it became available to a much wider social segment. Higher education expanded very rapidly. Initially the mood was rather quietist, even conformist. Certainly even political liberals were not particularly nonconformist in their cultural style. Those who were on the far left, in the sense of adhering to the authoritarian Marxism of that period, were often culturally puritan.

The Collapse of Puritanism

But then three developments occurred. First, the appeal of neopuritan, authoritarian, atheistic Marxism collapsed, more particularly after the invasion of Hungary and the revelations about the appalling brutalities perpetrated by the Communist regime in Russia. Adulation of Russia by the Communist left largely ceased. The problem became one of devising a socialism with a genuinely human face, and when Czechoslovakia followed Hungary it seemed impossible that any human face could appear behind the iron curtain. Thus the puritan ethic at home and the puritan ethos of authoritarian socialism abroad fell into equal disrepute. Any discipline of the self, as in classical puritanism, any discipline in society as exemplified in Marxist regimes was rejected. All authority was labeled "authoritarian," all centralized decision or decision by older people and by experts was automatically ruled out as paternalistic.[1]

With this double collapse of puritan values went the other two developments I mentioned: the appearance of a pop culture appealing to the young *in general* through the mass media and the growth of a vastly expanded university population educated *as if* it were to be part of an elite or part of a leisured class. Pop culture I leave on one side, except to refer to the obvious: the link with the deprived culture of the American Negro, and the "protest" element which achieved its first prominence in the public eye through Bob Dylan. My main concern here is with the young people who made up the

---

[1] Yet, of course, all the "reforms" desired by radicals required structures of authority and large bureaucracies for their implementation.

expanded university population in a situation in which the imperatives of the cold war had been weakened, money was available, and military service had been abolished.

These young people had literally nothing to fear and had been brought up in atmospheres in which whatever they did they were not subject to serious consequences for their actions. From school and home to university their environment was easy and supportive in a way no environment had ever been in the history of mankind, that is, apart from the very rich. Many of them had been brought up on systems of progressive education which assumed that life consisted of personal exploration rather than tasks and challenges. I can develop this later, but at this juncture it is relevant to one single point: Large numbers of people were given an education based on the style developed in elite schools by the semianarchic section of the middle class. Such middle-class people were often concentrated in key positions in the education system and encouraged their own free style within the state schools. Now this meant that by the time young people reached university and encountered its extremely open and traditionally liberal atmosphere, they had been trained to anticipate levels of self-fulfillment which even the university could not provide and to which society in general was largely indifferent. They had been given humanist tastes without the availability of humanist roles. They had been taught to relax, and found a world still at work and schools where there were still tests of competence. In short, they became candidates for educated unemployment. Only one further element needs to be added: The politics of conventional reform through the central structures of society moved but slowly and were plainly controlled by the reality principle. For young people brought up on the pleasure principle an alternative had to be found to conventional politics and this was provided by the student movement, in particular by its concern with psychic subversion of everything to do with the puritan cultural style. Curiously enough, this tactic worked on the principle of social salvation adopted by puritan evangelists: Each one convert one or, if you like, each one contaminate one. Psychic subversion took the place of political reform, iconography took over from carefully argued political programs. What static icons were to religion, casual graffiti and explosions of paint are to student ideology.

The point to begin with is the erosion of the character structure of puritanism. My main thesis will be concerned with the way a classical Protestantism, based on discipline and "works"—indeed, on disciplined work—has been attacked by the anarchism which goes back first of all to the romantic movement and Rousseau, but ultimately to the anarchic, radical wing of the Protestant Reformation. Weber's Protestant ethic has been suborned by an antinomian theology based on faith alone. Yet this doctrine of faith *alone* is different from the Reformation doctrine, since the radical implications of faith alone were normally controlled by the fact that the extremists among the reformers were concerned with faith *in Christ* alone and they usually added *sola scriptura* to *sola fide*. The modern extension of the Reformation has become just a celebration of faith for which there is no *object* of faith. It is a *pure* subjectivism. With this general and oversimplified thesis stated, let us look at the ways in which the "puritan ethic" has been eroded. We have a situation in which the subjectivism of the extreme, antinomian wing of the Reformation is conjoined with elements derived from Catholic culture and above all with anarchic mysticism, much of it now more easily based on eastern sources than anything contaminated by the cultural history of Europe.

What do we mean by the Protestant ethic? Many things, but in this context I mean guilt and work, and above all guilt about not working. Protestant character structure was based on literacy, self-improvement, conscience, saving, thrift, paying one's way, preparing for the future, personal control, honest dealing, veracity. It was pragmatic and empirical, dedicated to practicality, utility, and hard fact. It appealed to common sense and, in doing so, it overlapped an important strain in Anglo-American philosophy. This syndrome of virtues became otiose with welfare and affluence, at least for part of the educated young and a section of the youth culture. At the university they encountered a life style which contained certain of these Protestant virtues, but which included more aristocratic values of relaxation, aesthetic appreciation, contemplation. Disproportionate numbers of those socialized in old puritan styles entered the university because their self-discipline enabled them to succeed in the education system. And alongside them came those who had been reared in the new "progressive" style of education and large numbers affected by the relaxed values of the general youth culture. Unfortunately, most of those who entered into the humanistic inheritance of the university were unable to stay there. You cannot have an elite of hundreds of thousands. The scientists were employable, the humanists were not, or else they were forced to practice what some of them thought a low-grade form of humanism through schoolteaching. Thus they felt cheated and the semimonastic disciplines of a contemplative style were stigmatized as irrelevant. They had been encouraged to pass judgment on the universe but their destiny was a limited and limiting role. Industry seemed unrewarding and industrial vocations appeared sordid. Being failed aristocrats and thwarted humanists they despised commerce. So they turned either to personal exploration outside the disciplines of the university or else rejected contemplation in favor of a union of theory and political practice. They would educate themselves by the practice of subversion and in that respect humanism provided very little guidance. It was, as they said, irrelevant. Parenthetically, one must note that their own personalist philosophy also proved irrelevant. Whenever they tried to organize, they were confronted by the necessity of authority and discipline. This proved impossible to achieve, and even the most authoritarian student organizations which attempted a secular version of the puritan character foundered on the question of authority. Would-be Leninism found no characterological base on which to operate.

What has been said makes it quite clear why conventional politics have very little appeal. Messianism has no commerce with political pragmatism, and messianic aspirations for total liberty are affronted by the limitations on personal freedom inherent in the political role. The politician must take what shifting balance of advantages are available, jettison his personal life and even some of his beliefs for the wide cause.

The exigencies of party organization or of any coherent political grouping demand discipline. Moreover, this discipline is exercised in the context of the two largest and most impersonal forms of modern organization: the bureaucracy and the state. Size and impersonality are the two most anathematized features of contemporary liberal society; hence the almost total withdrawal of student revivalists from the political scene. Furthermore, of course they believe not only that conventional politics are ineffective but also that politics are positively responsible for the evils of the world, above all Vietnam. Political action in parliaments in the arena of corruption; pure souls and pure persons should have no part in it.

The Collapse of Humanism

I now turn more precisely to the relationship between student culture and humanism, particularly so far as the question of religion is concerned. I used the word *humanism* in two senses. The first sense is easily dealt with: humanism defined as a devotion to the human as distinct from the divine. This kind of humanism is continuous with the rationalist and ethical societies of the nineteenth century and is concerned to show that orthodox religion is incompatible with reason and science and detracts from human autonomy. Humanists of this kind hold that ethical standards are properly achieved not by virtue of transcendental rewards or divine edicts but by responsible choice of what is recognized as inherently good or of what is appropriate to the best and richest kind of human life. Of course, the humanist movement, though always against orthodox Christianity, has wavered between attempting to find a ritual and emotional substitute for religion and rejecting everything to do with religious forms. It was always ready to join with the reformist, progressive wing of Christianity in ethical crusades, and often the moral outlook of reformist Christians and puritanical atheists and agnostics was very similar. Both the Christian progressiveness and the puritan agnostics tended to recruit from the middle class. A movement like Unitarianism, which flourished in the nineteenth century and now languishes, combined the two. There is, however, only one thing to be said about this type of humanism: its moral outlook has been bypassed and its devotion to science and reason deprives it of interest. Humanist societies used to have quite an appeal to students, but they now have about as much éclat as a liberal-minded body like the Student Christian Movement (SCM). The SCM fell victim to its own "openness." It espoused the early stages of the present style and thereby destroyed itself, leaving the field to the closed cells of the Christian Union. Liberalism taken beyond a certain point plays into the hands of right and left extremes.

The second sense of humanism refers to the life style of the academic and the intellectual insofar as it relates to the ideal of Renaissance man. More narrowly, this kind of humanism connotes a culture rooted in the classics. This ideal and this culture found no great difficulty in coexisting with a rather aristocratic, stoical variant of Christianity. After all, Christian civilization had harbored the classics in its monasteries and Latin was its language. True, the Renaissance had included an explicit theoretical extension of secular political realism and an unbridled celebration of the individual, but it had also combined Christianity and the life-enhancing arts together in some of the sublimest achievements of civilized man. So there was no great difficulty in combining a stoic, civilized, and civic ethos with a proper regard for Christian decencies.

Humanism in this mode is now under as much pressure as the kind of humanism which is devoted to science and reason. It is clear that any acquaintance with classical civilization is rapidly disappearing and to use a combination of Roman stoicism and Christian ethics to socialize the young is now barely possible, even in public schools. But the erosion of humanism goes much further than this: not only is the tradition of the classics forgotten but the very notions of a "classic" and of a tradition are in disrepute. History itself is devalued and replaced by sociology. The urge towards relevance rejects cultural standards and continuities. Moreover, humanism involved the notion of a discipline, particularly grammar and rhetoric, and while today grammar is condemned for formalism, rhetoric is condemned as hypocritical. This occurs because an ideology of the naked person celebrates immediacy and therefore has to reject standards which are imparted from the past and cannot see the point of mastering rules which have no personal appeal. Such an ideology holds that ordered, elegant speech is treason against the existential vagaries of genuine emotion. This means, incidentally, that so far as religion is concerned there is a prejudice against the ordered formality of divine worship. A collapse in humanist cultural standards can mean a rebellion against traditional beauty in the ordering of liturgy. Where classics are despised, access to a whole tradition of speech is made more difficult. Indeed, speech itself becomes suspect. Humanism is the attitude of the scribe, and the scribes are rejected on the ground that they are pharisees. In a way this runs parallel to the rejection of puritanism. Puritans delighted in the Word, humanists delighted in words; puritans studied scripture, humanists studied manuscripts. But the new anarchistic personalism despised both sermons

and speeches and aspired to a condition of all-round reaction in which words
and music, sight, sound, and touch are one.

When the devotee of the youth cult rejects the rational and cumulative
ordering of words, he rejects a sequential mode of thought and the notion of
logical argument. Words also involve categories and categories divide up the
world of experience when in his view the world should be experienced as a
whole. It is this desire to embrace the world as a *totality* which spills over into
naturalistic mysticism. The devotee of personalism falls into a relationship
with the "All," and because this defies rational expression he can only witness
to the overwhelming nature of the experience without being able to give an
account of it. Like the oriental mystic he can only ejaculate the word "Om."
Like the Zen adept his religion defies both categories and expression. The
ineffable can be expressed only in inconsequential nonsense. The pregnant
silence of Zen complements the augmented decibels of pop music production, designed to "stone people out of their minds." Since the religious adept
experiences the world as a totality and as a totality preceding words and
categories, he is effectively returned to the world of the newborn infant: a
world of uninterrupted noise or uninterrupted silence. As we shall see later,
this return to angel infancy is an important motif in contemporary student
religion. Infancy is amoral and natural, and nudity is an appropriate symbol
for an ideology of infantile delinquency. This condition is exactly the reverse
of the mature, ordered, rational, and acquired autonomy desired by humanists.

There is, however, one particular in which the youth culture seems to
resemble classical humanism: that is its desire to relate the knowledge gained
in particular disciplines within a universal perspective. It desires a total view
of the world. This is why student ideologies ransack one discipline after
another to produce a general perspective showing how everything is related
to everything else. The phenomenon of left-wing functionalism is interesting
here. Functionalists like Parsons showed the systemic and (perhaps) benef-
icent interrelation of social structures. Radicals accepted this overintegrated
view of society, differing only in their estimate of its beneficence. This
ecumenical movement of the intellect can look like a proper disdain for
artificial boundaries, but it is actually part of the fear of categories. Levels
of judgment are confused; the specific gain of different subjects is ignored;
fact and desire are jumbled together; no considerations are possible based on
more or less or a calculation of if *this*, then not *that*. All that is necessary is a
chanting of the favorite slogans of the youth cult, one of the most important
of which is the notion that all knowledge is absolutely relative. Total
relevance ends up in total relativity. There is no external knowledge or
reality "out there" which can impose itself on the sacred psyche. Just as
there is no God out there, so there is no external world. Everything should
be malleable to the demand of personal vision. If it is not malleable, one
can retire into a world where the visionary becomes real: the world of

drugs. Thus the attempt to encompass all knowledge ends up in a denial of the possibility of knowledge, just as the attempt to achieve total communication concludes in a skepticism about the possibility of making contact. The susceptibility to drugs links, of course, to the espousal of naturalistic mysticism. Similarly, the skepticism about rational knowledge concerning the world plays back into fideism. It is only a short step from extreme skepticism to salvation by faith alone. When reason fails, what is left but faith?

Powers of Light and Powers of Darkness

So far I have discussed tendencies favorable to religion in general, but not particularly to Christianity. After all, Christianity is a historical religion and the ahistorical nature of the youth consciousness is hostile to it. Moreover, Christianity, at least in some forms, is in favor of reason, and though it has had its moments of conflict with science it has recognized the importance of objective knowledge about the universe. Indeed, it is one of the complaints of contemporary radicals that Christianity has too easily embraced the ideal of scientific truth. Christianity further involves a moral outlook, a continuing commitment to a defined and bounded religious community, and an attempt to give an intellectual account of itself, all of which are contrary to an ideology of the unrestrained self. So in all these respects Christianity is under pressure. In other respects, however, it finds points of congruence with the new cultural mode.

The most obvious case is the Jesus People and overlapping movements like the Festival of Light. In the Festival of Light the salvationism of the young is linked to an attempt by more staid older people to control the spread of pornography. By a concession to the contemporary style pornography is labeled "moral pollution." The appeal to youth is primarily through a lively, charismatic mode of evangelism remote from conventional Christianity though not, of course, from the tradition of American evangelism. "Jesus" becomes a "happening," above all so in the immensely popular musicals *Godspell* and *Jesus Christ Superstar*. The Jesus Christ of these productions is a contemporary "Lord of the Dance." Nevertheless, it is worth remarking that the Jesus People form a link back to traditional American culture, though their anti-intellectualism probably disqualifies them from full contact with the university tradition.

One of the major events of the hippie culture lifestyle is the pilgrimage to Glastonbury Tor, traditionally the most sacred spot in England, to which Joseph of Arimathea is believed to have brought the Christ child. The Glastonbury cult lies closer to the Christian pattern in several ways. It invokes a savior figure, expects a transformation of mundane reality, and espouses a gentle pacifistic communitarianism based on apostolic sharing. The hippies share their goods and beg like early Franciscans. On the other hand, the bands of hippies are not a disciplined order or sect but a shifting agglomeration of like-minded persons. (Not that the early Franciscans were so very well disciplined!) Their savior might be Christ but, equally, might be the legendary King Arthur and Merlin. It seems uncertain whether hope wells up from the sources of goodness deep in the earth or descends from heaven in traditional manner—perhaps with the help of modern technology in the form of a flying saucer. The pollution from which the pilgrims flee is not merely the moral evil of the City of Destruction and of its concrete jungles, but the scientific pollution of the sacred earth. A similar attitude animates those who adhere to the Doomsday cult.

This pilgrim devotion to myths intertwined with Christian motifs and partially based on Christian patterns also finds expression in the cult of Tolkien. Tolkien writes some of his books for children, but his adult followers absorb his work as a kind of imaginative shadowing of Christian ideas in which the white power of good confronts the powers of darkness. In Tolkien, therefore, moral categories are restored and the theme of childish innocence is not so much a return to presocial conditions as a re-creation of the New Testament theme of the "little ones" who enter into the Kingdom of God. It is, therefore, not far removed from a Christian mysticism which endeavors to see a world conformed to the vision of Isaiah. Nature itself shines as before the Fall and after the Restoration. This condition is not beyond good and evil but envisages the containment of evil. The mythical history envisages the various phases of the battle against darkness and when the light shines it shines on the yeoman virtue of England's green and pleasant land.

Yet it requires only a marginal shift of emphasis for these gentle, idyllic, and pastoral themes to be transmuted into darker colors. Not so far from Glastonbury Tor is Silbury Hill, a pre-Christian mound whose origin is unknown, and here the pilgrims seek power from the earth as much as they seek goodness. The mystic quest for salvation can switch into the acquisition of magical potencies and once power is invoked the gentle pilgrims can become violent deliverers. Add magic and amoral potency to the Christian myth and there emerges the figure of a Charles Manson: not crucified but crucifying. This figure *inverts* the Christian story: his disciples are his sexual slaves; those who suffer from their activities are victims of the divine. Similar motifs appeared in the notorious child murders known as the "Moors murders"; they were violent and sadistic, reenacting a blasphemous model of the Crucifixion.

The invocation of the powers of darkness by an inversion of the Christian means of salvation is, of course, an ancient practice. But in its modern forms it has links with magic and voodoo: the figure of Jimi Hendrix symbolized this link. The invocation of magic and the empathy with African and West

Indian cultural forms found its expression in the Afro hairdo. Hair sticking out in all directions signified sexual potency, primitivistic sympathies, and alienation from European social control.

Student commitment to irrationality also taps a somewhat different substratum of non-Christian religion: divination and astrology. Since a major motif in student consciousness is immediacy, choice, and existential openness, the growing interest in divination is curious. It is even more curious in that one of the most popular forms of divination, the Tao Te Ching, belongs to a Chinese civilization where roles were very sharply circumscribed. But of course the Taoist undercurrent to Confucian civilization was an anarchistic and quietist nostalgia for the small community, and as such highly congruent with student ideology. So too is the penchant for macrobiotic foods. The really surprising element is the overlap between the culture of the young and educated with the magical aspect of Taoism. However, systems of magic and divination, though not concerned with freedom, do tend to be individualistic. They give a prognosis for personal destiny; they present an impersonal prediction which can be worked to the individual's advantage. Thus we have a paradox: the belief in the sacred individual rejects science and its predictions in favor of quasi-science and divination. It also fills in the gap left by the rejection of traditional ways of doing things and by the rejection of moral rules, thus easing what becomes the intolerable burden of existential choice. How much the sections of the youth culture which embrace antinomian anarchy overlap the sections which consult systems of divination is a matter for further study.

The fundamental point underlying all the foregoing analysis has been the tendency to eliminate categories, and I will now try to bring together in a highly schematic manner the variety of ways in which categories are undermined. In the first place, the new attitude tries to achieve identity without initially accepting badges of identification—whether those of a particular religion or of a country. Then it tries to break down distinctions between fathers and sons: to accept paternalism is as corrupt as identifying with the fatherland. Similarly, a religion of the sons rejects heavenly fathers along with earthly fathers: it seeks to be submerged in a totality which engulfs man, nature, and God. Man returns to the bosom of nature and sees his unsocialized desires as inherently "natural." Nothing is unnatural, except the division of sex and role. Sexual differentiation is seen as imposed by society on an irrelevant biological base: men become feminized and clothing barely distinguishes male from female. Finally, the new female man rejects all categorization of himself in terms of competence and hierarchy: his precious psyche is not to be contaminated by tests nor his faculties assessed in a tested hierarchy of qualifications. He is, in fact, a pure person, nothing else but a mortal soul freed from all contingent labels. For him there is neither male nor female, Jew nor Greek, Christian nor pagan, public nor private, sacred nor profane. The only distinction is that between those who have recovered wholeness and personal authenticity and those who have not: the bond and the free. And the old are, by definition, bond and the young, free.

So we may conclude with a double contradiction. Humanistic liberalism has been destroyed in the most paradoxical way by a doctrine of the natural person freely expressing himself in the natural community. The assumption behind this doctrine is a classical liberal notion: the "invisible hand" harmonizing individual desire and social structures. Religion, too, has been destroyed in the most paradoxical way: by engulfing the secular in the divine. The former is not possible, the latter not even desirable.

The Mining of the Ivory Tower

Bernice Martin

IN THE 1960s the universities of Western Europe and America were rocked by an upsurge of progressive radicalism; then in the 1970s, as other contributors to this volume have noted, calm gradually crept back so that today, with the partial exception of West Germany, universities and students are barely newsworthy any more. The industrial disputes in mass higher education have cooled and production has been resumed. But it may be worth looking at the syndrome that characterized the disruption period and asking what deposit it has left in the apparently normalized university system which survived the inundation of radicalism.

My thesis is that the "student revolution" was only one facet of a general cultural movement popularly known as the avant-garde or the counterculture. It was one link in a chain of paradoxes the logic of which has not yet fully exhausted itself. Industrialization has produced, as Talcott Parsons has put it, first the educational and then, hard on its heels, the expressive revolution. Western societies, within the space of a mere century, have moved through the stages of mass elementary and mass secondary education and are now entering the era of mass higher education. Industrialism and its resultant material affluence have created what Ralf Dahrendorf refers to in his article as the "educational class" to staff the institutions of mass literacy. More than this, they have made it possible for modern societies to afford a large cultural class divorced from material productive processes and devoted to nonmaterialist and nonutilitarian pursuits of an artistic, intellectual, and expressive kind. Thus there evolved a whole stratum of society distanced and partially protected from the instrumental activities and material priorities of society's existence and able, by a characteristic modern process of structural differentiation, to embody and assert the values of cultural and expressive primacy in human life.

The counterculture was in essence just a further differentiation within the cultural class itself: the alter ego of the established cultural elite. Both are equally parasitic on the world of materially productive work and in this sense both are natural successors to the church and the universities of the preindustrial era, though their numbers are vastly greater, their institutional focus much more diverse, and their links with the structure of power more tenuous. At bottom, the expressive revolution was an extravagant statement of the self-affirming and anti- or noninstrumental values of the new cultural class. The ideas and motifs of the counterculture were not so much a radical break with conventional culture as the logical development of some of the central expressive values of that culture. The radical wing of the Expressive Revolution was making a bid for *absolute* autonomy for the "leisured class," for *total* divorce from the political and economic paymasters. The universities became the most spectacular battleground of the revolution because they were strategically poised with a foot in both the expressive and the instrumental camps. The arts, even though they may sometimes assist in legitimating the status quo, are *inherently* expressive and therefore not intrinsically problematic for the forces of the Expressive Revolution. The "hard" areas of economic and political expediency may be the logical target of the expressivist rebels but they are well defended and significantly distant from the influence of the cultural class. The university (and, to a lesser extent, the school) is closer, less powerfully armed, and the most obviously disputed territory. It is expected in part to service the labor market and the material scientific and administrative needs of industrial society and in part to bear witness to timeless human values— the pursuit of intellectual excellence and moral truth regardless of the consequences, of perfection, of spiritual and aesthetic insight, of innovation, of beauty, of personally satisfying uselessness.

At one level, then, the expressive revolution is not in any necessary sense politically radical. Indeed, its essence is to be *a*political and *a*economic, that is, not to assert a *new* politics and economics but to affirm the supremacy of values other than those of politics and economics. In this sense, the music students who went on playing their instruments and ignoring student assemblies throughout the troubles were more complete examples of the expressive revolution than were the philosophers and social scientists who ran the assemblies. At another level, of course, politics was a crucial part of the syndrome. Here one needs to introduce another consideration about the nature of radical politics in the sixties in Western Europe and North America. The degree of potential social conflict and political polarization in these societies is very varied: no modern Western society is without its institutional focus of political protest and class antagonism. But two points need to be borne in mind. First, the experience of Russian communism has made the puritan and politically realistic variant of left-wing utopianism very suspect (a) on nationalist and (b) on expressivist grounds: Eastern Europe is clearly no paradise of free-floating individualism as its own rebellious cultural class makes abundantly clear. Second, the intellectual stratum rather than the proletariat always tends to articulate radical ideologies—this, after all, is part of the natural function of a leisured elite whose raison d'être is ideas. Ideological though not necessarily pragmatic political leadership therefore tends to be characteristically middle class. The more the cultural and educational class can be differentiated from the hard areas of politics and economics, the more likely it is that a substantial minority of this protected enclave will be contemptuous of and outraged by the political compromises, maneuvers, and privileges of the ruling group: thus for many of them *every* politician, general, and business-man *must* have his own Watergate to hide. So the phenomenon of middle-class expressive politics evolves: political action designed to express the value premises and manifest the moral cleanness of the participants rather than to achieve a concrete end.

For these reasons among others hard variants of radicalism—classical Marxist socialism, national socialism, and doctrines of proletarian revolution —were relatively weak in the 1950s and 1960s. The proletariat in even the most polarized Western societies showed little or no sign of spontaneous combustion, and among the intelligentsia the Protestant ethic of work, diligence, and control was discredited by its contamination with capitalism and bureaucracy and was being replaced by a revamped romantic individual-ism more in tune with expressive values. Political ideologies on the left accordingly tried the expedient of anarchic expressivism, preaching the conversion of souls through drugs, psychodrama, sexual license, and the wholesale breaking of taboos in the hope of eroding the fabric of what Marcuse calls "repressive tolerance."

Now this syndrome contains a twin possibility—the politicization of culture or the transformation of politics into a system of purely symbolic gestures. The first makes the "soft" areas of culture serve the "hard" political battle, the second retreats from hard politics and economics and takes refuge in the expressive arts which then stand in for political action. In the first, anarchic techniques largely deriving from the arts—Dada, sur-realism, and the ideology of romantic individualism—are used aggressively as weapons of psychic subversion and political resocialization by would-be revolutionary movements (usually of the left, but it could just as easily as in the 1920s be the right). Continental Europe and in particular France and Germany have had some recent experience of cultural politics of this variety. Specifically, the student revolutions of the mid to late sixties took precisely this form. Alfred Willener's account of the troubles at the Sor-bonne in 1968 is a perfect example of the whole syndrome.[1] The success of this tactic has been very limited even if one attributes to it the French government changes after the 1968 student rebellions. Even in the most polarized Western European societies, the main impact of the attempt to political culture has been confined to the universities and the radical intelligentsia.

Much might be written about this continental mode which has fused without much difficulty with several variants of Marxist ideas and tactics

[1] A. Willener, *The Action Image of Society* (London: Tavistock Publications Ltd., 1970).

and which one sees illustrated in some of the contributions to this volume on the problems of the universities in West Germany. However, I shall concentrate on the second mode, which is more characteristic of Anglo-American cultural patterns. Here one finds not the politicization of culture but the politics of cultural symbolism. Here radical politics merely translate themselves into a style of cultural gesture which employs the same anarchic techniques but primarily as a form of self-display and a badge of in-group solidarity within the progressive intelligentsia. When this happens, anarchic expressionism becomes a cul-de-sac instead of the high road to revolution. Radicals avoid the hard, "masculine," "instrumental" areas of industrial and agricultural production: business, politics, and administration. These are seen as citadels still too well rooted in the "false consciousness" of all social classes to be easily toppled. Progressives in these societies therefore huddle together in the esoteric temples of elite culture (or counterculture, if you prefer). Through the arts they can preach to the converted and symbolically reaffirm their mutual righteousness through cultural gestures the impact of which is largely confined to the avant-garde itself. Thus their chosen field of operation is the "soft," "feminine," "expressive" area of modern life: the arts, education, the "caring" professions, and so on. Part of my thesis is that in British (and, to a lesser extent, American) society, much of the revolutionary potential has been drained off into self-affirming orgies of expressivism among the radical middle classes. So Britain offers the world a Vanessa Redgrave instead of a Rosa Luxemburg, a Lennon rather than a Lenin.

Yet there is still a further paradox. In spite of the self-induced political impotence of the avant-garde which results from their avoidance of the power centers of the economy and the polity, they have had a not negligible cultural impact. Not on the whole through Machiavellian cunning, but more through the unintended consequences of the fact that the progressive middle classes feel more comfortable with each other than with the philistine and unenlightened, they happen to have clustered in important agencies of socialization as well as in the hermetic world of the elite arts. Thus, in most Western liberal societies, progressives hold some of the commanding positions in educational institutions and the mass media and hence can induct the norms and distribute the symbols of the expressive revolution to society at large.

At this point one must note some very crucial developments in the structure of the universities—and, indeed, in the whole system of higher education—which began to play into this situation. As higher education is extended to an ever expanding proportion of the population two important developments occur. First, the universities are supplemented (and, in some cases, even swamped) by other institutions whose raison d'être is less the embodiment of humanistic culture than the production of trained personnel for technological and other useful professional and semiprofessional roles in society. The universities may either be infiltrated by the latter set of functions or may be specialized as the "purer" nonvocational and non-utilitarian institutions. There are dangers in both possibilities, of course: in the first place, the risk voiced so extravagantly by the "expressive revolutionaries" of the sixties that humanistic ideals may be distorted and corrupted by the pressures of immediate expediency; and, in the second place, the danger of being regarded as a socially irrelevant luxury and starved of funds and manpower by an instrumentally oriented ruling establishment.

The second important feature of the universities of the mid-twentieth century is the fact that, even when one has allowed for the impact of other institutions of higher education, larger numbers of relatively underprivileged segments of the population begin to receive a university education with its systematic exposure to humanistic values which set themselves apart from and above mere utility. Now humanistic culture has traditionally meant elite culture and its values are certainly most easily operable in the lifestyle of the wealthy, cultured gentleman: Renaissance man is essentially patrician. This has several interlocking consequences. It means that universities retain an elite label while the new institutions of instrumental higher education are commonly granted less status deference in spite of their frequent efforts to become more like traditional universities. The educationally mobile student of relatively lowly origins is more likely to find his way to the new vocational and technological institutions: the children of the privileged classes go in greater proportions to the humanist institutions. There is even an implicit status differentiation within subjects: the humanities and pure sciences—traditional gentlemanly subjects—carry more status than do applied science and technology or vocational subjects, even within the universities themselves, and are differentially popular with the students from privileged and professional strata.

All this parallels the war within the middle classes between a pragmatic and a humanistic ethos. The older preindustrial professions were a combination of pragmatic and technical elements inside a humanistic package: medicine, for instance, was and is not merely pragmatic but manual. Often the elements of gentlemanly humanism appeared not in the nature of the activity itself so much as in the assumption that its incumbents were educated men who happened to practice medicine or law. Humanistic rhetoric also tended to suffuse the self-definition of these elite occupations and in particular to express itself in the concept of professional ethical codes. The new middle classes created by industrialization were much more riven by the distinction between a pragmatic and a humanistic or expressive ethos: while the distinction between the two is far from total (it is an ideal type rather than a simple empirical description), the process of structural differentiation has tended to institutionalize a specialization in the pragmatic/instrumental or the humanistic/expressive in the new middle-to-high-status occupations of modern industrial societies. Thus, although there are innumerable mixed cases, one can crudely place in the first category a group running from accountants and bureaucrats to engineers and, in the second category, the caring professions and the higher rungs of personal service alongside the arts, the mass media, and education. The first category concerns itself mainly with commercial and technical pragmatism; it is often unashamedly modern and instrumental in its self-definition and may even glory in scientific and technological progress.

The second category includes the main body of what I earlier called the new cultural classes, tending to concern itself with the quality of relationships, with the creation and transmission of cultural symbols, and with values which transcend the practical. Even here the distinction between the two categories is impure. *All* the new professions and semiprofessions tend to use some traditional humanistic rhetoric in the process of professionalization—in part, because this is the status-confirming surface legitimation of a profession. And, on the other hand, even the most expressive of the new middle-class occupations is at some level dependent on modern science and technology and shares to one degree or another the characteristic ambivalence the older professions embody in relation to modern technology. The ambivalence probably finds its most piquant expression in the mass media: a television producer may pride himself on his skill in shooting, cutting, and editing; but he can use his expensive equipment and technical skill to make either a commercial for frozen peas or a documentary about environmental pollution and the negative feedback of scientific progress. If the cultural class in general feels this ambivalence, then the same applies a fortiori to the counterculture. The hippie road to Katmandu was literally strewn with the detritus of electronic guitars, tape recorders, amplifiers, and the like.

Now, although there is a relative institutional specialization of the humanistic/expressive values in the second group of new middle-class occupations, all these institutional specialties exist by courtesy of industrialism and in a not inconsiderable sense because they are conceived of as "useful" to society. However much their self-definition may appeal to timeless human values, they are also expected to fulfill certain pragmatic functions—to reduce or control delinquency, ease poverty, minimize social and personal discontent, produce a trained and efficient labor force, and so on. In short there are *very* few niches in which the life style of the leisured humanistic gentleman is an easily available option unsullied by some instrumental, material, economic, political, or other impure intrusions. The safest places are the arts, entertainment, and the mass media, although even these are subject to some considerable commercial pressures. Or, alternatively, there are the universities.

Western educational systems are so structured that the universities are intellectually the freest and most humanistic sectors: they are ideally conceived of as devoted to the life of the mind for its own intrinsic and self-justifying sake. If knowledge qua knowledge can be pursued anywhere it is in the universities. It is true that traditionally universities have concerned themselves also with the vocational training of gentlemen (or, at least, with the symbolic legitimation of fitness to enter the gentlemanly professions) and have never worried much about the vocationalism of medicine or law or divinity faculties as demeaning. But these were the old elite professions: the new technical professions of the industrial state are hived off where possible either to lower status technical institutions or to enclaves of postgraduate vocational training. Thus the universities have, if anything, *increased* their emphasis on education for its own sake and underlined their own definition of themselves as the main bastion of humanistic values in a materialist world dominated by economic and bureaucratic norms. Moreover, they could in this century as well as the last usually count on the sympathy and support of the economic and political elite who, even if some were themselves philistines, had a traditional respect for gentlemanly culture and for the life of the mind as pursued by the best brains of their generation. Indeed, they often saw this as, in part at least, the "civilization" which morally justified the material success of modern industrialism.

Yet, while universities were specializing out the humanistic ethos, they were also expanding with the mass education industry itself. Industrial societies more and more came to use (or believe they were using) education to sort out the various levels of talent and skill and assign the labor force to its "appropriate" point of entry on the occupational hierarchy: more and more occupations required educational qualifications as an entry permit. So the universities found themselves at the apex of a system of occupational selection, with the vast majority of both the old and new upper-status occupations expecting incumbents to have passed through a university degree before embarking on vocational training either on the job or in a specialized vocational course. Universities played along with the development to the extent that they justified and promoted their own vast expansion on the grounds (unsupported by anything other than rhetoric and extrapolation from existing trends) that modern societies "needed" graduates.

Thus our middle classes pass through a very long process of formal education, the unequivocal ideal goal of which is academic pursuits for their own sake, culminating in three or more years of intensive socialization in humanistic values and life style in the university. At this point society expects them finally to face the world of work—economics, bureaucracy, power, compromise, instrumentality, conflicting and only partly realizable goals, time limits, compartmentalization, and the rest. Is it any wonder that one of the favorite slogans of the London School of Economics

(LSE) student militants of the late sixties was "Who *wants* to join middle management at £1500 a year?" The problem is that in our expanded universities life is a rather loose but tempting induction into a pattern of activities and values which cannot easily be exported intact into the outside world. It sows the seeds of a taste for the life of the ivory tower which can scarcely be satisfied except by staying there. But, however many modern annexes it builds, the ivory tower cannot accommodate all who would prefer to take refuge there.[2] The problem is worst in the humanities and social sciences and least in technology where utility and vocation are more easily justified.

Here one needs to draw attention to two processes which affect these developments. The first, noted above, is the process of self-recruitment in the cultural classes. Certain professions and occupations are more successful than others at distancing themselves from material and instrumental norms: as we remarked earlier, these are par excellence the free-floating cultural professions in the arts, entertainment, and the mass media and, to a modified degree, the caring professions and the educational growth industry itself. Thus families already entrenched in these areas tend to predispose their children to follow the same circular route around the educational feeder plant back into the expressive professions. The second process which supplements this is the constant expansion of education and the expressive professions alike, so that each generation provides new recruits from lower status origins to join and extend the circular flow.

These two processes have important consequences. In the first place, because of the circularity of the process the anti-instrumental ethos is self-confirming and likely to be exaggerated rather than modified over time. In the second place, it gives rise to a phenomenon which one might call "status drip." As the system expands, so many of its products have to search lower down the status hierarchy for occupational niches. Exaggerated and crudified forms of humanistic values stripped of subtlety, complexity, and fertilizing paradox are thus "dripped" down to ever lower reaches of the occupational hierarchy; it becomes more accurate at this point to refer to an "anti-instrumental'" rather than a positively "humanistic" ethos. One result of this, especially in the education system itself, is the persistent erosion and disconfirmation of the instrumental functions which the system partly exists to perform—occupational selection, the possibility of social mobility, the acquisition assessment and measurement of skills, and so on. A further result, which the student troubles of the 1960s materially assisted, is the erosion of the confidence of the commercial and political classes that

---

[2] At the Venice Conference, Professor Tenbruck emphasized strongly the view that the counterculture is likely to continue to grow as more and more people gain access to higher education, swelling the numbers of the disenchanted among both intelligentsia and "cumparintelligentsia."

universities (or their lower-status analogues in the expressive half of the system) are either safe or sensible investments: the paymasters begin to have nagging doubts as to whether there is either "civilization" or "use" to be found there.

We should now, perhaps, return to the counterculture and the student troubles. Why did the explosions take place in the universities if they are, as the argument runs above, havens of protection for humanistic values and the gentlemanly life style? The point is that, though the universities are the safest home for the children of the expressive revolution, even so they are not pure havens of repose from the realities of twentieth-century industrial society: they still have their instrumental functions—in terms, say, of occupational selection, status legitimation, recruitment to elite positions, practical payoffs from research in natural and social science, and so on. Moreover, because they are part of a massive growth industry they cannot easily avoid taking on features which characterize modern bureaucracies—largeness of scale, impersonal administrative procedures, standardization, specialization, compartmentalization of operations, and the like. Many of these features are bound to be encouraged by the political and economic paymasters in whose sphere they form part of the normal life style: any other pattern will be under suspicion as inefficient and anachronistic. One should remember, too, that my description of the circular process of self-recruitment to the cultural classes involves an element of caricature: the circle is not perfect and some participants (often the new recruits) are imbued with models of progress and efficiency culled more from the economic than the humanistic enterprise. Or, again, the instrumental elements may be strategically emphasized as part of the rhetoric justifying universities in terms that will convince the paymasters through a vocabulary they understand. Such strategies have a nasty habit of turning rhetoric into necessary fact as a quid pro quo for expansion, research funds, or what you will.

Thus we see the universities as a fair field for battle between the humanistic/expressive and the pragmatic/instrumental ethos. Although this was not the only factor in the situation, the expressive rebels of the sixties plausibly could see themselves as so many Odysseuses slaughtering Penelope's suitors. They entered their only real home to find it polluted by alien intruders trying to take over the true master's functions. So we have thus far the first two of the series of paradoxes which describe the course of the mining of the ivory tower:

1. Industrialization creates and finances a leisured or cultured class which can then afford the luxury of despising and condemning the instrumentality and materialism of its creators.

2. The children of the educational and expressive revolutions use the counterculture's extension of humanistic values to attack the only safe home of those values, the universities.

It may worth examining the counterculture in a little more detail as a logical extension of established values. What were its lines of continuity with and divergence from the traditional humanistic culture of the universities? Where the traditional values of humanism have always asserted the worth of the life of the mind and imagination outside the cash and power nexus, the counterculture retranslated this into a total devaluation of any other kind of enterprise—in particular, anything which was useful to a stratified and materialist industrial state. To express it programmatically, they replaced a distant respect for utility by a celebration of uselessness. Expressiveness became its own justification with a consequent preference for the ephemeral (and therefore immediate and personal) over the lasting (and therefore fixed and to that extent impersonal). Rationality and objectivity had been a crucial part of the universities' traditional understanding of humanism: these were the powers and disciplines by which only the human mind could transcend animal immediacy and domination by instinctual and environmental forces. They were nevertheless rejected by the counterculture as ideologically tainted through their association with bourgeois science, technology, and bureaucracy; they were condemned as the bases of personal inhibition and psychic impoverishment and awarded only the creation of "capitalism" to their doubtful "credit." So rationality and objectivity must go and in their place arose cults of anti-, non-, or irrationality backed up by rhetoric derived from sources as diverse as Wordsworth, Nietzsche, de Sade, popularized post-Freudianism, and the whole ragbag of secondhand romantic individualism. Instead of objectivity as an aim and positivism as a method, subjectivism and relativism came to prevail as the only adequate vehicle for expressing the uniqueness and diversity of humanity. So magic could become superior to science and, by one of many such ironies, only reason came to be seen as truly subhuman.

Curiously, certain forms of individualism were also casualties of the countercultural ideology, despite the fact that "doing one's own thing" was one of the treasured values of the anarchic radicals. Individualism in academic matters became suspect the moment it smacked of achievement orientation, which again was polluted by its links with capitalistic competitiveness. So individualism was acceptable only as part of the cult of the loser, the deviant, and the dropout: individualists who were winners ipso facto "must" have sold out to the "system." And in this context loser-oriented "individualism" was quickly indistinguishable from peer group conformity. Tolerance of diversity, especially in politics, was similarly thrown out of the humanistic package. Liberal tolerance was seen as a patronizing confidence trick; it was the psychic violence of the powerful who had already socialized the powerless into rough conformity. Surface tolerance was the sneer of the Establishment at impotent minorities it did not even need to martyr. And Herbert Marcuse coined the endlessly useful phrase "repressive tolerance" to express the point and to justify the use of totalitarian repression and censorship by the enlightened against the conformist tools of the system.

Thus certain humanistic values were taken through the twists of their own logic to become their own opposites. Rationality turned to irrationality, objectivity to subjectivism and relativism, tolerance to "justified" violence against the unenlightened; individualism became peer group conformity, and intellectualism spawned anti-intellectualism to undermine the very foundations of the university's unique rationale. The life of the mind was well and truly blown.

The counterculture had evolved originally not in the universities, but in the so-called Underground and in the avant-garde arts. In the 1960s all these movements converged, and ideas which had been very esoteric for decades were ripe for popularization at the hands of the most footloose segments of the cultural class—protected adolescents and media operators, in particular. Thus the counterculture was assiduously proselytized by the student radicals (and some of their elders), pop art, and the mass media. The motifs of the movement had been around for a very long time. At one level the source material was the politicoreligious millennialism of proto-protestant antinomianism. This was supplemented and reworked by the romantic movement and topped up by the anarchic and surrealist move-ments of the early twentieth century. And, of course, there were the obvious political inspirations of the left. Adepts of the counterculture were some-times expressivist on principle—immediate experience as superior to the historic cumulations of culture or the hard-won skills of individual achieve-ment—and sometimes on tactical grounds which favored techniques of psychic subversion designed to shock the conventional mind so that hitherto unquestioned regularities could be seen as "absurd" instead of as intractable "givens."

The aspect of the counterculture to which I want to draw particular attention is its essential hostility to structure. It attacked ritual, form, boundaries, categories, roles, and certainties in every conceivable sphere. I have shown elsewhere the way in which this worked itself through in the avant-garde arts and pop music, both of which had crucial roles as vehicles of expression, and (simultaneous) symbols of identity and protest for the student rebels. Here it may worthwhile to summarize the main recurrent themes.

The separate arts all produced their own modes of eroding or denying structure and became increasingly involved in multimedia enterprises which sought to break down the distinctions between the separate arts themselves and provide the social basis for the experience of group euphoria: what, after all, were "happenings" if they were not instant ritual for the counter-cultural elite? Student demonstrations and protests had the same quality. The boundaries most frequently under attack were those between the public and the private sphere, between decent and indecent, tabooed and available, sacred and profane, between art and ordinary life, good taste and vulgarity, between creator and creation, artist and observer, between human and inhuman, male and female, animate and inanimate, man, animal, and nature. The rejection of control in all its forms showed itself as a preference for randomness or chance over plan, for excess over balance, for the fantastic over the normal, for emotion over reason, for the ephemeral over the lasting, for immediacy over hard-won comprehension, for the purely personal or topical allusion over the historically rooted image.

So far as subject is concerned, all the avant-garde arts were particularly intent on breaking the taboos concerning sex, violence, and good taste. The body symbolism of sexuality is a particularly potent symbolic instrument: all orifices become infinitely penetrable, sex becomes public not private. This both attacks convention by breaking taboos and provides an easy focal point for avant-garde identity: the "uptight" are patently not enlightened. All the arts used both the pastoral idyll and the daemonic in relation to sex—sex as "natural" lyricism or sex as salvation through the ultimate degradation of the self and others. In literature, for example, this takes one from Lawrence through to Genet and Burroughs. There was widespread use of sexual ambiguity and of what would be conventionally regarded as sexual perversions; another barrier to fall was that between art and pornography.[3] Much of this involved the sanctification of violence even, paradoxically, when one was preaching an end to violence. The other most favored taboo which the avant-garde delighted in violating was that which protects high culture from vulgarity—from culturally "low" forms like advertising, grand guignol, the horror film, or pop music. Thus "camp" became a cherished part of avant-garde culture providing the opportunity for the superior sneer, sadomasochistic immolation in vulgarity, and the key to the identity of fellow members of the progressive elite all at the same time. The cult of the object also assisted in eroding the distinction between art and the everyday or commonplace: the new novel with its minute and seemingly irrelevant details of material objects, the "objet trouvé" as sculpture, Duchamp's "ready-mades," and so on.

As well as themes which are common to all the arts, there are concerted attacks upon accepted style and form in each separate sphere, so that what one might call the grammar and punctuation of the various arts was largely discarded in favor of free, structureless expression.

The avant-garde arts and pop music flowed naturally into student radicalism, providing the latter with themes and perspectives and above all a vocabulary. Both in terms of fashions in taste and in terms of models of behavior the motifs summarized above were at the heart of the counter-culture's onslaught on the universities. Many of the ideas could be translated

---

[3] Professor Egerod reported in Venice the establishment of two lectureships in porno-graphic literature at the University of Copenhagen.

straight into educational panaceas for purifying the social system of the universities and the intellectual content and packaging of the education on offer. Thus, for example, student rebels tried to eliminate the distinction between teacher and taught in all kinds of ways: by demanding an equal say in curriculum content, by either eliminating or participating in assessment methods; by taking control of student recruitment and staff appointments; by abolishing or invading separate staff dining and common rooms, studies and offices; by denying staff the right to privileged access to personal information about students and colleagues. Many of these demands also constituted a denial of the distinction between public and private (places, information, behavior, roles); between relevant and irrelevant (knowledge, roles); between different subject areas (no departments, faculties, or expertise); between cognition and feeling; between "book knowledge" and random sense impressions; between high culture and triviality or vulgarity; between the university and the outside world—thus occupying a public park or squatting in empty property "for the people" could be regarded as at least as valid as academic work in defining the students' proper role. "Are you a sociologist or a human being?" was the persistent opening gambit of one of my own students during this period. The boundaries between individuals were symbolically attacked in innumerable ways—conventional, role-distinctive forms of address were dropped, instant personal intimacy was claimed, the protective walls around private or vulnerable parts of the personality were indignantly assaulted. The concept of academic production as individual private property in knowledge was anathema to many radicals and gave way to the collective project; thus as late as 1974 Dr. Halsey could receive a collective essay from fifteen self-styled Maoist students in one British university.[4]

Curiously enough, while the assault on boundaries was producing undifferentiated group phenomena like this, certain selected boundaries and categories were given a new salience. In particular, the conventional academic assumption that all scholars are in a certain sense equal and alike through their acceptance of basic humanist and intellectual norms met resistance on the new grounds of subjectivism, relativism, and the superior worth of the underdog. Women and ethnic minorities especially came to be treated as special ascriptive categories with their own world view, value system, and self-oriented subject matter. Women's studies, Black studies, and the like deny the possibility of objectivity, comparability, and equality in scholarship.

Many of these examples show individualist and anarchic notions twisting on their axes to become collectivism of various kinds. In part, this is a consequence of the assault on boundaries and structure: without boundaries distinctiveness is unattainable. But it was a result, too, of a basic dilemma

---

[4] A. H. Halsey, "Personal Column," *The Times Higher Education Supplement,* August 9, 1974.

which the whole counterculture built into its own position. Those involved were caught in a permanent and unresolvable tension within their own ideology between motifs of structurelessness and the need for rituals expressing their own collective identity. They used the language of what Mary Douglas has called "zero structure." [5] But zero structure as a rhetorical ploy is very different from zero structure as a life pattern. It is one thing to attack the roles, boundaries, and structures of other men's systems when you see them as the prison bars of convention and inauthenticity, but it is quite a different matter to pursue pure zero as one's own life pattern, consisting as it must of fleeting or tangential human contacts and weak or nonexistent bonds.

Most student radicals—and indeed most initiates of the wider counterculture—really hoped to replace old, conventional structures ("artificial" and/or "evil") by a new community ("real," "natural," and "good"). Here one encounters a bifurcation in the counterculture which echoes that between gentle utopian and violent adventist millennialism, or between the pastoral and the daemonic wings of romanticism. In the former it is held that the dissolution of existing restrictive structures in academic, social, and personal life will clear the way for the natural earth harmony to assert itself, which only perverse human meddling is preventing. In the latter, the belief is that most of mankind is (for the moment, at least) doomed to inauthenticity while only the enlightened individual or chosen elite has the power to ride the daemonic forces of the human psyche, social development, history, nature, or whatever. The road to illumination and salvation for the saints is often the path of excess, and if they see themselves as the Lord's sword to scourge the unrighteous, then this variety of radicalism seldom sees beyond Armageddon to the New Jerusalem. In Britain and America, most student radicals were in the last analysis almost exclusively the former type. Continental Europe suffered more serious adventist millennialism of the latter type.

The rhetoric and praxis of zero structure brought dilemmas and contradictions for both styles of radicalism. The main problem is that if one's whole symbolic system is geared to attacking ritual and structure *as such*, it becomes immensely difficult to prevent the natural logic of such a stance from undermining all one's attempts to breathe life into the community principle. If the dogma of zero structure is taken too seriously it can result in frustration rather than liberation. Instead of the prison of convention, one may find the lonelier prison of self unconnected with other thrashing and alien selves all incapable of building the arches of human communication because the acid ideology of liberation has destroyed the building materials. The unhappy experiences of some new universities

[5] M. Douglas, *Natural Symbols* (London: Barrie & Jenkins, 1970). See also M. Douglas, *Purity and Danger* (London: Barrie & Jenkins, 1966).

founded on all the best progressive ideas may be explicable in these terms.[6]

One can of course achieve a pseudoresolution of the dilemma by stylizing and restricting the motifs of structurelessness to a narrow range of symbols, so that they act as a badge of belonging: another middle-class student fashion such as Afro hairdos, John Lennon specs, patched jeans, or Vietcong headbands. These intellectual, verbal, visual, and political fashions then become mere peer group convention, the essential prerequisite of staying in the social race, labels worn to show one has rejected all labels. A good deal of the 1960s student protest was of this type, of course: as Professor Charles Townes pointed out, what else can one expect but conformity and tribalism of this sort if society isolates adolescent peer groups in ever larger numbers on our still expanding campuses?

The radicals wanted personalized experience, not impersonal submergence in the mass; they valued expressive not instrumental values; they sought openness and spontaneity rather than closed, formal, and inhibited contacts between human beings. They wanted to belong to a community, not to be cogs in an institutional machine. But they treated expressive values rather as if they were water, a life-giving force. They saw society as if it were a landscape cut through by rivers and canals, dikes and dams. If water is good then restrictive channels must be bad, their argument ran. Too often they failed to see that without the canals and dike the landscape would be less fertile: if they were removed, the lack of barriers would cause destructive floods drowning landscape and man alike.

In fact, one can seldom find examples of social systems which provide their members with a deep-rooted sense of belonging except through the medium of clear and all-embracing role specification. If you want to belong you must know your place. Yet the student radicals wanted belonging without role specificity and constriction. The history of medieval sectarianism and of contemporary commune experiments point the same lessons. If the principle of group belonging triumphs, then the end product usually is a totalitarian system more like the total institutions of prison, army, or monastery than the looser conventional structures of ordinary society. If the internal contradiction is maintained, then rituals of group belonging will evolve expressing collective euphoria and emphasizing badges of belonging and internal equality at the expense of real individuality. This was one of the most potent sources of all the fashionable cults of Indian mysticism, with and without drugs, in which individualized ecstasy was the sense of fusion of the One with the All. But social systems resting on such foundations tend to be ephemeral: task orientation, which at the very minimum is necessary to cope with the exigencies of continuity, is well-nigh impossible to achieve in so unstructured a milieu. When social disintegration ensues, as it often does,

---

[6] See, e.g., Mary Douglas' own analysis of what went wrong at the University of Essex in a letter to *The Times* (London), August 3, 1974.

a countermovement may spring up emphasizing clear role structures, simple but demanding criteria of belonging, certainly in place of drift. Thus the Jesus movement could sweep like wildfire through the campuses in the wake of hippie anarchism.

Though neighborhood community normally rests on clear, and indeed rigid, role structuring, there is another model available and (at least sometimes) appropriate to a university: the model of the family can embody a more flexible and less rigidly ascriptive pattern of behavior. The family, after all, is the main sphere of expressive behavior in the modern world. While it rests on age- and sex-based role specifications, the family nevertheless allows for flexible development and highly personal and idiosyncratic remolding of the basic social masks. The most successful traditional universities operate socially in something of the same way. Common socialization, shared values, smallness of scale, careful initiation into a personalization of role playing, and a subtle combination of role and status differentiation alongside selected symbols of common scholarly endeavor can combine in a delicate balance of ritual distancing and personal spontaneity. These are the safest homes of humanistic values. The model is very difficult to reproduce in a large-scale university, however: the multiversity cannot easily resemble a small and beautiful Oxford college. The large university therefore is trapped between massification and bureaucratization, on the one hand, and well-intentioned experiments in structurelessness, on the other; these are almost inevitably doomed to create maximum discontent and distress. There is no easy solution but it is quite clear that any serious erosion of roles, categories, limits, and rules is a recipe for disaster.

These considerations also help to explain the chronological sequence of student troubles. Let us take some crosscutting hypotheses:

1. Other things being equal, high-status and therefore heavily humanistic/expressive universities are likely to produce countercultural minorities most easily.

2. Smallness of scale and personalization of operations will largely counteract the effects of (1).

3. Large-scale and traditionless new universities emphasizing humanistic/expressive values are most likely to produce sizeable countercultural minorities.

4. In the case of (3) the difficulties will be maximized by (a) bureaucratization and depersonalization or (b) by progressive policies which erode role specificity and internal structuring.

5. In (4b) or other cases of institutional pursuit of structurelessness, the situation will be aggravated by the tendency to self-recruitment: the more an institution appears to favor the values approved by the counterculture, the more members it will attract who hold or flirt with progressive ideology.

Thus in America it was not Yale and Harvard but Berkeley which predictably proved front runner, and in Britain it was not Oxbridge but London and the new "progressive" universities. The spread of the pattern can largely be explained as an example of "status drip," so that today in Britain the fashion has percolated down to a few remaining polytechnics with a high social science component, and to the schools—in America to the smaller state colleges and high schools.

And so, finally, what were the consequences for the universities of the countercultural revolution? Though the troubles have receded, they have altered many universities both in their social organization and in their curricula and course structuring. As I insisted at the beginning of this essay, the student counterculture was only an exaggerated manifestation of a more general phenomenon—the Expressive Revolution. For this among other reasons its motifs had a wider resonance in the culture at large than the sheer numbers of serious revolutionaries could possibly account for. Many of its ideas popularized, vulgarized, and adulterated have passed into the common currency and, at another level, still affect the intellectual fashions and academic predilections in the universities. Positivism, objectivity, and reason are still widely suspect. Theories and philosophies stressing subjectivity and relativism are now entirely respectable. In sociology, to give only one example, phenomenology and ethnomethodology may have had a long history in German philosophic thought, but it took the university troubles of the 1960s to raise them alongside the accepted classics as a normal part of the curriculum.

The final paradox of the series is in many ways the saddest as well as the most inevitable. The major consequence of the radical sixties has been to strengthen the thrust of the bureaucratic ethos at the expense of the traditionalist and personal. If one looks at the fate of all those wild demonstrations to inaugurate student choice, flexible, personally tailored curricula and assessment methods (or none at all), student participation in decisions, and the rest, one finds that every one of them has altered the university system in a mechanistic and bureaucratic direction. More committees, minutes, documents, and bureaucratic prose. Fewer integrated subjects and more mechanized "choice"—modular degrees, course units and the like. A multiplicity of types of assessment which range from the dissertation and the course essay (encouraging either the commercialization of cheating or the total relativization of assessment) through to "objective testing" and other forms of programmed and mechanized assessment, all increase the burden on student and staff alike.

The expressive revolution achieved its most extravagant institutional flourish in a decade in which it still looked as if material progress were automatic and standards of living would go on rising effortlessly and indefinitely. At the popular level Western societies had not then seriously faced the possibility of zero material growth and retrenchment in living standards. Indeed, many radicals believed that we were on the verge of an era in which all work could be relegated to machines and computers, freeing human beings for "life." Pure expressiveness as a way of life looks a shade less plausible on a large scale now than it did in the 1960s. Moreover, expressiveness in all sorts of fields had been pushed to its own self-destructive limits and had nowhere new to go. Even more crucially, it had lost its exclusiveness: by the late sixties it was no longer the preserve of the upper reaches of the cultural class but had passed down into popular culture. So its more esoteric forms have begun to retreat back into compartments, to become again a purchasable private luxury in limited packages for the elite. Its stronghold remains the cultural class in the educational system and in the freer-floating professions, and its destructive potential is far from spent, especially in the lower reaches of the expressive occupational structure. But the universities in the 1970s are far more endangered by the steady infiltration of the bureaucratic mode, of short-term utility and pragmatic exigency, as the price they progressively pay both for their own expansion and as an ironic retribution for their conspicuous uselessness in the 1960s.

PART 2

NATIONAL EXPERIENCES

The German University in Crisis

Thomas Nipperdey

1. To CHARACTERIZE AND explain the present crisis of the university in Germany within the framework of the social, political, and cultural conditions of this country, one should start by reminding the reader of some of the well-known basic characteristics of the traditional German system of higher learning. The German universities are state universities, financed by the state; their constitutions or statutes are dependent upon legislation of the state; a member of the government (normally the minister of education) is in charge of university affairs; professors and junior faculty members are civil servants. Full professors are appointed by the state, though normally according to the nomination by the university. Due to the federal structure of the republic, responsibility for university affairs rests with the eleven *Länder* and many of the recent differences among German universities have been caused by the difference in legislation and executive policy of the dominant political forces within the *Länder*. It was only a short time ago that the federal government was given the right to set up some general and basic rules, a kind of framework or skeleton *(Rahmenkompetenz)* for university systems; a federal law on those matters is in preparation. In spite of their legal and financial dependence from the states, German universities have developed a very high measure of autonomy (appointments, budget, curricula, and examinations) during the last twenty-five years.

Before the "reform," the internal structure of the university was dominated by the full professors, with representatives of the various groups of junior academic staff (including representatives of the student body in Berlin) sitting and voting in the councils of academics self-government. The university was divided into several divisions *(Fakultäten)*, for example, theology, law, economics and social sciences, medicine, arts and letters, sciences. There was no difference between undergraduate colleges and graduate (and professional) schools; the Humanities Division does not serve as an undergraduate college but is mainly a professional school for high school teachers, journalists, librarians, and some other professions. It is also, but not exclusively, a graduate school for scholars. The basic units of the university were the so-called institutes or "seminars," mostly administered by one full professor as a "director."

2. During the sixties a growing need for a substantial reform of this

university system became evident. The university had become a mass enterprise, with an increase in the number of students of about 400 percent from 1945 to 1970; in consequence, the size of the academic staff and the costs had grown enormously (although not at all in proportion to the increase of students). The educational explosion led to a transformation of the university from a republic of scholars to an institution of mass instruction. So a university reform was needed designed to adapt research and teaching to the altered conditions, to solve the problems, and to ease the tensions which had developed in the meantime.

The first problem was to restore the declining effectiveness of instruction and learning (*Bildung Ausbildung*), to reform the curriculum. There were several reasons for this:

a. Normally, the German university is an institution with open admission, that is, unlimited free access for all high school graduates. Only in recent years was it felt necessary to introduce a limited admission (*numerus clausus*) for the departments of medicine, psychology, pharmacology, and some other scientific subjects. But, apart from these exceptions, one of the main causes for the reform was and is this system of open admission. Now the traditional system of studies was based on an elitist or aristocratic principle and enjoyed an enormous measure of liberality; students, especially in the humanities and social sciences (with secondary effects on almost all the other subjects), were allowed to study quite freely—without a definite scheme of courses and classes, without grades or credits, without examination before the termination of their studies, and without a definite limit for this termination. Up to the last decade, strong internal motivation and economic pressures took the place of the absent institutional pressure; in fact, studies were planned for (relative) effectiveness and finished within a limited time. Pressure of this kind has diminished, if not disappeared, over the last few years: parental means in an affluent society, relatively generous state grants, modest living in the communes of modern youth culture, the possibility of part-time jobs, and a still promising job market for graduates (especially with regard to the rapidly increasing public bureaucracies, e.g., within the school system)—these were some factors which allowed studies to go on for quite a long time, especially during the last years.

Thus, motivation and informed control of accomplishment ceased to be effective in a sufficient measure. In view of the increase of the costs of university and the menace of a total *numerus clausus* during the next years, when about 22 percent of an age group will attend the university, it became imperative to introduce a somewhat more rigid kind of studies, a curriculum. There had been some changes in this direction during the sixties but in general the reform was still pending.

b. Professors (i.e., the main bulk of the teaching staff), guided by the old Humboldtian ideal of unity of research and teaching—and ude to the growing specialization of scholarship—did not always adapt their teaching functions to the new conditions of the university as a mass enterprise and to the legitimate claims of the students.

    c. The change and the diversification of the German high school (*Gymnasium*) since 1945 became effective. Standards differ widely among German high school graduates and often fall short of the level required in universities.

    d. The problem labeled "multiversity" (in America) had to be solved; studies should be meaningful in human terms (at least in some respect).

    e. In our rapidly changing society with its need of academically trained personnel, students must not be trained for their chosen careers alone; they must develop also the capacity to respond to changes and challenges during their professional work which are not as yet even foreseeable; their training must be thorough and research oriented.

The second problem of university reform might be called staff reform. The teaching personnel of a German university consists—very roughly—of

    a. full professors;

    b. *Dozenten* (sometimes with the title of professor), a position similar to that of reader and lecturer, or associate professor; and

    c. assistants.

Groups (a) and (b) hold a postdoctoral degree, the *Habilitation*, which is a proof of continued and successful research activities, and entitles everyone who has passed it to give lectures and seminars within the university. In view of specialization and the fact that an academic career is often a strange mixture of chance, talent, accomplishment, and good luck, the differentiation between these groups (except for salaries) and certain hierarchical structures had become relatively obsolete. The homogeneity of the professoriate within the corporation, the abolition of hierarchical structures within the faculty (and some misuses of the old administration by the *Ordinarien*, i.e., full professors)—these were not only reasonable claims, but needed reforms. Much more difficult to answer was the question of group (c), the assistants. These assistants, mainly young Ph.D.s (or similar grades), had to assist a professor in his duties, give some courses and classes for beginners, and work towards their own *Habilitation*. One might call them, with some reservations, junior faculty. The majority were without tenure, but a certain group of instructors did have tenure already. Unfortunately, during the sixties this group was disproportionally expanded in order to cope with the rising student enrollment and at the same time to save money by avoiding the creation of new professorships. This state of affairs had, of course, led to a number of abuses. Needed were better safeguards for academic freedom and the independence of junior faculty, a certain representation and say in faculty and department affairs, especially matters of teaching, and—in the long run—a better (and more promising) balance between professors and junior staff.

The third need was for administrative reform: the administration dignitaries could not be expected to cope with the problems of mass instruction. The traditional divisions (*Fakultäten*) had grown so much that the introduction of a department system—which would perhaps improve cooperation within the professoriate over the old system with full professors as heads of separate institutes—was at least a very reasonable proposition. The introduction of a presidential system instead of the traditional rectorial system (full professors chosen by their peers for one year) promised greater continuity, better planning, and more administrative efficiency.

These were the themes of necessary reform; the dominating liberal majority of the academic community did not fundamentally question this need. Obviously, there are many other aspects and problems of the crisis of the university in Germany: the procedures of financing; academic freedom versus social accountability, or the legitimate claims of society and the legitimate autonomy of the university; the future needs of graduates; the relative roles of teaching and research. For the present crisis, however, the first group of problems was much more important. It is useless to quarrel about responsibility for the fact that these reforms were not implemented (only partial reforms came about). And, although one can only speculate how things would have developed otherwise, I think a certain measure of frustration and radicalization among junior faculty could have been avoided. In any event, the reform became de facto the task of the single states; it was a reform from above, just after the rebellion from below had started.

3. As in other highly industrialized Western societies, the radical student movement in West Germany began and reached its peak in the late sixties. It is not my task in this selection to discuss the basic problems, the causes, the aims, and the consequences of this upheaval. One should, however, say something about the causes of the movement which are specific for Germany, and accordingly about the specific character of the movement in Germany.

a. Because of a different school system, and the "liberal" system of studies I have described before, the average German student is some years older than are students in Anglo-Saxon countries.

Since students in their mid-twenties often feel too old to be dependent on others, the psychological situation strengthened the potential of the rebellion. The lack of motivation and informal control of accomplishment fostered the opportunity and the tendency to concentrate on political questions. The appeal of the new left against the repressive principle of achievement found a broad resonance just because some students were living in a situation in which the principle of achievement was suspended for an undefined time. The result is a specific German feature of the movement: the alliance of the radicals with the dull and the lazy.

b. One of the causes of the movement is probably the young generation's trouble in identifying themselves with the political and social, cultural and moral values, and institutions of the existing societies; it creates the problem of a growing moral and political relativism, the loss of a meaningful and convincing interpretation of our world and one's own life, the lack of a challenge, an emotional (and sometimes intellectual) vacuum. If there is any truth in such a hypothesis, the crisis between the young generation and the existing society was sharpened by the specific conditions of Germany after World War II.

After 1945 there has been (and still is) a specific crisis of national identity; the ties with tradition and/or heritage were much weaker than in other advanced societies. The young republic did not appeal to those in search of identity; the affluence of our society caused the very rapid spread of relativism. Moreover, this identity crisis had produced a crisis between the generations. The rebellion of the "kids" was sharpened by the question of what the parents had done during the Nazi period or what they had done in the fifties, the time of economic recovery (*Wirtschaftswunder*), and of their alleged preoccupation with earning money.

c. Furthermore, the traditional German orientation towards a non-pragmatc, nonempiristic philosophy of principle, the heritage of Hegel's dialectics, made itself felt again, with all its enthusiasm for theory and theoretical problems.

Philosophers of the so-called *Frankfurter Schule* became foster fathers of the intellectual brains at the beginning of the movement. The metaphysical element in the German branch of the movement is due mainly to this intellectual tradition.

d. The movement thrived on the German habit of financing student organizations; there are compulsory union fees and additional public means for the "official" student body of each university, and once a radical minority has conquered such a body (with less than half of the students actually voting) it achieves considerable means to finance radical propaganda almost without control, at the same time that most antiradical groups are suffering from the lack of money. So much for the specific German causes of the movement.

Now to the movement itself. As in most Western countries, the movement consisted mainly of young men and women of the upper middle class, the ones who styled themselves as protagonists of the exploited and oppressed masses or the people's interest. Germany differed from other countries in that the counterculture and the hippie movements were rather unimportant for the general trend within the student body. Compared with conditions in the United States, it is obvious that the movement was (and is) very little concerned with the real political or social problems of the country. The demands are abstract and artificial; one is preoccupied by the task to overcome "alienation" and "the system." The original practical goals of protest—grievances within the university—soon ceased to play a decisive part, and were used only as levers for other objectives. Even concern over Vietnam and the Third World, as much as one might respect the basic idea of human solidarity, was abstract because it was devoid of practical objectives or results and often factual information; and it was one-sided, as regards Israel, where the vast majority took an exclusively pro-Arab position. Similarly, the opposition to alleged abuses in Germany consequently had something artificial about it, as can most easily be seen from the rapid change of topics in the course of time.

The movement is guided by a secular faith in the salvation of society, by the utopia of a new society and new human beings. On the whole it is Marxist oriented, opposing the wicked, capitalistic, and bourgeois "system" of the Western world. The ultimate political objective is to abolish liberal and constitutional democracy. Within the university context, the movement advocates the abolition of what is called bourgeois scholarship and the introduction of "critical" scholarship in the sense of the new left. In the long run its members want to replace pluralism and diversity within disciplines and departments by a partisan creed, by scholarship in the service of what they pretend to be "the people's" interest. By and large, they want to turn the university into a factory for ideological products, into an agency designed to overcome the existing system of society. This is not only true for the humanities, the social and political sciences, but also for the rest; attempts are being made to establish such things as "red physics," "red mathematics," or "red medicine." Knowledge and the search for knowledge are judged according to political principles and the political functions of truth. In addition, they oppose the repressive principle of achievement which they say is aimed at adapting all human beings to the needs of a capitalistic and bureaucratic society: thus they oppose examinations, any scheme of courses and credits, the intended curriculum reform—at least, as long as they cannot have their own creed made the basis of a curriculum. Through this (in a way anarchistic) opposition they win support among the dull and the lazy.

Although the radical movement of the late sixties has consolidated its position, there are some remarkable changes. The anarchistic, antiauthoritarian, and spontaneous phase—the time of "radical democrats" and "new" left—has been replaced by a new phase with a strong revival of the old left. Within the movement we can very roughly discern three wings, with slight local differences:

a. the orthodox cadres of neo-Stalinist Communists of pro-Soviet persuasion—the law-and-order Communists (*Spartakus* in West Germany ADS in Berlin);

b. the so-called antirevisionist Communists—Maoists, the remnants of Trotskyites, anarchists, Palaeo-Stalinists, anti-Stalin Leninists, and other more or less sectarian groups—still very active in promoting violence and disrupting classes and examinations;

c. the left-wing radical socialists—a minor part still within the Social

Democratic party—who pursue a popular front policy with the Communists and have succeeded in infiltrating the teachers' union in university cities.

These groups are in opposition to each other—there are fundamental disagreements about principles and there are separations, dissolutions, shifts in the majority—but until now this has not really weakened radicalism. In university matters they usually march together. It is difficult to rate the proportion of the radicals among all the students; it is continually changing. I estimate the proportion at the present time at about 25–30 percent; all of these, however, are not part of the hard core. On the other hand, according to recent polls, an even stronger percentage opposes the system. This, of course, varies from campus to campus. During the last years most Western democracies have been experiencing a fading out of the protest movement and many of their schools appear to have gone back to regular and responsible academic work. Not so in a considerable number of West German universities where the crisis is still going on. Why so?

4. The radical movement was not decisive for the permanence of the crisis of the universities, which were able to survive it even in those places where it was strengthened by radical teachers. Nor was it the introduction of the necessary reforms we mentioned. More critical were the governmental and parliamentary policies, the change of university constitutions through new legislation and new university laws. What was the main purpose of this legislation and what were the main provisions? The underlying idea was simultaneously to calm the movement and to implement crucial reforms. Hence the structure of the university, the organization of decision-making institutions, was to be modernized. The basic principle was the so-called democratization of the university, the introduction of participatory democracy. The university was supposed to be made up of four groups—professors, assistants (junior faculty), students, and nonacademic personnel—each group sharing representation in decision-making bodies. There was a continuous struggle about the proportion according to which each group should be represented, as well as the proportion of group representation—and the definition of those groups is different in the different *Länder*. But the general point was and is that full and associate professors, or all tenured academic staff, were to be in the minority. Democratization was aimed at depriving professors of their decisive influence over academic matters. They were to be stripped of what was called their "power" or "privileges." The Berlin University Act of 1969 is a typical example. A university parliament (*Konzil*) was created, including thirty-three each of professors, junior faculty, and students as well as fifteen representatives of nonacademic personnel; its main tasks are the election of the president and the vice-presidents and the passing of bylaws. The academic senate consists of eleven professors, six assistants, five students, and two nonacademic personnel, responsible for central decisions but up against the strong executive power of the

president. Finally, there are department committees—seven professors, four assistants, three students, one nonacademic personnel—responsible for teaching, research, examinations, and appointments within the department.

These provisions for "democratization" of the university administration were completed in Berlin as well as in various *Länder* by "democratizing" the group of professors: certain large groups of assistants were promoted to tenured professorships by bureaucratic fiat—without consideration of their scholarly achievements, or by a rather easy *Habilitation,* and without the usual requirement of a second publication in book form.

This increase in the number of professors was deliberately combined with lowered academic standards for tenured positions. Thus at the Free University of Berlin the increase in the total number of professors (full and other) between 1968 and 1972 was 85.8 percent; the provisions mentioned above are the chief reasons for this 10 percent increase. To take another example: in the Department of Social Sciences of Marburg University in 1971 there were eight full professors and six other members of the faculty; by 1974 there were forty-seven tenured professors and seven members of the faculty without tenure. There were similar provisions for the group of assistants—an enormous increase along with lowered standard prerequisites. Most of them in fact are postgraduate students, but as a rule they teach independent courses of their own planning. The entire legislation was based on a philosophy of conflict, politicization, and participation. One basic idea was that each of the groups within a university had its own specific interests. and the best way to run a university was to combine them together on boards where no single group would have a majority; therefore, they would have to find compromises and be forced to cooperate. This "interest theory" was combined with a strong accent on the political implications of all academic decisions—and, politically, all groups were equal. Thus qualifications and competence had only a relative importance. Everyone was thought competent to make decisions (i.e., a secretary, for the appointment of a professor), albeit in varying degrees. The philosophy of participatory democracy was constructed on the hypothesis that those who are most immediately "affected" or "concerned" *(betroffen)* by a decision must have a big say in the matter. In Berlin students have half the seats on the curricular and teaching commissions. It is obvious that society at large is greatly affected by the academic training of the young generation; society at large, however, is almost excluded in this model. The assumption is that democracy can be transferred without differentiation from the political community to any functional area within society. (In the doctor-patient relationship alone is an exception always made.)

What were the reasons for these strange policies?

a. There was a common misunderstanding about the relationship between the need for reforms and the radical movement; the movement was thought to have been caused by abuses and failures of the old system and was supposed to be aimed at a reasonable reform. So it seemed natural to force a rapid reform and give adherents of the reform movement an important say within the new structure. Responsibility within the institution would—that was another idea—calm certain irresponsible and even violent features of the movement, and would separate radical reformers from extreme radicals within the student body. One might say that this was a rather provincial outlook, because the movement was an international phenomenon regardless of what the national university system happened to be. This misinterpretation was strengthened by some peculiarities of public opinion in Germany in the late sixties (and partly in the early seventies, too).

Leading liberal papers, as well as radio and television, depicted the university as a reactionary hierarchy hostile to progress. Cultural and university affairs were generally in the sphere of leftist (and sometimes very young) editors and there were quite a few students who had dropped out of studies or whose ambitions had been disappointed with a resulting strong resentment against the academic world. Reporting, in the first stages, was largely biased in favor of the movement. Excesses were played down, their causes looked for among reactions of the wicked; the ostensibly ideal goals of the young were offered as excuses for certain methods. Unrest was considered something good in itself. A certain group of educationists who wanted to change society by changing the educational system played a considerable role in convincing the public that reform by democratization was reasonable and sound; democratization was believed to be the crucial tool for necessary reforms.

This kind of thinking, perhaps wishful thinking, also was enormously popular with politicians, the public, and even within the professoriate. Many well-intentioned older gentlemen, pleased by the marvelous and idealistic youth movement, were ready to share responsibility with them. Moreover, the radical attack on the legitimacy of existing institutions in the name of a "new democracy" revealed not only an astonishing lack of self-confidence but also of faith in the values, institutions, and legitimacy of our system. The normal reaction was to understand and more or less to justify the attack. There was a kind of vacuum, which may explain the high measure of helplessness among the liberal community faced with the movement.

b. This feeling—responding to the challenge of the movement by rapid constitutional reform and shifting the base from staff, curriculum, and administration reform to the brand new "democratic" participation of all groups in academic decisions with less "power" for the professors and more for the students—was, of course, mixed up with a strong tendency towards appeasement as, notably, in Berlin where the main objective was to get radicals off the streets and back to the campus, to integrate the major part of a radical young generation into the liberal democratic systems by being soft and making substantial concessions to them. Probably most of these appeasers—professors as well as politicians—had not considered the consequences of such a policy. However, the principal point remains that these concessions were not (as in some places in the U.S.A.) concessions in special situations but, rather, general concessions within the university constitution through changed laws. This made at least the direction of concessions almost irreversible.

c. The leading political group responsible for this was the left wing of the Social Democratic party (SPD). This left wing was (and is) formed by radical intellectuals, not by blue- and white-collar workers. Among SPD members of the state parliaments and the *Bundestag*, university questions were considered more or less as a domain of these left-wingers, partly as a result of the distribution of labor among specialists, partly because of an informal compromise within the party whereby its left wing is kept loyal to majority policies in general. So the left wing is disproportionately strong in the parliamentary committees and among the SPD ministers for "cultural affairs." The latter have almost succeeded in monopolizing discussions on educational affairs within the party. Since part of the movement is integrated in the growing left wing of the party (the so-called Young Socialists), this group and this pattern have become more and more influential during the last years. The left-wingers strongly resent the allegedly elitist university and the principle of meritocracy, and cherish the rebellion of the upper-middle-class kids. They advocate participatory democracy—sometimes as an end in itself, sometimes as a means for other purposes. Because the working class is no longer the real subject of class struggle, they want to use the university as an instrument for radical change of the social and political system.

The fact that public sentiment and the majority of the voters do not favor the movement did not matter in the first years of the reform. University affairs do not rank high among the motive forces of the voters; and, although the reforms were extremely expensive, politicians did not suffer pressure from taxpayers: in German politics the spending of public money is unfortunately less influenced by grievances of the taxpayer than in Anglo-Saxon countries.

The result of these tendencies and development was that university reform by democratization was promulgated in several *Länder*, especially those with SPD governments. We now have this kind of law in Berlin, Hesse, and Lower Saxony. The Hamburg law is similar but a bit more moderate, and it has been introduced in an extremely radical form in the newly founded University of Bremen with a 1:1:1 proportion for professors, instructors, assistants; students; and nonacademic personnel. In North Rhine–Westphalia similar plans were developed; each university had to develop an assembly with an almost equal representation of the three main groups (plus the nonacademic personnel) to work out a new constitution. The results are different (and in some institutions there are no results at all), but some universities, especially the new ones, have already established group representation (in varying proportions).

The federal government and the Bundestag are preparing a skeleton law for the universities on the basis of democratization; in its first version, at least, the goal was to establish the majority of nonprofessors in all decisive academic bodies. The CDU-governed *Länder* also have promulgated new laws which pay their tribute to the idea of participatory democracy and the "group university," as it is now called.

In the first phase, in the late sixties, there were strong tendencies to adapt oneself to the current stream of feeling among the student generation. Thus in Bavaria, normally thought of as a conservative state, the statute of the newly founded university at Regensburg provided that professors were to have exactly half the seats of the decision-making bodies. In Baden-Württemberg the government introduced constitutional assemblies in each university with a strong representation of the nonprofessorial groups; and in Heidelberg and Constance this led to results similar to those in Regensburg (some councils even ended up with a minority of professors). In the Heidelberg senate, for instance, there was a majority of professors, because each department was represented by its dean (who was required to be a professor); but these deans were elected by department councils with a majority of nonprofessors, so, often these deans did not really represent the professoriate. This method of election called "integrated election," which was introduced in other universities too, in effect often meant a premium for left-wingers among the professors.

But in the universities just mentioned there were some rules functioning as checks and balances against the obvious dangers of a radical "seizure of power"—rules which have been stiffened by the governments in question during the last years. Thus it became possible to unseat the radical rector of Regensburg and the rector of Heidelberg—a fellow traveler of radicalism. Methods of containment may include provisions to assure a small majority of professors in decisions on professorial appointments and on examination requirements, to secure the principle that no professor could be appointed against the majority of his colleagues (which sometimes led to a prolonged stalemate within a department council), or even the "principle of *pares*" (peers): only those can decide on appointments and examinations who themselves have passed these examinations or have been appointed on an equal level. The latter rule, however, is a very rare exception. This is the type of university constitution now valid in CDU-governed *Länder*, such as Schleswig-Holstein, Rhineland-Palatinate, Saarland, and Bavaria—either a small majority of professors (i.e., all university teachers with tenure), from 51 to 58 percent, plus, in some, differentiations due to the type of decision.

Furthermore, the way in which governments were using their executive and controlling powers was critical. If, for instance, one compares the situation of Heidelberg and Berlin, which was sometimes rather similar (although the Berlin law was more radical than the Heidelberg *Grundordnung*), one of the decisive differences was that the Baden-Württemberg government took a first course against radicalization and appeasement while the Berlin government—although not especially happy about the development—continued to follow the course of appeasement, supporting the position of the more or less radical university presidents. In Hesse the radical minister of cultural affairs, a professor of sociology, used his executive powers extensively in favor of the radicals.

A new chapter in this story of legislation has been produced by a decision of the Supreme Constitutional Court, won by professors from Lower Saxony, according to which some principles of the laws in question have been judged unconstitutional. The court decided that, in questions of the appointment of professors and in questions of teaching, professors must have a majority; in questions of research, a "sufficient" majority; and that nonacademic personnel should have no vote at all in such matters. The university councils, which elect the president and pass the bylaws, and university senates are not bound to such a restriction: a 30 percent minority of professors there is thought to be constitutional.

Now the *Länder* governments whose legislation has been found at least partly unconstitutional (especially Hesse, Lower Saxony, and Bremen) are trying to sneak by the ruling through numerous tricks, for example, by claiming that the so-called assistant professors—assistants with a Ph.D. (or similar degrees) but without tenure—are part of the professoriate. The first version of the federal university bill, a skeleton law, which is still pending, was characterized by similar tendencies. Further constitutional conflicts can easily be predicted. On the national level, parliamentary discussions may result in a compromise which will fulfill the minimum demands of the constitutional court. The question is whether this minimum shall also be the maximum and what will happen to the central executive and legislative bodies of the university. This development might prevent academic life in Germany from further deterioration. The consequences of the reforms already implemented or planned, the politicization and the atmosphere of political conflict, however, will last for many years to come.

There is not only a great diversity among the university laws; the situation of universities under the same law differs also. This is due to special circumstances in each institution, to the reservoir of active personalities, and to the voting behavior of faculty, students, and assistants. The personality of the elected president and his relationship with those who have voted for him is often decisive. Hence the radicals were able to seize power in the central administration of the University of Marburg, while they failed to do so at Frankfurt, although both are situated in the *Land* of Hesse. At Frankfurt the president took a firm stand against radicalism and succeeded in holding together his rather small majority on the top level of the university; in Marburg, on the other hand, the president is collaborating with the radicals. And, of course, the same difference holds true for various departments; even in those universities which are generally characterized as radical there are several moderate or even quite normal departments, although much hampered by a radical central administration. By contrast, there are radical departments in those universities which are on the whole not radical.

At the present time we can speak roughly of three groups of universities:

a. those which can no longer be called normal universities insofar as a great number of their essential departments are under radical rule—for example, social, political, and economic sciences; psychology; arts and letters. Berlin and Marburg belong here. Bremen, even worse, is a kind of cadre school for the extreme left. The new universities—Kassel, Hesse, Osnabrück, and Oldenburg (Lower Saxony)—belong to the same type;

b. those where a permanent conflict is going on in essential departments and/or on the top level, where academic freedom and academic standards are not lost but frequently at stake. This group includes Hamburg, Frankfurt, Münster, universities in Hesse and Lower Saxony, and some of those in North Rhine–Westphalia;

c. those that still function relatively undisturbed, such as Munich or Freiburg. But the transitions are fluent and the problems are always similar.

5. We must now discuss the consequences of the reform bills, especially in the less moderate version. This is not a description of what one might call the average German university department. It is necessary to glance at those places and departments where legislative wisdom has resulted in a loss or a permanent threat to academic freedom and academic standards— necessary because until now this has been the dominant tendency; this pattern of democratization will be the pattern of further reforms in the future. In almost all universities there are departments with the same kinds of conflicts and problems which I will describe; and there are very few university teachers who have not experienced these conflicts and these problems. Academic freedom and academic standards are at stake because of the new legal framework. It is misleading to differentiate between average institutions and exceptional ones (the latter filling the headlines of newspapers); what we are discussing is the general effect of reform by democratization on academic life. In every particular situation there are differences in the amount but not in the quality of the problems resulting from the new legislation—and this is the main difference in most of the Western industrialized countries.

a. The institutionalization of the movement: its development was fixed by legislation for years and perhaps decades to come. So the radicals in a certain phase of a rapid development are the ones who have profited from the reform. It is their important share in decision making (or power, as they put it) which keeps the movement alive. The fading out of the rebellion (and, from a purely intellectual and psychological aspect, there are hints of such a development among high school students in 1974) was successfully prevented; once institutionalized, the movement has been perpetuated.

b. The second result is politicization and polarization, that is, the atmosphere of permanent confrontation and conflict. Sometimes one might call it an institutionalized permanent clinch. In the universities and departments most affected, no decision in any question whatsoever is made without a struggle for power and without regard to political goals and implications. Academic life consists of conflict and political tactics to secure or to prevent majorities, without even a basic consent about the rules of conflct as it exists between political parties in a democracy. The two fundamental errors of the legislators were: that antidemocrats would behave as democrats when they are involved in "democratic" institutions and that the appeal to the group interest and the claims of different groups for power should result in a better cooperation and in maintaining that measure of objectivity which is still needed in academic matters. Instead, it ended in confrontation and in abandonment of former standards of academic decisions. Sometimes a compromise is reached, normally that of the lowest common denominator; in other instances the boards are completely paralyzed, or the time-consuming, harsh, and occasionally violent confrontations end with a reasonable or unreasonable majority decision. What is more, the sessions of all board councils, and so on, are open to the public, meaning to other radicals, sometimes big crowds; the result is a frequent danger of disturbance and disruption (see below); thus a climate of pressure often prevails. The institutionalization of confrontation lent itself to an easy interpretation in terms of "class struggle" between the "ruling class" of professors, conveniently reduced to a minority position, and the "oppressed class" of students and—perhaps—junior faculty and nonacademic personnel. It is exactly this interpretation which has helped the Communists attract fellow travelers.

c. To understand why this conflict is so permanent and why the results are so often disastrous, we have to analyze the situation of the main groups within the framework of democratization. Professors are handicapped in this struggle. They are individualistic, difficult to organize; they do nothing but defend tolerance and pluralism against the aggression of a new and absolutistic doctrine of salvation, a secular creed. They are often neither physically nor psychically fit to meet the new situation (such as sessions lasting from 2:00 to 10:00 p.m.); they want to get on with their real job instead of being endlessly molested by university politics. They are less numerous and therefore more heavily burdened. Moreover, they are not a homogeneous group with a uniform vote.

One premise of some legislators hoping to secure decisions resting on the authority of those professionally responsible was that the professoriate would vote as one on vital matters. This assumption has been proved false. There is a not unimportant radical faction among the professors which has been strengthened by the bureaucratic increase of the professoriate described before. It is unfortunate that there are not very many German university scholars with a Marxian or, indeed, any other "deviant" point of view who are nevertheless prepared to stand for academic freedom, tolerance, and qualification by achievement. The majority of the new professoriate can by no means be described as conservative and status-quo-minded; it represents instead the normal moderate liberal and liberal type of Western academic communities.

Within the group of the so-called assistants the adherents or sympathizers of radicals play a relatively dominant role, at least in the social sciences and humanities. Some former grievances and misuses that I mentioned before—the inflationary increase of this group, the bringing in of people with smaller scholarly achievements which damages the prospects of the good ones as well, the radical wave of the late sixties—all this had far-reaching results. Those who agitate for the professional interest of this group often combine it with agitation for a radical ideology: they are the stronger activists. The appointment policy of the new majorities—either in favor of radicals or of those soft towards radicalism—had had its effects on the voting behavior of the group. Moreover, the newly won power has a great attraction and there is, of course, a lot of opportunism—one adapts oneself to conditions on which one's own career depends.

Now for the students: If the majority are not radical, why then do radicals play such a decisive role? Why are they the ones who profit from the reform and get the important share in the decision-making process? Almost always they win a majority in the elections of student representatives; only 40 to 50 percent of the whole student body are likely to vote. These are the stronger activists, theirs is an intense ideological commitment, they are able to invest all their time and energy in politics for a certain (normally very long) period. These students possess the financial means described before. And, what is most important, radicalism is still "in" and thrives on its gains in certain universities and departments. The opponents of radicalism are weaker, in a minority position; they had some remarkable gains only where vital interests of the majority of students were endangered by permanent disruptions of lectures and examinations and "strikes." But, always competing with the radicals' commitment to student power, it is difficult for the nonradicals to develop a positive platform of their own in university politics. The majority (especially those who do not vote) remain silent, hardly taking any stand against the radicals. In the face of the obvious antagonism between professors and students, they do not want to be found on the side of the "Establishment." And, though not supporting radicals, some think they might be of a certain value as an innovating force. This makes the majority of the students' actual vote in favor of the radicals— and the general public often thinks them to be representative of the student body as a whole. This is, of course, a dangerous error, because there is no such thing as "the" students.

The nonacademic staff representatives are in an ambiguous position among the other groups. Whether they are radical, nonradical, or neutral (and abstaining) depends very much on specific conditions Occasionally, before the decision of the Supreme Constitutional Court, the vote of this group has been decisive in academic matters (cf. p. 130).

In the new institutions of the "group" university, however, the political cleavage does not run simply between these groups, or between professors and nonprofessors. The cleavage is between radicals and moderates and both are, as I have described, represented in each group, although in different proportions. The specific situations of each group may explain why in so many departments (and in several universities) the political struggle over academic questions still goes on and why these politicized departments lack a sufficient or secure majority of reasonable representatives (regardless of whether the professors have half the seats, half plus one, or half minus one).

d. In some universities the combination of democratization and the introduction of a presidential system (with relatively strong executive powers for the president) has become the turning point of its further development. The election of semiradicals, or proradicals, or radical liberals soft on radicalism—or of people who were the prisoners of a radical coalition to which they owe their election—proved to be fatal for the development of the university. In university parliaments (councils) formed according to the model of a 30:30:30:10 representation, such an outcome of the election of a president was not at all impossible. Apart from Bremen and other recently founded universities with a strong leftist majority in the founding institutions, Marburg and the two universities in Berlin are notorious, as also, for a certain period, are Regensburg and Heidelberg. I omit some other cases, which would need further discussion. In some, such as Hamburg and the two universities of Berlin, young assistants with unfinished doctoral theses and without administrative and academic experience were elected presidents. In the Free University of Berlin the president elected in 1969 received the votes of only two professors. These presidents frequently succeeded in setting up a rather uniformly leftist administration; they make extensive use of their legal powers and apply the laws in favor of their clientele; perhaps they may even block decisions of nonradical department boards by means of massive pressure and various tricks.

e. It is quite obvious that outbreaks of violence and terrorist activities cannot be counted among the consequences of the new legislation. We had these things before and we find it in other countries which do not have our "reforms." But there is still a link. The hope of the legislators that participation of radicals would be the best means to avoid violence has proved to be wishful thinking. The twenty-fifth anniversary of the Free University of Berlin was celebrated by the nonradical academic world (an audience of 300 listening to political scientist Richard Lowenthal's address on "Democracy and Freedom") far away from the campus. On campus a Communist group gathered 1,000 people in the *Auditorium maximum* to present their version of the founding of the university: a hand-in-glove affair between U.S. imperialism and Social Democrats.

Terrorist activities are still going on, although the number has decreased. They have included disruptions of classes and examinations, and of board and council sessions, resulting in the necessity of teaching off campus, even in private homes; physical attacks against professors and students who want to attend classes (or even to build up a nonradical organization); such threats as "CIA agent Professor X off campus," and so on; and violent pickets. Several groups involved in these affairs are operating from office space (worst of all in the two Berlin universities, Frankfurt, or, until recently, Heidelberg). The experience of the weak reaction of such establishments towards organized pressure probably makes it seem profitable for those who still try to put through their goals by violence. The discipline committees of democratized universities are also democratized and now are totally ineffective; but a prevailing climate of liberal softness, unforeseeable difficulties of the legal process, and the opposition of left-wingers against new legislation on these matters made it impossible to come to grips with the violence. Finally, sometimes terrorist activities are covered or shielded by central university administrations. If the president, for instance, is the head of a leftist coalition he will react to such measures with a policy of appeasement, differentiating between the methods, which may come in for some mild criticism, and the "rational nucleus" of the radical claims. Violence is not the consequence of the new legislation, but it is fostered and not at all discouraged by the new system. I want to stress that the crisis of the university in Germany exists irrespective of terroristic and violent activities. The real and serious problems—politicization, incompetence, and lowering of standards—result from the curious idea of "democratization." Even one instance of violence, however, is one too many.

f. In politicized departments the question of appointments is normally a political one. The question of the applicant's political orientation —his ideological credentials, whether he is a Marxist (or at least fellow traveler) or not—often takes precedence, even if the council pretends the decision is based on his scholarly qualifications. We find the same arguments and pseudoarguments in Germany as Hans Daalder has discussed in his report on universities of the Netherlands (page 195), for example, the argument of "balance" (normally referred to as "pluralism"). A common practice, especially in the social and political sciences or in modern literature, has become the styling of advertisements in the intended ideological direction ("critical," "Marxist," or—understandable only in the context—the new interpretation of good old terms such as open-minded and cooperative, i.e., cooperative with radicals, etc.). Almost every important appointment leads to months of conflict and countless meetings. Younger applicants are tested in hearings as to their quality as appeasers, and put through questioning which has nothing to do with their subject or their teaching competence. In especially "wild" departments terrorist campaigns, "tribunals," and so on are mounted against nonradical candidates. My point is, of course, not the exclusion of nonconformist scholars or any kind of discrimination against them but, rather, the radical demand to appoint radicals because they are radicals and not because they are good scholars, and thereby to take lesser intelligence and minimal achievement into the bargain. If one analyzes the voting of the professoriate in the Free University of Berlin between November 1969 (when the new reform constitution was intro- duced) and February 1974, it is easy to see the results of such an appoint- ment policy (see Table 1). During this period the number of professors has risen from 494 to almost 1,000 (including the increase of the professoriate by bureaucratic fiat, as described above).

In the department of philosophy and social sciences—the most radical department except the department of political sciences—in 1974, 20 (41 percent) of the 49 tenured professors supported pro-Communist candidates, 8 voted for left liberal and reform socialist candidates, while the others just kept quiet. Among junior faculty (assistants) there were only Communist or pro-Communist slates. In the political science department in 1968 none of the professors belonged to the Communist or pro-Communist left; in 1973 there were 5, or 18.5 percent. The same figures for the assistants: 5 or 18.5 percent in 1968, 37 or 45.7 percent in 1973. These are, of course, extreme examples, but the general tendency in such departments which are "democratized" and dominated by proradicals is similar: not a Communist, but a left-wing political persuasion, and adherence to the principles of democratization are of the utmost importance. Consequently, there is now a kind of self-protective appointment policy within nonradical departments;

TABLE 1. Free University of Berlin Faculty Voting

	PERCENTAGE		INDEX FIGURE 1974 (1969 = 100)
	Nov. 1969	Feb. 1974	
Moderates and Liberal Centrists	84.3	52.7	63
Left Liberals and "Reform Socialists"	15.7	17.8	113
Communists and Other Leftists	0	20.4	2,040
Not Clearly Definable	0	9.1	910
And the same figures for the group of the "assistants":			
	35.8	20.6	58
	33.4	40.1	120
	30.8	36.8	125
	0	0.7	70
And the figures for the nonteaching staff:			
	33.6	25.2	75
	31.2	27.9	89
	21.2	32.5	153
	14.0	14.4	103

they feel obliged to take into account possible shifts of the majority. Where political conflict does not dominate to this degree—for example, in the sciences—the fact that a majority of other than full professors is responsible for all promotions and appointments leads very often to a cartel of mutual assistance—a system which guarantees a good career within the department from the first appointment onwards. Where the new method of decision making does not serve political ends, it tends to advance mediocrity. Only in the most extreme situations do some governments use their legal right to neglect the nomination by university institutions and not appoint the nominee. On the other hand, other governments do not appoint moderate nominees but this, of course, is no solution to the problem.

g. A further decisive point is the question of examinations, especially in the humanities and the social sciences. The radicals oppose the principle of achievement and disciplined work as a principle of capitalist repression and enforced adaptation or as a means of perpetuating social inequalities. According to the radicals, examinations should be basically simplified. A thesis (M.A. or Ph.D.) is to become a "collective paper" with no way of ascertaining individual achievement. Examinations are still set by teachers, but some radical faculty make a farce of examinations themselves, and candidates whose ideological commitment follows the party line can easily reach a high degree. Others in the role of the appeaser (or terrorized people with a rather human lack of courage) no longer risk setting a genuine examination or perhaps incline towards giving higher grades; so, in some departments an A now has the value of a C of some years ago. Manipulation and cheating are on the increase.

The decisive point, however, is that the requirements (and decisions on doubtful cases) are decided by democraticized councils with nongraduates voting. There is thus a vested interest in lowering requirements on the part of those who have not yet passed examinations. In several departments collective papers are now permissible and interim examinations bitterly opposed and disrupted by radicals have frequently been replaced by noncommittal "consultations." In the course of two years the rate of failure in economics in Berlin dropped from 25 percent to less than 4 percent and four out of five students of architecture were given the highest grade in the Technical University of Berlin. Even the examinations for high school teachers—organized by the state but set by professors—are affected by this lowering of standards. Until now this development has probably affected only those universities and departments which are hurt most by the radical pseudoreform, and the newly founded ones. But, more important for broad segments of academic life, there is a permanent tendency to erode academic standards; the eternal discussion on a reform of examinations is now an exhausting and only partly successful struggle against lowering standards.

h. With respect to teaching, the radicals aim to put through a program in the service of the so-called revolution. They demand compulsory "political economy" courses, that is, a chapter-by-chapter study of *Das Kapital* and other Marxist-Leninist bible lessons, or courses to prepare a revolutionary practice of "countercourses" against the normal lectures. In the Department of English Language and Literature in Marburg, for instance, the curriculum reform aimed at a broad field of interesting leftist topics—working-class literature, labor movement, "imperialism," education for "emancipation," economy of education, curricular theory of language instruction, Marxist theory of literature, position of teachers in *Spätkapitalismus*, comics, communication systems (and emancipation, which is always the right label). In short, it all adds up to antibourgeois English studies—all perhaps useful topics, but awkward for students and faculty in the context of the English department. The normal readings for these topics are German paperback books. The fundamental requirements—a practical knowledge and command of the English language and the ability to interpret historical and literary texts, which play an important role in understanding British and American culture and society—are neglected.

Now one has to realize that in universities such as Berlin or Marburg, to say nothing of the new ones, students have a very important voice in all curricular matters, either through special committees on the departmental level or, more important, on the central level, where committees on teaching matters are often nominated by the president. In the universities and departments most affected by the new rules we often find a mixture of "old-fashioned" and "reformed" teaching programs and a continuous and tiresome conflict about these problems, about particular classes each semester, as well as about curricula in general. The radicals' program is implemented by the support of the radical part of the senior faculty, the majority of the enormously increased junior faculty, and by classes given by graduate students (called tutors) or (outside the official program) student workshops. Student "guidance" by radical groups serves to denounce nonradical staff and to recommend those who are proradical. Comparing course schedules of 1967 and 1974 in certain departments, one finds a remarkable shift, especially if one knows the changing fashion in the wording of radical topics. Some curricula now include compulsory political economy courses, and some have been revised in ways which permit a student to get through a complete course of studies in classes and seminars which offer only the Marxist position: thus dogmatic indoctrination takes the place of scholarly instruction. There is also a slightly less dogmatic way: In the new University of Kassel, for example, a curriculum of social sciences (including history) is totally aimed at emancipation, so called, the creation of a new society and new human beings. Where radicals cannot command sufficient institutional support, they try to force teachers to abandon guidance of their courses or to "integrate" a radical "countercourse" into their own program. This is called *Umfunktionierung* (redirection), and is still rather frequent. Appeasers among professors often give up trying to guide their course and let the revolutionary chatter run its course. "Redirection" often takes the form of an insistence on "discussion" which gives radicals a chance of addressing a silent majority as an audience—rarely found outside classes. In several places hard-line tactics are still the order of the day: there are sit-ins, lockouts, organized boycotts with pickets, violence, and forced discussions. Such tactics—as in the campaign last year against Professor Wolfram Engels—are directed not only against teachers but also (and equally) against nonradical students.

There is, of course, a lot of teaching going on unhampered—but disruption and violence as described above are by no means exceptions. It is a typical and foreseeable development, as soon as radicals win a strong position in the decision-making institutions of the university. In most the introduction of a relatively fixed curriculum is still pending, because there is either a confusion as to who is to lay down what is going to be taught or a deadlock between radicals—fighting against all curricula in the name of academic freedom, or trying to establish an exclusively radical curriculum—and nonradicals. This struggle will become most important during the next years, when society at large will be expecting practical results. Democraticized institutions do not seem to be suited to this task.

Where useful and reasonable plans are put forward to reform the curriculum and teaching methods, the adherents of radical "didactics" (one of the most fashionable reform labels) appear on the stage. They do not stick to their proper job but talk about the "relevance" of other people's research, disciplines, and topics; they also claim the right to decide what professors should teach and what students should learn. Pretending to be "agents of the meaningful and the universal" (*die Agentur des Bedeutsam-Allgemeinen*) in our present society, they try to make all teaching conform to the labels of "liberation," "emancipation," "dialectic critiques," and so on. The "didacticians" are very influential in the committees on reform of the curriculum because normally professors are rather reluctant to sit on these committees. Radical didactics is a new and dangerous weapon in the struggle against free and pluralistic scholarship.

Finally, introduction of a definite limit for the termination of studies, which exists in almost all industrialized countries, has not been achieved. The legislators, who intended to make studies more effective, have essentially abandoned this task to those who wish the contrary (which includes the remnants of old-style, conservative professors). So one of the most urgent reforms is neglected and until now we have had only pseudoreforms.

i. No wonder scholarship does not flourish in this atmosphere. The struggle for the prerequisites of scholarship and academic freedom; endless sessions in the large number of committees, with at least one caucus for preparation; frequent confrontations, intimidation, and stress—all this means an immense waste of time and energy and preoccupies every scholar during term time. Experts of the Technical University of Berlin have discovered that, compared with the former system, the time spent in committees has increased by 270 percent (and costs by 280 percent). Unfortunately, the efficiency of the university has not increased at the same rate. In some institutions—for example, in the University of Marburg—democratization of decision-making bodies responsible for research funds or appointment of auxiliary personnel has led to a kind of equalization of all funds: in fact, this means the end of all serious research insofar as it is dependent on the financial means at its disposal. Sometimes majorities almost "expropriate" nonconformist professors by taking away from them all necessary means of work (rooms, secretaries, etc.). Often the fact that the legislation has stated no clear responsibilities leads to a growing feeling of irresponsibility. One result of the malaise is a kind of withdrawal from the university. Once an institution is totally or almost captured by the radicals, many great scholars, especially among the older generation, will no longer actively participate in the struggle for academic freedom, and no one taking part in this struggle can do so for long without neglecting his own research.

j. In the course of this development we find an astonishing new interpretation of the autonomy of the university. Up to now autonomy has been an instrument to secure academic freedom, that is, freedom of individual scholars and teachers (and of the institution) from social, political, and ideological pressures. Now autonomy is sometimes used to restrain this freedom and to prevent the government from stepping in to uphold this freedom. While until recently radicals have opposed the traditional notion of the university as an ivory tower and have claimed a reorientation towards active involvement with a changing world (as did some liberal reformers), they now try to establish a new ivory tower of their own—painted red. They talk about the responsibility of the university for a democratic society. They do not mean the existing society, however, but rather their own idea of the "society of the future." In fact, their concept is that of an elitist educational dictatorship; universities are to be the driving force of social reform regardless of professional standards and the scholarly pursuit of truth. They style themselves as an avant-garde, as the spokesmen of the hidden "true" consciousness of the masses, which until now has been manipulated in the interest of oppression. It is this for which they claim autonomy from parliament and society, while expecting to be financed by the taxpayers. A university based upon the ideal of academic freedom, which includes the freedom to criticize society as it is now, is nevertheless part of the democratic system and has its responsibility for society. Radical democratization destroys not only academic freedom as an individual right but this responsibility for society in its present form also. It is the emancipation of the self-appointed "democrats" from real democracy.

In the long run it is a dangerous development because scholarship will decline and because some results of the new laws, especially the countless tenure appointments, cannot be changed. The development is dangerous also because scholarship will be given an ideological bias in the service of the pretended "objective interest of the people" and the well-known "society of the future." It is still growing among younger scholars and remains the order of the day for a lot of politicians; one law (in Hesse) even demands denunciation of the results of scholarship if they are found to be running counter to the alleged interest of society. Further, the development is dangerous because graduates from "reformed" universities are becoming influential in the professions. Within the educational class, the school system, and the mass media, their position has already become very strong; so the movement nourishes the movement. The menace to freedom in the schools and the replacement of liberal ideas by enforced ideological indoctrination in some school systems—as in Hesse, for example—is perhaps even more dangerous than its development in the universities.

6. In 1970 we founded the *Bund Freiheit der Wissenschaft* (Association for Freedom in Science) to defend academic freedom, oppose pseudoreforms, and promote implementation of a reasonable and necessary reform. The bund is a nonpartisan organization with members from all democratic political parties. I myself, now one of the three chairmen of the bund, am a member of the Social Democratic party like my predecessor, political scientist Richard Lowenthal. The bund comprises university teachers (about 35 percent of the membership), assistants, students, and concerned citizens from academic and nonacademic professions. We try to inform the public about the present "mess" and the dangerous tendencies in universities and schools, to lobby in the legislature, and to organize resistance within single universities where it is necessary, following the example of the Berlin *Notgemeinschaft*. The decisive question in Germany is unfortunately a question not of the universities, but of politics. The bund is not led by bad reactionaries, as some of our opponents tried to show, but by the liberal reformers of the sixties. We have succeeded in changing public opinion and, to a certain degree, even the opinion of some politicians. In some, unfortunately rare, cases, we have won the battle as, for instance, at Heidelberg. But we have not succeeded in realizing our final aim, namely to render our organization superfluous after academic freedom has been restored. We have to expect the struggle to last for many years.

The immediate future of higher education in West Germany seems very grim indeed. There is, however, a chance that in the long run the tide will be turning. Those recently graduated from high school seem to be getting fed up with radical rhetoric; and within the silent majority there is an increasing opposition to the disruption of lectures and "redirection" of courses. The recent forecasts about a possible surplus of university-trained people in the late seventies and a worsening of the job market situation in certain fields (especially the humanities and social sciences) may act as incentives for achievement, in the same way as the limited access (*numerus clausus*) has for medicine and several sciences. The general public seems tired of the unrest in the universities, of the extremely expensive reforms through democratization and ideological "university politics." In fact, several politicians who until recently were bent on democratization have realized that the first need is for curricular reform and that radicalism, ideology, and permanent conflict—which were the results of democratization—are not always in line with their intentions. The ruling of the Supreme Constitutional Court, mentioned before, has declared at least some of these extreme measures to be unconstitutional. And, although this ruling is bitterly opposed by all left-wingers even within the democratic spectrum, it has set up limits which legislation will not be allowed to ignore. So generally we see a certain countercurrent running against the leftist trend towards democratization. But the danger is in no sense over. We do not know whether this countercurrent will prevail.

The vested interest of politicians and political groups in the ideology and the facts of democratization are extraordinarily strong, especially in the *Länder* which have "reform" laws—Bremen, Hesse, and Lower Saxony. While a certain group of Social Democratic politicians have abandoned the extreme left-wing ideas of university reform, the Free Democrats (FDP), strongly influenced by the radical movement, are promoting a new radical pattern for universities. They try to outrun the SPD with a new left policy. However, the trend to compromise with the opposition against these reforms and to submit to the ruling of the constitutional court is limited to a group management model on the basis of a 51 percent majority for the professoriate. If this turns out to be true, many universities so far unaffected by democratization will move in that same direction I have tried to describe. The left-wingers are now concentrating their forces on curricular reform and on committees working on this—with the intention of embedding strong ideological bias in the new curricula. So the struggle in the legislation as well as in the departments is bound to go on—and academic work will still be seriously hampered. Faculty affairs (appointments and instruction) will remain political questions in many departments of the humanities and the social (and political) sciences, even in those universities which could be described as at least somewhat normal. Academic freedom is not at all safe in Germany today.

The American University—1964–1974:
From Activism to Austerity

Seymour Martin Lipset

BERKELEY IN SEPTEMBER 1964 was where and when it began, the wave of student-based activism which ultimately toppled university presidents from Berkeley and Stanford to Columbia and Harvard, and set political processes in motion which contributed to the downfall of two American presidents. From the United States the activist wave diffused to Europe where student radicals, impressed by the successes of their American comrades, took to the use of civil disobedience tactics, sitting-in in university buildings, striking, and demonstrating.

A decade later, the picture has changed considerably. Widespread campus-based civil disobedience is gone almost everywhere in the developed world. The United States, which led in the disturbances, once again leads in the "calm." Radical protest groups, while larger than in the 1950s, are once more reduced to the status of relatively ineffectual sects holding meetings on a variety of issues to small audiences. Politics generally seems to be of little interest to undergraduates. The Watergate events, which seemingly confirmed much of the radicals' analysis of the corrupt character of the American society and polity, served to deepen political cynicism but failed to arouse political involvements. Various traditional student activities which declined sharply in the 1960s have had a gradual but steady revival in the seventies. These include membership in fraternities, recruitment in ROTC (Reserve Officers Training Corps), sales of class jewelry, proms (dances), and the like. Perhaps the most significant change, commented on in a myriad of journalists' articles, has been the increased emphasis on studying and concern for grades. At school after school, faculty report that they have never seen a college generation as interested in getting high marks, a goal to which they are ready to sacrifice all other activities. Perhaps the most

This selection incorporates some of my previous writings on the American university and American society. The references documenting much of the materials presented here may be found in S. M. Lipset, *Rebellion in the University* (Boston: Little, Brown, 1972); E. C. Ladd, Jr., and S. M. Lipset, *Professors, Unions, and American Higher Education* (Berkeley: Carnegie Commission on Higher Education, 1973); S. M. Lipset, *Opportunity and Welfare in the First New Nation* (Washington, D.C.: American Enterprise Institute for Public Policy Research, 1974); and E. C. Ladd, Jr., and S. M. Lipset, *The Divided Academy* (New York: McGraw-Hill, 1975).

startling development of all, in light of the comments made but a few years ago about the emergence of new cooperative, participant, and egalitarian values among American youth, has been the widespread cheating by students, particularly those hoping to enter medical school after graduation. From Berkeley to Minnesota to Harvard, faculty have noted students not only cheating but engaged in deliberate efforts to undermine the competitive chances of fellow students by sabotaging their experimental equipment. Psychiatrists employed in university health services report an enormous increase in those seeking assistance from difficulties exacerbated by competitive anxieties.

Ironically, the charge levied against American academe by some of the undergraduate critics of the 1960s—that it forced them to read for grades and jobs rather than for intellectual sustenance—was much less true in that decade, when the protests were voiced, but it is characteristic of the mid-seventies and has occasioned few objections.

Faculty behavior is also quite different. The crises of the 1960s politicized many of the leading universities. Intramural controversies as to how to treat student militancy, particularly sit-ins and strikes, severely divided the professoriate. On many campuses across the country, formal faculty caucuses or "parties" were formed, seeking to control faculty meetings, elect members of faculty councils or executive committees, and generally to influence university policy. The more left or liberal caucuses generally sympathized with student activism and sought to restrain efforts at hard or punitive policies. They favored the passage of resolutions against the Vietnam war by the faculty. The more moderate or conservative factions saw in student activism a threat to the autonomy of the university, an effort to politicize the scholarly side of the institution. And they tended to oppose the passage of political statements by the faculty as a body. Generally speaking, the more left-oriented faculty drew support disproportionately among the younger teachers and the social scientists; the more conservative ones had their stronghold among the older science and professional school professors.

During the politicized period, faculty meetings were frequent and heavily attended. Generally speaking, the more activist-oriented faculty secured majority support immediately after an event (often a sit-in in the university buildings, which led the administration to call the police on to campus). This traumatic event, often involving physical conflict between police and demonstrators and mass arrests, motivated the less committed "middle" among faculty and students to initially turn against the administration, to support student strikes, and to vote against punishments for those involved in the sit-ins, actions which ultimately brought down presidents in many schools.

In response to faculty pressure, many universities made major concessions to the demands of the militant students. These included dropping many, if not almost all, the regulations affecting student conduct and activities, not only with respect to politics but also those dealing with social affairs and behavior in university-owned student residences. Some schools, such as Columbia, Cornell, and Rutgers, incorporated student representatives within the governance system. Black students secured many of their demands for Afro-American or black studies departments and for separate black-controlled residential units. Research programs financed by the Defense Department, as well as ROTC, were also weakened or dropped in a number of institutions.

These changes won the support of many faculty who sought to restore the university to a house of study by eliminating student grievances. Subsequent events did not sustain these hopes. The growing radical movements —whose basic concerns were to gain adherents and to use the permissive university as a protected bastion from which to attack the larger political structure—continued their protests, including attempts at civil disobedience. Continuation of political unrest gradually alienated many faculty initially sympathetic to the manifest aims of the protesters—for example, opposition to the Vietnam War, increased support for black demands, and the like. And, within a year or two following the initial dramatic polarizing crisis, the majority of the faculty at the various divided institutions usually accepted the views of the moderate faction and supported the restoration of faculty and administrative authority. The disputations, however, left a bitterly divided professoriate, a situation which affected collegial and social relations in many places.

By the early seventies, as student unrest declined almost as rapidly as it had emerged, professors also left the political arena. Faculty meetings, once held in packed auditoriums, often could not even secure a quorum for meetings called to discuss important academic issues. Administrators and committee chairmen found that they could gain swift assent for major changes since few wanted to get involved in disputations of any kind. The debates of the 1960s had been painful for many faculty, who much preferred a "house of study" to a "house of politics."

Why did the political era decline so rapidly? Clearly, there is no simple answer to this question. The fact that an activist cycle ended should not have come as much of a surprise to those few in academe who had any sense of their own history. American higher education has witnessed a series of waves of student political and campus protests, some of which had involved even larger proportions of the total (much smaller) student cohort. Protests against intramural defects in the early nineteenth century were perhaps even more violent than those of the late 1960s. In the twentieth century, the pre–World War I decade and the era of the Great Depression witnessed relatively high levels of radical student activism. The 1920s and the 1950s, on the other hand, produced a moderate to low level of campus protests. Writing in 1953 during the "quiet" of the McCarthy era, historian of academic affairs Ernest Earnest concluded that "unless history fails to repeat itself, there will be another revolt of youth."

During the 1960s student radicals bitterly resented and attacked efforts at scholarly analysis which pointed up the cyclical character of campus activism, a conclusion which implied that their wave would also ebb, that they were not living in an age of revolution. But in 1973 Bettina Aptheker, a leader of the Berkeley revolt in 1964–1965 and an acknowledged Communist, urged her fellow radicals to take heart from the fact that "all social movements go in waves. You cannot sustain a level of intensity for an indeterminate length of time. . . . If that analysis is right the movement will recur."

To analyze the sources of political cycles, on or off campus, would require moving beyond the scope of this discussion. It may be noted, however, that the historical evidence suggests waves of protest constitute responses to politically relevant events—wars, depressions, and so on—much more than to basic structural trends, such as those inherent in the increased size of the university or its involvement in diverse "multiuniversity" activities. The mass character of the American campus revolt of the 1960s occurred as a response to a political event, the Vietnam War, and the draft. When conscription and American military participation in the war ended, the "movement" quickly disintegrated. Generally speaking, as this development suggests, as events change, and particularly as the issue or situation giving rise to a particular activist wave is satisfied, the movement ebbs, the cycle shifts. Periods of intense politicization rarely last more than a few years. Conflict situations are painful and people move away from them if at all possible.

Political cycles take on a special pattern in universities since the student population turns over almost completely within half a decade. The freshman class of 1969–1970, which witnessed the final major events of the ebbing antiwar activity, the Cambodian protest, and the killings at Kent State and Jackson State, graduated in June 1973. The seniors returning to campus in the mid-decade year 1975–1976 entered college in 1972—after the militance was totally over. For them, Vietnam and the movement are part of history. They respond to a different political era and, even more important, to a period of economic uncertainty in a depressed labor market. This latter consideration has seemingly pressed students entering in the 1970s to study hard and compete strenuously with each other for the good grades which will help determine their personal economic futures.

The protest wave of the 1960s may have ended, but clearly it has had some enduring effects on society and the university. On the cultural and ideological level, it intensified the commitment to greater permissiveness or freedom in personal behavior—particularly with respect to sexual activity and the power of adults to control youth, and also with respect to the strength of equalitarianism, especially the claim for "equality of results" by ethnic and racial minorities and women.

These changes in the norms have had a particular effect on higher education. Universities, for the most part, have yielded their claims to restrict undergraduates. Coeducational dormitories have become common. Health services distribute contraceptives. Course requirements, such as foreign languages or mathematics, have been dropped at many schools; sometimes this has resulted in the closing down of some language departments. Although for the most part the grading of students continues, the average mark given to students has increased sharply.

The equalitarian tendencies which have given birth to the demands by deprived and excluded groups that they be accorded rights as a *group* have had extraordinary consequences for general conceptions of equal rights in America, and for the traditional values of academe. Historically, minority groups which had suffered discrimination, institutionalized prejudice, or handicap with respect to education or jobs have demanded the elimination of barriers denying *individuals* access to opportunity. Jews, Orientals, and Italians objected in previous decades to the *numerus clausus* (quotas) established by institutions of higher learning against qualified members of their groups.

Liberal and socialist intellectual opinion has always assumed that the egalitarian creed meant advocacy of universalism or meritocracy, enabling all to secure positions for which they qualified in open, fair competition. Felix Frankfurter, who came to Harvard Law School from the City College of New York (CCNY) as an immigrant Jewish youth before World War I, never lost his awe of the meritocratic system. "What mattered was excellence in your profession to which your father or your race was equally irrelevant. And so rich man, poor man, were just irrelevant titles to the equation of human relations. The thing that mattered was what you did professionally." Randolph Bourne (Columbia graduate and the most creative and celebrated of the young socialist intellectuals of the pre–World War I period) also argued in similar terms: "Scholarship is fundamentally democratic. Before the bar of marks and grades, penniless adventurer and rich man's son stand equal."

Scholarship emphasizes the need to apply pure meritocratic and universalist criteria (treatment of all according to impersonal standards) in evaluating those who would take part in its world. For scholarship, intellectual abilities, and achievements—not family, race, wealth, or other aspects of social background—must be the primary quality associated with any award within its scope. Committed to advancing the frontiers of knowledge, the scholar ideally seeks only the best available.

This standard for university life has been rejected in recent years by those who argue that it is necessary to speed up the process of gaining equality for underprivileged minorities and women by applying the principle of equality of results, requiring institutions to establish quotas for admission and for hiring which would bring the numbers of such groups up to their proportion in the population. Compliance with these demands, which have increasingly become government policy since the 1960s, means denial of access to some with great qualifications for study or creative scholarship. It involves accepting a version of the principle of *ascription*, or hereditary placement, as a method of advancing opportunity.

Not surprisingly, specific issues stemming from the emphasis on ascription as distinct from achievement has sharply divided academe. Giving preference to some means denying position to others. And, in a declining labor market, filling black or female quotas reduces the chances of white males. Admitting less qualified students at given levels of higher education affects the level and nature of teaching. Introducing standards other than the meritocratic as criteria for choosing faculty may reduce the general emphasis on scholarship.

The more intellectually oriented, research-involved scholars, though generally more liberal than others, are highly committed to the competitive emphasis on originality and creativity. They seek for themselves and their students the rewards for being the best scholars, in much the same framework as an athletic contest is conducted. To deny access to the best qualified, to the brightest, is for them comparable to dropping a player from a championship sports competition because of some social characteristic. Hence, though often quite liberal on other social issues, they seek to retain the principle of meritocracy in their university, department, or research team.

Few in academe openly resist the policy of judging the commitment of universities to equality for minorities and women in terms of willingness to use quotas. In fact, however, many white males and some members of minority groups are troubled. Their resistance often appears in discussions over specific candidates for admission, hiring, or promotions. And, as a form of covert but real politics, the issues stemming from efforts at affirmative action for minorities will continue for many years to come.

Black economist Thomas Sowell has pointed up the demoralizing consequences of emphasis on quotas for students and faculty. He suggests that the effort of universities to fill such quotas has meant that large numbers of black students are enrolled in schools for which they are ill prepared. Thus when the most scholarly, prestigious, and selective universities admit black students who are less prepared than whites, they set up a situation in which blacks can only feel inadequate. He describes the problem caused by the admission policies of the elite white institutions this way:

> When black students who would normally qualify for a state college are drained away by Ivy League colleges and universities, then state colleges have little choice but to recruit black students who would normally qualify for still lower level institutions—and so the process continues down the line. The net result is that, in a country with 3,000 widely differing colleges and universities capable of accommodating every conceivable level of educational preparation and intellectual development, there is a widespread problem of

"underprepared" black students at many institutional levels, even though black students' capabilities span the whole range by any standard used. The problem is not one of absolute ability level, but rather of widespread mismatching of individuals with institutions. The problem is seldom seen for what it is, for it has not been approached in terms of the optimum distribution of black students in the light of their preparation and interests, but rather in terms of how Harvard, Berkeley, or Antioch can do its part, maintain its leadership, or fill its quota. The schools which have most rapidly increased their enrollments of black students are those where the great majority of white American students could not qualify. However, since such schools typically do not admit underqualified white students, they have no "white problem" corresponding to the problem posed for them by underqualified black students. This problem must also be seen in perspective: the College Board scores and other academic indicators for black students in prestige colleges and universities are typically above the national average for white Americans. Special tutoring, reduced course loads, and other special accommodations and expedients for minority students are necessitated by programs geared to a student body which is not only above the national average but in the top 1 or 2 percent of all American students. The problem created by black students who do not meet the usual institutional standards may be grim or even desperate for both the students and the institution. Yet it does not arise because students are incapable of absorbing a college education. They may be incapable of absorbing an M.I.T. education, but so is virtually everyone else. . . .

[B]lacks at all levels of ability are systematically mismatched upward, so that good students go where outstanding students should be going and outstanding students go where only a handful of peak performers can survive. The net effect of this "pervasive shifting effect" is to place students where they do not learn as much as they would in schools geared to students of their own educational preparation.

According to Sowell, a comparable problem has been created by the efforts of universities to fill faculty quotas. As is obvious from the statistics, the past record of inferior education for blacks means that black America

has included very few persons trained to be academic scholars. . . . In short, there are relatively few black scholars in existence, and the number cannot be greatly increased in the immediate future. And it is in this context that faculty quotas must be considered. Any "goal," "target," or "affirmative action" designed to make the percentage of blacks on faculties approximate that in the general population can only mean reducing quality standards.

And this creates a situation in which black faculty are identified with "substandard" teachers, a phenomenon which can only create demoralizing stereotypes among both black and white students.

Faculty find it hard to resist the antimeritocratic tendencies in the seventies because the equalitarian valves strengthened by the events of the past decade are stronger among them than in any other stratum. As a more or less permanent estate of the university, they are much less likely than students to exhibit drastic changes in views and behavior. Although they too respond to shifts in the overall mood and to varying salient events and issues, the large majority of them carry the experiences and commitments which form their underlying values with them into new eras. Since academe has entered a "no growth" period in the 1970s with a relatively young senior faculty, the turnover rate for the next two decades will be very low. Earlier moods, waves, and experiences should continue to inform academic orientations for a long time to come.

The steadier character of faculty political predispositions was demonstrated during previous cycles. Thus, during the quiet and more conservative fifties, surveys of academic opinion indicated that faculty remained consistently to the left of the electorate generally, and of most subgroups in the population. In 1948 and 1952, left third parties found considerably greater strength among professors than among other strata. The same cannot be said for undergraduates of that period who were much more likely than their teachers to have preferred Tom Dewey and Dwight Eisenhower.

Faculty were also more disposed to take part in campus protests against violations of academic freedom than were students. Thus the celebrated fight against the imposition of an anti-Communist loyalty oath at the University of California in 1949–1950 was almost entirely a faculty affair. Student groups did little to support the faculty in its opposition. A study of social science reaction to McCarthyism conducted by Paul Lazarsfeld and Wagner Thielens, Jr., in the mid-fifties concluded that supporters of McCarthy stood in more risk of being sanctioned (ostracized) by their colleagues than did Communists. Liberal faculty were critical about the mood of students. Thus in May 1953 Arthur Schlesinger, Jr., then a history professor at Harvard, wrote to the Harvard *Crimson* complaining about student groups canceling an appearance by author Howard Fast, and a movie starring Paul Robeson. Schlesinger stated: "I gather that in these cases the students acted on their own, without orders or even hints from the Faculty. It is a stirring commentary on the courage of this new generation that the faculties and governing boards of the university should be more in favor of free speech than the students." In 1972, when the country swung to the right, faculty gave a slightly higher majority to McGovern than did college students. The shift of the latter from undergraduate preferences four years earlier was more in tandem with the mood of the electorate than was that of the professors.

The sense of alienation from the dominant establishment culture, identified with business and materialist values (and strongly felt in academe) should be reinforced during the late seventies and possibly the eighties by two factors: the financial squeeze mentioned previously and the disproportionate weight which the very large number entering faculty ranks in the

1960s will continue to hold in a period of no expansion. The decline in financial support during a period of rapid inflation—which implies reductions in real income, the laying off of some tenured faculty, and increasing difficulty in securing tenure—has led many academics to support collective bargaining and to vote for faculty unions.

Unionism has emerged as a potent force in higher education. As of Fall 1974, close to 100,000 faculty at approximately 350 campuses were represented by bargaining agents. Even more impressive than the sheer numbers is the placing of collective bargaining prominently on the political agenda of academe. A decade ago professorial unionism was hardly even considered; but today, in all but a small sector of higher education, the possibilities of unionization are actively considered.

From the broadest perspective, the rapid growth of collective bargaining in higher education during the past half decade should be seen as the extension, to the level of university governance and faculty life, of the powerful trends toward equalization and away from elitism that has characterized many sectors of American society since the mid-sixties. As recently as 1968, Christopher Jencks and David Riesman stressed the extent to which the postwar decades had witnessed throughout the entire system of higher education the triumph of meritocracy and of the values of the creative research culture fostered by the leading faculty of the major institutions.

They called attention to a "redistribution of power" within the universities that had given the faculty control over courses, curriculum, standards for admitting students, and, most importantly, complete power with respect to selecting and rewarding colleagues. As they noted, at the better schools faculty were appointed "almost entirely on the basis of their 'output' and professional reputation. . . . The claims of localism, sectarianism, ethnic prejudice and preference, class background, age, sex . . . are largely ignored." These emphases and values, first largely centered in the major graduate institutions, permeated out to the lesser ones. As a result, there was "a rapid decline in teaching loads for productive scholars, an increase in the ratio of graduate to undergraduate students at the institutions where scholars are concentrated, the gradual elimination of unscholarly undergraduates from these institutions, and the partial elimination of unscholarly faculty." Administrators came to "see their institution primarily as an assemblage of scholars and scientists, each doing his work in his own way. Most university presidents see their primary responsibility as 'making the world safe for academicians.' "

Today it is obvious that the scene has changed considerably. The egalitarian pressures of the late 1960s have broken the hold of meritocratic values. Universities have altered their admission policies to give special preference to students from "culturally deprived" backgrounds, defined in ethnic, racial, sex, and class terms. As we have seen, under pressure from the federal government, and reinforced by the belief of many faculty in liberal-left egalitarian values, affirmative action programs—often including informal but real quotas for people belonging to deprived groups—have been accepted by many leading institutions in their faculty appointment policies. Moreover, the rapid spread of unionization has served to reduce meritocracy even further as a basis for differentiation within the professoriate itself. Organizations of academics successfully oppose merit increases and seek to reduce the ability of universities to emphasize competitive judgments about scholarly excellence as a basis for granting or refusing tenure. Such policies, of course, represent the "interests" of the less privileged and less prestigious components of the professoriate who not only form the base of the electorate which votes for collective bargaining, but also are much more disposed to become dues-paying and active members of organizations which serve as legal bargaining agents for the entire faculty and professional staff.

It may be argued that faculty unionization represents an effort by the mass of academe to overthrow the domination of a relatively small group of distinguished scholars. Writing in 1968, Jencks and Riesman noted that "in the course of trying to strengthen their faculty, administrators of upwardly mobile institutions also usually offend many of the 'weak' faculty currently on the payroll." They did not anticipate, however, that the offended faculty would so soon be in a position to strike back. A combination of factors—the change in the larger sociopolitical atmosphere from the stress in the 1950s on achievement and meritocracy to egalitarianism and particularism in the 1960s, together with the drastic shift in the economic circumstances governing budgets for both salaries and research—have given the less privileged and the younger academics the opportunity to challenge the main direction of much of higher education.

Yet the reversal of emphasis was inherent in the earlier commitment of the society to widen access to higher education for the majority of youth, to make the academy a "mass institution." Since World War II the great growth has been (1) in the public as compared to the private sector, and (2) in the "lower-tier" teaching institutions compared to those that are concerned with basic research and the training of scholars. In the proto-typical state of California, there are now 96 community colleges with 900,000 students and 13,000 faculty; 19 campuses of the state university and colleges system with close to 300,000 students and over 11,000 faculty; and 9 units of the University of California, which have over 100,000 students and 6,000 faculty. The community colleges and the state university and state colleges are explicitly defined as "teaching" institutions; the latter system does not offer work beyond the master's degree. Standards for both student and faculty selection appropriate to graduate and research-oriented universities clearly do not apply to the larger teaching systems. But many of the policies implicit in unionization *do apply* to the latter. For them, the need is to institutionalize their relations with public authorities, to bargain collectively; for, unlike the "scholars," they have little individual bargaining power.

"Class" or vocational interests in the late seventies may enhance the traditional "adversary culture" associated with higher education. One may even identify in this process a countercyclical trend in the academic community whereby the more conservatively inclined "teacher" segment at less research-involved schools takes on socially critical views in harmony with their support for militant unionism. The (initially) more liberal views of younger faculty, reflecting the dominant orientations of the 1960s when they entered the profession, may be reinforced rather than moderated as they suffer frustrations imposed by a declining labor market and scarce financial resources.

The growth in "vocational consciousness" and consequent union organization among faculty appears, however, to have quite different effects among undergraduates. Many students, including more militant groups such as the National Student Association, have identified faculty unionism as a threat to the gains in "student power" secured in the 1960s, or to the interests of students with respect to issues such as tuition and teaching quality.

The assumption that unionization may stimulate student conflict with faculty is not simply a hypothetical prognostication. As George Bonham notes: "Already, some student organizations are questioning the merits of faculty tenure, while others are looking askance at teaching efficiency, both in terms of classroom effectiveness and in terms of hours worked and classes taught." Student leaders at the first major university to be unionized, the City University of New York, have openly expressed their opposition at times to the high-pay package given to a "mediocre" faculty, which aroused the natural ire of union leaders.

At the State University of New York (SUNY), a comparable clash developed. Student representatives from the different SUNY campuses who met in Albany on February 6–7, 1972, to discuss the projected master plan for the university seemingly saw little good in the emergence of collective bargaining. A detailed report of that conference summarized their conclusions:

> The formation of faculty and staff unions to further the self-interest of their members will inevitably clash with student interests. . . . The potential impact of these unions on university governance is particularly frightening. Negotiations between the University and the union on the terms and conditions of employment can and will cover every aspect of operation of the University. With students playing no role in these negotiations, the resulting contracts could nullify every gain which students have made in terms of increased participation in university governance. . . . Unfortunately, faculty and staff unions are a reality in American higher education. Now all possible steps must be taken to ensure that unionization does not lock students out of

university governance. . . . It is unacceptable for students as consumers and participants in the learning process to be locked out of decision making.

Some professors view the growth of faculty unionism favorably for the same reasons that student leaders fear it, seeing in it a way for the professoriate to regain power given up to students during the activism of the late 1960s. Writing from experiences at SUNY, William McHugh suggests that "unionism may well appeal to . . . traditional elements of a faculty as a reaffirmation of the faculty guild concept in face of student pressures. Faculty unionism may result in a collision course with the newly emerging tripartite governance patterns. . . ." A report by a Michigan State professor, Robert Repas, on the 1972 bargaining election there maintains that many MSU faculty "supported collective bargaining because they looked upon it as a device to keep students out of the decision making process." During the campaign, an article in the campus newspaper made the same point from the student side, arguing that "unionization could jeopardize student gains in academic governance [since], the faculty generally would not be swayed by any concern for student input. . . ."

The shift in power—or at least in representation—that excludes students may be seen in the experience at Rutgers University organized by the American Association of University Professors (AAUP). A Rutgers professor, Richard McCormick, notes that it was anticipated that collective bargaining "would develop as a new base for faculty power . . . because the university senate included representatives of faculty, students, and administration, and the AAUP could claim to be the whole university wide faculty body." A delegate assembly, with members elected by faculty from departments and campuses, was set up by the Rutgers AAUP. The assembly "moved to strengthen its function as the only university-wide body that exclusively represents and expresses faculty opinion," by passing a resolution "to petition for a University Assembly called for the purpose of disbanding the University Senate and recognizing the Delegate Assembly as the Faculty Senate."

The conflict between the interests of professors and students made evident with the growth of faculty unionism has served to modify the image presented during the 1960s by campus activists that students were the exploited "underclass" of the university, the equivalent of the workers in the factory. In fact, students are the "consumers," the buyers, the patrons of a product sold by the faculty through a middleman, the university system. In economic class terms, the relationship of student to teacher is that of buyer to seller, or of client to professional. In this context, the buyer or client seeks to get the most for his money at the lowest possible price. He prefers that an increased share of the payment to the institution should go for more direct benefits to him—teaching, student activities, better housing, and so forth. The faculty seller of services, on the other hand, is obviously interested in maximizing his income and working conditions. Lower teaching loads and greater research facilities are to his benefit. Tenure not only reduces the power of administrators over faculty, it protects teachers from consumer (student) power as well.

The conception of students as consumers is not simply an analytic one. It has been explicitly argued in these terms by student leaders at CUNY and SUNY. Conversely, the CUNY union, in objecting to the students' demand to participate in negotiations, has editorialized, saying: "Management and labor do not invite consumers to the bargaining table, though consumers, of course, have rights and recourse elsewhere in the business sector."

Efforts, much more successful in Europe than in America, to give students a major role in university governance serve to weaken faculty power. Student power reduces the faculty's freedom to choose their colleagues, to determine the curriculum, to select research topics, and to control their work schedules. It does not, however, affect the power of those who control the purse strings to determine how much shall be spent on higher education, and the ways it will be distributed among alternative sectors. Hence, even conservative politicians have been willing to support systems of student-faculty governance in a number of European countries.

Student groups, of course, may ally with faculty factions for common extramural sociopolitical objectives. Given a similar political position—on racism or the Vietnam War, for example—they can work together against common opponents. Students may join with junior nontenured faculty, close to students in age and style, in opposition to senior professors. Such alliances, too, often reflect similar ideological leanings in both strata. But where the issues are purely of the marketplace, where they revolve around the faculty's desire to maximize income and reduce the direct service (teaching) that they give to buyers (students), a conflict of interests exists that cannot be easily bridged. There may, in fact, often be a congruence of interests between student buyers and the middlemen public authorities and administrators. The latter may also be more interested in optimizing the services rendered to the students than in the conditions of the faculty. Students, their parents, and alumni form a much larger voting bloc than do professors. Thus, in spite of the "antiestablishment" sympathies of most politically active students, tacit alliances between administrators and students against faculty may emerge.

In the long run, it is likely that those who view faculty unionism as a way of enhancing faculty authority and reducing student power are right. Faculty unions, employing experienced permanent professional negotiators, public relations staff, and so on, and allied with the labor movement, are at a considerable advantage in contests with student groups, which are dependent on a rotating leadership drawn from a highly transitory student population. The unions, once institutionalized, press on from year to year for "more." Student groups rise and fall, have little memory, and in the long run will be unable to best the faculty in any adversary relationship.

The extension of trade union policies (successfully applied in elementary and high schools) to academe clearly will require some drastic modifications of practice, particularly in the major more research-oriented sector. The more scholarly productive faculty, though much more liberal than other academics on societal questions and hence ideologically more receptive to the norms of unionism in general, tend to be opposed to intramural changes that will reduce the emphasis on research, meritocracy, and the ability of the academically successful to determine who will gain permanent status (tenure) in their institutions. Many of them see the competitive aspects of the system—the high regard given to presumed intellectual achievement as reflected in national and international peer judgments—as desirable ways of motivating the successful to continue to innovate and the able young to work hard to prove themselves. Further, as Riesman notes, "a college faculty needs to combine the individualism one associates with artists and free-floating intellectuals with the cooperative-competitive collegiality, not of a submarine crew, but of a research group, a private medical clinic, or the partners in an elite law firm."

Even these concerns may dwindle, however, in the face of the financial crunch that reaches all across academe. Faced with declining monetary support, faculty even in elite schools may decide that unions are necessary.

As academe moves from an age of activism to one of austerity, it remains a troubled institution. The "golden age" in every sense of the term—which followed the end of World War II and lasted through 1964—will not revive soon, if ever. Unionization portends a much more bureaucratic system, characterized by a more rigorous emphasis on rules and regulations and due process, and on adversary relations among the estates of the university. The end of growth implies a gerontocratically controlled institution, one in which innovative emphases stemming from small cohorts of young professors will be minimal. There is need for imaginative leadership, but administrators faced with the need to curtail existing activities to balance budgets are increasingly conservative and defensive. The austerity age breed of presidents have little to propose. The times call for imagination from the institution supported by society to supply it with new ideas and imaginative analysis. Whether academe can turn from reacting to externally imposed crises to new ways of stimulating intellect remains for the future. The portents, however, are not good.

Problems of Academic Freedom in Canada

Charles Hanly

ACADEMIC FREEDOM may be considered from two points of view: that of the individual professor carrying out his scientific and scholarly work of research, teaching, and publication and that of the university as an academic institution. These two aspects of academic freedom are somewhat independent. The university as an institution may be subject to financial constraints which prohibit it from undertaking academic work that ideally it should be engaged in without there being any inappropriate constraints on the exercise of academic freedom by individual professors. But the imposition of fiscal restraints—either by the university itself but more especially by government —may use considerations of economy in order to control what is taught. In this circumstance, individual academic freedom becomes linked to institutional academic freedom. This review of problems of academic freedom in Canada employs both perspectives.

The issues are complex. They can easily be oversimplified by the facile identification of one group or another as the principal threat to academic freedom. It is easy for professors to point the finger of blame at groups of student radicals, university administration, government bureaucrats, or politicians while overlooking their own indifference and complacency or their wish to impose their own ideological or scholarly investments on their students and colleagues. This survey of issues and problems focuses attention on relations between governments and universities, on student activism, and on faculty unionization as the three currently most important areas of concern about academic freedom in Canada.

Universities and Government

In Canada education is a provincial responsibility. The universities (with the exception of the Queen's University which has a federal charter) are chartered by provincial governments. Although the federal government contributes half of public financing, these funds are transferred to the provincial governments which then completely control the manner of their expenditure. This procedure was designed primarily to safeguard the rights of French-speaking Canadians who live for the most part in the province of Quebec.

157

Unlike the United States and Great Britain, Canada has no private universities; nor do any universities enjoy significant private endowment. Furthermore, financing universities has undergone a major change in the last decade. Prior to the 1960s universities were financed from three independent sources: federal grants (then paid directly to the universities), student fees, and ad hoc provincial support. This arrangement gave the universities a very large measure of fiscal autonomy. However, the constitutional problem referred to above caused the federal government to abandon its policy of direct grants in favor of payments to provincial governments (one half of provincial expenditure on higher education with adjustments for interprovincial equalization). During the same period student fees remained relatively unchanged. As a result provincial government funding increased sharply to cover the costs of a very rapid increase in the number of students, number of institutions, and inflation. As a result, at the present time, student fees represent about 15 percent of university revenue and public financing controlled by provincial governments makes up 85 percent. Universities have quite recently become financially dependent on provincial governments and consequently are exposed to provincial control and interference as never before.

This erosion of financial independence can be better appreciated when it is understood that most provincial governments have adopted systems of formula financing. These formula systems provide grants which are tied to the numbers of students registered and weighted according to categories (arts and sciences, professional, graduate, etc.). They also tie student fees to public grants. Consequently, universities are unable to finance new academic programs by revenue generated by fee increases because these increases would be offset by reductions in public grants. Hence, universities are now completely dependent on their provincial governments.[1] And this situation, in practice, is the same for those provinces which have not yet adopted a formula system of financing.

Nevertheless, the systems which have formalized this dependency also contain some important safeguards for university fiscal autonomy. Grants are paid to the universities without being linked to specific programs and universities are free to expend funds thus received according to their own academic priorities. In this respect universities are, in fact, subject to no greater fiscal constraint in their academic planning than they would be if they relied to a greater extent than they now do on cost related student fees.

Second, most provinces have established bodies which act as buffers between the universities and the government ministries responsible for university affairs. These bodies are appointed by government, but they usually contain university as well as public representatives. (Recent British

---

[1] A more detailed exposition and analysis of this type of grant system is found in C. M. T. Hanly, *Who Pays? University Financing in Ontario* (Toronto: 1970).

Columbia legislation which allows for university administrative representation but excludes faculty and students on its provincial buffering body is an exception to the general pattern in Canada.) Their basic task is to interpret and advocate university needs to government and to insure an equitable and academically sound distribution of the global amounts made available by governments for university financing.[2]

Third, as a consequence of the grants system and the work of the buffering bodies, neither government ministries nor legislatures become involved in a line-by-line scrutiny of university budgets. Hence, university academic policies including the setting of academic priorities and the appointment of faculty (what is taught, what is researched, and who undertakes teaching and research) are not subject to direct or indirect government control or influence. Consequently, although Canadian universities are public institutions, they enjoy a considerable measure of the fiscal autonomy as well as the administrative and academic autonomy of private institutions. For the most part, the financial and institutional mechanisms currently at work in the provinces provide a reasonably secure defense for the exercise of institutional academic freedom.

The basic qualities of the relationship between universities and provincial governments are determined by implicit tradition-sanctioned habits of conduct on the part of governments. In the final analysis no better safeguard is available. The question is to what extent new pressures and events may erode the traditional respect provincial governments have shown for university academic autonomy. Are there any storm warnings on the horizon in Canada? The shift to complete financial dependency of the universities on provincial governments described above constitutes a general condition that has potential for danger.

Recently (1973), the Alberta government abolished the buffering body between its ministry of education and the universities of the province in favor of direct dealings with the universities. However, within the last year British Columbia, as noted above, has created such a body and Ontario has decided to create a similar body under statute to replace a former body which had been functioning under orders-in-council (act of the cabinet). Consequently, Alberta is the only province which does not recognize that a buffer is an important institutional corollary of the traditional autonomy vouchsafed by governments to universities.[3] (Prince Edward Island and Newfoundland do not have this institutional safeguard either, but both

---

[2] A general discussion of issues involved in relations between universities and society is to be found in André Côté, "University Administration and Nationalism in Canadian Universities," in *Nationalism and the University* (Toronto: 1973), and in R. Hurtubise and D. C. Rowat, *The University, Society, and Government* (Ottawa: 1970).

[3] *University Affairs*, October 1974, pp. 7–8, and the *Bulletin* of the Canadian Association of University Teachers, XXIII, no. 1, 1974, pp. 102, 104, offer discussions of buffering bodies in British Columbia, Saskatchewan, and Nova Scotia.

provinces have only one university so that the boards of the universities concerned, in effect, do act as buffers.)

Of greater concern is a recent incident at the University of Quebec Montreal campus. The university had approved a program in law aimed at equipping students to provide low-cost legal services for working-class communities. It was claimed in the press that the professors involved were selecting students for the program on ideological grounds. The minister of education made a statement in the Provincial Assembly criticizing the program. Government and professional pressure was brought to bear on the university. As a result the university administration decided to suspend the program and then to reconstitute it under the direction of a committee dominated by nonacademics. An investigating committee established by the *Fédération des Associations des Professeurs de Québec* found that the allegations of ideological bias in the selection of students were unfounded and has accused the university administration of failing to protect a program and its teachers, which had been fully approved by all the appropriate academic bodies within and without the university. It has called for the reinstitution of the original program, including academic control over it by the committee of professors who originally held that responsibility.[4]

This episode is disquieting for a number of reasons. Quebec has a buffering institution, *Le Conseil des Universités*, but here it proved ineffective. The fact that the conseil had approved funding for the program did not serve as a deterrent to those who wished to suspend it. Quebec also has a formula grants system. It provided no protection. These defenses are no defenses at all when the senior administrative and academic officers of the university are willing to submit to inappropriate governmental, professional, or other societal pressures.

Thus the financial dependency of the universities on provincial governments is not in itself so directly dangerous to academic freedom as the indirect consequence of its corrosive effects on administrative and academic officials who may come to identify themselves (and to function) as middle managers in a government-operated educational system rather than as leaders of academic communities. Such a development could seriously erode the capacity of universities to discharge their educational responsibilities in ways that will not only sustain society but also improve it.

To place this episode in perspective, it must be pointed out that it is unique in recent Canadian university experience. At the same time, there can be no question that it is a danger signal to universities which must be taken seriously. However, the loss of university fiscal autonomy which does bring with it a diminution of administrative independence need not result in a loss of academic autonomy so long as the universities themselves, and

[4] *Fédération des Associations des Professeurs de l'Université de Québec Rapport no. 59*, October 1973.

especially their professors, clearly understand the nature and purposes of the universities and fully appreciate that these rest upon the responsible exercise of academic autonomy which they are willing to join ranks to defend. The institutional instruments by which academic autonomy can be defended exist in university senates, most of which are faculty dominated, and in the voluntary professional associations of professors at local, provincial, and national levels. In the final analysis, if academic autonomy is lost in our universities as a result of the corrosive effects of fiscal dependency, it will be partly because, out of lack of foresight or indifference, professors have failed to use these instruments effectively.

There is one further aspect of the relation of the university to governments that merits consideration. For several years governments have been forced into positions of retrenchment because of escalating public debts and increased rates of inflation. At the same time public programs in health, welfare, the environment, transportation, and urban problems have made increasing demands on public resources. The sixties were a period of major university expansion; the seventies have become a period of curtailment. University planning decisions were made in the last decade which cannot be realized in the present decade. In particular, and with few exceptions, every university including new ones began establishing graduate programs in a wide range of disciplines, some of which have experienced difficulty in achieving academic viability. Many have encountered problems in achieving fiscal viability because of the rapid decline in new university teaching and research positions and in the demand for Ph.D.s in the public and private sector.

In Ontario (1971) the provincial government imposed an embargo on funding new graduate programs in any discipline until a province-wide assessment of the academic feasibility of graduate programs, discipline by discipline, has been carried out. To the credit of the government and the universities, it has been agreed that these assessments should be worked on by the universities acting collectively rather than by any government agency. This program, which is being executed by the Council of Ontario Universities, has worked reasonably well, but there remains the danger that the universities will not be effectively able to plan and discipline their own academic development in graduate studies and that the government—which has the means for doing so, through the financial arrangements described above—will intervene directly by selectively withdrawing support from graduate programs on the basis of its own views of social need. Such a step could sharply curtail the capacity of the universities either individually or collectively to plan their own academic development. It could seriously diminish institutional academic autonomy. Also it would leave the door wide open for the intrusion of political and ideological influences into the process of academic planning, especially in times of social crisis. There is no real and present danger of this happening. But the nature of the relation between governments and universities must be evaluated not only in terms of their current functioning during a period of social stability but also in terms of how they might operate in periods of social instability.

It is not hard to see why universities have difficulty in carrying out collective discipline planning. The universities are individually autonomous institutions and the basis of cooperation among them is voluntary, there being no provincial university systems—as there are state systems in some U.S. states, or in some European countries—with the one possible exception of the Université de Québec which has several campuses. Therefore, there is no interuniversity institution apart from the government, or an agency it may establish, to sanction collective agreements about discipline development. Thus the universities must exercise voluntary self-discipline sanctioned only by the threat that, if they are not successful in doing so, they may become subject to direct government regulation.

This exercise of voluntary self-discipline is not easy because real problems for discipline groups within the universities are caused by the assessments. For example, it has been decided by the Council of Ontario Universities on the basis of an assessment that university X, which has a full undergraduate program in chemistry, will be allowed to offer a doctorate degree in only one limited area of the subject. As a result, funds will be provided only for a limited number of students in the approved program; the result will be that only a small number of chemistry professors at university X will be able to teach graduate students. Because research productivity is so dependent on graduate instruction in the natural sciences and in the professional schools, professors permitted to continue graduate instruction are substantially advantaged relative to others who are denied this opportunity. The problem is exacerbated by the fact that research productivity is an important criteria for success in research grant applications. As a result, groups of professors in scientific and professional disciplines in various universities can find themselves working under serious handicaps in their efforts to undertake research in their own fields of specialization. Unless solutions are found for these problems, there is danger that the quality of undergraduate instruction may suffer. In addition, professors, especially those of outstanding ability, may choose to leave the university when such conditions prevail. Fortunately, this difficulty does not occur to the same extent in the humanities and social sciences, in which research depends far less on the work of graduate students in laboratories. It is incumbent on individual universities and the discipline groups within them to work out solutions to these problems because the causative economic conditions are not likely to ameliorate in the foreseeable future. The risk attendant upon the failure of the universities and their disciplines to work out the adjustments voluntarily (in terms of their own scientific and educational objectives) is that governments will impose regulations according to their own lights. In such a circumstance nothing would be gained and the autonomy now enjoyed by the universities would be lost. In this respect, the task of protecting academic autonomy rests squarely on the shoulders of the universities themselves.

Student Activism

Universities in Canada, as elsewhere, have been made the objects and the instruments of the aggressive reforming zeal of youth during the last decade. Earlier generations of students sought to reform society but they exempted universities themselves from this process because students saw them as the best available means for realizing personal social goals and for equipping themselves with the knowledge and skills needed to tackle the social problems that concerned them. By responding to the accelerating demands for higher education, universities grew in number and size until they became themselves major social institutions. As a result, they were inevitably perceived as being themselves both unique foci of social problems and bridgeheads for social change.

Student demands for change have focused, accordingly, on the university as an academic community and as a social institution. Students have demanded equal access with faculty to university library research holdings; equal representation with faculty on appointment, promotion, and tenure committees, on academic divisional councils, university senates, and governing bodies. They have agitated for day care centers and for various improvements in the quality of their educational experience. There is insufficient space here to comment in detail on these issues, the tactics used by students to promote solutions to them, or the resolutions that were eventually worked out. Suffice it to state that the disruptions of classes, academic councils, or administrative offices that have occurred seldom reached such severity that ongoing academic or administrative work was seriously disrupted. Only on a very few occasions has it been found necessary to call upon the local police to remove student demonstrators and their supporters from university buildings to safeguard academic or administrative functions.

By far the worst incident during this period occurred at Sir George Williams University in Montreal (1969). Black students alleged that a professor in biology had been prejudiced in assigning grades to their work. When a faculty review of the professor's grading practices exonerated him, the students and their supporters occupied the computer facility of the university. After several days of occupation a fire started in the computer facility. Firemen and police moved in. The students and their supporters were forcibly removed. Though the building was saved, the heat of the fire totally destroyed the computer. The university took no disciplinary action,

but here civic authorities did bring charges in the courts against those involved. This kind of destructiveness had not occurred in Canada before nor
has it since. And the precipitating issue—allegations of racial bias in grading
—has not been a serious one in Canadian universities.

To be sure, some professors believe that academic standards have been
eroded. But this state of affairs (which is disputed) cannot be attributed to
the fear of incidents of the Sir George Williams variety. Rather, some faculty
do fear that they will become redundant and be dismissed for financial
reasons unless they can attract substantial numbers of students to their
classes. This fear has led academic departments which are subject to this
pressure to offer "relevant" courses and employ a less demanding standard
in evaluating students enrolled in them. This process is much more damaging to that component of academic freedom which consists of the autonomous exercise of responsibility for standards of work in scholarly or
scientific fields than any of the efforts students have made to curtail the
rights and responsibilities of professors to set academic standards. It is easy
for us to envisage ourselves as a beleaguered profession defending academic
standards from the subversive attacks of activist or radical students, and to
be sure such attacks must be resisted. But reality is seldom as simple as neat
value dichotomies allow. There is a more subtle subversion of standards
when faculty exploit student demands for facile relevance and an easy passage to a devalued degree in order to maintain the appearance of academic
"productivity" as measured merely by the numbers of students enrolled in
particular courses.

The Sir George Williams episode was not typical. More characteristic
are two examples from the recent history of the University of Toronto. The
General Committee of the Faculty of Arts and Science at the University of
Toronto was unable to transact business for one academic year (1971)
because of student disruptions; the chairman of the Department of Mathematics (1972) found it inconvenient to use his office and chose not to do
so for several weeks as a consequence of a sit-in protesting departmental
academic policies in the teaching of first year mathematics. By and large, the
approach of the universities to these situations has been to avoid direct
political confrontations with student demonstrators and, if at all possible, to
avoid physical force. Instead, an effort has been made to identify substantive problems and seek remedies to them through the normal processes of
academic planning and decision making at the appropriate departmental,
divisional, or university level. A major advantage of this approach has been
to resolve conflicts without altering or undermining established university
procedures or structures for academic decision making. In this way universities have been successful for the most part in avoiding the politicization of
these processes. And, insofar as universities have responded constructively to
legitimate student grievances, the outcomes have been beneficial. For example, the mathematics sit-in at the University of Toronto dramatized the

need for improvement in the teaching arrangements, especially for large introductory courses in the faculty. The demonstration catalyzed efforts that were already being made to remedy the problem and probably contributed to the early acceptance of a far-reaching plan to reorganize instruction in the faculty—one which should result in educational benefits not only for students in mathematics but also for students in a number of other disciplines which have large first-year enrollments.

In the incident of the mathematics demonstration, certain of the demonstrators' demands were not accepted. They insisted also on the reinstatement of three instructors of first-year courses whose employment had been discontinued by the department. The university has a procedure for considering appeals against dismissal. Those dismissed teachers who exercised their right of appeal had their cases reviewed in the usual way; and departmental decisions were upheld by the review committees.

Among the faculty there are those who would take a much harder line against student demonstrators than the one described here as being generally operative. However, most faculty at Canadian universities are convinced that students have the same right to orderly demonstrations on behalf of their grievances that society extends to any citizen group so long as these manifestations do not infringe upon the rights of others, do not damage university property, or interfere unduly with the ongoing work of the institution. What constitutes undue interference is a matter of judgment. This writer shares the opinion of many colleagues that, had the chairman of the mathematics department been physically constrained from using his office, such an action would have constituted undue interference. In the event, he chose, probably wisely, not to test the issue since departmental business could be successfully carried on elsewhere. It is unlikely that the student demonstrators would have barred his way physically had he gone to his office. If they had done so, no doubt charges would have been laid against them before the university's disciplinary body and if the charges were substantiated the students would have been penalized for their actions.

But universities are by no means perfect institutions. Problems affecting the quality of students' educational experience can develop and persist without remedy. For this reason, universities have been prudent in their willingness to accept orderly demonstrations aimed at seeking improvements where improvements are needed. The danger has been that universities would overreact to these manifestations either by trying to suppress them or by capitulating to them. Aristotle's concept of virtuous conduct as a mean that avoids polar extremes provides a useful guiding principle which, fortunately, the universities have for the most part been able to follow in responding to student protests.

These practical maxims have emerged: universities need to have a well established and widely accepted operative understanding of what does and what does not constitute an orderly demonstration; university authorities and student protesters must be prepared to work together to identify the nature of the grievances and steps that might be taken to remedy them; the problems thus defined must then be referred for study, recommendation, and action by the appropriate deliberative and executive bodies and offices within the university. In this way the worst outcomes can be avoided even if the best may not always be achieved. The worst would be either to have legitimate grievances go unremedied or to have the university adopt policies imposed by student demonstrators on the basis of threats—something that would destroy those normal processes of university government which are essential to the health of academic communities. It is fair to say that Canadian universities have been able, for the most part, to sustain these maxims in dealing with student protests during the past decade and that they have emerged more strengthened than weakened by the experience.

Credit for this happy state of affairs rests not only with university administrations and their governing bodies which, naturally enough, have not always acted wisely in situations of stress. Credit must be given also to student demonstrators who usually have acted with constraint, and with the student body as a whole which has occasionally refused to support those who would mobilize it to engage in extreme actions on behalf of dubious causes. An episode at the University of Toronto will serve as an illustration.

It was inevitable that the right to protest would itself become an issue. Moved by what, in retrospect, was an exaggerated fear of student unrest, the presidents of the universities in Ontario met (1969) and adopted a policy for dealing with student demonstrations which was perceived by student leaders to be repressive. The presidential disciplinary document itself became the motive for mass protests. The president of the University of Toronto agreed to attend a student-organized rally where he gave assurances that the document was a study paper the provisions of which would be examined for their relevance to the university by the appropriate bodies within the university. He explained the rationale for its recommendations and did not retract his support for it.

Radical student leaders insisted upon a retraction by the president and his concurrence with a set of proposals of their own which would have deprived the university of its ability to deal effectively with disorderly demonstrations. Confident of their success on the basis of the first meeting, radical student leaders insisted on another mass meeting to debate the issues with the president in the hope of being able to force from him capitulation and full acceptance of their demands. But this meeting was attended by an overwhelming majority of students who vigorously demonstrated their support for the president and rejected the demands of radical student leaders. This situation—probably the most severe crisis the university had faced—might well have been successfully resolved in any event. But the outcome was uncertain until the majority of students, in effect, disciplined their own elected leaders by demonstrating their confidence in the president and their opposition to the tactics and objectives of the radical student leaders. However, one should not idealize the significance of this event. Many of the students who came out against the radical leaders —probably a substantial majority on this occasion—were from the engineering faculty whose professors had canceled lectures so students could take their places early and dominate the auditorium. No doubt their motives were mixed and included feelings that had little to do with the issues at hand—including a traditional rivalry with students from the Faculty of Arts and Science (a group from which student leaders had garnered most of their following). Nevertheless, their action had a decisive influence because it represented the attitude of the majority of students on the campus, irrespective of the motives involved. The student leaders were unable to claim any longer that they represented predominant student opinion on the issue.[5]

Two problems persist currently: students want greater representation on university governing bodies and on departmental personnel committees which decide on professorial appointments, promotions, and the granting of tenure. The aim has been to achieve parity of student and faculty representation. Although some faculty support this as a principle of composition for all university deliberative bodies, the great majority firmly oppose it. Also it is necessary to differentiate between student membership on university policy-making bodies and on appointment, promotion, and tenure committees. Most faculty, while rejecting parity, support student membership on curriculum committees, departmental councils, faculty councils, senates, and so on. At the same time student membership on appointment, promotion, and tenure committees is generally opposed. Academic freedom is not only the enjoyment of a privilege, it is the exercise of a responsibility. This responsibility has three obvious components: responsibility to students and society for the best possible education; responsibility to and for the scientific, scholarly, and professional disciplines to insure their preservation and growth through learning and research; and responsibility for academic standards. Most faculty take the view that this responsibility can be shared in matters of curriculum planning, fixing academic priorities, and the like but that it must finally rest with faculty because of their experience in and lifelong commitments to their fields of expert knowledge. This view entails that faculty should occupy majority positions on bodies at every level dealing with these types of academic issues. Thus most universities have encouraged and provided for student participation on academic policy-making bodies. But most faculty are reluctant to share responsibility with students for setting academic standards or for appointments, promotion, and tenure of faculty and there has been general opposition to placing students on committees charged with such responsibilities. A reasonably accurate impression of the current situation, as far as student representation on

---

[5] C. T. Bissell, *Halfway Up Parnassus* (Toronto: 1974), pp. 144–147.

academic governing bodies is concerned, can be formed from the pattern of composition on university senates in Ontario. In no senate in the universities of Ontario does the number of student representatives exceed 25 percent of the sum of elected faculty and academic administrative representatives. It is significant that six of fourteen universities in the province, some of which have recently reviewed their charters, require either that 50 percent or a simple majority of their senates be elected faculty. The significance of the general pattern is evident. Senate compositions are premised on the assumption that effective academic policy making depends on a substantial and usually predominant faculty contribution, with a significant but by no means equal student contribution.

The pattern for committees dealing with academic standards and appointments and tenure committees is more complex. Insofar as academic standards committees are committees of senates, these will usually have student representation on them. But, although they may develop policies concerning examinations and so on, the responsibility for assigning grades, and often the responsibility for determining the basis for the grades, will rest with the individual instructor. And the review of grades will be carried out by committees at the departmental and faculty level with only faculty representation. Similarly, although some departments have personnel committees which include student representatives, these committees are usually advisory to the chairman of the department. In the final analysis, the departmental chairman must decide whether or not to accept the recommendations of the departmental personnel committee whatever its composition. In addition, he will have to secure the support of the dean of his faculty, and of the academic vice- president and/or the president, as well as the ratification of the senate for his appointments. Tenure committeees are usually faculty committees and for the most part do not include student representation. Thus it is fair to say that, however far "democratization" may have proceeded in some instances, there are two important bulwarks that protect the exercise of academic responsibility in these areas: one is the tradition of individual professorial responsibility for grades; the other is the line responsibilities and powers of academic officers.

But let us return to the issue of parity of faculty and students on governing bodies. This issue, after all, is crucial since parity could result in a profound shift in the balance of power within the university and could mean, among other things, legislative enactments that would alter drastically the bulwarks identified above. For example, students have demanded recently that deans of faculties should be executive officers of parity faculty councils and be uniquely responsible to them. Parity is not an important issue at most Canadian universities. A form of parity exists at the University of Alberta at Edmonton. There the General Council of Faculties, which exercises the functions of a senate, includes 40 percent students, 40 percent faculty, and 20 percent academic administrators and others. Thus, while there is parity of elected students and elected faculty, the body does not have parity of students and professors, since most academic administrators are also professors. This composition was strongly advocated by the president of the university and was accepted reluctantly and skeptically by a majority of the faculty. It was created in 1971 and thus far appears to have worked reasonably well. Contributing to its success has been the absence of a strong student government on the campus which could impose its view of issues on the student members of the council. Consequently, these members have not tended to act as a political party within the council. Efforts to use this composition formula for other bodies within the university have been successfully resisted. For example, there are no students on tenure committees at the university.

The issue of parity came to a head at the University of Toronto last year. The university recently adopted a unicameral governing structure which has replaced its senate and board. Student demands for parity of faculty and students were not met by the provincial government which legislated a new act for the University of Toronto in 1971 in order to establish the unicameral system. However, a mandatory review in 1974 was written into the legislation. The great majority of faculty adamantly oppose parity on the governing council in part because, if the principle of parity were adopted in government legislation, it would be very difficult to avoid applying this composition formula to every council and committee of the university, including staffing committees. Unlike the University of Alberta, student government at the University of Toronto has been strong enough to exercise a decisive influence on student members of the council. On crucial issues these students have asked the president of the student government to state its position and have voted accordingly. And, whereas both students and faculty occupy minority positions on the council (it being required by the act that public and alumni representatives should equal the total of internal representatives), because of the absence of public and alumni members on other governing bodies the application of the parity formula would give one half of their membership to students. At succeeding meetings, the governing council voted first to reject parity and then to alter the number of students so as to provide for "token nonparity." The act of 1972 provided for eight students and twelve faculty. The council has since recommended to the government that the composition be changed to eleven students and thirteen faculty, and there the matter still rests in 1975 until the provincial government decides whether to accept this recommendation.

If the government changes the composition of the university's top governing body in this way, it is likely that this body will become crippled by political conflicts and that decisions will be determined by political compromises (which was already true of the decision to change the composition of the council) rather than be grounded on academic principles and university needs. If, in addition, students were to use this victory as the motive for further pressure to make similar changes at other levels of the university, the faculty would probably respond by organizing itself into a professional union and insist upon direct negotiations with the university administration on a broad range of issues in order to bypass university governmental structures in which the faculty could no longer place confidence.

Thus we come upon the issue of faculty unionism. But first let us briefly consider the way student groups have sought to embroil the universities as institutions in some of the larger social issues which have aroused student concern. Typical of these activities were the demonstrations (1968–1969) against the Dow Chemical Company representatives who came at the invitation of universities to recruit scientific and engineering personnel among prospective graduates. The Dow Chemical Company was alleged to be selling war materials to the United States (under a U.S.–Canadian arms-sharing agreement) which were being used in the Vietnam War. There has been, of course, a long tradition of student activisim on public issues in Canada. What was different was the choice of the university as the target based on the rather tenuous premise that by permitting this company to recruit on campus the university was implicated in endorsing the policies under which war materials were being supplied to the United States and which in turn found their way to Vietnam. The aim of the radical students, of course, was to enlist universities as institutions on the side of opposition to the war and, further, to force them to become ideologically committed.

Universities do have a responsibility grounded in academic freedom to examine critically all ideologies, including liberal ideology. They have a responsibility to provide opportunities for the study of alternative ideologies in an environment which encourages free inquiry. They have, finally, a responsibility to refuse to adopt any ideology as the basis of the intellectual life of the universities that would compromise this critical function or destroy the environment which makes its exercise possible. Despite efforts of the radical students to get them to do so, universities have not, as institutions, taken positions on contemporary social and political problems; at the same time they are safeguarding the rights of professors or students to do so as individuals or as members of groups. Almost all professors and administrators as well as the great majority of students reject the ideological university in order to protect the critical university.

The major threat to academic freedom in recent years has not been autocratic government or university bureaucrats or reactionary board members but groups of students, small in number but highly visible because of their actions. These groups want to censor what is taught at the university and to choose who may teach on the basis of their own radical ideological commitments. These groups are usually of the left. But there have also been incidents of right-wing disruptions. Only the content of their demands is different. Their wish to suppress ideas that they oppose, their attitudes towards the universities, and their tactics are similar.

An incident last year at the University of Toronto is instructive. An American sociologist had been invited to the campus to deliver a series of lectures. Local SDS members accused the professor of being racist and by means of various acts of intimidation, harassment, and disruption were able to prohibit him from delivering a lecture. Though a few professors came out in favor of the disruptions, most faculty were shocked and angered by the incident and strongly criticized the administration for failing to act to protect the professor's right to speak. The administration and the governing council of the university acted quickly to adopt a set of procedures for dealing with any future incidents of this kind. (Within a week of the SDS incident a right-wing group from outside the university violently disrupted a meeting on racism in East Africa.) An investigation of the incident was made by the administration as a result of which two graduate student leaders of SDS were charged before the university's disciplinary body. The students were found guilty of conduct prejudicial to the interests of the university—insofar as they had with intent interfered with the visiting professor's right to deliver a lecture, and had taken actions without excuse which interfered with an authorized university activity and with the lawful use of university premises. The students were suspended from the university, one for three years and the other for four years, with the provision that a notation of the suspension would appear on their transcripts for five years, after which it would be removed. The disciplinary body stated an important principle in reaching its decision:

> We see freedom of speech as a fundamental right in Canada. It is subject to the punishment the law provides when it is abused. But it is not subject to prior restraint. In particular it is not subject to advance censorship by any one. . . .[6]

No other comparable incidents took place at any other Canadian university during the year. Should such incidents occur in the future, it is likely that the action of the University of Toronto would serve as a wholesome precedent. Two further points need to be made. The University of Toronto disciplinary body was not attempting to stifle dissent or the orderly demonstration of dissent. In protecting the right of free speech of a visiting professor, they were protecting the same right of free speech for radical students (and anyone else) from prior restraint and advance censorship subject to the constraints imposed upon the exercise of this right by Canadian law.

It is probably true that most universities in Canada are now better able to deal constructively with student activism simply because of the experience of the last five years. But one can easily exaggerate this factor. Student

[6] *University of Toronto Bulletin*, July 1974, p. 1.

activism directed at the universities is on the decline largely because new generations of students want to find new issues rather than warm up the old ones. Additionally, the new generation of students has been sobered by the greater difficulties that now exist in finding desirable professional employment upon graduation than existed before.

Unionism

There has been a growing interest in unionization among professors during the last six years.[7] A major cause is the decline in the purchasing power of faculty salaries during the last four years. But two other factors are important. At some universities unionization is seen as the only means available to the faculty for gaining some measure of influence upon university budgetary and academic priorities. This led recently to the formation of a faculty union at the University of Manitoba. Unionization is also seen as a strategy for avoiding the consequences of undue 'student influence on university governing bodies and on appointment, promotion, and tenure committees should universities and government accede to student demands for student-faculty parity. At the present time, faculty unions exist or are in the process of formation at some six universities in five provinces.

The major reservation faculty have about unionization is the change that it may bring about in the relation of professors to the university. Over the past decade, many universities have become "worker-controlled industries" through the formal and informal participation of faculty in policy and decision making at every level. Academic administrators are drawn from faculty and return to full-time teaching and research after their terms of office. Unionization under provincial labor law presupposes relations between management and labor that are inappropriate to these relations as they operate in most universities. Many professors fear that not only would their identity as scientists and scholars be distorted by unionization of this kind but that their contributions to university policy and decision making would be severely curtailed by it. Unionization in this form becomes attractive only when faculty are already significantly excluded from participation in important decisions affecting the operation of the university (as at the University of Manitoba) or where labor legislation does not require that members of a legally recognized bargaining unit be excluded from university policy-making activities.

An alternative, which has been under active consideration in the hope that it would avoid these difficulties, is special legislation to provide for

[7] A detailed study of faculty unionization and its problems is found in G. L. Adell and D. D. Carter, *Collective Bargaining for University Faculty in Canada*, (Queen's University Industrial Relations Centre, 1972). See also Ontario Confederation of University Faculty Association, *Newsletter*, VIII, no. 1, September 1974, 4ff.

faculty bargaining rights based on a professional rather than an industrial model. Unfortunately, legislative precedents are not encouraging. Currently, in Ontario, community college teachers have bargaining rights under special legislation of this type. However, this legislation contains provisions which would curtail rights and, indeed, responsibilities which university professors should exercise. The legislation which provides bargaining rights for community college teachers in Ontario prohibits them from any form of involvement in politics, even to the extent of forbidding a letter to a newspaper "on any matter that forms a part of the platform of a provincial or federal political party" (Crown Employees Collective Bargaining Act, Section 14). Such provisions in any legislation providing for negotiating rights for faculty would strike at the heart of the critical function of the university and would severely curtail the professorial exercise of academic freedom.[8] Although this particular hazard was not involved, the faculty associations at the four universities in British Columbia rejected a proposal to have their bargaining rights established under special legislation, preferring instead to seek recognition under the province's labor law.

Yet another alternative under active exploration is voluntary collective bargaining at the provincial level based on a model derived from British practice. This format consists of a three-stage negotiation. First, representatives of the universities and representatives of the faculty associations of the universities would negotiate an agreement defining demands for increases in the salary component of provincial grants. Next, representatives of this group would negotiate with a government-designated body to reach an agreement on the amount available for faculty salary increases in the provincial grants. The disposition of this increment would then be decided at each university by a negotiation between the local faculty association and the university. This procedure could be carried out with only a minor modification of the formula grants system, namely, the segregation of the faculty salary component.

This procedure has a number of merits. The first stage of negotiations between universities and faculty associations would provide a mechanism for adjusting general institutional financial needs and faculty salary needs. The second stage would provide for an adjustment of faculty salary demands to available public resources based on considerations of equity and so on among competing demands of professional groups who depend on provincially funded programs for their income. The third stage would provide for an adjustment of the amounts thus negotiated to the circumstances of each university.

But its greatest merit is that it would provide a mechanism that would preserve a valuable feature of the formula grants system, namely, it would protect institutional autonomy. Formal negotiations at the individual

---

[8] *Free the Servants*, a brief to the Ontario government by the Civil Service Association of Ontario, May 1974.

university level are ultimately meaningless for any portion of a university budget as large as that represented by faculty salaries. Union negotiations now occur for certain segments of support staff. The outcome of these negotiations can be honored by the universities because they have a relatively small impact on the overall budget, and can be met by attritions in faculty salary increments or other budgetary stratagems. But universities do not control their income; they cannot increase their revenue by service price increases as can the private sector. Consequently, universities must work out some mechanisms for direct negotiations with the source of their income— the provincial governments—if they are to meet the legitimate salary demands of their professoriates and avoid the problems consequent upon a chronic failure to do so.

The danger inherent in any direct negotiation is that governments would respond by insisting upon a much greater direct control over university programs than they now exercise. By agreeing to subject itself to the outcome of a negotiation on a major part of the university grants, the government would in effect be abandoning its control over a portion of its expenditure. Assuming that it would not want to allow this arrangement to affect the priority it attached to total university funding, it might well insist upon establishing other controls over total university expenditure, which could very easily take the form of government control over academic programs, opening the door wide to the intrusion of political influence. We have already described the developments that tend in that direction quite independently of the unionization issue. We are well aware that some state legislatures in the United States have been enacting legislation concerning academic programs in state universities.[9] This has not happened in Canada, but the danger is real enough that many faculty find themselves in the dilemma of being loath to finance university autonomy out of foregone earnings (a state of affairs that would likely have damaging long-term effects upon the recruitment of individuals of outstanding ability to the professoriate) and being equally loath to do anything about this problem that would tip the scales further in the direction of greater government control over the universities.

This dilemma may be resolved shortly by the actions of governments themselves. In several provinces governments are now demanding program cost information, university by university and discipline by discipline. It is still not clear to what end this information is to be used. If it is used to institute government-controlled program financing on a discipline basis, a situation will then exist in which nothing is to be lost by unionization. If provincial governments move further in this direction, it is very likely that unionization will proceed rapidly across the country.

However, unionization need not make universities vulnerable to direct government intervention. Canada enjoys a strong tradition of individual

[9] "Colleges in a Steady State," *Economist*, September 1974, p. 67.

university autonomy which has, on the whole, been respected by governments despite the extent of their financial commitments to universities. Most politicians and senior government officials are aware, as well, that universities are complex institutions the operation of which is best left to those who have had many years of experience as teachers and administrators. Professors and administrators, for their part, are sensitive to the dangers inherent in increased government control. The format for collective negotiations with government based on the British model described above has been formally adopted by the faculty associations in Ontario as their preferred solution for this reason.

Finally, unionization may damage university academic autonomy and the pursuit of academic excellence by imposing salary and personnel policies on the universities which protect and reward mediocrity at the expense of excellence. In Canada faculty associations have always strongly supported the principle of merit increments. Typically, a portion of the salary increment (usually in the vicinity of 3 percent, since this is the amount applied annually which would produce the average career pattern of progress through the ranks) is set aside for merit increments. It is agreed that these increases may vary from 0 to 6 percent depending on the individual's performance. The amount distributed uniformly is one that offsets inflationary increases. At some universities it is accepted also that there may be individuals who should not receive the inflationary increase. Although departmental chairmen whose responsibility it is to make individual salary decisions may not exercise this discretion, it is not because faculty associations have approved its exercise.

Similarly, the faculty associations have insisted that appointments, promotions, and the granting of tenure should be done according to fair rules which allow for appeal when these rules have not been properly observed; but they have not favored protecting incompetence or even mediocrity from its just deserts. The Canadian faculty associations have thus acted as voluntary professional associations. These same associations at the university, provincial, and national levels have now responded to pressure for unionization. In doing so, they have usually insisted on retaining their traditional approach to salary and personnel policies. In this respect universities can be grateful for the existence of strong faculty associations which have, on at least one occasion (St. Mary's University in the Maritimes), jealously and effectively warded off the efforts of a trade union to organize the faculty of the university. Whether this approach to the crucial issue of professional excellence in teaching and research can be maintained as unionization proceeds, it is still too early to tell, but present indications are that the faculty associations will make every effort to preserve it.

It is easy to let wishful thinking influence one's anticipation of the future. But, on the whole, Canadian experience to date encourages one to believe that our universities will be able to preserve both their institutional and their individual academic freedom despite the difficulties they face.

The British Position

Donald MacRae

"HAPPY IS THE COUNTRY WITHOUT A HISTORY." There has been an illusion
—at least I think it is part an illusion—that by comparison with other
countries British universities have been decorously at peace and that there
has been no history of problems, of emergency, or of crisis in the last
decade. In a period widely felt to be one of decline in British affairs, the
history of higher education has been one of expansion both in the number
of universities and of their students. In addition, a new system of nearly
thirty polytechnics has been brought into being and all three institutions
—and some other new arrivals, too—teach to at least the first-degree level
and, most often, beyond. In this area, at least, for scholarly and scientific
standards remain high, the British story seems to be one of success. The
features of success are real enough; the achievement of a wider, more democratic higher education system with decent standards is remarkable. But
it is not the whole story.

What is a university crisis? How does one identify it? Most people
would agree with me in saying that at least one of the new British universities is chronically sick and that at least one of the new polytechnics is in
a state of dismal disarray. Are interferences with freedom of speech, teaching, and inquiry serious or critical things? I think they are. And such things
occur, if infrequently. Yet in my own instituton a visiting professor has been
assaulted and silenced because of the unpopularity of his views on the
nature-and-nurture components in intelligence. An American scholar has
been silenced in a new university because of his views on foreign policy
matters. In a great provincial university the vice-chancellor, once an
eminent and liberally minded parliamentarian and minister, withdrew the
conferring of an honorary degree on a distinguished American scholar. This
extraordinary event was justified by the argument that the views of the
scientist in question were of a kind likely to be unpopular with the young
—not that they were untrue or in some way dishonest. Even an obscure
professor like myself has been written anxiously by another vice-chancellor
before I lectured in his university in the hope that what I had to say would
not, please, disturb the local socialist society. As my theme was as remote
from politics as is imaginable I must own to surprise. Such things may not
signify a crisis. Neither do they cheer me up particularly.

There has also been in Britain a record of student unrest and liveliness going back even before the events of the Fall 1964 in Berkeley. Such affairs —I am thinking, above all, of Glasgow—remained obscure for the odd reason that Britain has a national press and broadcasting system. This press does not normally think provincial or regional universities news. This is a source of consolation to people remote from London, but it has meant that for well over ten years much that has been threatening or worse has gone unnoticed.

When the Venice conference was first thought of I asked Lord Annan, provost of University College, London, if he would attend. He had just wisely and thoroughly defended the free university in his Dimbleby Lecture on BBC television. He declined because I think he believed that, while there was a university crisis in, say, Germany, nothing comparable or even serious existed in Britain. As you will gather, I agree about comparability, but not about seriousness.

Yet it is certain that in the 1970s things have become less disruptive. Some of our conservative politicians profess an alarm that our dons are in some measure corrupted. Some of our labor politicians believe that our dons are lazy and otiose. Yet I think good sense has, save in a few places, triumphed through firm moderation. But the atmosphere has changed and is changing. David Martin has written of our revolutionary students— primitivist, populist, Maoist, Trotskyist, Stalinist, anarchist, and so on— as numerically insignificant. But they have acquired legitimacy in the general student body. Many of them are able, most are sincere, many of them are ardent, and they have been able to—and perhaps still can—exercise great influence, mobilizing to their ends up to 85 percent of a given student population. Professor Martin referred to an antinomian element in our culture. This is the base of that influence. This is what gives them legitimacy. This is what is threatening to the law-bound culture of free rationality.

Now this conference was not about student bashing. We were in Venice to defend the traditional values of the university transmitting, extending, defending, and rationally criticizing the realm of knowledge. Some students, in a dangerous time, attack these things. So do many nonstudents. This attack is not confined to students, nor yet to youth. Some of our malaise comes from inside the academy, from the dons themselves.

Kenneth Minogue has ascribed this to the new prevalence of sociologists. As a sociologist, I am unconvinced. He reminds me of that close student of barometers who, having studied these instruments exhaustively and extensively, came to the conclusion that, as barometers presage storm and flood, they therefore cause storm and flood. You can, if you will, believe this. To us sociologists it is even flattering. Yet it is unlikely.

Let us look at the expansion of the student body to which I referred earlier. Students, widely defined, are now some 16 percent of the age group in Britain. (I believe 20 percent more accurate, but the official figures are hard to interpret, so let us be conservative.) In 1960 they were only about 4 percent. Such an expansion Mr. Kingsley Amis claimed, could have but one result. "More," he said, "means worse." I do not think he has been proved right. But "more" has certainly meant "less."

Let me explain: Expansion has meant more dons. Their quality has deteriorated. This has not been, I believe, a deterioration in intellectual ability. But the constituency of young dons has been extended and they have been drawn from those sectors less imbued with the culture of the intellect and they have found that culture very demanding and worrying. They have had to teach very hard—our system tries to achieve, by and large, in three years what in America takes four, in much of Europe six— and the burden of doing this, achieving doctorates, and publishing research has worried them into resentment. The number of junior researchers and research assistants, inevitably insecure, has also grown. A continuum of anxiety unites these dons to the students. Private fear is mediated into public revolt. Vocation in some parts of the new constituency has become rare and less complete. To be a don is to have a vocation or to be in bad faith—and bad faith can lead to worse acts. At the same time a university career now carries less public prestige and status, if only because of the very prevalence of dons. To be an elite, with its burdens and rewards, a profession should not be too numerous.

It is quite clear, too, that among the young teachers were some who thought of the university with disapproval just because the academy is predicated on tolerance. Populism is less strong in Britain than in, for example, Australia, but it does exist. The academy cannot, by definition, be populist. Populism, also by definition, cannot be tolerant. Thus there was and is an attack from within; if you like, a fifth column. What is more the general devaluation of a literate, verbal culture meant that many of the new dons were genuinely puzzled by the interests, the attitudes, of their colleagues in the universities. Such people are an easy prey to populist pressures, for the main vehicle of our academic culture, including such fields as pure natural science and technology, is one of the word, of the open, flexible, and skeptical use of language. Those unskilled in language, suspicious of its sophisticated use and puzzled by its centrality, provide a fertile field for the rhetoric of populism and practice of intolerance to grow and flourish.

So, too, with the new extended student constituency. In the sense I have already employed, more here has also meant less. Students are certainly no less able than in the past, but their constituency is also certainly less formed and less socialized into the traditional high culture of British society than it was. Now this is a subject about which there is much cant. That culture had and has many defects requiring criticism, innovation, and reform. It is far from true, thank God, to say that all previous student generations came from book-filled homes, sang madrigals, played upper-class team games, and discussed high issues rather than money or sex. There is untruth and false nostalgia in such assumptions. As a Scot, one from a country that far more than England has invested in education, in the "democratic intellect," I cannot deplore the birth pangs of a wider university. Nor, however, can I deny the high cost involved.

These points, in some sense cultural, all connect with another aspect of the seventies. This is cultural and geographical provinciality. I am not putting down the strengths, real enough, of provincialism or holding that provincials are somehow more stupid than metropolitans—an absurd and indefensible view. Yet between 1966 and 1969 university malaise was metropolitan or a feature of culturally central institutions, whatever their geographic location. Since then it has been rather the physically and physically remote places—Stirling, for example, or Lancaster—that have suffered. Or it has been places which are culturally remote, even though geographically metropolitan (like the Northern Polytechnic in London), which have been at risk. This migration of our troubles to the provinces suggests to me that they are nearly over, which does not mean, of course, that they will not flare up again. If they do, they will, I think, be somewhat different in that the protests will become economic and be powered by the new national strength of the National Union of Students—a body now politicized and important, which at an earlier period was trivial and essentially welfare oriented. (It is worth explaining that the NUS had at earlier times been highly politicized for brief periods; but in the fifties it was, as I said, essentially a welfare body.)

I now leave the survivals of the sixties and turn to newer matters. The Venice conference has turned much on a discussion of "pluralism." My usage is an old one. By pluralism, I understand the independent being of corporate bodies within our societies and the claim that corporate and collegial bodies have an important claim to independent and special rights. With six exceptions[1] British universities are modern and all are financially creatures of the state. Yet all our universities have about them a collegial claim and nature. They are like medieval guilds, guilds of scholars. (The word university is after all *universitas*, the word for a guild.) For nearly half a century this independent collegiality, this pluralism, was maintained by the ingenious device of the University Grants Committee, mediating between universities and the state. In the last decade the system has begun to change. Pluralism in my sense is at risk. More and more, the UGC seems not the agent of the universities dealing with the state but, rather, the agent of the state vis-à-vis the universities. The Department of Education and Science is now directly concerned with the academy and with

[1] Oxford, Cambridge, St. Andrews, Glasgow, Aberdeen, and Edinburgh.

the official grant-giving research councils. A junior minister guides—and politicizes—our business in Parliament. The quasi-universities or polytechnics are the creatures of local government. And so on. . . .

Now the state and local government in Britain are not ill-disposed entities. My fear is that they are often inappropriate, short sighted, moved by fashion and by a desire for tidy uniformity. They are inevitably, over time, the enemies of a pluralistic academy. They are particularly dangerous in a hard economic climate of the kind into which we are now moving. They are coarsely utilitarian. They are moved by short-term accountancy. The universities of Britain are therefore at risk if you believe that academic freedom is freedom, under law, to be disinterested, critical, exploratory, and judges in their own cause which is simply the cause of learning itself. I am confident that all the unrests of the recent past have been contained, and with little loss. Britain in these matters has indeed been fortunate in having, for once, so small a history. I am, alas, less confident about our ability to weather the gales of the economic climate and the well-meant activity of the state in its various forms.

Danish Universities in Transition

Mogens Blegvad and Steen Leth Jeppesen

SINCE THE SECOND WORLD WAR, higher education has seen great changes in Denmark, as it has in many other countries; since the end of the sixties changes have been so extensive and dramatic that they may be called revolutionary. To a certain extent violence or threat of violence on the part of students has played a role, but it is also a question of deliberate attempts on the part of political and administrative authorities to adapt higher education to new social conditions. Under slogans such as "democratization" and "flexibility," systems of administration, positional hierarchies, and study programs have been changed; former attitudes toward academic studies and their social functions have more or less deliberately been undermined. As for giving students a voice in the running of institutions, Denmark has gone farther than any other country with comparable academic traditions. Thus, understandably, the question has been raised as to whether some things might have taken place which in the long run can cause irreparable harm to the country and to its democratic system of government.

Around 1960 the Danish system of higher education included two universities (Copenhagen, founded in 1479; and Århus, founded in 1929) and a number of other institutions ("Højere læreanstalter," colleges) which provided instruction in engineering, dentistry, pharmacy, business administration, veterinary medicine, architecture, and so forth. While university studies were free—both in the sense that anyone who passed the *studentereksamen* (high-school graduation examination requiring 12 years of schooling) was admitted, and in the sense that attending lectures was voluntary—the colleges, on the other hand, accepted only a limited number of students each year (selection based mainly on marks obtained in the studentereksamen), and many of the courses were compulsory. The universities, for which the Ministry of Education was responsible, had extended self-government, while various other government departments were responsible for some of the colleges. The universities were divided into five divisions ("Fakulteter"): theology, medicine, law and economics, humanities and science. Each division was governed by a council consisting of all full professors. Each of these councils in turn chose a number of its members to sit on the supreme

181

governing body, the senate ("Konsistorium") whose chairman was the president ("Rektor") of that university, elected for two years among and by all full professors. Each divisional council chose for one year its own chairman ("Dekan," dean) who was automatically a member of the senate. It was customary for professors to serve as deans in order of seniority.

No departments as such existed, but when there were several professors in one field of study, they were considered to constitute a unit. To many fields of study were attached research institutes or laboratories which also served educational purposes.

University studies were relatively lengthy and scientific in character—in most fields of study graduation required presentation of a thesis. There was no distinction (as known in the United States) between undergraduate and graduate or professional studies; the general education which the first two years in particular of an American college education provide was assumed to have been acquired in high school. The prescribed duration of study varied between 5 and 7 years; the actual study time was usually a few years longer, one of the reasons being that many students had to undertake part-time employment and their studies were thus slowed down. In the colleges the required duration of study was somewhat less and delays were shorter and less frequent, due partly to the fact that their more compulsory and compact studies did not permit any work on the side.

During the sixties, the higher education system expanded very rapidly. As the damage inflicted on the production apparatus of the country during the war years was remedied and foreign trade increased once again, economic conditions improved to the point where expansion of secondary education could be afforded. Therefore, by taking the high-school graduation examination, many more youngsters than before won the right to matriculate at universities. The rising standard of living also made it possible for larger segments of the population to give their children more education than they themselves had enjoyed. At the same time, financial support given by the state toward the daily expenses of the students was considerably expanded.

The sixties, therefore, saw a dramatic rise in the number of young people who could and would aspire to a higher education. As there was a great demand for engineers, architects, dentists, and so on, existing colleges were expanded and new ones were founded (an engineering academy in Copenhagen, 1957, and one in Aalborg, 1965; a dental school in Århus, 1958; an architectural school in Århus, 1965). Nevertheless, many students could not find a place in these institutions and sought the university education to which they were fully entitled after they had taken the high-school graduation examination. This trend continued until just recently, when a decline in the rate of increase of students began. It is significant that a considerable proportion of the dramatically increased number of students was borne by the largest and oldest of the universities, the University of Copenhagen, where the number of students doubled over a five-year period. (From 1960 till 1970 the number of university students increased from 9,100 to 35,400, while the number of students at the colleges grew from 5,600 to 10,000. Out of 100 19-year-olds in 1960, 4 entered a university, 2 a college. Comparable numbers for 1970 were 11 and 3.)

It is worth mentioning, furthermore, that a disproportionately large part of the increase fell to the humanities and social sciences, subjects many of which are of lesser practical use. For a number of years the dangers of this were hidden by the fact that the expansion of higher and secondary education created a demand for graduates for newly established teaching positions, so that even in very specialized and traditionally low-paying fields it was for a time easy to obtain jobs. Even more important, a stronger growth in Denmark's public sector than in any other Western country created another great demand for many types of academically trained people.

Although the number of new teaching positions thus rose to a hitherto unknown level, the student-teacher ratio at the universities worsened to the extent that many fields of study had more than 30 students per teacher. This, of course, meant accommodation problems. The University of Copenhagen in particular, many of whose buildings are in the center of the capital, was forced to adopt shortsighted, expensive, and incomplete solutions to these problems.

The government rejected any suggestions for regulating the increase; instead it tried to expand the capacity of existing institutions and to establish new ones. This applied to universities as well as to colleges: In 1964 a new law established a university in Odense (Denmark's third largest city) which opened its doors to a limited number of students in 1966. By 1973 its student body had reached some 3,000. In 1970, legislation called for a new type of institution, called a "university center," to be established in three provincial towns. Of these, the one in Roskilde began operations in 1972, while that in Aalborg opened its doors in September 1974. In Esbjerg-Ribe, where a third one may some day be built, small research groups have been established locally.

In these university centers, the kind of education which in Denmark has been traditionally divided between universities and colleges is being combined. However, none of the university centers will offer all of the traditional university programs (e.g., medicine will be reserved for the three "old" universities). It is hoped that changeovers and combinations between different studies at the center will be facilitated, particularly by the introduction of the so-called base studies. A more detailed discussion of the university centers follows; here it should only be mentioned that it became clear in the course of the sixties that expansion would require certain changes in the administration of both the individual institutions and higher education in general.

In 1962, the Minister of Education set up a committee on administration of universities and colleges. In the following years this committee produced a number of recommendations, several of which were put into effect. In order to further cooperation and coordination between the institutions three new bodies were established: a Planning Council for Higher Education (1964), a Joint Committee for Research (1965) and "Rektor kollegiet" (1967), a conference of the heads of all universities and colleges. Problems concerning the governance of the individual institutions were also discussed by the committee which—without reaching unanimity—reported on them in 1965.

Before the recommendations embodied in these reports could be put into practice, a development gained momentum which made them of no further interest. One of the most pressing problems in the governance of universities dealt with by the committee was the status of nonprofessorial teachers. These teachers, who had become far more numerous than the professors (4:1), belonged to several categories ("docenter," "lektorer," "amanuenser," "undervisningsassistenter"), none of which was represented on the governing bodies. These teachers felt that they had less influence than the students, who (although without the right to vote) were able to state their views to the divisional councils and in the senate of the university through an officially recognized student council ("Studenterrådet"). The nonprofessorial teachers organized and worked for what was called "integration"—i.e., complete equality between professors and nonprofessorial teachers in matters of influence. They did not, on the other hand, contest the position of professors as tenured public servants: nor did they contest the professors' slightly higher wage scale. The university administration committee did not support integration, and suggested only certain limited representation for full-time nonprofessorial teachers. Many professors were also unwilling to go further than that. The tension between the two academic groups and the problems of governing became acute in April 1968 with the occurrence of the first violent student demonstrations and the occupation of the psychology laboratory at the University of Copenhagen.

It is not surprising that the trouble began there. For some years psychology had been a popular subject—in Denmark as elsewhere. Because of the free-admission policies and the fact that the University of Copenhagen was the only place in the country where one could obtain a complete education in psychology, the number of students had increased enormously, and conditions had become very poor. There were only three professors and a very limited number of other teachers to teach approximately 1500 students. Responsibility and authority was vaguely distributed between the divisional council for the humanities, the senior professor of psychology as director of the laboratory, and the group of professors of psychology; clearly the radical students were fishing in troubled waters. The students made a series of demands, and, when (according to the students), the negotiations regarding these demands went too slowly, the laboratory—situated in one of the older university buildings in the center of Copenhagen—was occupied. ·

The president of the university, neurologist Mogens Fog—well-known for his participation in the resistance movement during the German occupation, and for his left-wing political sympathies—intervened (disciplinary cases came under his jurisdiction according to the rules). During a series of negotiations between the psychology students and the different groups of teachers in the psychology faculty, it was agreed that the occupation would be discontinued on the promise that two of the three professors would sign a declaration delegating their authority as leaders of the department to a new temporary body, a study board ("Studienævn"). This board would consist of equal numbers of teachers and students. Thereby a principle was introduced from which it proved impossible to break away during the following months and years: Study-related matters are to be settled by bodies with equal teacher–student representation.

In the following months demands for similar study boards were made in other parts of the university and at other institutions. Copenhagen's humanities division decided, at an October 11, 1968 meeting, on temporary rules for study boards which, among other things, gave these boards authority to hire and fire all teaching assistants paid on an hourly basis. It also established the following principle: The study boards would be the highest tribunal in all study and examination matters. All of the higher-education institutions were then asked by the Ministry of Education to prepare suggestions for administrative reforms, it being understood that the proposals from 1965 were superseded. This work went on on several levels throughout 1969, and the ministry, on the basis of the results, prepared a bill which was presented in parliament in March 1970. It became law in June—without any changes. The law differed in many ways from suggestions made by the institutions, but it cannot be maintained that the new law was dictated from "higher up"—its most important principles found support in the original proposals.

The Governance Act for universities ("Styrelsesloven") introduced a number of decisive changes in university administration. The most important were: (a) governance of individual subject areas' educational affairs by study boards; (b) implementation of the integration principle, according to which all full-time university teachers and researchers are regarded as equal—professors deprived of their former special administrative duties and rights; and (c) the introduction of representation for students in governing organs, and representation for the technical–administrative personnel in management of the institutions. The act contained a series of general structural principles which were to be supplemented by the individual universities' specific regulations or by ministerial order—for example, election rules, study board and management conditions, and so forth, were subsequently stipulated for the University of Copenhagen.

The Act sought to maintain the universities' autonomy, economically and professionally, to about the same degree as was true before the Act was implemented. It still reserved to the Ministry of Education the right to lay down more specific administrative rules for the individual university as to the establishment and appointment of professorships, conferral of academic degrees, the admission to study and to enter an examination, examinations systems, and the awarding of marks.

A university was to be headed by a president acting in conjunction with a senate ("Konsistorium"), and the divisional councils, departmental councils, and study boards, which were to be established. The president and vice-president were to be elected from the university's professors by all the full-time academic associates and teachers, as well as the student representatives in the divisional or sectional councils. The senate consisted of the rector (chairman), vice-rector, deans for the various divisions, and a number of full-time academic associates and teachers elected by and from among the members of the divisional and sectional councils. Finally, one-third of the total number of senate members was made up of representatives elected by and from among matriculated students. The electoral period was three years for the teacher group, and one year for students.

The Act asserted that the university's academic research and instruction should take place within various divisions (theology, social science, medicine, the humanities, and natural science). Research and instruction within a particular division was to be governed by a divisional council. This council was to consist of a number of members elected by and from among full-time academic associates and teachers, and at least one representing those employed part-time. Representation from the students was to make up one third of the total number of members of the divisional council. Any divisional council member could be elected dean (chairman). A division could be divided by the senate into two or more sections, thereafter to be headed by a sectional council operating with the same rules as divisional councils regarding composition and competence.

With regard to departments, the supreme body has to be the departmental council, made up of all of the divisional or sectional full-time academic associates, part-time lecturers, and representatives of the remaining personnel and students taking part in the department's program of instruction. More specific rules on this were to be established by the senate and the divisional or sectional councils. The department's council elected a director and/or a board of directors, representing the department externally and responsible for day-to-day management. A study board was to be appointed for each individual subject area. It was to consist of an even number of teachers and students, elected by all teachers and students within the area of the study board in question.

The distribution of competence among these different governing bodies, according to the Act of 1970, was not clear. As mentioned, instruction and research in individual divisions (sections) were to be regulated by the divisional or sectional council. The study boards, however, were to regulate matters concerning curriculum content, instructional organization, and the holding of examinations. As for financial matters, authority for matters concerning a division as a whole (e.g., grants for projects) rested with the divisional council, whereas matters concerning the individual subject area went to the departmental council.

As far as academic matters are concerned, responsibility for research lay almost wholly with the individual departments and the individual researcher, although there was a tendency to accept the authority of the study boards regarding instructional areas. These study boards were to make decisions in matters relating to course content and so forth. It is not clear how this responsibility related to the requirement of the Act that the divisional or sectional council should head the studies. Also, it is unclear as to how the study board's sphere should be delimited with respect to the individual teacher's own competence and responsibility and to the authority of the department.

It was not intended that decisions made in bodies with equal teacher–student representation, such as study boards, should be appealed to differently constituted bodies, such as faculty councils. Among other reasons, that is why an order at the University of Copenhagen of October 30, 1972, called for using the Governance Act as the instrument to appoint an equally constituted, central study board for each division. After that time, appeal matters from the departmental study boards went to the central study board. This, however, did not make it any easier to understand the Act's rule that the divisional or sectional council head the instruction in every division or section. For the most part, the attempt to distribute the authority (as to decisions about subject areas) among the divisional council, study board, and departmental council was never successfully resolved. Practice has varied at different universities and even within different divisions and subject areas at individual universities.

As far as appointments are concerned, the situation is somewhat clearer. For professors, the appointing authority was to be the Queen; the university president deciding for the remaining categories. The recommendation for appointment was to be decided by relevant divisional councils on the basis of a recommendation from an expert ad hoc committee (of which no students could be members). Instructors were to be appointed by study boards; appointment of technical-administrative personnel was to be carried out by the president upon recommendation from the department involved.

In the initial period following the establishment of the University Governance Act, several disputes arose at the country's three universities, particularly at the University of Copenhagen and the University of Århus.

The teachers (more or less quietly) selected representatives to the governing bodies. But strong disputes arose, not only among and within the different student groups, but also between some of the groups and the Ministry of Education and the government.

Traditionally the student council has been the students' main organization at the universities. Historically, this organization has been nonpolitical. Since the latter half of the 1960s, however, student councils have become continuously more politicized; they have appointed themselves spokesmen for points of view which—at least within the existing political spectrum in Denmark—must be regarded as extremely "left-wing." The result has been increasing polarization in the student world, which became manifest when student organizations such as "Conservative Students" and "Moderate Students" sought to influence universities in opposition to the radicalized student councils.

During early discussions of drafts of the Governance Act, the Ministry of Education, however, took the position that student councils must continue to be recognized as legitimate organizations with the right to appoint student representatives to the governing bodies. Demands were made that bylaws and election rules which these councils would use be approved by the Ministry or by another public authority. The councils indignantly refused this demand. Thereafter, the Minister of Education decided that student councils should not have any special prerogatives over other organizations in student elections. In practice this meant that now the other student organizations had the opportunity to have their representatives elected.

This decision—when included in the final Act—aroused great excitement in the student councils, which went on to boycott elections of student representatives to the governing bodies of the fall of 1970; thus the only representatives elected came from the remaining student organizations, notably conservative or moderate. (This applies only partially to the medical division.) As the governing bodies began to hold their first meetings in January, 1971, a number of students tried, especially in Copenhagen and Århus, to prevent the meetings from taking place. Especially in Copenhagen, a direct intrusion of unauthorized persons disrupted the senate's first meeting. The harassed senate thereafter held its meetings in different places during the first six months of 1971; their locations were made known confidentially to members immediately before each meeting. But meetings of other bodies such as the Council of the Humanities Division had to be cancelled. Different improvisations were made to permit student councils to participate, but these in turn evoked protests from the conservative and moderate students, and made regular meetings of some groups such as the Council of the Science Division, impossible. The student council's attempts to prevent the governing bodies from holding meetings died out during the spring of 1971. However, the councils maintained their boycott at the election of representatives in the fall of 1971. Not until the fall of 1972 did the councils make nominations over a broad front.

The Governance Act provided that motions to revise the act had to be proposed to the parliament ("Folketinget") no later than the legislative year 1972–1973. The intention was to regard the first three years as a trial period, where one could find out how the new system worked in practice. However, completing the provisions of the Act took this entire period. The Ministry of Education was very slow in issuing the different supplementary decrees required by the law. For instance, rules regarding study boards and departments were not issued until October, 1972, and February, 1973, for the University of Copenhagen. This university complained insistently about the slowness and uncertainty up until the time of the law's revision.

A new Act was passed in June, 1973. The fundamental principles of teacher integration, study boards, and departmental councils as a whole have been transferred unaltered from the old Act. Certain changes were made in a number of areas. The new Act applies not only to the universities but also to all other institutes of higher education under the Ministry of Education. The Act framed a number of principles for the management of the institutions, whereas more specific rules for each individual institution were to appear in a subsequent statute, which would have to be approved by the Minister of Education.

Among important changes in the new Act compared with the old one are these: The new Act reduced teacher representation in the senate, and in divisional and sectional councils. As mentioned previously, this teacher representation earlier had constituted two thirds of the total number of members of those bodies. However, representation for the technical–administrative personnel (TAP) was now introduced. If the TAP group makes up at least half of the total number of teachers at the institution, employee representation must equal half of the total teacher representation. However, if the number of TAP is below this number, the share is reduced to one-fourth of the number of teacher representatives. Representatives for this group are elected for one three-year term at a time. Student representation in all cases is to equal half of the total teacher representation. Thus the ratio for teachers, TAP, and students will be 4:2:2 or 4:1:2.

The offices of president and vice-president can now be filled by any of the full-time lecturers as well as any of the professoriate; previously, only professors had been eligible. Whereas originally the president and vice-president were elected by an assembly consisting of all the full-time academic associates and teachers at the university, as well as of the student representatives to the divisional and sectional councils, now the assembly is made up of all members of the divisional and sectional councils and members of the senate not represented in these councils. A significant consequence of these changes is that now a unanimous action among representatives for students and the technical–administrative personnel will be able to elect a president, since one would hardly expect it to be opposed by a unanimous bloc of teachers.

The election rules have been changed so that, in the future, senate members will have to be elected by all teachers, TAP, and students within the individual divisions, although the president, vice-president, and chairmen of the councils for each individual division are members *ex officio*. At least one teacher must be a part-time employee.

The new Act also introduced an additional governing body when it formalized the concept of a central study board for each division, made up equally of teachers and students. The Act specifies that decisions of individual study boards, including appointment of instructors, can be submitted to the central study board for review. The Act also added the new requirement that so-called commissions of appeal must be established for handling complaints from examinees about an examination or awarding of marks. The commissions will have the power to change the mark, demand reexamination of both oral and written examinations, or let a reevaluation be made. Their decisions cannot be appealed.

As the foregoing discussion indicates, universities and other institutions of higher education in Denmark have enjoyed a rather considerable amount of self-government. Ultimately they have been dependent, of course, on the Ministry of Education, which has been responsible for establishing different regulations regarding examinations, the form of appointment for professors, admission to study at the educational institutions, and so forth. In the implementation of the 1970 Governance Act the Ministry's powers changed somewhat. The Planning Council for Higher Education, created in 1964 as an advisory to the Ministry regarding educational matters, was abolished in 1973. The Central Education Council (CUR) was established, as an advisory body to the government for the educational area as a whole, and as part of a structural change in the Ministry of Education. CUR consists of 20 members, half of whom represent different interest groups, while the rest are personally appointed by the Minister of Education. Under CUR four area education councils must function, one of these being an area council for higher education (which presumably means any education three years or more past the twelfth grade.)

Further, as part of the structural change a Directorate for Higher Education (DVU) was established. The budget administration for the educational institutions hereafter lies with DVU; advisory bodies, the so-called professional committees, also must be appointed for major subject areas. These committees have the task of assisting the DVU in questions pertaining to their discipline. It must be assumed that, essentially, universities and colleges of higher education will retain a high degree of self-government even after these administrative changes.

The extensive changes in the organizational structure of Danish higher education, brought about by the two Acts and attendant reforms, have of course created an intensive debate in academic circles. The general public, surprisingly indifferent for a long time, has begun to take an interest in what is happening, alarmed now by sporadic reports about conditions. It is, however, not easy to evaluate objectively just how well the reforms have worked. The reforms came at a time when growth alone was responsible for many poor conditions within the system. The very effect of so many extensive reforms has been to create a tremendous workload and many additional difficulties which have not yet been overcome. Certain developments of a negative nature might be a consequence of the reform process itself and thus would not necessarily be grounds for criticizing the content of the reforms. Without more careful study it is difficult to establish what actually has happened; the development seems to have taken very different forms even in related subjects within the same institution. The total effect of the reforms has not yet been seen, although a few general tendencies can be pointed out now.

There are reasons for concern about research in the three universities. The increased teaching load, attributable to the rapidly increasing student population, has had a restrictive effect on research. Frequent changes in study plans, the proliferation of individual curricula, and the like, have further increased this burden. Finally, the complicated new organizational structure—even after transitional difficulties have passed—requires scholars to spend an amazing amount of time and energy at meetings and in other administrative work.

Another reason for concern about research lies in the government's attitude. Certain measures taken in connection with efforts to economize have shown a tendency to limit the role of the universities as domiciles for free basic research—a tendency also expressed in statements by administrators and politicians. For instance, the practice whereby publication expenses for doctoral dissertations were partially covered has been abolished, and doctoral candidates must now apply for support from research councils. Also, a special class of research fellowship is gradually being phased out. These fellowships could be granted to established researchers without permanent tenure, to allow them to use their full time and energy for research of their own choice. Finally, the rule whereby a full-time university teacher should spend 45 percent of his working hours, on the average, for research, 10 percent for administration, and 45 percent for instruction, has been changed so that research time is reduced to 40 percent. To be sure, these are norm figures somewhat out of touch with reality. Actually, administrative work takes far more time and effort than the equivalent of 10 percent. Politicians and other opinion leaders have put forward a demand that faculty research be financed through the research councils. In that way it could and should be directed upon topics of immediate public utility. The demand that research be relevant to social needs has also been raised from quite another quarter by those who wish to expose deficiencies in the existing social order, and in this way work for its overthrow. Those demands have greatly influenced the nature of research, especially in the social sciences.

All in all, there is reason to believe that university research has suffered, and that a decline has taken place, at least if the increase in personnel is taken into consideration.

Regarding instruction, there is no doubt that the influence given to the students through the study board arrangement has been exploited. Most teachers would agree that this has led to a deterioration of studies. Also, the contents of studies have been ideologically biased in several departments. In many places there have been lengthy, embittered struggles about this subject.

A popular student concept is the ideal that anyone, regardless of qualifications, should be permitted to study at a university and thereby either develop personally or qualify for whatever he or she wishes—and, moreover, be paid by the government for so doing. Any evaluation of the individual which could significantly affect his career later on ought not to occur. Instead, cooperation—for example, in the form of group work—ought to be encouraged.

The student councils have continued to dominate student representation in the governing bodies despite the fact they do not have a majority of students behind them, and despite the changes made in their power by the Act of 1970. The many changes in study plans and examination rules that they have carried through (supported by some, mostly younger teachers) invariably mean that professional requirements have been lowered and examination procedures weakened. Curriculum content varies widely, making it enormously difficult for teachers to discover what level of insight and knowledge an individual student has attained. Changes have also been made in the form of the examinations with the same effect. Regular examinations have been replaced with unsupervised take-home ones on self-chosen subjects. Jointly written exercises make it impossible to ascertain the quality of an individual student's efforts.

One way in which the Governance Act challenges established, fundamental principles, is in the method of procedure for appointments. The study boards, as previously mentioned, have been given authority to appoint teachers who are hired for a semester (or a succession of three semesters at the most) to teach basic courses. This means that students take part in the evaluation of applicants for positions for which they themselves are not qualified. Technical–administrative staff and students similarly take part—through their membership in divisional and departmental councils and the senate—in filling permanent positions, including professorships. An evaluation of the applicants has to be done by expert committees, but these committees are appointed by divisional and departmental councils which in addition make the final decisions.

At the university centers, especially, the new structure of governance may have lasting effects on education as well as on the quality of research. There has been, first of all, the problem of staffing these institutions. Until recently, there have been few qualified teachers to draw from, even for university positions. The university centers, therefore, have found it very difficult to find sufficiently qualified applicants within the borders of the country.

A second problem is the tremendous freedom in curriculum planning that has taken place at university centers—radically different from what is available to most other university students in Denmark. At both Roskilde and Aalborg, programs begin with the so-called basic studies. For two (Roskilde) or one (Aalborg) year all students of—for example—social science follow the same program. They work together in groups on projects, whereas systematic, compulsory courses are very few. Only after these basic years do students specialize. As a result, there is no way to compare the first two years of study at Roskilde with those of other institutions. No comparable evaluation of student learning is possible. The Ministry of Education seems to be aware of this, and a special evaluation project has been organized, under the leadership of a Swedish professor, to assess the results of the basic studies at Roskilde. Until further notice the Roskilde basic studies are to be considered only as an experiment, one which the Swedish professor in question has described as "the most extensive of its kind in Northern Europe."

Regarding Aalborg, the record is slight, because the center began so recently. The basic studies program is required only for one year. Again, it is organized into projects, as at Roskilde. Unlike at Roskilde, project choices must be approved by the teachers at Aalborg; nevertheless, this form of study continues to make it very difficult to evaluate the student's professional level. The program at Aalborg, it must be feared, will be less than satisfactory, even though it may not be catastrophic.

One reason why balanced development is more likely at Aalborg is that people have been frightened by developments at Roskilde. Also, Aalborg has incorporated already existing engineering and other studies at the local college of business administration into its program, thus gaining faculties which possibly may be able to create a more normal atmosphere for education.

The picture is more varied for other Danish institutions of higher education. The colleges functioned according to separate regulations until the new Governance Act. No significant data exists at present as to what effect the Act will have on them. It can probably be assumed, however, that the impact on the quality of education and research will be less pronounced at institutions with a professional base, especially in the economic, technical, and scientific fields, such as the Technical University of Denmark, the Royal Veterinary and Agricultural University, schools of business administration, the Royal Danish School of Pharmacy, and the dental colleges.

Less hopeful is the prospect for such schools as those of architecture and journalism. Here, governing rules in line with the ones the Act now prescribes generally have been in effect for several years. At the schools of architecture, extremely far-reaching provisions regarding students' influence have now been implemented, creating problems even more enormous than the ones that have been confronted elsewhere.

The Dutch Universities between the "New Democracy" and the "New Management"

Hans Daalder

IN THE AUTUMN OF 1970, the Dutch parliament passed a new University Government Reorganization Act. It was introduced by the Catholic minister of education and science, Dr. G. Veringa,[1] under a coalition cabinet composed of members of the Catholic, two Protestant, and Liberal parties—the latter occupies the place of a moderate conservative party in Dutch politics. The bill was opposed within parliament by the left-wing opposition parties —most notably the Labor party and a new radical party, Democrats '66— and was attacked bitterly by radical students outside it. The bill was the government's response to the Dutch *événements de mai*—that is, May 1969 —the month in which conflict suddenly flared on one campus after another, one full year after the events in France. The new University Government Reorganization Act did not meet the opposition's demands for some form of "parliamentary" university government. But it introduced far-reaching reforms.

Four basic questions have arisen from its passage and from the slow process of application which has followed since: (1) What is the basic structure of the act, denounced as a compromise by dissatisfied radical students, hallowed by some as the "democratization of the university," hated by others as a threat to the very heart of academic freedom? (2) How are we to account for the passage of this act, which is more radical than similar legislation in other countries and which came unexpectedly in the traditionally sober atmosphere of the Dutch universities and of Dutch society in general? (3) What consequences does the execution of the act have for the functioning of Dutch universities? What conflicts are emerging? What is the character of present university politics? And to what degree is the university becoming an arena for political conflicts beyond the immediate issues of teaching or research? (4) How can the "new democracy," on the one hand, and the seemingly antithetical trend towards the "new

---

[1] The bill was in fact introduced jointly by Dr. G. Veringa and the minister of agriculture, Mr. Pierre Lardinois, as the latter was formally responsible for the School of Agriculture in Wageningen. The definitive text of the act may be found in *Staatsblad* 1970, no. 601.

management" on the other—both of which are characteristic of Dutch as well as other contemporary Western societies and which are both pressing on the university—be brought into balance?

The "crisis of the university" obviously comprises many things beyond the present conflict about "university democracy." These include expansion of numbers of students and staff, procedures of central government financing, arguments for curricular reform, debate on the balance of teaching and research in the universities, future demand for university graduates, academic freedom versus social accountability, and so on. My selection concentrates almost exclusively on the problem of university organization; I do this for two reasons above all. The Dutch case represents in many ways a unique experiment in revolution from above, in response to student activism from below, and all these other significant things will be greatly affected by the impact of the act on the organization of the universities.

The University Government Reorganization Act of 1970

Before we trace the effects of the new act on Dutch university life, it is first necessary to describe its main formal provisions.[2]

CENTRAL UNIVERSITY ORGANIZATION

Traditionally, the Dutch universities were governed—in a phrase dear to *rectores magnifici* in assembly oratory—by a *duplex ordo:* a mainly honorific board of regents *(curatoren)* which oversaw the administrative side, and the senate and the faculties, composed of full professors only, which were in

---

[2] The following description of the new university organization refers particularly to the large state universities of Leiden, Groningen, and Utrecht, the newly established Erasmus University in Rotterdam, the formerly Municipal University of Amsterdam, the more specialized State Technological Schools in Delft, Eindhoven, and Enschede, and the Agricultural School in Wageningen. Somewhat different arrangements prevail in the private confessional universities, the (Calvinist) Free University of Amsterdam, the Catholic University of Nijmegen, and the Catholic School of Economics, Law, and Social Sciences in Tilburg. These latter institutions are entirely supported by the central government, however, and the University Government Reorganization Act in fact prescribed that these universities should reform their own organization in accordance with the general spirit of the act. The main differences between the state universities and the private confessional universities lies in the somewhat smaller powers the minister of education and sciences exercises over the latter. In particular, he does not appoint or approve the appointment of members of the executive board, the *rector magnificus,* or full professors or readers.

charge of education and research.[3] The new reorganization act substituted a condominium of two bodies—a university council *(Universiteitsraad)* and an executive board *(College van Bestuur)*.

The university council consists of a maximum of five sixths of elected members, and a minimum of one sixth of persons chosen to represent society at large; these are appointed by the Crown on the nomination of the elected members. The elected members are chosen by and from three distinct "constituencies": the academic staff irrespective of grade but excluding student assistants, all nonacademic staff members, and students of more than six months' standing. The act requires that a minimum of one third of the elected members of the university council must be chosen from the academic staff, and it limits representation for each of the other two categories to a maximum of one third. In order to be allowed to fill all its allotted seats, a minimum turnout of 35 percent of eligible voters is required in each constituency. If the actual turnout is lower than 35 percent, the number of seats is reduced proportionately.

The executive board is a *mixtum compositum* of elected and appointed members. In most universities the board has five full-time members: two elected for two-year periods by the university council from members of the academic staff, two appointed for a four-year period by the minister of education after consultation with—but not necessarily with the assent of— the university council, and the *rector magnificus*. The latter is nominated by the board of deans, and is appointed by the minister for a minimum period of two years after consultation with the university council.

The board of deans is composed of the deans of faculties—who must be full professors or readers. It has mainly advisory powers in relation to the other two central bodies on all matters relating to education and research. Apart from its role in nominating the *rector magnificus*, its chief function is the granting of doctoral degrees, for which it appoints ad hoc committees of professors and readers.

The relationship between the university council and the executive board is complex. Article 20, section 2, gives the university council

---

[3] The legal structure of the Dutch universities was extensively regulated in the *Wet op het Wetenschappelijk Onderwijs (Staatsblad 1960, no. 559)*. Formal degree requirements are contained in the *Academisch Statuut (Staatsblad 1963, no. 380)*, a royal decree frequently adjusted on the basis of consultations among the universities which take place under the aegis of the Academic Council. This Academic Council is an advisory body composed of twelve Crown appointees, including the chairman and the deputy chairman, and three delegates from each of the universities. In presenting advisory opinions each university delegation, which always includes the *rector magnificus*, casts one vote. The Crown appointees do not take part in formal voting but they may submit individual opinions, as may individual university delegations. A large number of committees operate under the Academic Council. There are ad hoc committees on special problems as well as standing committees for disciplinary fields; faculty councils send three-member delegations to the latter which must always include a full professor or reader in the discipline.

"authority to regulate and administer all matters of the university as a whole insofar as these have not been entrusted by or under this Act to the executive board."

Article 31 charges the executive board with the daily administration of the university and stipulates that it has, as a minimum, the performance of the following tasks: (a) to prepare, publish, and execute the decisions of the university council; (b) to take charge of buildings, efficient financial administration, and all university property; (c) to appoint and dismiss all personnel, and to be in charge of all further personnel management insofar as the authority in such matters has not been reserved in the Higher Education Act by the Crown or the minister;[4] (d) to enter into contracts and represent the university in all other legal actions; (e) to carry out all correspondence on behalf of the university; (f) to supervise permanently all matters which concern the university.

These clauses were the subject of bitter contention at the time the bill was passed in parliament. The left opposition parties demanded that the elected university council be the sole sovereign body in matters of university government, that the executive board should have no independent powers, and that its members should be responsible to, and removable by, the university council through a vote of no confidence, as in a parliamentary system. The minister and the government parties resisted this demand. The executive board was given powers of its own and guaranteed tenure for a fixed period. The board was to keep the university council completely informed, but it was responsible not only to the university council but also to the minister for the proper exercise of its powers. The executive board was given authority, moreover, to suspend decrees of the university council, by referring them to the minister who can quash council decrees on grounds of conflict with the law or the general interest. In extreme cases of neglect or of the illegal functioning of a university or part of it, the Crown may by decree withdraw the powers of a particular university organ and charge another university organ, a group of persons, or even a single person with the exercise of such powers.

FACULTY ORGANIZATION

The chief divisions under the central university organs are the larger faculties (e.g., theology, law, letters, sciences, medicine, economics, and social sciences), often subdivided into subfaculties (e.g., mathematics, physics, psychology, sociology, and languages). Each faculty or subfaculty

[4] Full professors and readers are appointed by royal decree, so that the faculty councils and the executive board can only submit nominations; they cannot make actual appointments. The Crown also prescribes such things as pay scales, grades, and conditions of promotion for all university personnel.

is governed by a faculty council. In these councils, the three separate categories which elect the university council—academic personnel, nonacademic staff, and students—are again represented by direct election, albeit in a somewhat different proportion from the university council. The council members chosen by and from the academic staff must have at least one half of the faculty council seats, the distribution of the remainder of the seats among the three categories to be determined by the faculty rules which must have the approval of the university council. The faculty council elects a dean and a faculty executive, of whom only the dean must be a full professor or reader. The faculty council is responsible for all faculty matters— in particular, the organization and coordination of the teaching and research programs. For the latter, it must consult special education and research committees of which the majority of members must belong to the academic staff. The faculty council appoints examination committees of at least three members from among the academic staff on permanent tenure; at least one member must be a full professor or reader. It institutes committees to prepare nominations for full professorships and readerships; these committees must be composed of full professors and readers but the faculty council may decide to add "other experts." The faculty council votes on the nominations by such a committee, and can change or refuse the nomination. But it must always add the advice of the nomination committee when it refers its decision to the executive board of the university; the committee report, therefore, becomes part of the documentation on which that body and the minister base their final decisions.

"VAKGROEP"—BOARD FOR DIRECT TEACHING AND RESEARCH TASKS

Responsibility for actual teaching and research in a particular academic discipline[5] is entrusted to newly established collective entities, the so-called *vakgroepen*. These bring together academic and nonacademic staff as well as advanced students who work in a given academic field. They are governed by *vakgroep* boards. The act prescribes that all full professors, readers, special lecturers in the discipline, and any other academic staff members in the field who are appointed on permanent tenure are automatically members

[5] The usual study program in the Netherlands consists of a number of disciplines which must be taken in conjunction with the major field of specialization of the student. A faculty or subfaculty council for a given study program has therefore separate chairs and staff for each discipline which forms part of the degree program. In recent years, there has been a tendency to establish more specialized chairs within the major discipline, and to reduce the share of additional subjects. The establishment of *vakgroepen* presupposes a delimitation of the major and minor subjects—and possibly of subspecializations within the major discipline. This causes considerable problems and sometimes open conflict.

of the *vakgroep* board. It further stipulates that representatives of academic staff without permanent tenure, nonacademic staff, and students who contribute to the work of the *vakgroep* may be added to the professional nucleus. The explanatory memorandum accompanying the bill stipulates that the permanent core should at any rate have at least one half of the seats of the *vakgroep* board but the text of the act leaves it to the faculty council to decide on the actual proportion of staff with tenure, on the one hand, and of representatives of staff without tenure, nonacademic staff, and students, on the other hand. The chairman of the *vakgroep* board must be chosen from among the full professors or readers, and he may appeal to the faculty council from any decision of the *vakgroep* board with which he disagrees.

Such were the main clauses of the new act which received royal assent after a difficult passage through parliament on December 9, 1970. Ever since, Dutch universities have been engaged in the arduous process of carrying out its main stipulations. Hundreds of persons have labored in meeting after meeting, to draw up rules at the level of the *vakgroep*, the faculty, and the university. As faculty rules require approval from the university council, and the university rules need the consent of the minister of education, who is in turn advised by a special, high-level committee of experts,[6] this process is still far from ended. The new act is to run for an experimental period of six years, ending on August 31, 1976. At midpoint, it looks as if the universities may be in labor for almost that full period.

Why Such Drastic Legislation in the Netherlands?

It would be difficult to argue that the drastic changes contained in the new act were the result of particularly strong action on the part of militant students. Compared with other countries, Dutch student agitation came relatively late. General student life had been dominated by the *corpora*,

---

[6] Article 56 of the University Government Reorganization Act established a Committee on University Reorganization, called the Polak committee after its present chairman, Professor J. M. Polak of Wageningen. This committee, which has a number of persons with considerable experience in government and business as members, advises the minister and the universities on application of the act. It presents an annual report to parliament and must evaluate its operation before the present legislation runs out in 1976. The committee's main activity so far has been a close scrutiny of the new rules which each university must establish and present to the minister for approval. The committee has adhered strictly to the letter of the law. For this reason, it has become increasingly unpopular with the advocates of "more democracy" in the university who would like to go further than the legal framework of the act permits.

traditionalist recreational associations not dissimilar in style from American fraternities. These associations for the most part propagated the belief that the student body was an elite which should deliberately isolate itself from society at large. Next to the *corpora* there were general associations of students in particular faculties—these might form an ad hoc representative body for the entire student body on the university level. Bodies such as these in turn sent delegates to a national *Nederlandse Studentenraad* which was often consulted by the ministry of education on student matters. Since 1963 a new student unionism had begun to develop which attempted to organize students—particularly those outside the elitist *corpora*—on behalf of particular demands such as student housing, scholarships, and so on. Active members of this *studentenvakbeweging* began to contest student elections at faculty and university level. Its sympathizers eventually captured majorities in a sufficient number of universities to obtain a majority at the level of the *Nederlandse Studentenraad*. But the new student unions soon lost their organizational impetus and coherence, as a belief in direct democracy made them abolish earlier representative procedures in favor of amorphous mass assemblies which in turn fell prey to increasing dissension among different political and ideological factions: reformist democrats, Communists, anarchists, other revolutionary groupings, proponents of a new "underground" culture, and so on.

Looked at in an international perspective, neither student ideologies nor student tactics were particularly original. Ideological writings were little but a somewhat turgid mixture of ideas derived from various new left and "underground" movements in the United States, from the Parisian rhetoric of May 1968, and from German revolutionary writings. The latter were particularly influential at the Catholic University of Nijmegen, the university closest to the German border; the *Studentenvakbeweging* had originated there. For a long time student militancy was purely verbal, and even when militant actions erupted they hardly ever became violent. A critical event occurred in late April 1969 when a small group of militant students at Tilburg tried to press their demands for reforms in the structure of university government by occupying the telephone exchange of that university. The authorities at Tilburg reacted by closing the university. This led to mass occupation there and provoked a bout of similar actions at other universities. But once the initial enthusiasm wore off, disillusionment soon set in among most of the new recruits. Most eventually returned to their studies. Others dropped out and joined a new hippie culture. Only a few became quasi-professional agitators with a career lasting a number of years. Since Dutch student agitation was therefore not particularly original or persistent, its considerable impact must be explained by reference to other factors. These may be found in the particular condition of the Dutch universities, and in the larger changes taking place simultaneously in Dutch society.

Changes in the Structure of the Universities

Traditionally, Dutch universities tended to be the preserve of a small elite, catering for at most 3 percent of any age group. All teaching was in the hands of university professors or readers. There was almost no junior staff beyond an occasional student assistant. There was little planning of curricula or supervision of student progress. Most studies for a final degree took five to seven years at a minimum.

From the early 1960s onwards, the demand for university education soared, as a result of the high postwar birth rate, on the one hand, and growing interest in higher education among the relevant age groups, on the other. The number of full-time students registered rose from 40,000 in 1960 to over 100,000 in 1970. The increased numbers posed an entirely new challenge. Lecture rooms became crowded. Examinations became massive written affairs rather than the traditional oral examination of a single student by the professor in charge of a given field. More formal patterns of study were laid down, with clear specifications on courses to be followed and tests to be taken. New administrative controls by the university and the central government became necessary to cope with the soaring costs of higher education.

To meet growing demands, the cabinet decided deliberately to expand the existing institutions of higher learning—including the subsidized confessional universities—rather than to establish new institutions. The student bodies of the larger ones grew rapidly to between 15,000 and 20,000. A number of new professorships and readerships were established, but there was a much more rapid expansion of junior academic staff, who were ranked and paid according to civil service grades. These new staff members were in an anomalous and frustrating position. No clear criteria were established for their appointment, which rested on little but the personal preference of the holder of the chair. Promotion and permanent tenure usually followed after these staff members had served on temporary appointments for four years.

There was no particular efficiency bar of any kind. Neither a doctorate nor other special academic qualifications were needed, only the nomination of the holder of the chair to which these staff members were attached. At the same time, all formal teaching responsibilities, all setting of detailed examination requirements, and all other matters of university government remained the exclusive right of the full professors or *curatoren* only. In consequence of the expansion of the university, there were rapidly burgeoning staffs with little guarantee for their quality and without effective rights for their members.

As business mounted and numbers increased, the senate as constituted became unmanageable as an institution of university government. Day-to-day management of teaching and research matters at central university level became concentrated in a sort of representative executive body chosen from within it, usually consisting of the *rector magnificus*, the secretary of the senate, the deans of faculties, and a few professors selected at large. At the same time two contrary demands arose for further reforms. On the one hand, impatient professors and civil servants pleaded for a professionalization of university administration by full-time officials. On the other hand, junior staff members demanded a redistribution of authority along more egalitarian lines. Yet both the entrenched position of autonomous professors and the problematical qualifications of junior staff stood in the way of improvement.

Another paradox became visible simultaneously. On the one hand, structure of university government, fundamental requirements for degrees, procedures and criteria of professional appointments, and so on had traditionally been promulgated by explicit national legislation. On the other hand, actual authority within the universities remained with the autonomous holders of chairs and the relatively weak *curatoren*. New initiatives for curricular reform, for shortening academic courses of study, for changing the position of the junior staff were proposed at central government level. But there was no effective follow-up within the universities. The entire situation was ripe for an attack on two flanks—national intervention from above and rebellion from below, with the junior academic staff providing frustrated candidates for easy mobilization under the banner of reform.

The Challenge to Authority in Dutch Society

University reform by itself could conceivably have been settled through the time-honored procedures of reform committees and the introduction of piecemeal changes. Even the confluence of student agitation—largely under foreign influence—and demand for structural reforms—chiefly motivated by internal university friction—might still have had little impact were it not for the more fundamental political and social changes which were taking place simultaneously in Dutch society. The attack on vested interests in the universities coincided with an effective challenge to the tradition of rule by elites in the Netherlands.

The traditional forms of rule in Dutch society were not unlike the practices of university government. Just as the universities were administered by a body of prominent regents (*curatoren*) and the holders of professorial posts, so Dutch rule rested for centuries on a complex system of "offices," rather than on centralized rule by officials, on the one hand, or accountable representatives, on the other. Ministers, members of estates, provincial dignitaries, mayors or aldermen, and judges all tended to rule by inherent right. They often did so in a responsible manner, but they did not hold themselves accountable to the electorate or regard themselves as sub-servient to some central sovereign. Dutch rule tended to be pluralist, "accommodative," collegial, with little trust in concentration of power, or in the will of an electorate.

This system—originating in the structure of the Dutch Republic—had seen the development in the nineteenth and twentieth centuries of a strong system of segmentation along religious and other doctrinal lines, as Cal-vinists, Catholics, and socialists developed strongly organized cultures of their own. This had increased the possibility of mass participation, and introduced a new element of modern organizational life. Yet it did not supplant the older pluralism; in fact, it reinforced it as every culture sought to make sure of its "inherent and sovereign right" to settle its own affairs. The system retained its abhorrence of unified power, and preference for "accommodative" styles at the top, with a free hand for a plurality of leaders in their relations to one another and to their own followers. Elaborate rule by committee, sharing of power, carefully circumscribed regulation of com-mon affairs with full preservation of the rights of autonomous cultures were the most characteristic feature of Dutch social life.[7] It was this system which made it possible to have both national legislation in university matters and total dependence on central government financing—even of the private religious universities—while at the same time the autonomy of the universi-ties in general, and of individual professors within them, was fully respected.

In recent years, however, this long-established and apparently stable system has come under great strain through a combination of factors.

The Change in Religious Cultures

Perhaps the single most important change has been the fundamental reorientation of the leadership of the churches—the Catholic church above all, but the Protestant churches as well. The churches had long been inward looking; their chief preoccupation was with sin, salvation, and eternity. In worldly life they were well satisfied to keep the faithful together through a

---

[7] For an analysis of the traditional structure of Dutch politics, see Hans Daalder, "The Netherlands: Opposition in a Segmented Society," in Robert A. Dahl (ed.), *Political Opposition in Western Democracies* (New Haven: Yale University Press, 1966), pp. 188–236, and Arend Lijphart, *The Politics of Accommodation: Pluralism and Democracy in The Netherlands* (Berkeley: University of California Press, 1968).

system of strong social control. As Catholics and fundamentalist Protestants encompassed more than half of Dutch society, the religious cultures were the natural props of a stable social order. Socialists and liberals knew themselves to be minority movements which could only hope for a role in government if the religious parties were willing to enter into a coalition with them. This forced them into sober and moderate positions.

In recent years, however, revolutionary changes have occurred in the outlook of clergy and laity alike. A desire to break out of their isolation, to bring the lessons of the gospel to this world, to intervene actively in its structure and operation, to concern oneself with man's immediate condition and not only his ultimate destiny, came to replace the formerly conservative outlook of many of the religious leaders. The religious universities tended to be the center of this movement, with students, lecturers, and some individual professors forming its vanguard. As a result, the tight unity of the religious cultures was broken. Many of the new evangelical radicals were as confident of their newly won insights as they had once been of theological dogma. Others showed no such certainty, and split into moderate reformers and fundamentalist keepers of the old faith. Dissension among the leaders made the religious cultures lose their monolithic hold. The masses began to waver between conservative reaction, intellectual disorientation, and growing indifference. In three successive elections the total strength of the three larger religious parties declined from 49.2 percent of the national vote in 1963 to 31.3 percent in 1972.

THE EMERGENCE OF THE SOCIALIST "NEW LEFT"

The disarray of the religious cultures coincided with considerable changes in the socialist left. In the postwar decades the socialist movement had steered a pragmatic course, its leaders being absorbed in practical action at central or local government levels. This mode of action proved insufficiently inspiring for a new political generation, once Vietnam destroyed confidence in Western supremacy. The success of postwar reconstruction policies made economic welfare issues a matter of secondary concern—or even a negative item in the romantic revulsion against a hedonistic society which destroyed the environment in pursuit of materialistic values. "New left" forces, in which students and young academic staff members were again particularly prominent, set out to capture leading positions in the Labor party. They possessed strong resources: ideological fervor, articulateness, and ample free time—the latter a rare resource in a country where the few professional politicians were usually occupied with political work in local or central government, and where other citizens were very lukewarm about politics.

THE DEMAND FOR DEMOCRATIZATION

Both the socialist new left forces and the new religious radicals began in an emphatic manner to pose challenges to the existing political regime. Instead of the older accommodative style of the elite at the top, they demanded direct participatory democracy from the base. They challenged the tradition of coalition politics by demanding opportunities for direct electoral choice. Many campaigned for the introduction of a system of a directly elected prime minister or elected mayors. All desired a reorientation of the party system in such a manner that mutually exclusive groups would contend against one another for a direct electoral mandate. They not only became active in existing institutional channels, but they also had recourse on numerous occasions to the tactics of direct action.

These new developments coincided with a rather fundamental change in the mass media. Both newspapers and wireless networks had traditionally been closely allied with particular political and religious groups. These ties were increasingly severed, however, as the social cohesion of these groups declined, as the economics of newspaper production led to mergers and less "exclusivist" newspapers, and as television began to break up the fairly closed communication networks which had existed previously. A new type of yellow press—and somewhat comparable television broadcasting—emerged. At the same time, the socialist and religious organs tended to move increasingly towards the left. There were three causes for this. The more innovative intellectual movements were oriented towards the left. The media were to a considerable extent—and television almost exclusively—in the hands of younger journalists who shared the outlook of the newer generation. These new elements possessed color and an air of conviction, unlike the more prosaic representatives of intricate and incrementalist rule.

THE REACTION OF THE OLDER ELITES

The Dutch political elites were confronted by a series of unwonted challenges. They faced a large number of groups employing the tactics of direct action which were magnified by radio and television coverage. Television cameras exposed political leaders to new forms of direct access, whereas in the past they had conducted their business in relatively sheltered committees. They faced, moreover, an increasingly volatile electorate. These new developments undermined the tight organizational structures of Dutch society, and made politics less calculable. This caused considerable uncertainty within the elite and as a result accentuated electoral instability. As long as strong institutional structures had given the older elites a secure base, they could afford to greet such challenges with disdain. When these crumbled—or were thought to crumble—they acted diffidently in the face of the demands of the "new democracy." [8]

The Universities as a Microcosm of Dutch Society

The revolutionary changes in Dutch university government since 1969 may be viewed as a process internal to the universities, where an effective onslaught on an existing elite has occurred; this process in its turn should be seen as part of the larger changes in society.

The demands for university reform which were put forward by students and members of the lower ranks of the teaching staff—separately or in coalition—closely resembled demands for participatory democracy expressed elsewhere. They ranged from a minimum of representation for students and teachers in existing governing bodies to the introduction of "one man–one vote" systems and government by general assembly. The first effective challenges took place in the religious universities, notably the Catholic institutions at Tilburg and Nijmegen. But in May 1969 they spread like wildfire from one university campus to another when agitating students confronted senates and *curatoren* with ultimata. These demands were often accompanied by flamboyant but mainly symbolic occupations of university buildings. The initiative came from small minorities, but the

[8] This brief sketch of changes in Dutch society is, of course, far from exhaustive. A fuller analysis would deal with such diverse phenomena as conflict over the monarchy in 1964 and 1965 as a result of two unexpected royal marriages; the rise and fall of the Provo movement; the rapid entry of new parties into parliament, such as the Peasant party (1963), Democrats '66 (1967), the Religious Radicals (PPR, 1968), and Democratic Socialists '70 (1971). Such an analysis would also deal with the slow countergrowth of fundamentalist Calvinist and Catholic movements; two traumatic *renversements des alliances* among the main parties of the traditionally dominant system and their common decline; the hitherto unproductive attempts to merge parties of the left and the religious center; the attempt to attract a new mass base on the part of the Liberal party; a debate on the merits of economic growth; demographic developments; increasing tensions between different groups of society such as employers and workers or young and old; the erosion of institutionalized social organizations by tactics of direct action, and so on. For the present selection, I regard as most important: the growing ability and lack of "calculability" of the system; the leftward shift of some of the more articulate religious and socialist sectors of society; the attack on the legitimacy of existing institutions in the name of the "new democracy"; the increasing political role of the media; the uncertainty and possibly greater strain and more rapid erosion of political elites; and the greater prominence of youth.

The instability of the political elite is vividly illustrated by the rapid turnover in the Ministry of Education: the Catholic Dr. Veringa was followed by a Democratic Socialist '70 minister (1971–1972), a Christian-Historical minister (1972–1973), and a Labor minister (May 1973 to the present), who in practice leaves matters of university government to his undersecretary, Dr. G. Klein, a professor of electrical engineering, who was active in "new left" politics.

exhilaration of sentiment and romanticism of outlook soon led to enthu-
siastic participation by larger numbers.

The demands of the students did not meet with a coherent front of the
teaching staff or with consistent attitudes on the part of *curatoren* or even
the minister. The *curatoren* wavered between stern measures and con-
ciliatoriness, giving little guidance to an equally uncertain academic staff.
The latter was itself divided in more than one way. There was a considerable chasm between the full professors and younger staff, since the latter had
no direct responsibility and could mainly gain from such changes as were
likely to be introduced. Individual professors, departments, and faculties
were accustomed to operate on their own. They often averted their eyes
from trouble elsewhere, believing that they could weather the storm better
if they worked out their own solutions. Thus the traditional aloofness and
autonomy of Dutch university life prevented the development of strong
links of solidarity within any given university, or among universities.

For these reasons university reform was very diffuse from the outset.
Curatoren and senates agreed in principle to some form of partnership with
junior academic staff members, representatives of the nonacademic staff, and
student leaders, by admitting them to governing bodies as members or
observers, and by establishing committees to look into the need for further
structural reform. At the same time, individual faculties, departments, and
professors—and even some university institutions as a whole—went further,
in some instances yielding authority to general assemblies in which all
individuals—professors, junior lecturers, students, secretaries, and porters
—could cast an equal vote on all matters.

Such developments led to curious realignments within the universities.
Two vague blocs were formed. The first consisted of once sturdy proponents
of the established order which suddenly became apprehensive and joined
with outright protagonists of democratic reform to plead for far-reaching
concessions to militant students. The other comprised the outspoken
traditionalists, and a number of erstwhile reformers who had earlier pleaded
unsuccessfully for fundamental reorganization of the universities but who
now refused to jump into the dark under duress and intimidation. The
former spoke of the need for democracy and of a new social role for the
universities, the latter pointed to the dangers to academic freedom and
intellectual standards.

A series of lengthy struggles followed. Upon these student agitators,
those junior academic staff members in coalition with them, university
authorities, and individual professors brought very different resources to
bear. If the latter had the backing of an admittedly crumbling legal
authority, the former had the precious resources of the absence of direct
responsibility and of ample free time. Eventually, many university authorities began to yield, possibly in the hope of preserving good personal relations
with opposite partners, or perhaps simply to get out of the wrangle of interminable meetings which interfered with their normal work—and which in

some cases began to threaten their health as much as their happiness. Occasionally, there may have been deliberate ambiguity. Many of the *curatoren* were relatively old men who knew that they were not likely to return to administrative office under a new university regime. They may have offered token concessions to buy time. They may have done so with more conviction because they expected that the cabinet would eventually have to step in anyhow to impose some degree of order in an increasingly chaotic situation.

In the larger Dutch society, student demands for university reform fell on fairly favorable soil. Although there was some popular revulsion against too militant student actions—notably, the occupation in May 1969 of the *Maagdenhuis*, the administrative center of the University of Amsterdam— student actions received considerable publicity and often a sympathetic press. Paradoxically, student activists benefited from two seemingly contradictory images: they were both an elite and underdogs. Society had long been tolerant about student frolics, such as traditional initiation rites. So why not applaud students when their antics now concerned more serious matters such as university reform or a reorientation of an unworldly university enclave towards active involvement with a changing world? In a struggle between students and professors, the latter could easily be pictured as the defenders of authoritarian privileges. The expansion in their number had whittled down the strong prestige which university professors had carried in less volatile days. And mutual denunciation and dissension did further damage to their status.

Differential access to the new media may have been a further factor. Student activism provided more news, and students knew better how to exploit the strategic weapon of publicity. When the universities suddenly became a continuous source of dramatic news, some newspapers and radio and television networks recruited student activists as reporters. Professors, however, had traditionally conducted university affairs in confidentiality, and they continued to regard the activities of the news media as improper intrusions into the internal affairs of the universities. They put their trust in traditional procedures and regulations, and often hesitated to bring conflicts into the open for fear the main effect would be the disruption of their immediate environment.

The Intervention of the Central Government

The rapid and disorderly flow of events in the universities presented the political parties with a difficult dilemma. Articulate spokesmen in favor of university reform—notably, young members of the academic staff—were often as active in political parties as they were in their own universities.

Youth in the Netherlands had generally achieved greater prominence and visibility, and the prospective lowering of the voting age from twenty-one to eighteen promised to augment their voting power. Public opinion polls began to show a marked shift of younger voters towards the left. This concerned the religious parties—the main prospective losers—as much as the left parties which stood to gain from this trend. The cabinet could not avoid seeing a rapid erosion of the existing legal constitution of the universities. It was confronted by demands from the left for replacement of the existing university law by a blanket provision which would permit every sort of democratic experiment.

The minister eventually stepped in. On June 27, 1969, he presented a memorandum (*Nota Bestuurshervorming van de Universiteiten en Hogescholen*) to parliament in which he outlined a number of principles for the reform of university government. It would be necessary, so read the memorandum,[9] to insure the participation of all members of the university community in university decision making, and to see to it that the university also fulfilled the task—ascribed to it in Article 2 of the Higher Education Act of 1960—of promoting a sense of social responsibility. Hence, each unit of the university should be as autonomous as possible. Professors, junior academic staff, nonacademic staff, students, and representatives of society at large should henceforth jointly decide on university matters, though not necessarily in arithmetically equal proportions at every level of university government.

The minister agreed that direct democracy might be an ideal form of making decisions in the smallest unit, and that general university assemblies could serve a useful function for purposes of discussion and information, but actual university government could be based only on the principle of representative democracy. New organs of university government should not follow the principle of "one man–one vote." This principle, argued Dr. Veringa, was purely formal and schematic and implied that the university was a mere sum of individuals, and not an organization of persons and groups, each of which had its own place, task, and responsibility. Democratic accountability should be insured by public meetings of representative organs and by public access to all documents, except those which would involve personal interests. The old division between *curatoren* and the senate should be replaced by a new undivided university administration which would be responsible for the whole field of education, research, and administration. Authority at the top should be divided among a university council and an executive board composed of full-time experienced administrators, chosen partly from inside, partly from outside the university. The board should have powers of its own on certain matters and should share powers in other

9 See *Handelingen van de Tweede Kamer der Staten-Generaal, zitting 1968–1969,* no. 10194, 2, for the full text of this memorandum. The *Handelingen* contain the parliamentary records of the *Tweede Kamer* (lower house) and the *Eerste Kamer* (upper house).

matters—notably in those involving the budget, planning, and general university government—with the university council. At the same time it would be important to work for greater unity of the academic corps by diminishing the distinction between full professors and other ranks. Finally, the memorandum laid out a schedule by which reforms could be introduced in phases.

Following the presentation of this memorandum, the education committee of the lower house held a number of public hearings on October 8, 10, and 23, 1969, and the house extensively debated the situation in the universities during the four-day debates on the budget of the ministry of education in November 1969. On February 17, 1970, the minister promulgated a draft of a bill embodying his views. This was followed on April 27, 1970, by the introduction in parliament of the bill itself.[10] An elaborate written exchange[11] took place between the minister and the lower house in preparation for the public debates. These ran from September 22 to 24— with the relationship of the executive board and the university council and the amount of freedom for further experimentation beyond the framework of the bill providing the chief bones of contention. The lower house eventually passed the bill by 64 votes to 44, and the upper house did the same on December 8 by 51 votes against 16.[12] The bill received royal assent the following day, and it became the basic law of university government for the next five and a half years. The left opposition parties had voted against the bill in the lower house on the ground that they deemed it insufficiently democratic.

The University Government Reorganization Act at Work

The application of the new law began in 1971, when the period of most acute conflict in the universities was over. The struggles of 1969 and 1970 had left an atmosphere of weariness, and many prominent protagonists on both sides had withdrawn from active battle. Untold numbers of meetings were necessary at all levels to carry out the act. They attracted little attention beyond the circle of persons most directly concerned. Yet the details of the process were vital, because they concerned nothing less than the establishment of new organs of university government. The discussions were shot through with political controversy, even though they lacked some of the

[10] The text of the bill may be found in the *Handelingen, zitting 1969–1970*, no. 10636 no. 2.
[11] See the reports of the written and oral exchanges, *ibid.*, nos. 5–9.
[12] *Handelingen Tweede Kamer, zitting 1970–1971*, pp. 103–141, 144–199, 207–222; *Handelingen Eerste Kamer, zitting 1970–1971*, pp. 152–178.

color and excitement of the more direct confrontations and struggles of the preceding years.

The application of the law was further complicated by having to start from very different situations. In some places the old legal structures had remained fully effective until the day on which the act came into force. To this day, the traditional structure lingers, notably in faculties such as medicine or science where the new democracy demanded in matters of teaching and research lives uneasily with the hierarchical structures of large clinics and laboratories. In other departments and faculties—and even in certain of the universities—new structures had been worked out independently in ways which went much beyond the provisions of the new law. Here the beneficiaries of the new distribution of power found it undesirable—and those who had reluctantly conceded the new forms found it distasteful and politically hazardous—to bring the new situation into conformity with the University Government Reorganization Act.

The Principles of Parity and of Minimum Guarantees for Academic Staff

In the early days of the struggle in 1969, many university authorities had conceded the principle of parity in representative bodies. This decision—which went beyond the minister's memorandum of the end of June 1969—was based on the assumption that there would be at least five distinct "corps," each of which would be given an equal voice in university affairs: *curatoren*, full professors and readers, the academic staff below these grades, nonacademic personnel, and students. Because *curatoren* went into eclipse soon afterwards, and because professors and lower ranking teachers were merged eventually into the one undivided corps of the academic staff, the number of distinct constituent bodies was in practice reduced to three. If the parity principle were applied, the proportion of the nonacademic staff and of the students in governing councils would each increase automatically from one fifth to one third. The University Government Reorganization Act—though endorsing the principle that there would be three constituent corps only—qualified the full force of the principles of parity, as it descended from the higher organs of university government to the lower levels which were charged with particular teaching programs. It stipulated that the academic staff should have a minimum of one third of the elected members of the university council, at least one half of the seats in the faculty council, and the majority of the seats in the educational and research committees; it gave staff on permanent appointment automatic membership in the *vakgroep* boards and reserved the membership of examination committees to them; it stipulated that each examination committee should include at least one professor or reader; and it required that deans of faculties and chairmen of *vakgroep* boards be chosen from the ranks of full professors or readers only.

Minimum Guarantees as Maximum Claims

In the application of the act, the clear intention of these stipulations was often reversed. Guaranteed minima were often interpreted as maximal limits, so that the representation of the academic staff was reduced to the absolute minimum prescribed in the act. Several factors accounted for this development.

The act was applied from the top down: the university councils were established first, the faculty councils later, the faculty committees and *vakgroep* boards last. As the higher bodies set the more general "laws"— and also had to approve the rules of lower organs—the more powerful position of students and nonacademic staff in the higher bodies was easily extended to lower bodies, occasionally by imposition from above, more often by simple preemption from below.

Academic staff members were often hesitant to press their claims, lest they damage the possibility of good personal relations with student and nonacademic staff and their representatives. The academic staff rarely acted in concert on behalf of its own claims in any university. During the passage of the bill in parliament, the minister had defended the need for a guaranteed minimum in the representation of the academic staff by the argument that "decisions should rest on the authority of those professionally responsible." The argument rested on the premise that the academic corps would vote as one on vital matters. What often happened, however, was the formation of relatively coherent voting coalitions of student representatives and some academic staff members, with the remainder of the academic staff representatives in opposition, and the nonacademic staff representatives in an ambiguous position between them.

This tendency became more marked once partisan groups entered elections in one university after another with the contention that democratic university government should rest on particular views about the social functions of a modern university—views which might be shared by teachers, nonacademic staff, and students alike—rather than on special responsibilities which distinguished teachers from students. The partisan groups were organized across the boundaries of the different constituent corps—unlike other candidates for election who sought votes within their own corps only —and they often showed greater cohesion. Groups of this type often obtained a majority in university councils and faculty councils. Generally, their electoral platform demanded a maximum extension of the democratic principle in university government. In practice, this meant a reduction in the numbers of the academic staff, and in principle an increase in the representation of nonacademic staff and students alike. Usually, however, the latter benefited most.

The position was further complicated by the weak position of the non-academic staff in certain faculties. Especially in the arts and the social sciences, they had too few members to be able to claim more than an occasional seat, and in many instances these staff groups did not even claim seats to which they were entitled. The resulting vacancies could have been allotted to the academic staff, to student representatives, or to both. But, when the guaranteed minima of the act were interpreted as maximal limits for the academic staff, this made it possible to increase student representation. In faculty councils and faculty committees in these faculties, students thus came close to having a majority. At the same time, the potential value of the parity principle was not forgotten. Thus the faculty executives almost automatically came to be composed of representatives of all categories. Although the deans had to be chosen from full professors or readers, junior academic staff and students were also given guaranteed places, so that faculty executives often came to have a majority of relatively young and inexperienced personnel.

The Governing Councils of Departments of Sociology and History

In certain faculties and departments the situation has gone even further. A survey of the governing councils of the departments of sociology in the Netherlands in November 1973 reveals the following picture. In no university do members of the academic staff have more than a bare majority or half of the seats; and in three institutions—Amsterdam, Rotterdam, and Utrecht—they have not even this (see Table 1). In the University of Amsterdam, supreme authority lies in principle with a general assembly, which elects a steering committee; the committee is presided over by a junior staff member without permanent tenure.

A similar experiment in direct democracy undertaken in the Leiden Department of Sociology in 1969 faded out when the general assembly and its executive council eventually withered through lack of student interest. By February 1971 only twelve candidates offered themselves for the twelve places on the department council. Only one of them was a student—a military man on study leave who is alleged to have asked his superiors' permission to stand for election. The general assembly then decided to abolish itself, and after a while the department returned to a structure not dissimilar from that envisaged in the act. Of the six elected members of

TABLE 1. Governing Councils of Departments of Sociology
(Autumn 1973)

University	Number of Members of Academic Staff	Number of Members of Non-Academic Staff	Number of Student Representatives
Leiden	6	2	4
Groningen	11	1	10
Utrecht	7	2	7[a]
Amsterdam[b]	5	1	5
Rotterdam	6	6	6
Free University Amsterdam	6	—	5
Nijmegen	12[c]	3	9
Tilburg	8	2	6[a]

[a] Seats not taken up because of student boycott.

[b] General assembly with special subassemblies for subfields. The figures in the table refer to the executive committee.

[c] Six seats reserved for full professors or readers.

the academic staff, only two have permanent tenure. In two other departments of sociology—Utrecht and Tilburg—students formally boycott existing councils under the pressure of groups of militant students who prefer direct agitation to the representative process.

The situation in the history departments is not very different from that in sociology (see Table 2). In three departments the situation in 1973 was in direct violation of the act: in Groningen, Amsterdam, and Utrecht. In Groningen, seats on the governing council are divided into four categories: six seats for the academic corps elected by specialists in each of six subfields, six student representatives, one member of the nonacademic staff, and five seats at large under a system of one man–one vote. In view of the large number of students, it should come as no surprise that at the last elections four of these seats were won by students and one seat by a member of the academic staff, thus making for a majority of ten students over seven staff members. Formally, the council is in charge of "general policy," with staff members responsible for the "execution" of its decisions. But conflicts are emerging over the demarcation of these nebulous dividing lines.

The Amsterdam history department formally instituted a general assembly, and four subassemblies for subfields; in these, decisions were to be taken on the principle of one man–one vote. These various assemblies have practically died and decisions tend now to be taken in an executive council composed of twelve staff members, twelve students, and two nonacademic staff members. The subfield assemblies must now be converted into *vakgroep* boards and this leads to considerable conflict between the staff and

TABLE 2. Governing Councils of Departments of History
(Autumn 1973)

UNIVERSITY	NUMBER OF MEMBERS OF ACADEMIC STAFF	NUMBER OF MEMBERS OF NON-ACADEMIC STAFF	NUMBER OF STUDENT REPRESENTATIVES
Leiden	8	—	7
Groningen[a]	7	1	10
Utrecht[b]	9	3	9
Amsterdam[c]	12	2	12
Free University Amsterdam	6	—	5
Nijmegen	12[d]	—	12

[a] Actual composition, resulting from voting for six seats reserved for academic staff, six seats reserved for student representatives, one seat reserved for nonacademic staff, five "free seats" elected on a one man–one vote principle.

[b] Ultimate sovereign body: general assembly of all staff (two thirds) and student representatives (one third).

[c] General assembly with special subassemblies for subfields. The figures in the table refer to the executive committee.

[d] Six seats reserved for full professors or readers.

militant students. In Utrecht, the Historical Institute is governed by an institute council of nine members of the academic staff, three members of the nonacademic staff, and nine students. This arrangement conflicts with the act's requirement that the academic staff should have at least one half of the seats. To meet this objection, a formal assembly has been established —composed of all staff members (two thirds) and students (one third)— which meets once a year to endorse decisions of the council of the institute.

A comparison of the departments of history and sociology shows that almost everywhere the academic staff has been reduced to its absolute legal minimum and sometimes well below it. In contrast, student power has been pushed to the maximum limits of the act in practically all places, and in some departments beyond these. History departments have had less strife than sociology departments. The reasons for this are various. Departments of history are very much smaller than departments of sociology and have expanded more gradually. Personal relations between staff and students have remained closer and more friendly and revolutionary students have not attained critical numbers as easily as in sociology departments. History is the older academic discipline. Professional standards are more clearly established. Recruitment for professorships is based on stiffer competition and the successful candidates have more solid achievements. There are also differences in the professional ambitions of students. A history professor is likely to encounter in most of his students future teachers of history—if not archivists. A sociology professor, on the other hand, is frequently confronted by students who, from the secure base of the university, demand social "action" and "revolution," and show little interest in theory or research and little love for books except those which could reinforce a priori beliefs. Standards in the writing of history are more widely shared between professors, junior staff members, and students—whatever their political persuasion or choice of subject. But the situation in a number of history departments remains delicately poised. If conflicts have not raged as fiercely as in sociology, this is not because history departments have had more effective arrangements for governing themselves or greater cohesion of their teaching staff, but because there has been so far less effective challenge.

Appointments Committees and "Vakgroep" Boards: Minimizing the Special Claims of Rank and Tenure

In principle, Article 12, 2 of the University Government Reorganization Act reserved membership on appointments committees for professorships or readerships to full professors and readers, but it also contained the clause that the faculty council might add "other experts." Although the minister had stated explicitly that students or nonacademic staff members could be regarded as experts only if they possessed demonstrable special knowledge in the particular field in which appointment was to be made, many faculty councils chose to give this their own interpretation. Students were held to be experts simply because they had an interest in the selection of good professors. Who could judge better than students whether candidates had pedagogical ability? Student participation in appointments committees, it was argued, would guarantee that proper procedures were followed and that the committees would make their decisions on the basis of merit rather than under the influence of an *esprit de clique*. Because a single student was held to be too isolated—both in the committee and in his relation to his fellow students—the Leiden Faculty of Letters decided in 1971 that as a matter of principle appointments committees should have two advanced students as members. In circumstances such as these, the inclusion of academic staff members below the rank of professor or reader was a foregone conclusion. In some, appointments committees for professorships have as a result not even had a majority of professors or readers. Needless to say, such arrangements have not guaranteed that the criterion of merit would dominate: as future junior colleagues or students, committee members might very well have a personal stake in the appointment or nonappointment of particular persons, for reasons other than academic qualifications.

The act does not regulate the procedure of appointing junior academic staff members. This has made it possible to establish appointments com-

mittees for junior grades in which academic staff members have only half
the number of seats, or even less. One of the history departments recently
established an appointments committee, composed of three students and
three staff members. One candidate was preparing a dissertation on Marcel
Proust; none of the "expert" student judges had heard of Proust.

As for the *vakgroep* boards, the decision to include or not to include
representatives of the academic staff without permanent tenure, of nonacademic staff, and of students was left to the discretion of the faculty councils, although the permanent core of academics with permanent tenure was,
in the minister's view, to carry the chief responsibility. Again, this intention
of the act has often been evaded. Student representatives could qualify on
the ground of "the contribution they made to the work of the *vakgroep*";
this was thought to be true of any student who prepared himself for special
examinations in a given subject. Academic staff without permanent tenure
could be added through elected representatives. Democracy was thought to
require that all should automatically become members of the *vakgroep*
boards. The component of permanent staff members was generally reduced,
on the basis of an incidental reference in the explanatory memorandum
which accompanied the act, to about half the seats in the *vakgroep* boards.
But in the University of Amsterdam the university council went beyond this
in drafting the university rules. Democracy required, in its view, that all
academic staff members, whether on permanent tenure or not, should have
equal rights. Jointly, they were to have half the seats of the *vakgroep* boards;
the remainder of the seats were then to be taken up by students and the nonacademic staff. If the latter were few in number, this could result in an increase of the number of student representatives to almost one half. Not only
on the level of the faculty councils, therefore, but also in the most crucial
activities of the academic staff—in teaching, setting examination requirements, and research—students acquired considerable power. They could
gain the decisive voice if they could unite with only a few members of the
academic staff. It is expected that the minister of education will refuse to
approve this particular clause in the Amsterdam University rules. In the
meantime it has resulted in considerable friction on the academic staff between those who went along and those who resisted. Such wounds do not
heal easily.

The special position of academic staff members on permanent tenure in
the *vakgroep* boards has been used as an argument in many faculties outside
Amsterdam not to establish these professional groups at all. Thus, in none
of the sociology departments mentioned above have *vakgroep* boards been
officially constituted. There is either bitter conflict about this matter or the
faculty councils have avoided touching the issue. The situation in the departments of history is similar. Only one department—in Leiden—has
formally constituted *vakgroep* boards. Their membership comprises an
equal number of academic staff and students.

The Personnel of the Governing Bodies

Different principles and procedures prevail in the selection of personnel for the different bodies:

The larger part of the university council, all faculty councils, and the elected representatives of *vakgroep* boards are elected by and from the different constituent bodies; the usual system is proportional representation, with a single tranferable vote. This encourages the presentation of lists, but leaves individual voters free to express a preference for persons rather than parties.[13]

Executive posts are filled by council election. Thus the university council elects two members of the executive board, and the faculty councils choose the faculty executive and establish all other committees. If a faculty is divided into subfaculties, the different voting groups elect the subfaculty councils and these elect their representatives to the faculty council by simple majority vote.

Membership of some other bodies follows ex officio. Thus the *rector magnificus* is automatically a member of the executive board; the elected deans of faculties automatically form the board of deans; all academic staff members on permanent tenure belong automatically to their *vakgroep* boards.

Finally, certain important positions are filled by appointment by the Crown. The Crown appoints a minimum of one sixth of the members of the university council, the *rector magnificus*, and two members of the executive board. But, in drawing up proposals for such appointments by the Crown, the minister of education is under pressure from many forces. He receives nominations from the elected members of the university council for the Crown appointees to that body. As the number of nominees may be equal to the number of posts to be filled, this procedure can in practice imply cooptation by the sitting members of the university council. The minister has to choose the *rector magnificus* from a list of two nominees presented by the board of deans, and he can do little but choose the top candidate. He has more freedom in the selection of the two Crown members of the executive board of the university. But in this matter, too, university councils have actively pressed their will, by seeking candidates of their own

[13] Certain university groups have asked for the establishment of a system of proportional representation with list voting, arguing that this would make for better relations between candidates, and between voters and council members elected. The Delft School of Technology and Rotterdam have actually adopted this system, which leaves the ranking of candidates to the nominating group rather than to individual voters. In reaction to the practice, other observers have demanded the substitution of indirect election for the present direct elections. They wish to have the university councils selected by the faculty councils and the faculty councils by delegates of the *vakgroepen*.

who are then presented to the minister for appointment, or by expressing a strong preference for one ministerial nominee rather than any other.

These varied and complex procedures create a number of political problems. These include the following:

THE MINIMUM THRESHOLD

The Act prescribes that seats may be filled only if a minimum of 35 percent of all eligible voters of a particular constituent corps cast their votes. Academic and nonacademic staff have usually had turnouts considerably higher than this minimum.[14] The record of students has been more checkered. During the first elections for the university council in 1971, but also in a number of particular faculty elections since then, radical students called a boycott as they deemed the provisions of the University Government Reorganization Act insufficiently democratic. As other students came forward only hesitantly, or not at all, the minimum was not attained and in such cases the student seats on elected bodies were not all filled. Radical students resorted instead to demonstrations; they occupied university buildings when specific demands were not met, and occasionally they sought to intimidate and disrupt public meetings of the elected bodies through mass attendance with banners and even with bullhorns. Elected councils with minimal or no representation of student members have often felt less legitimate because of their absence. Many of the members leaned over backwards to prove by their actions that students had every reason to take their constitutionally provided positions in such friendly organs. In the elections of 1973 for the university councils, radical student groups generally gave up their boycott and systematically put forward candidates for the available seats. They often won such elections by large margins, not least because other student groups remained inactive.

ELECTION BY NOMINATION

The University Government Reorganization Act was based on the assumption that many individuals and groups were anxious to participate in university government. The actual record has tended to belie this assumption. The number of candidates coming forward for the fairly large number of elective places to be filled has tended to be small. The composition of the elected bodies has often depended on accidents of nomination and has not been the result of spirited contests between eager candidates. Small groups

14 The average participation in all elections to university councils was: academic staff, 72.4 percent in 1971 and 66.1 percent in 1973; nonacademic staff, 62.3 percent in 1971 and 51.3 percent in 1973.

which nominate candidates in sufficient numbers can win by default. Elections offer, therefore, little guarantee of representativeness. Nevertheless, they confer definite powers to persons thus fortuitously selected.

THE SELECTION OF OTHER PERSONNEL BY THE ELECTED BODIES

Those who are empowered to designate, or nominate, persons for particular executive office are often markedly influenced by partisan considerations. Groups enjoying majorities in the university councils have used their voting power to nominate the outside persons with whom they are politically sympathetic for appointment by the Crown. Thus they strengthen their voting position in the university council, even beyond the next election. They have similarly tried—often successfully—to reserve the elective positions in the executive board for persons who share their general political and social outlook; they have also sought to resist the appointment of the Crown-designated candidates for the executive board if they do not find them politically congenial. Similar practices have occasionally been employed in the selection of faculty executives and even in the election of deans. Although the dean must be a full professor, his election is by simple majority of the faculty council; this majority need not coincide with the majority of the elected members of the academic staff.

THE SUPERIOR CLAIM OF THE ELECTIVE PRINCIPLE

The legitimate force of the elective principle has been used as an argument to reduce the role of the board of deans as an advisory organ, to proclaim the sovereignty of the university council in all university matters, and to diminish the independent powers of the executive board.

The relationship between university councils which are mainly elected and executive boards which are composed by a complex combination of election, nomination, and appointment, has consequently tended to be somewhat tense and precarious. They must collaborate since they often have concurrent powers. The councils claim constitutional supremacy, the boards special responsibilities. But the boards may not be internally homogeneous, and they have often proved to be somewhat timid and ambivalent, whenever they anticipate possible trouble.

THE LACK OF CONTINUITY OF PERSONNEL

The elected councils have met with two further difficulties. Their personnel has been almost entirely new, and in the few years of their functioning there has been little continuity even among the elected academic staff members who are on permanent tenure in the university. Therefore, members often have little intimate knowledge of past events, nor are they directly responsible for the future consequences of their decisions. Understandably, they have often wavered between deliberate indecision and sudden flurries of uneasy decision making.

Attendance has been irregular. The making of decisions has therefore often been assured only by the requirement of a small quorum. This means in practice that there has been no definite guarantee of effective continuity of personnel in any given council, even from one meeting to another.[15]

Faculty Councils, Teaching, and Examination Responsibilities

In the relationship between the newly established faculty councils and the day-to-day teaching activities of the academic staff, two conflicting trends are emerging. On the one hand, there is an increasing separation between the two. In the faculties before 1969, the automatic membership of all full professors guaranteed a direct link between faculty decision and immediate teaching responsibilities. Such a link no longer exists. There is, therefore, no continuous communication among different fields. Many staff members increasingly concentrate only on their respective fields, and show little interest beyond them. Faculty councils and teaching staffs are thus becoming more remote from each other. On the other hand, some very active faculty councils demand comprehensive curricular reforms, as well as changes in particular fields. In these circumstances a fundamental conflict is emerging about the ultimate responsibility for power over teaching and examinations.

The demands of radical council members have different sources. Some simply have to do with instruction: students may want fewer lectures and more seminars and ad hoc projects as part of their training. Others have to do with questions of the amount of work: students may wish for changes in examination requirements—usually a lowering, sometimes a shift, in emphasis. Faculty councils sometimes use their power to settle old accounts:

---

15 Absenteeism in the university council at the University of Leiden was 20 percent during its first ten meetings, 25 percent during the following ten meetings, and 29 percent during the remaining twenty meetings before the council dissolved. Since the original quorum of 27 out of 40 members was often not reached when important decisions had to be taken, the quorum requirement was lowered to 21. A majority of 11 members can therefore make a valid decision. This arrangement has been criticized by the member of the executive board, Professor P. Th. Oosterhoff, in an address at the opening of the academic year, September 3, 1973: *Terugblik op het afgeopen academiejaar* (Leiden: Leidsch Universiteits-Fonds, 1973), pp. 17–18.

the formerly complete autonomy of individual professors occasionally led to idiosyncratic and possibly unjust situations which can now be effectively challenged. Often the demand for reform is motivated by political concerns. Certain staff members and students on the faculty council somtimes seek a fundamental political reorientation, demanding the elimination of less fashionable parts from the curriculum, and the substitution of more politically pertinent fields, topics, or reading lists.

These issues are raised in a complex legal setting. In 1960 new legislation charged the faculties with the "arrangement and proper progress of instruction." This phrase was held to empower existing faculties to override, if necessary, the special authority of the holders of individual chairs in setting requirements for particular fields. This was done on the assumption that the assembly of the full professors of an individual faculty was likely to exercise better and fairer judgment than an interested professor in a particular field making a decision without regard for the views of his peers. Such authority was in practice used only sparingly and only in answer to evident abuse. The new University Government Reorganization Act transferred most powers of the previous faculty meetings to the new faculty councils, without at the same time transmitting the guarantees of academic learning and experience which the earlier faculties had possessed. It abolished the relevant article of the Higher Education Act and substituted a new clause, which entrusted the faculty council with "the organization and coordination of teaching and research" in the fields belonging to that faculty. It also laid down that the degree programs in particular fields were to be submitted to interuniversity committees, which operate under the aegis of the interuniversity Academic Council. Faculties continue to be bound, moreover, to the general framework of the academic statute which lays down which subjects must be studied for particular degrees. Therefore, the law reasoned—as does Dutch educational organization, in general—in terms of collective authority and requirements, rather than of the individual discretion of teacher or students. Moreover, it replaced the earlier dual relationship of faculty and full professor by a quadripartite relationship of faculty council, *vakgroep*, individual teacher, and interuniversity committees of the Academic Council. It gave no clear indication for the resolution of conflicting claims about the modes and content of teaching and examinations.

Use or Misuse of the Powers of Faculty Councils

Reforming elements in certain faculty councils have resorted to a number of different procedures to impose their will on particular groups of teachers. The easiest way has been to set definite limits on the teaching and reading load in a particular field, through some quasi-objective standards such as number of lecture hours, total pages to be read, and so on. A more drastic weapon has been interference with content: specific *vakgroepen* were obliged to consult students about reading lists, and to accept their demands in whole or in part.[16] In more extreme cases, notably in faculties of social sciences, faculty councils have gone further and fashioned *vakgroepen* according to their own taste. Article 17 of the act, which makes the faculty councils responsible for the establishment of *vakgroepen*, has thus been interpreted as providing a mandate for the complete reallocation of personnel and responsibilities irrespective of scholarly qualifications and disciplinary specialization. In other cases, councils have refused to create *vakgroepen* altogether, thus substituting their own power for that of professional specialists. When the latter resisted, the councils have sidestepped them by a combination of further measures—for example, by charging a few cooperative teachers with sole authority to examine in that particular field, by packing examination committees with sympathetic staff members who would grant degrees against the will of professors or *vakgroepen*,[17] and by using their powers of appointment for junior staff as well as their nomination rights for professorships and readerships to change the physiognomy of a faculty. When faced with such action, some academic staff members have appealed to higher authority within their university, or to the committees of the interuniversity Academic Council to resist these developments. They have, however, met with little immediate response. Executive boards have argued that they have no authority in particular teaching matters. The Academic Council also has only consultative powers and, furthermore, is undergoing a thorough transformation of membership. Initially, the various sections of the Academic Council were thought to be the repositories of expertise in a special discipline. When faced with unwelcome opinions, faculty councils have increasingly tried to replace professional members with

---

16 In the case of the Amsterdam political science faculty, an ad hoc committee under the chairmanship of Professor A. de Froe decided that faculty councils were not authorized to prescribe lists of books for students as this would mean the substitution of the authority of nonexperts for that of professional specialists in a given field. A faculty council, according to the de Froe committee, could intervene only if there were objective proof that no competent professor or *vakgroep* board could reasonably have made up such a reading list or examination requirements. For the text of this verdict, see *Universiteit en Hogeschool*, XIX, January 1973, 195–201. Professor de Froe himself was later appointed *rector magnificus* in the University of Amsterdam. As a member of the university's executive board, he was responsible for transmitting to Professor Daudt and his colleagues the order of February 6, 1973, instructing him to return to his duties.

17 At the University of Groningen, four professors of sociology have for two years refused to sign academic diplomas because they regard the new study programs as incompatible with professional standards. After considerable conflict, they were permitted to offer a rival degree program of their own so that there are now two kinds of sociology degree in that university. A similar conflict in the University of Groningen faculty of economics caused all professors and readers to refuse to sign diplomas when the majority of the faculty council decided to eliminate major parts of the discipline. This conflict was eventually solved by a compromise.

their own closely instructed delegates, who now may be students, in addition to academic staff members. Only a few hardy persons have continued their struggles against these heavy odds. But, in many cases, those once professionally responsible have simply conceded defeat; they have gone along with the new regime or withdrawn from all activity except official teaching assignments.

The Appointment of Academic Staff

The most basic problem of academic appointments had been the complete lack of rights of the junior academic staff coupled with the absence of clear criteria for their appointment. The University Government Reorganization Act considerably improved the first of these conditions. The substitution of *vakgroep* boards for the monopoly of the professor gave the academic staff below the rank of professor or reader independent responsibility and a share in collective decision making. This provided the possibility of a wider spread of academic capacities and responsibilities, and left less scope for the possible idiosyncrasies of the professor who had formerly enjoyed a monopolistic position. However, the new act failed to remedy another fault. The staffs of Dutch universities fall in principle under civil service regulations which require appointment to permanent tenure of temporary staff after a stipulated number of years—normally, four years for academic staff. Under the old structure the junior academic staff were fully dependent on the holder of the chair to which they were attached. Professors could nominate their assistants for permanent appointment or propose a termination of their contract at will, without having to offer substantial proof of their academic qualities.

The new democracy has tended to strengthen the demand of junior staff for permanent tenure, not least because the new University Government Reorganization Act gave staff members on permanent appointment a special position. The replacement of the powers of the holder of the professorial chair by those of the *vakgroep* board extended the responsiblities for the academic ranks below professors and readers and brought a new group into decisions on tenure and promotion; it did nothing, however, to provide for new guarantees of academic quality. In many *vakgroep* boards only a tiny minority of staff members have a doctorate. As time served in temporary appointments rather than proven intellectual excellence is generally the basis for granting tenure, the special place which the act assigned to staff members on permanent tenure in *vakgroep* boards and in examination committees does not offer very firm assurance on this matter. The effect of this is even more pronounced when the permanent staff is given only a marginal majority over other representatives in the *vakgroep* boards.

The government is not unaware of this problem, and new rules for academic careers are being drawn up centrally. But in the meantime the permanent staffing of Dutch universities without clear criteria of qualification goes on. It carries with it two possible dangers. Intellectual quality may sink while responsibilities become more dispersed; this may mean a mortgage on the future of the university which will last a generation or more. And for a government in search of economies this very circumstance threatens to become an alibi to engage in a drastic reorganization of the pattern of university teaching. Occasionally, one hears pleas for the separation of responsibilities for research and teaching. The lower academic ranks would then be destined for persons who are exclusively teachers employed full time and who would work mainly in the junior years much like secondary school teachers. Such a reform might lead to a fundamental degradation of academic life, both in the kinds of teaching offered in different grades and in the kinds of persons recruited.

The Political Element in Appointments

As elsewhere in the Western world, there are vociferous demands in the Netherlands for a "politicization" of the university. These demands, often expressed openly, are sometimes dressed in the garb of the need for "new scientific approaches." As a result, political criteria have begun to enter into appointments, in at least three different ways. There is first the argument of "balance." Whether as a result of outside pressure or internal anticipation, certain vakgroepen go out of their way to find candidates who represent particular ideologies. One may now find occasional advertisements by a school of education demanding "an expert on Marxist economics" or find a department of sociology seeking a "critical sociologist"—the reference presumably being to the ideological orientation of the "Frankfurt school," without the guarantee of the intellectual qualities of some of the leaders of that group in the past. When demands for such appointments are resisted, their advocates employ the argument of "pluralism" to press candidates of their own particular brand. It is necessary, so the standard argument goes, to have a proper "ideological spread" of staff and anyone who resists such views is said not to live up to the ideal of democratic tolerance.[18] There is, secondly,

---

[18] The political science department in Nijmegen has a ten-member Sectieraad, composed of five students and five staff members. This body decided in April 1973, by a vote of the five students and one staff member against the four other staff members, to nominate a radical student as a teacher in the department, although he had not at that time yet completed his studies in Amsterdam. In arriving at this decision, they passed over other candidates who had finished their university studies. Professor Andries Hoogerwerf appealed to the Nijmegen executive board not to honor this vote and to refuse to make the requested appointment as it was clearly based on other than

the reverse mechanism of self-protective discrimination: *vakgroepen* may avoid the appointment of certain persons for fear they may create political trouble. Finally, there is an implicit tendency towards self-censorship: in drawing up lists of candidates for professorships, certain qualified persons may be ruled out in committee beforehand because the committee does not deem their appointment prudent, given the conditions of the modern university. The presence of politically committed student members can appointments committees reinforces this readiness to engage in a delicate calculation based on other than scientific and scholarly criteria.

The Great Withdrawal

The trends I have described are still far from universal in Dutch universities. They are found most frequently in the faculties of social sciences and theology, to some extent in faculties of law and letters, much less so in the more professionally oriented faculties of sciences and medicine. There standards seem clear. The influence of vocational bodies is stronger and organizational restrictions are greater. Student power is blunted by the presence of a large nonacademic staff, and student demands are usually less dominated by political ideologies. There are, moreover, wide variations from group to group in a given field, through local circumstances or personal factors.

At the same time, there is a growing sense of insecurity in parts of the

---

scientific criteria. The simple fact of his appeal precipitated a series of militant actions by radical students who for a time occupied nine university institutes and the university's telephone exchange. The executive board of the university at one time demanded that the department first establish formal *vakgroep* boards so that it could receive advice from a legally established professional group. Students successfully fought this decision, and continued to occupy the Institute of Political Science for 106 days. The occupation was terminated only when the student candidate was appointed for attachment to the chair of another professor—not Professor Hoogerwerf's and only for a trial year—after which his contract would be reviewed on the basis of his actual performance.

A few months later the student representatives in the *Sectieraad* submitted a document on the future of the department. According to this document, it would be necessary to replace "bourgeois" political science by a Marxist program of study which should have three phases: in the first period of "deideologization," students should be made conscious of their bourgeois prejudices and their home-fostered faith in bourgeois science should be shown to be unjustified. In the second phase, they should be made conscious of issues which would give a direct insight into actual social conditions by, for example, a study of student activism, anti-imperialism, political philosophy, economic realities, and so on. In the third phase, the artificial divisions between theory and "praxis" should be bridged in a program which was still to be elaborated. Present conditions in the department would make it impossible to establish such a curriculum immediately, but all future arrangements should be regarded as a step towards its full implementation. See "Socialistische Studentenbond Politikologie," *Over Maatschappij, Wetenschap en Politikologie* (Xeroxed document, November 1973).

university. Traditional conceptions of academic roles—in the relations between professors and junior colleagues and between academic staff and
students—are no longer accepted. Admittedly, these relations sometimes
assumed an arbitrary character in the past through the monopolistic position of the single professor. But their character was generally well understood. Now new relations must be worked out in legally ambiguous settings.
This causes considerable stress. Members of the academic staff may fall out
among themselves over student demands. Partisan elections may align them
formally in antagonistic camps. There is an extensive mixing of roles. Professors and students who meet one day in class or in examinations may
encounter one another next day in council rooms for a wrangle on matters
of deep professional concern. Such ambiguous relations require a large investment in time and tact and they may eventually impose a heavy toll. To
preserve harmony, academic staff members may assent to decisions in which
they do not really believe. Once this becomes a regular occurrence, they
sometimes experience a severe loss of self-respect. A false tone of jocularity
creeps in, a pose of good fellowship not really felt. A mask of optimism may
be worn in public which is only taken off in furtive meetings with like-
minded colleagues, or in the privacy of a suffering family at home.

Eventually, such artificial participation tends to give way to deliberate
avoidance. The transfer of authority from appointed to effective office
effected by the act has permitted a flight away from formal responsibility.
The tendency of academics to withdraw into their own specialized world is
therefore aggravated by the new university reforms, for what was once an
inclination only now becomes escape, which is accompanied by a curious
mixture of resentment and a sense of guilt. Although those who withdraw
deliberately refuse to avail themselves of the opportunities for election to
the new councils, they often still resent the legal mandate and the "political"
authority which such organs represent. Therefore, open entry does not lead
to willing participation, nor does election confer effective legitimacy.

The "New Democracy" and the "New Management"

The organizational revolution in the Dutch universities has occurred at
a time when they face other important structural problems of finance, of
curricular reform, and of a reorientation of science policy above all.

The budget of the ministry of education increased dramatically since
1960—from 1,420,633,000 D.fls. in 1960 to 6,707,422,000 in 1970 to
10,066,828,000 in 1973, that is, 15.4 percent, 23.2 percent, and 23.4 percent
respectively of the total government budget. The share of the higher edu-

cational division within it grew even more—from 8.9 percent of all educational expenditures in 1955, to 13.4 percent in 1960, 15.9 percent in 1965, and 18.9 percent in 1970. Competing demands from other departments, as well as from other sections of the ministry itself, led to a decision that expenditures on higher education should not continue to increase. Two possible measures were considered: these were to raise revenue by an increase in tuition fees and to curtail total expenditures.

The center-right Biesheuvel cabinet formed in 1971 decided to raise tuition fees from 200 to 1,000 D.fls., that is, from some U.S. $80 per annum to about U.S. $400 at 1973 exchange rates. In 1972 legislation to this effect passed in both houses of parliament—with considerable opposition in the upper house. Student activists called for an immediate boycott against payment of tuition fees. This action ultimately proved successful, not least because the law had certain technical defects, and because the university councils and executive boards generally went on record against the law and applied it only halfheartedly. The issue of tuition fees did much to reactivate and solidify the radical student movement; it weakened the authority of the executive baords; and it complicated relations between the ministry and the universities. In 1973 a new left-oriented cabinet decided to reduce tuition fees by half, without so far having appeased the boycotters.[19]

The control of expenditures was less controversial. The Biesheuvel cabinet simply froze the larger part of planned expansion of staff and university buildings from 1971, which necessitated limits on admission into particular fields of study. At the same time most parties began to agree on the need for basic reforms in the university structure, in the field of degree programs as well as in the control of scientific research.

Both financial and educational considerations eventually convinced most observers that the prolonged period of academic study traditionally prevailing in the Netherlands should be abandoned. Instead, a split was envisaged between a shorter first-degree program and later more specialized graduate training. During the first year, the ability of students to follow an academic course of study successfully would be tested; they would be allowed to repeat this year once in the event of failure. Then a three-year program would lead to a "doctorandus" degree. Afterwards, only a few carefully selected students would continue with a fundamental research training at

[19] The number of students at Dutch universities in the autumn of 1973 was estimated at slightly under 110,000. Only 53,090 were registered by November 20 and of these 31,125 had been registered automatically as part of student scholarship procedures, so that in fact only some 22,000 students had independently paid tuition fees. The actual payment had been set at 500 guilders pending the repeal of the 1,000 guilder tuition charge which the minister has proposed to parliament and which was to be decided only in February 1974. At the equivalent period in 1972 the number of registered students had been 86,815. See *Nieuwe Rotterdamse Courant-Algemeen Handelsblad*, December 7, 1973.

master's or doctoral level. These new plans, called the "Posthumus" reforms —after their initiator, the late Professor K. Posthumus—present much fuel for a new conflagration in the universities. Student radicals, as well as teachers of both the left and more traditionalist circles, have denounced the reforms as an attempt to force the university into a straitjacket. They proclaim, instead, that the university should remain a place for unfettered academic inquiry, with unlimited entry for all qualified persons.

In addition to these new reforms, a complex system of planning is being established which also looks into the possibilities of a division of labor among the universities. Many new committees are being formed, numerous discussion papers are being prepared, and information is being sought on very diverse points. At the same time new curricula must be drawn up. This will stir up further controversy as it will touch many vested interests, old and new alike.

The reforms are further complicated by the desire of the government to achieve a closer integration between the universities and many other existing institutions of higher education, such as teacher training colleges, schools of social work, technical colleges, and so on. This will require many new institutional provisions, and will impose additional burdens on overworked councils and university bureaucracies at central as well as faculty level.

In addition to all these problems, a reorientation is also taking place in the field of science policy. There are at least two reasons for this. The principle of complete freedom of science is being questioned because it is believed to be at the root of the technology to which many of the defects of modern society are attributed. Furthermore, the high costs and the diffuse organization of scientific research have led the government to demand better information on actual costs, so as to be able to allocate funds in accordance with a general science policy under the direct responsibility of a minister of science.[20]

These new developments create various problems for science in the universities. They demand an elaborate reporting system on research plans and on the progress of each research project; they force universities to separate budgetarily the costs of teaching from those of research; and they envisage exceedingly complex organizational arrangements, with separate committees for research at *vakgroep* level, faculty level, and university level, interuniversity organs, scientific research organizations, and ministerial policy advisers.

[20] The Dutch auditing office was asked by the Dutch lower house to inquire into the efficiency of expenditures on research in Dutch universities, and submitted a severely critical report on June 27, 1972. See *Handelingen Tweede Kamer, zitting 1971–1972*, no. 11 036, no. 3. Similar criticism was expressed in a report, *Science Policy of the Netherlands*, May 1972, which was drawn up by three foreign examiners for the Committee for Scientific and Technological Policy of the OECD.

The Crisis of Government

The confluence of the "new democracy," on the one hand, and the "new management," on the other, thus poses a fundamental dilemma. The government wishes to make the main decisions—so as to secure better financial control, to reorganize the entire structure of higher education, and to obtain a grip on the more fundamental decisions in science policy. But it must at the same time obtain consent. The new management requires centralization, the new democracy demands freedom and security at the periphery. Across these two forces pushing in opposite directions runs a host of institutional vested interests, of which the new "democratic" university organs are not the least forceful.

If one may speak in the Dutch situation of "the crisis of the university," this paradox offers perhaps its most conspicuous example. Dutch universities face a process of massive reforms which would create tensions under even the most favorable of circumstances. These reforms must now be carried through with the aid of institutions of doubtful legitimacy, in the face of a withdrawal by large groups of the academic staff. There are serious conflicts between ad hoc electoral mandates and professional qualifications. The banner of democratic reform often covers particularistic interests, which are backed by the pressure of direct confrontation. There is less willingness to abide by rules. There is an oppressive burden of information gathering and meetings. There is growing group egoism. Deliberate as well as unconscious politicization threatens certain parts of the university. There is often an unacknowledged lowering of standards. There is a notable fall from the high prestige which universities once enjoyed.

Some of these developments may be the result of ineluctable changes in society. But others are the consequence of the reactions of elites in society and in the universities who lost their self-confidence when they had to face sudden demands contended for by unwonted tactics. There is a deep tragedy in these developments. It is probably true that the traditional values of the university, as the seat of academic liberty and higher learning, can be retained only through rather substantial structural reforms. But, by allowing a process of drift to prevail within the universities, the responsible authorities may have deprived themselves of that very foundation of goodwill and civic spirit on which a fundamental reorganization must rest.

The French University as a "Fixed Society" or, the Futility of the 1968 "Reform"

François Bourricaud

THE SITUATION OF THE French university, both before and after the memorable date of 1968, can be characterized by three essential features. In the first place, I will point out the *dualism* opposing the *Grandes Ecoles* to the universities themselves. In the second place, it must be noted that legally the *bacheliers* continue to enjoy *virtually* free access to the universities. Finally, it must be stressed that the university remains *"un monde corporatif clos,"* despite sporadic outbreaks of violence, which are the acts of minuscule groups of the far left and far right.

A few words are necessary regarding the 1968 crisis and the so-called law of university orientation, prepared by M. Edgar Faure, then General de Gaulle's minister of national education. On the 1968 crisis, it seems to me that one can distinguish two principal orientations in the immense and generally mediocre literature which it has generated. A first group of authors tends to minimize the specific aspects of the university crisis and bury it in the larger and somewhat vaguer context of the "crisis of civilization." This first tendency is found as much on the left—among those who see a pattern of "new" social conflicts and the premonitory symptoms of postindustrial society diseases in the student revolt—as on the right—among those who proclaim the return of the familiar demons of our *intelligentsia* in the psychodrama of May 1968. A second group tries to limit the field of inquiry, accenting the crisis of university *institutions*, examining simultaneously the endogenous and exogenous aspects of the crisis. By *endogenous* aspects, I mean the problems relative to the university's organization, its mode of government, the prevailing pedagogical style, the hierarchy of activities (teaching, research, general or specialized training of students) which are represented there. By the *exogenous* aspects, I mean the relationship between the university and the administrative and political authorities who allocate its resources and control its use, the relationship between different institutions of the university, and finally the relationship of the university system taken as a whole with its various "clients" (the professions, business, public or private administrators—in short, all the groups who expect the university not only to contribute to the training of their personnel and their leaders but also to furnish new ideas and original inspirations). In reality, no matter whether preference is given to an analysis of the very special social system which makes up the university, or to an analysis of the "interaction" of this system with its environment, the primary interest of this second group of observers is the university and not the sociocultural environment—even if, of course, the "crisis of civilization" (supposing one can manage to arrive at even a somewhat clear idea of this) and the development of a different type of industrial society cannot fail to affect the functioning of the university.

I will not disguise my preference for the second approach which, having to explain the crisis of the university, begins with the university itself—at the risk of retracing the chain of events and conditions which led to the "events" of May 1968. I will add that those authors who look at the university crisis in a relatively restricted and university-centered way are significantly fewer than those more ambitious writers who adopt a more extensive point of view, at the risk of losing the specific character of the phenomenon. Finally, the second group of authors recruits from the left as well as the right, but more from the right, with one important qualification. Actually, the left–right opposition in the political realm does not mesh exactly with the left–right opposition on the university level. If one distinguishes a university right, defined by the attachment to the status quo, as distinct from the political right, I would say that the second group of authors recruits mostly from the political right, but also from the university left (that is, from the after all very heterogeneous group of academics who were critical of the situation prior to the events of May). But, since the crisis does not concern academics alone, it is instructive to ask oneself how political leaders themselves viewed it, and what solutions they proposed after the great commotion was over.

The inclinations and intentions of General de Gaulle are not difficult to determine. The university (the various educational levels and, in particular, higher education) had manifested as a body sentiments which ranged from scorn to the most constant hostility towards the general and his regime, through a sulky reserve on the part of a large number of its greatest dignitaries and through systematic pestering by its various corporate organizations. The relationship between the ministers of national education that he had named and the teaching staff at all levels had been almost constantly acrimonious, and the various reforms that the government had tried to introduce, particularly under M. Fouchet's authority, had been rather badly received by those affected by them. The university as a whole, and higher education in particular, appeared to General de Gaulle as an institution with a spirit of corporate demands, locked into its ancient and petty quarrels, both negative and excited, representing in his eyes "the spirit that always says no." And then its students and teachers had almost overthrown de Gaulle and the republic. Thus this decrepit institution that had gone astray need to be thoroughly reformed.

It does not seem that the general had very clear ideas about the nature and extent of the reform that he intended to introduce into the university. Not that he was held back by scruples and inhibitions. It is true that the general was very respectful towards the *grands corps de l'Etat*, but he saw no reason to spare professors, especially those who wanted status quo in the university and revolution in the state. Having insisted since his return to public life that France should be forced to "embrace the times," he was aware of the important contribution that a "renovated" university could make to the "modernization" of the economy of French society. In this connection, he certainly leaned towards the "technocratic" orientation of certain counselors and ministers who stressed the importance of the research and training functions in the complex of university activities. It is true that the prime minister, M. Georges Pompidou, a graduate of the *Ecole Normale* and a former professor on the secondary level, remained very loyal to the humanities and general culture.

During the ten years preceding the May 1968 crisis, the French government made a massive effort in the realm of educational expenditures. During the 1967 electoral campaign, M. Georges Pompidou declared that the Fifth Republic's educational policies had been its great success; to give an idea of the extraordinary transformations accomplished under his administration, he stressed that since he had been prime minister more university buildings had been built in France than during the entire Third Republic. In fact, this truly immense effort, although it was measured in tons of concrete and teaching posts, accompanied, with a certain amount of delay, a very rapid increase in numbers of students. Table 1 gives an idea of this.

According to the facts given by MM. Bourdieu and Passeron concerning the development of the distribution of students by discipline, there is a decrease in the percentage of students in law, medicine, and pharmacy, and a corresponding increase in students in sciences and letters, who "represent 65 percent of the student population today, whereas they constituted no more than a quarter at the beginning of the century." [1] Regarding the development of the numbers of teachers, M. Antoine Prost writes: "From 1960–61 to 1965–66, in the Faculties of Letters, Sciences, and Law, the number of professors and *maîtres de conference* increased from 2,120 to 3,254, the *maîtres-assistants* increased from 1,147 to 3,285, and the *assistants* from 2,164 to 5,477." [2]

The policies of the first ten years of the Fifth Republic can be accurately summed up by the expression "more means better." The other side of the coin is that the pedagogical and institutional problems that arose in the university due to various changes taking place in French society were evaded or treated in an essentially rhetorical, completely irresponsible manner, and

[1] *Les heritiers* (Paris: Les Editions de Minuit, 1964), p. 133.
[2] *L'Enseignement en France, 1800–1967* (Paris: A. Colin, Collection U.), p. 456.

TABLE 1. Public Education

Development of Numbers of Students (Male and Female)

	1958–1959	1959–1960	1960–1961	1961–1962	1962–1963	1963–1964	1964–1965	1965–1966	1966–1967	1967–1968
Number of students:										
French citizens registered in faculties:										
Law	29,808	29,394	29,716	34,522	41,084	49,732	60,121	70,530	80,107	96,974
Science	57,536	63,416	63,967	70,810	83,110	94,299	102,871	111,042	114,739	124,174
Letters	47,403	52,982	55,283	65,454	81,975	93,968	108,801	111,499	129,608	153,339
Medicine, dental surgery	27,989	28,454	26,787	32,312	36,137	36,869	37,812	39,514	46,384	56,268
Pharmacy	7,646	7,737	8,017	8,781	9,512	10,093	11,456	12,513	13,899	16,540
Total	170,382	181,983	183,770	211,879	251,818	284,961	321,061	345,098	384,737	447,295
Foreigners registered in faculties	21,746	20,079	19,605	20,731	21,630	23,960	26,872	24,304	24,410	30,219
Nonregistered French	{10,000	11,000	11,297	12,204	11,434	18,122	18,766	{16,078	19,013	19,937
Nonregistered foreigners								4,019	4,504	5,309
Miscellaneous (registered during year)							1,002	*24,267*	*24,101*	
IUT									1,644	5,359
General Total	202,128	213,062	214,672	244,814	284,882	327,043	367,701	413,766	458,409	508,119
Grandes écoles (not registered in faculties)	30,000	32,000	34,000	32,000	33,000	36,000	38,000	42,000	46,000	63,000

NOTE: Figures in italics are not included in the academic population.
SOURCE: "Tableaux de l'Education Nationale statistiques rétrospectives 1958–1968," 1969 edition, pp. 40–41.

I think it could not have been otherwise. It is of course natural that the professorial staff would demand an increase in the "means" (posts, buildings) put at its disposal. But, prisoners of habit, systematically hostile to every initiative of the government, divided between a minority of "reformers" seduced by the model of American universities (which in reality most knew only very imperfectly) and a majority dominated by an unconditional hostility towards the *pouvoir gaullist* and an attachment to corporate habits, the only grounds on which the professors could maintain their unity were those of quantitative claims. It is true that the most involved of them called for more or less reasonable pedagogical changes as well. But, taking into account the prestige of the traditional disciplines, the weight given to habit, and also the distribution of power—which at the various levels of the university organization favored the status quo—propositions for reform had little chance of survival, even if they had not been characterized by unreality and a discrediting maximalization, which so often was true.

Before 1968 university reformers stumbled over a fundamental obstacle: basically, they did not know very well what they wanted, and in the new regime's political world they had few sure allies. Reformers had to content themselves with more or less confused declarations of principles. And university institutions were no less indecisive. They pretended to rebel against both the administrative dictates of the "ministry" and against the narrow corporatism of the "Old Guard," but they had hardly any ideas about governing a modern university; the only theme that even began to be clearly articulated in this connection by the reformers was the autonomy of departments "*à l'américaine*," of which progressives were enamored and which, by constant references, they used to discredit the old faculties. On an issue as important as the access of students to the university, the reformers never could arrive at a consensus. A tiny minority maintained that the Imperial Decree of 1807, which made the *baccalauréat* the first university grade, opened the door of the faculties indiscriminately to all *bacheliers*, and should be replaced by more modern admission procedures. But the great majority proclaimed itself fiercely hostile to any idea of "selection," out of loyalty to the "ideas of the left" and to traditions of the "republican university."

The reformers' chances to be heard by the political authorities were reduced as much by their lack of unity as by the great hostility to the *pouvoir gaullist* which most of them flaunted. General de Gaulle's ministers therefore were led to believe that a strictly quantitative expansion policy, enhanced by technocratic declarations on the necessity of adapting the university to the modern world, was the only approach likely to preserve a minimum of agreement. Under the keynote of "more means better," not to be explicitly pronounced, of course, a convergence could be effected between governmental authorities and corporate authorities of the university, wresting an ambiguous agreement from professors—both from conservatives who realized, despite the disruptive declarations, that things went on in a status quo of sorts, and from the reformers who had some reason to rejoice that things were beginning to "move" in spite of it all.

The manner of perceiving the crisis, which could be predicted as far back as 1964–1965, diminished even more the chances of an effective treatment. What caught the attention of professors and students were the symptoms rather than the causes of the crisis. What professors and students felt first of all were the insufficient "means" (personnel, buildings, operating supplies) put at their disposal by the ministry. Secondary effects of poverty included first of all administrative disorganization, with "recovery" taking place in the midst of chaos and improvisation. Pursuing an analysis of the "sickness," it is easy to see that the "obstruction" produced a feeling of distance and inhibition at the level of the pedagogical relation. The university was seen as a general scuffle, the overflow where a chronic surplus piles up, for which a breathless administration never manages to allocate an adequate number of amphitheaters, libraries, and professors. But this first group of impressions, which trades on the amorphous, massive character of the university, was supplemented by an impression of coldness and separation. Denunciation of the *cours magistral* and recriminations against the barriers to contacts between students and teachers should be seen from this perspective. Naturally, to correct the anomie resulting from this obstruction, it seems entirely natural to think first (if not exclusively) of more generous budgetary allocations to abolish scarcities. Thus one falls back on the inevitable "more means better."

Did the events of May 1968 modify the perceptions that the persons concerned had of the crisis and their ideas about the necessary remedies? As for the professors' group, what remained of their unity has been lastingly shattered. Not only has the division between "conservatives" and "reformers" been aggravated, but reformers have the impression of being the playthings in an immense fraud. Having begun as a dispute among schools, the May movement developed into general and undifferentiated disruption. A certain number of progressive professors were led to ask themselves whether they were not becoming victims or accomplices of a mistake or a swindle. They had dreamed of university reform and they woke up in the midst of a pseudorevolutionary orgy. Not only were professors divided, but the most excited of them who rejoined the movement played at every turn in the great scenes of the night of August 4 and of the abolition of privileges. (As for the others, they stayed discreetly at home, waiting for the commotion to abate.) In this connection the vocabulary is characteristic: professors, anxious not to be given the ignominious designation of "mandarins," preferred to call themselves "teachers," and immersed themselves gleefully in the interminable "general assemblies" manipulated by the contesting students.

At the beginning of July 1968, when General de Gaulle and the government, reestablished by their electoral triumph, tried to "put their house in order," the situation of the university at first glance resembled that of France after the disaster of 1870 where, as a journalist amusingly described it, "there is nothing and no one left." In fact, beneath this apparent immense tabula rasa there remained many institutional elements that had stood up in the end for better or worse. As for the egoism and the corporate interests, their vitality was in no way broken down, as experience was to demonstrate. M. Edgar Faure (whom General de Gaulle named minister of national education), with infallible intuition, had the incomparable judgment to accept the relationship of the forces as it was left by the disruptions of May 1968. Unfortunately, M. Edgar Faure's tactical genius had no other objective but to push through a series of ingenious compromises which, in essence, confirmed and reinforced all the vices of the previous organization.

As a prudent lawyer, the new minister was aware from the start of the extent and limits of the concessions the interested parties could grant one another. First of all, it was clear that any attempt to restrict the requirements for admission of students to the university had to be abandoned. The refusal of any kind of selection having been one of the essential elements of the May credo, the minister decided to make that his war cry as well. In the second place, the distinction universities–Grandes Ecoles would be maintained. Several comments are in order on this fundamental distinction in the arrangement of the French system. The Grandes Ecoles (Polytechnique, Normale Superieure, Ecole Nationale d'Administration) recruit through a competition a small number of very select students who, in the most prestigious of these Ecoles, make up no more than a tenth of the candidates. In the second place, after leaving the Ecoles, students find positions giving them immediate access to the ruling classes of political administration or business. The elitist character of the system is thus affirmed by the mechanics of a very severe and restrictive recruitment policy, and by the hierarchical quality of the "openings" guaranteed to the students. Compared with this perfectly mandarin-like system, the faculties practice a very liberal admissions policy, since by law they are open to all bacheliers. As long as the students from the lycées came from the "upper middle" classes, with the rare exception of several brilliant scholarship holders, "sons of the people," the faculties easily could place their students in positions in professions such as law or medicine, more or less comparable in prestige to those available to the engineers from the Grandes Ecoles. The quality of students in higher education and their chances of securing a good position depended directly on the "level" of secondary students working towards the baccalauréat, and on the congruence of these studies with the professional careers the future bacheliers proposed to follow.

As long as most of them had the ambition and the probability of becoming doctors, lawyers, and even civil servants, the problem of openings was hardly a problem, and the faculties easily maintained their prestige—even if the quality of the services they offered to the students was sometimes rather mediocre, particularly regarding preparation for research. But things changed quickly as the number of students increased—faster than the number of positions in the fields the faculties usually led to. This disequilibrium between the increase of positions and the increase in numbers of students could be corrected only by a change in the curricula and the style of teaching. The least one could say is that the faculties delayed taking this step. Furthermore, out of the mass of students in the secondary educational institutions around 1955, even if most of them "dropped out" before taking the *baccalauréat,* many would find themselves trapped in a more and more anomic situation. Those who go as far as the university above all expect from it a certification that will guarantee them status as members of the middle classes. But, as M. Bourdieu and his school have clearly shown, students from modest or lower class backgrounds at the university are led into less prestigious studies which, even if productive, will assure them only modest positions in *petits cadres,* as secondary level teachers or schoolteachers.

The universities, therefore, must content themselves more and more with little or poorly motivated students who end up in mediocre positions and consider their university years a banal extension of obligatory education—while the *Grandes Ecoles* monopolize more and more strictly the recruitment and training for the ruling cadres. After several skirmishes, M. Edgar Faure resigned himself to this situation, which was violently denounced as "antidemocratic" by the most radical of the reformers, and he took care not to include the *Grandes Ecoles* in the application of his reforms.

The so-called law of university orientation not only sanctioned the monopoly of the *Grandes Ecoles;* it reinforced the corporate privileges of the professors as well. In the latter instance it limited the extension of professorial privileges to categories which had until then been "dependent": the *maîtres-assistants.* But, contrary to the requirements of the radical elements that students or their representatives take part in the selection of professors, cooptation remained the rule for all teaching positions; the possibility of involving individuals from outside the university, even provisionally, was as strictly limited as in the past. The fact that in France professors are civil servants, governed by the statutes of public office, allows the most radical requests to be blocked: As civil servants, how could professors be chosen by the students, who after all are the users of a public service? Are tax collectors elected by taxpayers or public works engineers elected by motorists?

M. Edgar Faure, a shrewd politician, took the greatest care to give his law a progressive luster, while preserving corporate interests. He accomplished this by putting forth three catchwords which then enjoyed the greatest prestige: *participation, autonomie,* and *pluridisciplinarité.* Naturally, the practical results of these noble principles were carefully contained by the restrictive framework into which the minister had placed himself. *Participation:* Students were invited to elect delegates who would sit with the delegates of all other categories affected by the functioning of the university institutions, on a series of councils charged with managing the business of the university. But the scope of the "principle" was cleverly limited. For participation to make sense, the councils would have to have had real powers. But their effectiveness was severely limited. The recruitment of teaching staff was left to the professors themselves; councils on which the students "participated" found themselves dispossessed. As for the curricula, to the extent that diplomas are conferred not by the universities but by the Ministry of National Education, they continued to be subject to the approval of the tutelar authority. As for the use of funds, since the universities have practically no resources of their own, they are financed as in the past by appropriations from the state budget and managed according to the rules of public accounting. It is evident that the "autonomy" referred to in the law is no more than a word. As for *pluridisciplinarité*, its aim was to prevent the development of strictly professional universities (like the *Ecoles de Droit* or *Médecine*). In practice, it has allowed above all for the formation of conglomerations of the most amorphous and motley character but, through application of the principle of *pluridisciplinarité*, and by means of certain contortions, the dismembered pieces of the pre-1968 faculties have been reassembled to form the most baroque arrangements.

The fundamental characteristic of these ingenious arrangements is that essentially they confirm the tendencies at work before 1968. The corporatism of the professors has been affirmed. The conditions for admitting students to the university will not be questioned. The dualism of the French system has been reinforced: the *Grandes Ecoles* will continue to take the "cream of the crop" while the universities will content themselves with the rejects and the ungraded products. Under these circumstances, how can one avoid concluding that the 1968 law takes account of the downfall of the university while it cleverly divides up its modalities?

Two facts are particularly important concerning the *Grandes Ecoles*–universities dualism. In the first place, the proportion of students of the *Grandes Ecoles* in the entire student body has remained very small. For the 1972–1973 academic year the total number of students in the engineering schools was 17,000 out of an overall total of 820,918. Furthermore, admission to these institutions continues to be controlled by recruitment through very selective competition. Thus French higher education, after 1968 as before, continues to juxtapose a "free" or semifree sector (the universities) to a numerically very small sector, the *Grandes Ecoles*, whose elitist privileges, on their part, have a tendency to consolidate themselves. This situation has multiple effects. In particular, it influences the composition of the ruling classes, in both the public and private sectors, and it helps "reproduce" certain of the most debatable of the characteristics of our "elites."

In the second place, the *baccalauréat* remains the first level of higher education. The result is that legally all *bacheliers* can register in the university, and in the disciplines of their choice. It is true that, by means of regulations, this freedom has been considerably narrowed down, at least in the fields of medical and scientific studies. In medicine, students must take an examination at the end of their first year of study; in scientific studies, a "mathematical" *baccalauréat* is required for future students of the Faculty of Sciences. Completely free access in fact is now assured only to students entering law or letters, which make up the "soft underbelly" of the system.

To appreciate this situation, it must be linked to one of the paradoxes of the present system of studies in France: while access to *higher* education is *free* (with the qualifications just enumerated) to all holders of any sort of *baccalauréat*, secondary education remains relatively specialized, differentiated, and stratified, due to an opposition between "strong" sections (the scientific, mathematical, and classical sections) and "weak" sections (the modern and technical sections). Furthermore, the distinctions between different types of secondary institutions remain very marked: CEG, CES, and *lycées*. These distinctions are very obvious if one considers the relative rates of success and failure, the aspirations of the students of the different institutions, and the professional perspectives offered to them. Thus the French educational system tends to be more selective in the earlier years (at the level of the second degree of education) and less selective at the level of the university, which is not true, for example, in England or in the United States. A whole series of consequences results from this—as much on the level of secondary education, where a growing resistance to the pattern of traditional teaching is evident, as on the level of the universities, which are having more and more difficulties reconciling the forms or "semblance" of traditional university organization with the "expectations" or "requirements" of their new customers, who have come to the university for a prolongation of the "moratorium" rather than for intellectual or professional training.

Statistics published by the Ministry of National Education on August 10, 1974, confirm that the social class distribution represented at the university is broadening (see Table 2). Comparing the figures for the last academic year (1973–1974) with those for 1964–1965—some nine years earlier—three principal tendencies can be pointed out. First, the percentage of children of industrialists and business executives—as well as the percentage of middle-level managerial children—has decreased: 11.8 percent (compared to 15.2 percent in 1964–1965) and 14.9 percent (compared to 17.7 percent), respectively. On the other hand, children of the middle classes (laborers, clerks, tradesmen, and service workers), who represented in 1964–1965 a percentage identical to that of the middle managerial level (17.7 percent), are increasing: 21.2 percent, of which 11.6 percent fall into the "laborers" category (compared to 8.3 percent in 1964–1965). In 1968 these categories represented 58.2 percent of the working population in France. Finally, sons

TABLE 2. Student Body Origin

SOCIOPROFESSIONAL ORIGIN	1964–1965	1973–1974	WORKING POPULATION 1968
Agricultural owners	5.5	6.1	12.1
Salaried agricultural workers	0.7	0.7	2.9
Industrialists and business executives	15.2	11.8	9.6
Professions and upper managerial	30.2	30.2	4.9
Middle-level managerial	17.7	14.9	9.8
Clerks and tradesmen	8.2	8.8	14.7
Laborers	8.3	11.6	37.8
Service workers	1.2	0.8	5.7
Miscellaneous	6.5	7.8	2.5
No profession	6.0	1.9	
Unknown	0.5	5.4	
	100.0	100.0	100.0

and daughters of members of the professions and upper-level managerial positions have maintained their high percentages (30.2), out of proportion with the percentages their parents occupy in the total working population (4.9 in the 1968 census).

It is difficult to determine the effects of this "democratization" of the student body on the functioning of the university institutions. I suppose the gap between the institutional *values* and the *ethos* of the students will be more likely to increase. I would predict—to the extent that the university is not in a position to guide its students and to differentiate its curricula—a risk of increased anomie.

Limiting ourselves to the university situation, and to what can be explained about it by the institutional facts just related, let us say that the distance between universities and *Grandes Ecoles*, far from diminishing, is augmenting; that the rejection of all selection, or even of all somewhat restrictive direction, remains dogma; that the differentiation of curricula and channels, especially when it takes the form of professionalization, is more suspect today than ever. Obviously, it would be excessive to derive this situation, very distressing in my eyes, wholly from the institutional privilege of the *baccalauréat* and from the rules of admission to the university which result from it. But two things seem perfectly clear: in opening the door to *bacheliers* simply on presentation of their diplomas, the margin of control that universities can exercise over the flow of admissions is severely reduced. And, pretending that the *baccalauréat* (since it remains the first university grade) still has a "level" it no longer possesses retards the evolution of secondary education towards more flexible, more pragmatic, pedagogical forms, which would probably be more acceptable to the "mass" of students.

I have strongly stressed the *corporate* character of the French university and I claim that, far from correcting itself, it has worsened since 1968. It would be well to distinguish between what results from organizational characteristics common to all university systems and what is peculiar to French university institutions. Every university is corporate *to a certain extent* as a result of the nature of the responsibilities of, and the method of recruitment of, the teaching staff. In the French system this situation is reinforced by the legal status of the personnel. Furthermore, in the last twenty years new categories or strata have proliferated and each has acknowledged very particular interests, which oppose or ally it to all others according to subtle modalities; at the same time, the "corporation" in its entirety finds unity only in resistance against external intrusions. These intrusions are particularly resented when they come from the hierarchical authorities, that is from the Minister of National Education, especially when its minister can be disqualified by teachers' and students' unions as conservative or reactionary. But the corporate defense mechanisms are called into play with equally merciless rigidity against the attempts of "users" to bend training programs or pedagogical style, for the purpose of taking into account the new "needs" of a professional, technical, or administrative order. Every attempt to relate university training to the kinds of professional openings offered to students brings about an insuperable distrust, which is expressed by the "refusal to subordinate the university to the demands of capitalism and the bourgeoisie."

Often contemporaries are more aware of the most immediately irritating aspects of a situation but do not see the most fundamental and durable aspects of it. This explains how the violence perpetrated by the leftists could have made front-page news for a long time when it was impossible to get any admission of the gravity of the institutional vices which disfigured the university and confirmed its lasting decline. The intensity and frequency of leftist violence have certainly diminished since 1969–1970. But I will avoid any predictions. In any event, the ease with which strike movements (which, even when they involve a small fraction of the students, disorganize classes for long periods) can be started, whether on behalf of corporate claims, or of slogans of a political nature, seems to be a well-established fact in the "reformed university." The *débilité* and complaisance of the institution towards pressures operating to transform it either into a place of security or into a war machine for the benefit of various extremisms, does not seem to have been corrected by student participation which, incidentally, remained at a constantly low level since it never exceeded a third of registered students (with of course certain definite variations between disciplines, institutions, and regions).

What seems to me more serious than the risk of politicization is the as-it-were constitutional incapability of the universities to manage their own changes. I would draw attention to two problems which cannot fail to arise for the university managers, whatever the political contingencies. It seems perfectly clear to me that we have made no progress in regard to these problems since 1968. More important than the rapid increase in the number of students is their distribution. Furthermore, the problem of the differentiation of curricula, pedagogy, and institutions is becoming all the more important because the old university structure was adapted, for better or worse, to an employment structure that is largely out of date today, and because the change in the social composition of the student body calls for adaptation of the institution to its new clientele.

Regarding the distribution among the various disciplines, everyone agreed before 1968 that it was bad—without necessarily defining the criteria for this judgment. Looking at a table prepared by the central administration, one can see that the number of students in letters increased from 93,032 in 1962 to 244,935 in 1972–1973, a rate of increase somewhat less than 300 percent, while the number of students in sciences grew from 92,204 in 1962 to 115,852 in 1972–1973, a rate less than 50 percent. In law and medicine, which lead more directly to professional careers, one notes that law has doubled and medicine has quadrupled. Analysis of these data is very sensitive, and it would be absurd to consider any increase—let us say, for example, in sciences and medicine—as "satisfactory," and any increase in letters and law as "distressing." But the magnitude of these often erratic movements involves both high social costs and grave consequences for the university institution itself. Now, in the present situation, it is almost impossible to correct this distribution in any way—as the many reform projects and their subsequent failure will attest. Theoretically, two corrective measures are conceivable. One is manifestly impossible; it would be to assign the greatest possible number of students to positions determined to be socially desirable. This approach presumes two equally unrealistic conditions, one concerning the validity of meritocratic criteria of selection, the other concerning the technocratic objectivity of the procedures used to determine optimal employment fields. A second solution remains, which is to diversify the university system and manage it on a hierarchical system. The open door policy for *bacheliers* could be maintained under two conditions: that not everyone could go anywhere and do anything and, of course, that there would be a relatively high number of really practicable doors and channels open. This method would differ from the two practices in use simultaneously today in French education: totally free access to the university and selection by competition, because those candidates who do not gain admission to their first choice university would have a good chance of admission to another. The preponderance of the university left today, and the egalitarian ideology, makes not only the first solution impossible but the second as well, and consequently condemns the system to remain as it is indefinitely, overcrowded and amorphous.

In the meantime, the university seems destined to a prolonged drift. I tend to judge the dramatic episodes connected with its politicization as less serious than the sort of anomie in which it finds itself today, through the weakness of the structures of authority and the laxity of the various disciplines. Several indications confirming its decline and assuring the lasting nature of it have been briefly described in this essay. And, anyway, a certain number of functions or activities will still be fulfilled for society whatever the prevailing situation in the university; it will still be necessary to train professionals and to assure the progress of knowledge and technology by basic and applied research. If our university is not in a position to assure these two functions through its incapability to modernize itself, as everything would seem to predict, it is condemning itself to a double marginalization and will exclude itself—which has already happened in the course of history—from the movement and progress of knowledge.

The Italian University System

Giovanni Sartori

FOR MOST OF THE WESTERN WORLD the watershed between "old" university and whatever is called and sought as the "new" university was 1968. That the student revolt spread in a flash across a very great variety of countries, cultures, and learning institutions testifies to the fact that the particular "sins" of each university in each particular country do not in themselves explain the events of the late sixties and early seventies. Each institution was challenged—regardless of its performance and structure—among other reasons, merely because it was in existence. Nevertheless, it is important to examine the old university in each country to see what were its specific features and vices.

In many respects the Italian university system has survived relatively unchanged. It should be understood, therefore, that the following description of the old system does not imply that all, or even most of it, is bygone. The first thing to note is that, with very minor and partial exceptions, all Italian universities (about thirty full-fledged ones in the late sixties) are state universities, and very much so in two major respects: that they are tightly regulated by state law; and the system is highly centralized and dependent on the Ministry of Instruction in Rome. As for structure, it adheres to the usual continental European pattern: universities are divided into some ten to twelve faculties (not to be understood as broad and loose assemblages of professors, but as the organic teaching unit) which hinge, in turn, on a "chair system," that is, on the tenured titular holder of one chair per subject matter. Vis-à-vis the Anglo-American structure, the distinguishing trait of the traditional continental European structure is that there is (was) no intermediate unit, such as a department, between the faculty and the chair holder. And while faculty affairs are entrusted to the faculty council (until 1968 exclusively composed of full or tenured professors), nevertheless the real system is a chair system—and a highly monadic and hierarchical one at that. Nor can it be denied that this structure had largely degenerated into an atomized feudal-type system, with almighty "barons" (as full professors are called in Italy) ruling over their institutes and their fields of specialization.

We have thus quickly arrived at *a* major vice of the system, and at *the* major target of the rebellion: the university "baron." In the heat of controversy the structural and personalized aspects of the issue have seldom been looked at separately—and yet it is important to do so. As a structure, the chair system is an anachronistic survival. It served its purposes when knowledge was not only entrusted to an elite university, but was far from being as specialized as it today; that is, when it was conceivable that one chair could embrace and be the equivalent of, one discipline. Under present conditions, therefore, the chair system is a nonworking, absurd structure.

But the "barons" as human beings are a much more diversified matter. The bad ones—those who largely abused their powers—were predominantly concentrated in the Faculties of Medicine. While professors of medicine have not discovered how to cure cancer, in many respects they have themselves been the major cancer of the Italian university system. It was within the Faculties of Medicine—closely followed by architecture—that a related, major abuse became offensive: the exploitation of university status for private professional benefits. It should be clearly stated, however, that for most professors of most faculties (including law) this abuse was by no means the rule. Aside from the University of Rome—a site with too many distractions —even in the good old times a large majority of the tenured professors of the center and north universities in fact had attended to their duties with full-time devotion. When the whole category became exposed en bloc to the joint accusations of students, junior faculty, and politicians, a majority of innocents paid for a minority of sinners. If the category deserved a condemnation en bloc this was not because it failed to comply with its academic duties, but because it had withdrawn to its well-fenced orchards, and had been largely insensitive and myopic about the pressing needs for reform.

Some ten years ago I was asked to prepare a report on the respective merits and defaults of a faculty vis-à-vis a departmental system. I argued that faculties could be conceived as the less costly way of running a mass university at the undergraduate level; but that a departmental structure was absolutely necessary for graduate or, at least, postgraduate training (a huge gap in the faculty system), and for scientific research. The general idea was that a departmental system could be grafted upon the existing faculty system with great advantages for both. I vividly remember that the proposal was received, and quickly buried, as a sort of subversive madness. This private story goes a long way to illustrate how one reform project after the other never managed—in the fifties and sixties—to get through parliament. Most of these projects (one of which, the Ermini project, became monumental) never bypassed the stage of reports. The philosophy of the enterprise was that university reform had to be "universal." Perhaps some propounders of the "universality" argument were in good faith. In practice, however, universality became a wonderful alibi for killing whatever change was immediately feasible and highly urgent. The most eloquent example of this state of affairs was that of the Faculties of Political Sciences, whose statutes and curricula had been established in 1934 under the Mussolini regime. It was obvious, therefore, that they required immediate and radical changes. The first demands for a reform of these faculties go back to 1946. However, it was only in 1969—twenty-three years later—that Minister of Instruction Scaglia dared to propose, and managed to obtain (by surprise), a presidential decree of reform of the Faculties of Political Sciences, which still elicited (at a time when most universities were "experimenting with chaos") heated criticism in the name of universality.

Reverting to the universal reform, only one project of law (the Gui project, Number 2314) came very close to enactment in the spring of 1968—but ran aground with the early dissolution of the legislature. However, the Gui draft reflected the prerebellion era, for it had been elaborated in the middle sixties. Its provisions did not meet demands for the democratization of the university and, surely, its enactment would not have averted the campus revolt. Yet the failure of any reform, epitomized by the failure of the Gui bill, confronts the guilts and responsibilities of the professorial class as a whole. The corporate interests of *academia* were best served by the status quo. And until 1968 *academia* carried a very substantial weight in the matter. One characteristic of the Italian parliament is that it includes a sizeable number of university professors (almost 10 percent). Since politicians had not been concerned about universities until the Paris revolution, the "hyperbarons" sitting in parliament largely had a free hand. And their common reason—across the ideological spectrum—for cherishing the status quo was that no reform was going to overlook their sitting in parliament *and* simultaneously occupying a chair.

It was, then, in the legislature elected in June 1968 and terminated in 1972 that parties and politicians finally realized that there was a university problem—indeed a problem that was shattering not only the universities but also the major central and northern cities of the country, from Rome up to Bologna, Milan, and especially (at the time) Turin. After decades of total neglect, far-reaching reform projects were drafted almost overnight by mysterious, self-styled "experts" in a rather common pattern of those years: the barons had to be punished and became the scapegoat; students had to be placated at all costs and, in any event, students meant votes; and "democratization" was the magic word for some magic solution. The new project of law (Number 612) was endlessly redrafted—off and on the record —to accommodate opposite pulls throughout the legislature. Three ministers of instruction unworthy of naming drifted along with the successive changes of the project—which was never extreme enough for the extremists, and ever too extreme for its adversaries. The bill never passed. Whatever its demerits and merits, one thing can be said for sure: it never was given teeth. In spite of three years of heated debate, its operative deficiencies and impossibilities remained unaltered. The university matter was a "political question," and this implied that expert advice and technical drafting were both unnecessary and suspect. If bill 612 had been enacted, surely it would have "smashed the machine," fulfilling the unveiled desire of many of its propounders; but little more than a tabula rasa would have followed. The new machine had been designed without wheels.

This does not mean that nothing was actually done. Awaiting the grand reform, Senator Codignola—a left-wing member of the Socialist party dedicated to destruction of the old system, and the real protagonist of that period—quickly pushed through to approval, in November 1969, a short bill (Number 910, but better known as the "liberalization" bill) of great consequence. It contained two provisions; open access to all the faculties from whatever secondary school and free choice of the curriculum by each student, albeit subject to approval by the faculties. Soon after, all appointments of full professors were frozen awaiting a new system of appointment. Let it be noted that in 1969 Italian full professors were, in all, just about 3,000, with a student population, before the Codignola act, of over 400,000 (while university buildings and funds had remained at very much the same level as in the early fifties, when the student population was about 200,000). Finally, funds were allocated for what was called a "presalary" for students of relatively deprived conditions; in practice, it went to a very substantial number of students, subject to their passing a modicum of examinations with sufficiently good marks.

The first consequence was the utterly unmanageable explosion of the student population which doubled from 400,000 to more than 800,000 in 1972. It has been argued that this boom was not caused by the liberalization bill, since it came in the wake of a comparable boom at the secondary school level. Nevertheless, the very strong presumption is that when powerful incentives are held out (remember the presalary) for opening the university to all, the university population will in fact escalate—and it did. Had the students attended classes, and had their presence been anything more than on paper, the buildings would have crumbled. The buildings did not crumble, but the load of examinations often became, for the examiners, too heavy to bear. In part, it was a matter of sheer numbers. The University of Rome, for instance, was already close to a population of 100,000 students (140,000 four years later), with some professors having to cope with several thousand students registered with their course. But the question was only partly one of magnitude. Let it be recalled that in 1969 the radical students (at the time the "student movement") were at the height of their protest against grade "selection," demanding collective (group) examinations and/or abolition of any tests. The joint impact of overload, intimidation, actual harassment, and overall demoralization produced, as one would expect, a drastic fall in standards or, what is the same thing, a generalized inflation of grades. Architecture examinations largely became a sham; at least in the field of the humanities (with most progressive teachers in most faculties) almost everybody was passed with high marks; and, in spite of very great individual differences, it is pretty safe generalization to say that the gatekeepers very much let the gates go. Even diehard resistors hardly could deny whatever mark was demanded by students in order to meet presalary minima.

The liberalization bill included a second provision: freedom of curriculum subject to faculty control. Since the curricula were largely frozen by law, in and by itself their defreezing had long been necessary. However, this liberalization arrived when the faculties were no longer in control of anything. Many faculties simply gave up; and nobody will ever know how many students used their freedom simply to become "doctors" via the Milky (i.e., easiest) Way. And faculties that did exercise control over individual curricula underwent a most taxing, nerve-straining experience. As was easy to foresee, the freedom-of-curriculum theme immediately became—for the radical students engaged in fighting examinations (viz., meritocratic elitism) —a major mobilizing device, No matter how they were conducted in substance, examinations were required by law. But the law now encouraged students to "develop their personality." Faculty control thus was denounced as authoritarian oppression—and the message was attractive both for the intellectually gifted and for students with no desire to study.

As I said before, the existing curricula were absurdly rigid and—thanks to the chair system—inadequately articulated and often outdated. The point was, and remains, that Italian doctorates have a legal status. Had the legislature been serious, freedom of curriculum included as its inevitable complement the idea that university degrees having a different make-up— individual by individual and faculty by faculty—could no longer claim a uniform legal validity. The *fictio* was, at this point, too fictitious to bear. The delegalization of university degrees was also very much in demand as a counter incentive to the boom of a student population seeking a piece of paper with no other prospect than unemployment. However, delegalization of the doctorate was sternly refused not only on the justifiable grounds that the liberalization law was emergency legislation, but in principle. Senator Codignola and the progressive chorus which backed him wanted—and still ' want—the legal fiction to remain and in its wake the inflation of unemployable and unusable (know-everything but know-nothing) "doctors" to continue growing.

In 1972, as the legislature that had taken up the student revolution was ending, the overall condition of Italian universities had improved in two respects and mightily deteriorated in three others. The first improvement was that the barons had lost all their arrogance and haughtiness. Along the way many of them had, hopefully, lost their self-respect. It is fair to add that many scholars who deserved respect were heartbroken. Nevertheless, the overall atmosphere had changed very much for the better. If not much democracy had entered the institutions (aside from a de facto inclusion of the junior ranks in faculty councils), a hitherto unknown "spirit of equality"—as Tocqueville would have called it—was a real novelty. The second improvement was that the surge of "contestation" had subsided. True enough, the student movement had largely given way to the extra-parliamentarians—a much more violent and violence-prone set of characters. This difference notwithstanding, in most universities (Milan, from 1970 onwards, being the most notable exception) class disruptions, occupations, assembly rule, and ultimatums had lost momentum. And here it is well to pause and to attempt to understand why.

The 1968 eruption can be imputed largely—given its simultaneous spread—to a mass-communicating world in which "events are in the media" and follow, to no small extent, media channels and circuits. Its relapse in the early seventies has been, instead, far less synchronous and far more diversified. It is my surmise that the best single explanation for the relative peace that reentered Italian universities points to a shift of the epicenter of conflict. That is to say, the university owes much of its relief to the fact that the turmoil now converges strongly on the secondary schools. This is hardly a paradox. For some four to five years freshmen entering the university have experienced the delights of daily chaos, unruly assemblies, intimidations, and virulent rhetoric. Most of them arrive at the university pretty exhausted. Since they have learned next to nothing, many of them have a fresh interest in learning something. Furthermore, at the secondary school level the quality of teaching and of teachers has deteriorated to such an extent that, by comparison, what students get at the university stands out—rightly or wrongly—as pretty good. In this respect the Italian situation closely resembles the French one—except that our collapse of secondary education is much more thorough and, I am afraid, beyond repair. But, of course, the university has not reverted to a relative tranquility only because the eye of the hurricane has moved into the secondary schools. Another major reason is that the student movement of the late sixties dissolved itself in two directions: either into extraparliamentary anarchy or the Communist order. And since the Italian Communist party abides by a legal-ascent-to-power doctrine, it follows that Communist students represent the organization that either guarantees or helps restore order. To be sure, nothing is given in exchange for nothing. But the Communists are solid realists. They do not demand "red physics" or "red mathematics." They are interested in recruitment; and, when they cannot get Communist teachers, they settle for proselytizing students. And here equally one finds an explanation—if only partial—for the otherwise inexplicable fact that many German universities have never recovered the relative peace of their French and Italian counterparts. In all three countries "redness" is widespread and expanding; but in Germany it goes loose while in Italy, and to a lesser extent in France, much of the opposition of principle (to the capitalist society) obeys a logic and is removed from extraparliamentarian violence and sectarianism. Finally, a third reason cannot pass unmentioned: cemeteries are peaceful by definition. If a faculty is dead—without lectures and without examinations (except pro forma)—and yields to whatever is demanded, then it is bound to be a very quiet place. And, while the extent of our teaching cemeteries is bound to remain a well-kept secret, surely peace has often been bought at a very high price.

The last point introduces one of the three aspects of the deterioration mentioned at the outset. Aside from the fatal casualties, there remains a very wide spectrum of lesser ones, related in the main to the so-called experimenting with "new didactics." The best argument in its favor is, presumably, that we all tend to rest on habits, to sit down, and resting is bad in itself. Correlatively, there is more than a grain of truth in the argument that change is good in itself, for a process of change as such is exhilarating. In Italy, the standard practice had been to deliver solemn lectures from a high stool (spiritually elevated, when not high above the floor). They were not bad lectures; but the monologue was often boring, authority flowed down with condescendence, and it is true that "relevance" was the last concern of the teacher. All this deserved to be challenged. But, as with all processes that get out of control, the baby often drifted away with the dirty water. Much of the new didactics turned out to be worse didactics, or no didactics at all. Lectures gave way to seminars; but few teachers knew how to conduct them, and the self-monitored ones produced more smoke than roast. In the main, the really new didactics corresponded to what radical students wanted to have: collective promotions on some "progressive" subject which had nothing to do with what the subject was supposed to be.

The second deterioration, and perhaps the one with more far-reaching implications, was represented by the extent and intensity of politicization. True enough, politics had been entering the universities. All along the old system for appointing full professors hinged on the election across the country of a five-judge commission which produced, in turn, a slate of three winners entitled to being called to a chair in some university. Since the electorates electing the judges were mobilized very much along party lines, the usual outcome of the slate was one winner for the left, one winner for the Catholics, and eventually one winner on its own independent merits. However, until 1968 this was generally done with a modicum of decency. In subsequent years faculties were left to enroll only lecturers (*professori incaricati*: a fusion of the American assistant and associate professor without tenure) and assistants. And in left-controlled faculties most of this quite massive recruitment occurred on the basis of ideological merit, of outspoken political discrimination.

The third deterioration related to the ratio between teachers and students, and particularly to the ratio between full professors and nontenured faculty. Since all new tenured appointments had been blocked, by 1972 the disproportion between barons and junior staff (let alone students) had become more intolerable than ever before. This disproportion, in turn, exacerbated the generational conflict within the faculties, and transformed it into a conflict between the force of the many and the feebleness of the few—with little if any room left for rational argument. The rational argument was that one thing basically was wrong, and another absolutely rotten, about the old system. What was wrong about it was that it had never been conceived as a career system: either one was "in," full professor for life, or one was "out," a badly paid, nontenured lecturer. Since chairs were distributed by the Ministry of Instruction and their trickle had been minimal since the thirties, most of its teachers had to remain "outs" as the university expanded. Not only was this wrong: it was also a patent distortion of the original design, in which the lecturer had been conceived as an emergency remedy and/or as an exceptional stage of transition to the chair. The rotten part of the story was the system of appointment. As we know, this system hinged on the national election of a commission. Now the rational argument was that this system had degenerated not because of the *election*, but because of the *electorates*. Bit by bit, the electorates for each discipline (chair) had been extended beyond any decent interpretation of affinity. Hence elections were decided by totally incompetent and unconcerned majorities; this is why and how the racketeers had a free hand in canvasing and obtaining votes. A professor of Roman law voting for sociology (a real, not an imaginary, example) could be easily persuaded to vote as advised by a friend.

The rational remedies to the foregoing state of affairs were, thus, quite obvious: (1) a career system, (2) a redressment of the proportions between tenured and nontenured positions, and (3) a drastic pruning of the electorate along criteria of competence. However, the demands of the "slaves" in revolt to which the politicians paid heed were of a very different nature: (1) all had to be tenured, and all had to be equal (in Italian: *docente unico*), and (2) their promotion had to be automatic, or quasi-automatic. If bill 612 —which basically incorporated these claims—never won final approval, this was in no small part because the demands, especially the latter one, verged on being unconstitutional (university professors are civil servants) and appeared excessive to any thoughtful mind. Translated in figures, it meant that in three years some twenty thousand new barons (for the *docente unico*, proclaimed as a revolutionary novelty at its inception, was nothing but the old system) would have occupied all the conceivable teaching posts for some thirty to forty years, and that this army would have to be promoted en masse simply because it was there (as a byproduct, incidentally, of a selection made by the very same barons now declared unworthy of selecting them). Hindsight might suggest that this exaggeration was fortunate, for it turned out to be the major stumbling block of a bill which responded to pressures and scares but hardly to responsible and informed judgment. Nevertheless, the legislature closed down leaving a dramatic, and indeed increasingly burning, issue totally unrelsolved.

The parliament elected in May 1972 inherited the defeat of the grand reform (of no less than 106 sections) relentlessly pushed forward by Senator

Codignola, while realizing that bill 612 reflected, in no small part, demands of a student revolution that were no longer in demand. To be sure, the Socialist party immediately reintroduced the bill; but Senator Codignola in the meantime had lost his seat and, with it, much of his impact and prestige. It was not that true, after all, that students and assistants carried votes. On these and other grounds, something that should have been understood at least twenty years earlier finally was grasped, namely, that feasible partial reforms are better than global reforms which are never accomplished. That is to say, the legislature was predisposed to settle for "Urgent Measures" (*Provvedimenti Urgenti*) dealing, in the first place, with the most unavoidable issue at hand: defreezing competitions for tenured professors, and thereby establishing a new system of appointment for the junior faculty which had been pushed aside since 1968. Another major unsettled problem which was equally incorporated in the Urgent Measures number 580 (issued by decree on October 1, 1973, and converted into the law number 766 on November 30, 1973) dealt with the reorganization and democratization of the university governing bodies.

As the dates show, even the "minireform" in question—known as the Malfatti bill—took more than a year of endless and exhausting bargaining. It should be noted also that its conversion into law not only occurred *in extremis*, the very last day, but was a near miracle. In all likelihood, even the urgency of measures actually labeled "urgent" would have fallen victim to the growing paralysis of the Italian governments and parliament, had it not been for a set of fortunate and lagely fortuitous circumstances. One was that the former "adviser to the prince" lost his seat. The second providential occurrence was that Senator Spadolini, a very skillful, respected, and well-known scholar, unexpectedly became chairman of the senate Committee of Instruction and took the matter very much to heart. Third, and conclusively, a responsible and capable minister, Malfatti, happened to enter the Ministry of Instruction after it had suffered almost five years of irresponsible or highly incompetent management. Had it not been—let it be stressed—for this combination of circumstances (unfortunate, to be sure, for advocates of the "all-the-worst, all-the-better" smash-all doctrine), by the time of the present writing the university would have sunk into such a state of paralysis that my conclusion might have been that Italy had no future—for, after all, learning institutions *are* the future.

As of the end of 1974, instead, something was finally moving. With regard to recruitment of full professors, the Malfatti bill accepts the last-resort solution: a lot system of appointment of the national judging commissions. Here, even more than for electorates of the former system, everything hinges on whether the disciplines are clustered according to real, meaningful affinities. While the professorial advisory body gave in to the temptations of gerrymandering, the minister saw to it that the apportionment made sense. The bill provides, over a three-year period, for 7,500 new tenured positions, which amount almost to a tripling, with respect to the number of actually surviving barons of the pre-1968 era. In spite of the fact that in 1973 the Socialist party still insisted on no less than 18,000 new posts, the increase provided by the Malfatti bill raises, if anything, the question as to whether 7,500 positions can be filled without a drastic lowering of standards. No Malthusian preference is implied by recalling that the Italian university system is neither devised for, nor capable of (for lack of a postgraduate level), training university teachers. However that may be, what matters most is that a first, essential wheel of the new machinery has been put into motion.

Let us now turn to the second major element of the Malfatti bill—student representation in, and democratization of, the governance of universities. After a first unsuccessful try in the summer of 1974, the quorum of minimal electoral participation that had been established along the lines of the French Faure reform was abandoned and replaced by a flexible criterion: more-or-less seats in relation to more-or-less voters. The first student elections were held in February 1975. They were boycotted and, in some cases, disrupted by ultra leftist groups on the grounds that the only solution to university problems is to destroy the university by revolutionary means. Although the turnout was low as a result of these tactics, the new student councils have been put into operation.

Aside from electoral unpredictables, student, clerical, and junior faculty participation in the governance of the university established by the Malfatti bill distinctly improves on the parliamentary orders of magnitude envisaged by the Codignola-inspired project. It would be saying too much to claim that the legislature had a clear perception of size thresholds and of decision-making overloads. Nevertheless, it is fair to say that the Malfatti bill does not create bodies crushed by their size: democracy is not converted, in practice, into nongovernance. As for the weight of the professorial body in the democratized university, the fact that the gates of tenure have been opened has deprived the "punishment of the baron" slogan of much of its firepower. After all, by insisting on their former slogan, the new entrants would be punishing themselves. The overall inefficiency of the political system, and the resulting time lag has also been very relevant. There has been ample time to realize that professors are a far cry from being a monolith to be neutralized—in the decision-making bodies—by equivalent countermonoliths. On these premises the Italian legislator has avoided the extremes of other more prompt (or more shortsightedly responsive) legislators, thereby maintaining, on the whole, a prevalence of the professorial body over the other so-called "components."

This appraisal of the emergency legislation enacted at the end of 1973 neither implies that the worst is over nor that the most has been accomplished. Tensions resulting from the politicization of the university—and impinging upon the university from the general state of collapse of the country—are strong, unpleasant, and menacing. While Italian universities are currently better off than German ones, Italy is far worse off than Germany.

Setting aside the outer world, one very major piece of reform—departmental reform—is still missing and, to say the least, flounders in deep water. All reformers have demanded departments; and, when one speaks of restructuring the university system at base and as a whole, what is at stake is transforming the faculty chair system into a departmental system. But here prospects are gloomy for the ideas remain as confused today as they were in 1968. If departmental reform proceeds as envisaged—without funds, without campuses, but maintaining the chair system—then the new and the old university will simply wreck one another. And it would be very sad to discover at the end that we have only managed to combine the worse of two worlds. Even if we have done comparatively well in recent days, nonetheless we are skating on very thin ice—at least in Italy. We cannot afford mistakes in what still needs to be done.

In universities, we have grown accustomed to unpleasantness. Intimidation and latent violence are an ongoing, if hidden, reality in many faculties across the country. If anything, ideological indoctrination and discrimination are on the increase. In short, the Italian university *is* territory for conquest. We should not be deluded into thinking that all of this can be cured by "good" reforms. But "bad" or wrong reforms can only make things worse.

Japanese Universities:
Student Revolt and Reform Plans

Ichiro Kato

Student Revolt in 1968–1969

THE CASE OF THE UNIVERSITY OF TOKYO

Universities throughout Japan experienced a wide-scale student revolt in 1968–1969; I will explain here what happened at the University of Tokyo, the oldest state university, established about one hundred years ago and recognized as the top university in Japan.

Since 1966 at this university there have been disputes between students and professors in the faculty of medicine regarding the postgraduate training of doctors. Students insisted that the University of Tokyo Hospital receive as many interns as possible, practically all the applicants, and recognize the student body as a negotiating body with the faculty. They protested against the faculty by means of a student strike for an indefinite period in January 1968, but the faculty refused to talk with the student grievance committee. In February there was the forced inquisition of a hospital doctor by a group of twelve students, to which the faculty responded with disciplinary action, including expulsion from the university in March.

Later, one of these students insisted that he had not been at the scene of action and submitted a sort of evidence in his support. As the disciplinary action had been proposed by the faculty of medicine through the president to the academic council, and formally decided by the latter, disputes about the affair now spread throughout the university; and many students criticized the one-sided procedure of discipline, the faculty's derogatory attitude towards the student's contentions, and the irresponsibility of the academic council including the president.

On June 15 of the same year, a group of 80 radical students violently occupied the main administration building. The president called in the police on June 17, but the students escaped before policemen (numbering around 400) entered the campus. The action of the president served to provoke many regular students, who had formerly been opposed to the occupation of the building by radical students.

In July a group of so-called new leftist students again occupied the main building. They won more students over to their side and blockaded or occupied other buildings as well. Students then went on strike within various faculties with the result that university authorities were compelled to re-examine the disciplinary action and later to withdraw it. Eventually, in November, the president, deans, and members of the academic council who had decided the disciplinary action resigned; but these concessions were too late. Students now criticized the university as being a part of the ruling power (the Establishment) oppressing them, and new leftist students called for the dissolution of the university itself.

I returned home in July 1968 after a one-year stay at Berkeley, California. When the president and deans resigned in November, I was elected the dean of law and immediately the acting president. I tried to talk with the different student groups and to find a new solution. By January 1969 the group of leftist and nonsect students had reached an agreement with us, while the other group of new leftist students occupying buildings rejected our proposal. Finally, the latter began damaging buildings and violently at-tacking the former group. At that point, I called in police to expel the students from occupied buildings. About 8,000 policemen were dispatched and during two days of combat the radical students were dispersed or ar-rested. After this incident we gradually resumed our ordinary activities of teaching and research.

GENERAL FEATURE OF STUDENT REVOLT IN JAPAN

What happened at the University of Tokyo was a typical example of student revolt in Japan during that period.

1. First, we have to admit that these revolts indicated a deep and wide-spread discontent with the university system and administration, as well as with the Japanese social system itself. These revolts originally had been a kind of struggle for the student's fundamental rights in the university, although the causes varied from one university to another: student dis-cipline, dormitory control, raise of tuition, dubious accounting practices in private universities, and so on. But a small spark, a minor incident, ignited widespread discontent and spread over the whole university system. Thus these student revolts indicated the necessity of university reform.

2. Second, a split within the student movement—the former famous *Zengakuren*, into a pro-Communist group (the so-called *Minsei*), and many new leftist groups (generically named *Zen-Kyōtō*)—spurred on the disorder. The two leading factions fought each other, a struggle which made the troubles even more complicated. The *Zen-Kyōtō* or *Kyōtō* groups took a hard line, being more radical than the orthodox Communists. Wearing

helmets and carrying sticks, they blockaded or occupied university buildings and dared confrontation with the president, deans, professors, and even with opposition students, sometimes resorting to force and calling for the dissolution of universities. An eminent professor criticized them for destroying academic freedom and went further to say that even the Nazis had not dared such outrageous actions.

University authorities often tried to solve problems through discussion with students; but on the whole they did not succeed, because their answers were usually too late to settle disputes, and because radical students refused any compromise. Accordingly, university authorities had to resort to police action in order to expel students forcibly from occupied buildings. Predictably, the students formed an interuniversity or transuniversity network and went to aid their fellow students at each university; most students who were arrested at the University of Tokyo, in fact, were not students there.

3. Third, universities were caught in a squeeze between attacks from radical students, on the one hand, and pressure from the Japanese ruling establishment (the government and ruling business circles), which criticized them for inept administration.

University authorities were especially troubled with regard to police power. The establishment criticized them for hesitating to call in the police, insisting that police should enter the campus at their own discretion. However, if this were to happen, it would arouse a heated reaction by students—not only radical groups, but students in general; and this would make the solution more difficult. Therefore, university authorities contended that the police ought not to enter the campus without the request or consent of the president or other responsible persons representing the university.

I talked with the chief of the metropolitan police and came to an informal oral agreement that police would not enter without the university's consent; the university, keeping contact with the police, would request or consent to having them come on campus at the right time. To date, this gentlemen's agreement has been honored by the police, at least concerning the University of Tokyo; I think it is a reasonable relationship between the university and the police, who also recognized the merits of such a setup.

THE NEW GOVERNMENTAL LAW

During this turmoil the government, that is, the Ministry of Education, enacted a law which was passed by the parliament in August 1969, named "Provisional Measures for the University Management Law."

It includes a provision that the minister of education may suspend the activities (of teaching and research) of a faculty which has been in trouble with students for nine months. This threat of suspension or closure aims at encouraging any wavering or irresponsible faculty to be active. In reality, it is a kind of bluff to university authorities, professors, and, moreover, to the students themselves.

Many university presidents and professors were opposed to the measure, since it would interfere with university autonomy; they felt that universities could solve their problems without such a law. In fact, the law has never been applied because universities found their way out of difficulties. However, the Ministry of Education insists that university activities have been normalized because the law exists; and we cannot deny that the position of universities vis-à-vis the ruling establishment has been weakened as a result of the student revolt.

It is a five-year terminal law; but the government can be expected to try to enact a stronger law controlling universities—or at least attempt to put off the termination.

University Reform in Japan

As I mentioned above, the student revolt showed the need for university reform.

STRUGGLE FOR LEADERSHIP OF REFORM

After the student revolts, the active students split into many factions and have lost the power to promote reforms. For instance, pro-Communist students were very eager to bring about student participation in the university administration, hoping eventually to control the university. New leftist students, however, were not interested in this participation, complaining that such student participation would compel students to become a part of the ruling university establishment.

On the other hand, ordinary students tended to be indifferent to political matters; soon they grew tired of radical activities and wanted a return to routine university life. Therefore, it would be very hard to establish a responsible organization representing all the students.

University authorities and professors ardently discussed university reform. They proposed many plans to implement this goal which stressed reform of the teaching system, reorganization of facilities, democratization and rationalization of the university administration, rigid discipline of faculty members, and so on.

They tried also to carry out such reforms independently at each university; but so far only a small portion of the proposed plans have been implemented anywhere at certain universities. On one hand, it is very difficult to obtain consensus among professors—let alone consensus with students, employees, and the Ministry of Education; on the other, the zeal of professors for reform gradually cooled as they began to enjoy a peaceful life again.

The Ministry of Education also tried to reform the universities. The Central Council of Education, which is an advisory committee under the Ministry, submitted a detailed report in 1970 advocating centralization of the university administration as well as a new classification of universities in response to the needs of society. Professors as well as students, however, fear that such reforms might strengthen the control of the government over universities.

The Ministry of Education just recently has enacted plans to establish a new university in Tsukuba in order to carry out the reform plan of the Central Council of Education.

To sum up, each group—that is, students, professors, and the government—struggled for leadership of the reform movement and checked each other; in the meantime, any chance for large-scale reform has been lost. We must be satisfied with small-scale reforms or modest improvements for the time being and wait for another chance for major reform. Many professors fear that the present stagnation concerning the reform may eventually result in a full-scale university crisis.

ISSUES OF REFORM

I will mention here important issues concerning reform.

Teaching and Research Innovations. Japan's educational system, revised after World War II, is patterned after the American educational system; students are to spend four years at the university after twelve years of primary and secondary education. The character of university education has been changed from a narrow education for elites to a broad education for the general citizenry.

The number of universities increased rapidly in the 1950s. They have generally been able to cope with the great expansion of students since the 1960s and also have contributed to the development of the Japanese economy. There are 79 state universities and about 300 private universities in Japan today. The number of students entering the university is about 25 percent of Japan's entire population of entrance age. This percentage exceeds that of the middle-school graduates in the prewar period.

Despite revision of the educational system and popularization of the university education, the teaching system and the curriculum retain many features from the past which are not suited to the new situation. The new four-year university system was established as a combination of the former three years of high school and three years of university. The course of study is divided into a two-year junior course of general education and a two-year course of specialized education. Campuses are usually separated according to this division. Such a teaching system hinders effective education and has caused discontent and frustration among students.

Most reform plans propose abolishing such a division and advocate reorganization of the general and specialized education to the four-year consistent and organic education system. There needs to be not only a fusion of curriculum but also a reorganization of professors and faculties—possibly campuses, as well. Accordingly, such reform is very difficult to carry out and is anticipated for only a few universities, including Tsukuba. Nevertheless, at many universities the curriculum has been improved in the direction of the proposed reform.

In the face of popularization of university education, it is feared that mass education and the easygoing attitude of students will lower the level of university education. Therefore, more intense education in the way of seminars and smaller classes is now being emphasized.

At the same time, the coincidence of education and research at the university is now being questioned due to the development of scientific research and popularization of university education. There are some experiments at a few universities to functionally separate teaching and research; for instance, at Tsukuba, a professor simultaneously belongs to a certain teaching section as well as to a certain research section.

Innovations in University Administration. There are two levels of decision making at the university. First, the faculty meeting—usually composed of professors and associate professors—decides on matters of teaching and research, including selection of professors in each faculty. Second, the university council—including the president, deans, and representatives of professors—decides on matters concerning the whole university.

Universities in Japan enjoy academic freedom and university autonomy; professors are usually selected by faculty meetings, and presidents are elected by faculty members. In state universities, formal appointment is made by the Ministry of Education, while at private universities the chairman of the board of trustees performs this function.

The reform of university administration has two phases—democratization and rationalization, the latter often being similar to centralization.

"Democratization" means participation of students or other personnel in the administration. After the student revolt, university authorities tried to talk with students and listen to their demands; this, however, was not institutionalized participation but, rather, informal consultation. In other words, students have not yet been allowed to participate in the decision-making process.

On the other hand, students have come to have some voice concerning election of the president at several universities. They have won a veto against presidential candidates or conditioned voting rights for the president; but the effect is limited. Besides, at some universities, assistants—that is, teaching and research assistants—participate in the presidential election as well as in the faculty meeting.

As to "rationalization," or centralization, Tsukuba University serves as a model. It has five vice-presidents, and the selection of professors is carried out by an upper-level committee under the central administration, not by the faculty meeting. The effects and outcomes, however, are still unclear.

I conclude my report by stating that universities in Japan have survived the critical situation of the period of student revolt, but we must promote and carry out innovations in the university system (that is, innovations in teaching and research) as well as innovations in university administration in order to revive the university vigorously.

The Condition of Australian Universities

James McAuley

ALL AUSTRALIAN UNIVERSITIES are public institutions. With the exception of the Australian National University, they have been created by acts of the six state parliaments. Since 1956, state financial allocations have been matched by substantial federal government grants administered by the Australian Universities Commission. Salary scales are uniform and determined by a Commonwealth salary-fixing process. Staff can be attracted only by the prospect of promotion elsewhere, except for personal preference for one city or one university rather than another. Students generally attend the university or universities of their own state or city. It is like having a single university system with campuses located in different places.

In addition to the universities, there has been created a new system of tertiary colleges, incorporating former technical colleges and teachers' colleges, and creating new institutions. These are called "Colleges of Advanced Education." Although they are meant to be more vocational in their aims, their mandate has remained cloudy in many important respects. They are being given degree-granting rights and there is a strong tendency to vie with the universities, for status reasons and also because the staff carry university patterns with them into their new situation. There is, however, no sign at present that they are likely to be major centers of political activity, because of their predominantly applied or vocational character.

This uniformity is now being completed by the Commonwealth government's offer to take over all financing of tertiary institutions. Also, tuition fees have now been abolished; the implications of this have yet to be seen.

Radical action in the Australian universities began in 1965 and followed the American pattern to such an extent that techniques of radical action could be predicted in outline months before they appeared. Even American expressions not applicable in Australia became standard, for example, "draft resistance" instead of resistance to being called up for national service. This predictability did not, predictably, prevent university authorities from being surprised, and did not prevent many commentators from gravely analyzing disturbances as though they were products of specific local conditions. The scope and intensity of radical action was never so great as in the United States of America or some European countries. But the time of troubles had generally the same effect in weakening legitimacy, and exposing the degree of confusion and decay under the smooth surface of academic dignity. I want to make two general observations about radical activity on the Australian scene because I am not sure how these observations match with experience elsewhere.

The first point concerns the intellectual caliber of the radical left. Whereas in the United States of America it was frequently said that the radical core was very bright, able, and gifted, in Australia the reverse has been nearer the truth. With a very few exceptions, the radical left has been intellectually second rate and shoddy. This is true also at the staff level.

The second point concerns the political structure of the radical movement. While there were some individual operators and a good deal of fluid association and temporary alignment, the importance of the organized Communist parties, based outside the universities and manipulating the situation, has been very great indeed, though the importance of this factor has been denied and derided both by people on the left and by people who regarded themselves as outside or above the struggle. Trotskyism surfaced almost from the grave and Trotskyite factions were of primary importance in some of the troubles of Sydney University and Queensland University. Trotskyist factions have recently appeared in the secondary school arena in Melbourne. Maoist organization, closely linked with the Communist party of Australia (Marxist-Leninist), dominated Monash University for some years, though it has lost its hold now; it was strong also in the third Melbourne university, LaTrobe. But the greatest continuing factor throughout has been the Communist party of Australia, which is the parent body from which the other Communist factions have split away at different times. Since the Czechoslovakian crisis, it has been at odds with Moscow—the latest split being the formation of a new Moscow-lining Socialist party of Australia, whose base is mainly industrial and which at present has little involvement in the tertiary educational field, though it has some importance in secondary teacher unions.

I want to mention here the growing importance of political activity in the field of secondary education, and will return to this point because no analysis of the problems in the universities can ignore it.

The first lesson which I would want to draw from the Australian experience is one that I believe has universal application. What we have seen is the effective use of the "organizational weapon." A very small number of activists operating in an amorphous mass can produce massive results. The technology of political organization is one of the most fateful developments of the twentieth century. The truth must be faced, even if one wishes it were otherwise: unless we face the necessity for *organized* resistance, we are unrealistic and futile. Organized resistance in the universities on a national scale—as coordinated as possible, matching as well as possible the organization of the disruptive left—was badly needed. Fortunately, it was to some extent achieved, though under great difficulties. Such counterorganization has to exist at every level where the left makes its challenge—at staff and student levels, and extending into the state and national political arena. It must go down into the secondary school system and contest the increasing power of the left there. The style of organization has to be appropriate to the situation. And the need for rational organization—determined, sober, dedicated, and on sound principles—needs to be complemented finally by international organization. I hope that our present international body will develop strongly as an international alliance which will do more than merely exchange phrases about "sailing with the winds of change."

In the past year or so we have seen the same subsiding of the froth of radical activity as elsewhere: few demonstrations, few buildings occupied. The future remains uncertain, but the main recent thrust has been to attack academic integrity as such: especially, of course, in the humanities. I will mention the latest and most alarming example in Australia. It concerns events in the philosophy department of Sydney University. Typically, the only philosophers in the department of any repute and achievement are liberal conservatives who have been unable to prevent the outbreak of barbarism. Typically, the organs of academic government—faculty and professorial board—failed to apply academic principles and betrayed their trust. The events, in outline, occurred in two successive phases:

1. A course in Marxism-Leninism starring such distinguished modern philosophers as Ho, Mao, and Che was imposed by demagogic action against the academic judgment of the head of the department. As a result of this activity, departmental government was handed over to an experiment in participatory democracy embracing staff and students.

2. In phase two, a course in women's liberation, *confessedly* nonobjective and tendentious, to be conducted by two female graduate students, was pushed through after weeks of melodrama in which faculty and professorial board again behaved ignobly.

The situation currently is that the philosophy department in Sydney University is in the process of being divided into two departments: a Department of Traditional and Modern Philosophy, which will teach what most of us would regard as philosophy; and a Department of General Philosophy, which will offer various things, but will make room for those who regard the teaching of philosophy as a means of furthering revolutionary aims. I am implying no criticism of the vice-chancellor for taking this action —on the contrary, this division is quite a sensible step under the circumstances. But it is a step that has become desirable because of a disgraceful situation in which a faction of students and staff have been allowed to trample with impunity on academic principles, and other students and staff have seen their rights ignored or threatened.

Let me conclude by stating the lessons which I believe should be drawn from the experiences which I have briefly reviewed—lessons which I think are of universal application.

Lesson 1.   I have already stated the need for organized resistance at all levels, in appropriate forms, coordinated nationally and internationally as far as possible.

Lesson 2.   The *doctrine of the university* must be explicitly taught. We have taken it for granted to the point where it has become unknown or misunderstood by students and many members of staff. It must be fully and explicitly redeveloped and firmly articulated and explicitly proclaimed. I take the heart of that doctrine to be that the university is a subject-centered school, not a child-centered, student-centered school; that authority can be legitimate and valid only if it flows from dedication to the teaching of real subjects. The subjects taught by universities are main structural members of our civilization. Any tampering with them, any betrayal of the disciplines of learning under the pressure of students demanding relevance, or political operators demanding the unity of theory and action, is a betrayal of our civilization. I stand with Antigone against Creon.

Lesson 3.   There is something wrong with a situation in which masses of students are being herded into universities when they are poorly motivated and therefore not capable of participation in depth in the academic process as defined by the pursuit of essential subjects. I believe that we are only pretending to follow an enlightened policy of wider and wider educational opportunity for more and more students. What we seem to be doing in the humanistic or general faculties is debauching education in the interests of an undeclared program of social administration; we are keeping adolescents and young adults out of the labor market in expensive tertiary compounds because we do not know what else to do with them. The academic system is deteriorating, though this deterioration is disguised as updating and enlightened innovation. The losers are those students and staff who would like to pursue the humanistic disciplines severely and in depth. I do not know what the practical remedy for this huge problem is. But let us start by admitting that we are being driven along by social administrative expediency, not by anything deserving to be called an academic policy.

Lesson 4.   The problem begins in the secondary sphere. Academics make a mistake if they abandon interest and responsibility towards what is happening there through the actions of a combination of progressive educationists and political progressives. Secondary teachers of the state of Victoria in Australia have just adopted a policy in their teachers' union that all examining should be abolished, internal as well as external, so that university entrance should be by ballot.

In the face of the sort of muddle and nonsense that this example typifies, the importance of scholastic integrity has to be stressed. This year a number of us in Australia, academics and other citizens, have sponsored the formation of an Australian Council for Educational Standards. I mention it to emphasize that the fortunes of university education are closely bound up with the primary and secondary school, and we ignore this at our peril.

University Autonomy in Sweden

Krister Wahlbäck

THE DECLINE OF UNIVERSITY AUTONOMY, in relation to government authorities as well as to students,[1] would seem to have proceeded more rapidly in Sweden than anywhere else in Western Europe. At present this trend is epitomized by a proposal for a thorough overhaul of the whole university system, which was submitted to parliament in the spring of 1975. The origins of this situation, however, are to be found in a series of long-standing characteristics of Swedish universities and their place in society.

I

The six Swedish universities are all public, financed by the state, and with no autonomous sources of income of any importance. This holds true for the old universities of Uppsala and Lund, which for many decades have not seen any major additions to the donations assembled in previous centuries. It also applies to the nineteenth-century universities of Stockholm and Göteborg—once supported by local industrialists, later by the city councils, only to be taken over by the state in the postwar years. The universities established in the 1960s in Umeå and Linköping do not even have a history of any nongovernmental funds.

Of course there are important advantages to this system. The universities do not have to cope with pressures from individual financial tycoons or anticipate reactions from traditional contributing segments of society. Nor do they need to deal with local public authorities of the complexion that may be found in Texas or California. There are no regional eccentricities in homogenous Sweden, and besides all public funding is on the national level. Government and parliament have scrupulously avoided infringements on

[1] By "university autonomy" I understand autonomy of the faculty, in contrast to another possible concept where faculty and students are both considered parts of the enterprise. Of course, a less essayistic discussion than this would require, among other things, distinctions between autonomy in different respects and on different subject matters, as well as between realities and formal arrangements. There are, however, no scholarly studies to draw on which define the changes in Swedish university autonomy during this century.

academic freedoms. There has hardly been a single instance during the last fifty years of a university teacher's having been forced out for left- or right-wing radicalism, religious unorthodoxy, or defiance of moral norms.

The obvious drawback, on the other hand, is the conservatism and stifling of initiative which follows from total financial dependence on government authorities. Beyond that a consequence of some political importance is the lack of identification with their university on the part of former students.[2] This may be unavoidable in a uniform system with negligible differences between a few big universities, and little sense of competition between them. But if a measure of financial support is expected from alumni, universities may draw some political strength from citizens who feel that they have a stake in their university.

There are more important reasons for the political impotence of Swedish universities. A number of university professors have been highly active in party politics, often in quite prominent positions, but this has almost exclusively been within the Conservative or Liberal parties, in permanent opposition. Moreover, outside economics departments there is very little of the American tradition of professors taking a few years' leave to work with the administration. Even if a number of professors in Sweden are engaged in an advisory capacity, somehow this does not seem to spill over to the benefit of university interests.

On the other hand, senior students active in local student unions or the National Union of Students used to collaborate intimately with the ministry of education to promote various reforms opposed by conservative professors. In the 1950s and 1960s many of these students were coopted by the expanding central bureaucracy supervising the universities, some of them entered successful political careers (as in the case of Olaf Palme, minister of education, 1967–1969, before he was appointed prime minister). It may safely be assumed that their experiences do not make for much goodwill toward the traditional university structure.

It is tempting to speculate on the more fundamental reasons for the vulnerability of Swedish universities as revealed in recent years. The social prestige of the doctor's degree and the professor's title remains very high in Sweden, and the importance of university education for social mobility has always been great. However, Swedish universities have never played a role in political life comparable to that in Norway and Finland. In these countries, during the formative decades around the turn of the century, the universities were vital instruments of national and democratic self-assertion against their culturally or politically hegemonial neighbors (for Norway, Denmark and Sweden—for Finland, Sweden and Russia). The fact that Swedish universities have never been perceived as having made a crucial contribution to

---

[2] Uppsala and Lund, the Swedish Oxbridge, where students are organized in "nations" according to their native provinces, used to be an exception.

progressive political change may be part of their ineffectiveness in the Swedish post-war political context. Indeed, some depressing episodes, such as the sad story of the new campus of the University of Stockholm, may be indicative of a still more fundamental weakness. The universities—at least their social science and liberal arts faculties—simply are not the domain in which modern Swedish society chooses to express its ambitions and keep abreast of international progress. Other sectors are preferred. This may of course be a perfectly sensible policy, even if university faculties cannot be expected to agree. And in Europe's richest country, this means that the universities feel quite well off, on the whole, in a European context. It is in relation to the United States that the difference is painfully obvious.

II

Well into the 1950s Swedish universities were very small establishments. In the faculties of liberal arts and of social sciences (on which this essay is focused), there was only one professor in each department, that is, if one can talk of a "department" where the professor had no more collaborators than maybe one assistant professor and one or two teaching assistants. A few seminar meetings were the important parts of teaching, and students were left pretty much on their own. With the rapid increase in student enrollment in the 1950s it was clear that this system was hopelessly inadequate. Reform measures passed by parliament in the late 1950s were based, however, on principles which—as we can see in retrospect—set the stage for the turmoil a decade later.

First, the tradition of free admission to the faculties of liberal arts and the social sciences was upheld. This decision had the political advantage of permitting the government to satisfy the enormous demand for university education without incurring the prohibitive costs of a parallel expansion in the sciences, medicine, and engineering. However, it meant that available resources were used to provide university education for anyone in the college age group of the day, while nothing was done to mobilize real talent in a slightly earlier generation—a generation which the universities had failed to attract because of social and economic barriers of the time. Further, it also meant that the Swedish university system received almost the same share of high-school graduates as the American system, but without the latter's differentiation. If the American system was able to combine mass education and excellence by maintaining a wide variety of private and public institutions, the prospects were obviously dim in a small uniform system like Sweden's, lacking both resources and flexibility.[3]

---

[3] Ingemar Dörfer, "Science and Technology in Sweden: The Fabians versus Europe," *Research Policy*, 1974, p. 148.

Second, the faculty was expanded almost exclusively by lectureships for basic undergraduate courses, with teaching loads so extensive as to deter from research, and with courses so broad in scope as to exclude treatment in any depth. The professor was to take care of graduate students only—in his spare time, that is, since inevitably, his most pressing responsibility was to administer his swelling department.

Third, an important part of a professor's burden was to cope with his overlords in an even faster swelling three-level bureaucracy. The administrators of his own university were perhaps less of a problem than in many American universities, since members of the University Board as well as the president who runs the administration were all professors, and were elected by their fellow professors.[4] But with the limited scope of university home rule it was as important for the professor to learn how to handle the national office of the chancellor of the universities and the ministry of education.

Bureaucratization was probably inevitable in a setting where the government disposed of every instrument of power but the faculties had not learned to behave accordingly. The government tended to regard universities as different from other administrative agencies mainly in that professors were less loyal than other civil servants to government decisions, or at least to the political intentions behind them, and thus required increased supervision. Professors resented such intrusion into their traditional position and thought that decisions were too often based on poor insight into their real problems. This mutual lack of confidence did not make for smoothness and efficiency.

Thus in the spring of 1968, when the sparks from Columbia and Nanterre were carried to Sweden, the ground was in a way well prepared. It is true that some crucial elements of the American or French setting were missing. There was no Vietnam War, no experience from recent civil rights campaigns, no nearby slum neighborhoods, no barriers to political activity on campus, no regulation of social and moral behavior. However, apart from the international new left *Zeitgeist* there did exist some very real reasons for student discontent. Some of them may be difficult to relate to specific student actions, but they certainly formed the general background.

Obviously, the quality of teaching was bound to suffer severely from the system evolved in the late 1950s. This was vaguely felt even by students who did not subscribe to the Marxist critique of the student activists. Furthermore, a scheme to subsidize study costs, which parliament had adopted in 1965, proved more of a burden than anticipated, particularly with the declining prospects of finding a job upon graduation. By 1968 it was obvious that there would be a vast surplus of graduates from the "free faculties," and that many would have to accept less qualified jobs at less pay than they had been led to believe. Also, the selective function of the

---

[4] Olof Ruin, "Universitetsautonomi och studentparticipation i Sverige och USA," *Statsvetenskaplig tidskrift* 1972, p. 473 f.

rejected *numerus clausus* system had been carried out by exams instead; even with reduced requirements many students failed and felt cheated, not to speak of their parents.

To this was added a particular action on the part of the authorities. The government had grown impatient with the costs of expanding universities and with paying for the student welfare system. They realized something must be wrong with universities when so many students dropped out or spent twice as much time as scheduled to pass the exams. However, the remedy they proposed was a reform which would cut down study time at the expense of quality and introduce the possibility of expelling students who consistently proved incapable of university studies. Furthermore, the reform would limit the students' freedom to combine courses in favor of a system of "educational lines," which would supposedly make university studies more "occupationally relevant."

The initial faculty protests against these plans were joined by intense student opposition in the spring of 1968. In effect the scheme provided a much needed rallying point for the diverse movement of student protest which erupted in May 1968. Eventually, the students did succeed in having the proposal watered down to the point of meaninglessness.

But there was little reason for satisfaction on the part of the universities. The government's discontent with university performance remained, and the retreat was clearly a temporary one, brought about much more by students than by professors. Moreover, the second challenge to the universities, that of the students, was much more successful. The government decided to propose that students should have an equal share with faculty in decision making on the department level.

III

Thus the issue of university autonomy was first brought to a head in terms of the university-student relationship.

Traditionally, departments had been run by the professor as a more or less benevolent autocrat. His authority had been much greater than that of the department chairman at American universities simply because there were no countervailing powers in the form of other professors of equal rank. The Swedish "one department, one professor" system could obviously be disastrous when the professor was an eccentric, a bad administrator, or inept at handling teachers and students.[5] In 1964 a separate function as chairman, or "prefect," was instituted, and university authorities did not necessarily

[5] Richard Tomasson, *Sweden: Prototype of Modern Society* (New York: Random House, 1970), p. 140.

have to assign that position to the professor. Moreover, the prefect was to consult with a department council, comprising all teachers and two student representatives. This meant substantial change, though sensible professors had always consulted broadly as a matter of course.

Such was the setup which had to cope with student unrest on the department level in 1968–1969. Now part of the student revolt was against their own student union leadership, described as an unresponsive lot of self-serving elitists collaborating with the government bureaucracy. As student representatives on the department councils had been appointed by this student leadership, they did not prove to be of much help in legitimizing the existing structure in the eyes of the student activists. The government very soon indicated that it did not intend to stand by the 1964 system but, rather, would propose a reform broadly in accordance with student demands. In the spring of 1969 the new system was introduced. Teachers and students elected four or five members each to a department board, to which most of the decision-making powers of the prefect were transferred. The prefect was to execute the board's decisions, and the independent authority which he retained varied according to four "models" for student participation to be tried at various departments in an initial experimental phase.[6] Appointments to the faculty, however, were consistently kept in the hands of the teachers.

It may well be that dated images of professorial authoritarianism still prevailed among the politicians who settled for this reform, and that the division of power favored by the students seemed to them at least as legitimate as the one in place. We do not know, however, since no real debate preceded the reform. It was presented as part of a general democratization of working conditions. Within public administration the universities were to make the pioneering try. Cynics may argue, of course, that this was simply the politically convenient solution of the moment. Radical students and obstinate professors—none of whom were very popular with the government—were left to sort things out as best they could; and, if the assignment were to keep professors too busy to do their real job properly, at least no vital part of the administration would be disrupted.

However that may be, it is obvious that some potential flaws in the official argument were not really faced. Would students who spent a year or less in a department feel the same responsibility as industrial workers or white-collar employees with real stakes in their place of work? Were freshmen on a department board really competent to decide on reading lists for their own courses, let alone for courses on higher levels? To the extent that such decisions must reflect political bias, would it be progress in

---

[6] Formally, it is still (1974) an experiment. Out of the 550 departments at Swedish universities about 220 take part, mainly in the liberal arts and social science faculties. There is also a measure of student participation on higher levels of the university organization, but this will not be dealt with here.

democracy to have them heavily influenced by a group whose active representatives were political extremists in the national context? [7]

Any attempt to sum up the way that the new system has worked in the past five years must be based on subjective impressions.[8] Clearly, much depended on the political skills of individual prefects, including their capacity to handle the maverick teachers who turn up in any faculty and who relished their increased influence under the new precarious balance of power. Understandably, prefects tended to minimize their troubles, somewhat like high school teachers who fear that disciplinary problems might reflect on their reputation. Student attitudes varied sharply from department to department and from year to year. A few departments were taken over by Maoists, and you might find Stalin's speech at the 1926 Party Congress on the reading list. Other departments changed into an agglomeration of committees.

On the whole, however, there is no doubt that in many places the system caused no problems and that the difficulties decreased with time. Students grew passive and disillusioned as they found out how narrow the scope for department initiative is, and how often their pet projects, even if accepted on the department level, were thwarted by regulations in force or by higher authorities. There was a general decline in student radicalism, and increased concern with down-to-earth problems of the kind that used to occupy student unions. The decrease in student enrollment and the austerity mood which succeeded the expansive 1960s may have contributed as well.

By 1973 it could be argued that the change in relation to the pre-1969 situation was not really that great. Of course, the formal structure kept departments potentially vulnerable to sudden shifts in student attitudes. But for the time being the main effect seemed to be increased inertia. Even minor changes required so much effort in persuasion and coalition building that those involved tended to leave things as they were, except when forced to implement decisions from above. There was little left of the genuine optimism with which many teachers had originally looked forward to the positive effects of the reform, such as increased involvement and satisfaction on the part of the students, and improved teaching as a result of ideas and information from students.

[7] This holds true even some years later, after the change in student mood. The elections to the student union council of the University of Stockholm in the autumn of 1973 were rather typical. A non-Socialist party, roughly corresponding to the national Conservative Party, carried 24 seats, two Communist parties 12, and the Social Democrats 5. In national elections the same autumn, the Conservative Party polled 14 percent, three Communist parties 6 percent, and the Social Democrats 43 percent. Of the national electorate, 90.7 percent went to the polls, as against 30 percent of the student body. Student union elections have been based on political parties since the early 1960's.

[8] There is no later study available than a 1970 evaluation on the basis of interview data published by Nils Elvander and Birger Lindskog *Nya samarbetsformer på institutionsnivå* (Uddevalla: Utbildningsforlaget, 1970). My own experiences are from the social science departments of the University of Stockholm, in particular the Department of Political Science.

IV

Meanwhile, the government continued planning a major reform much more comprehensive than the abortive 1968 proposal. A commission on post-secondary education, including the universities, finally presented its report in the spring of 1973.[9]

Parts of the report are rather ambiguous, and the recommendations do not really provide more than an incomplete framework. The main proposal, however, is clearly to bring universities into a common administrative system with the vast number of postsecondary vocational schools. Sweden is to be divided into nineteen "higher education areas," each run by a board of higher education appointed by the government. A majority of the board members will be "representatives of public interests," which in effect means politicians on the local and regional level, and representatives of interest organizations such as trade unions and business associations. The faculties of a university in an educational area will retain responsibility for research and research training, though in fact only within the limits set by decisions on teaching taken by the board.

The university departments will largely be reduced to service functions for "programme committees," responsibility for "educational programmes," each of which will guarantee a "clear occupational relevancy" of university education. These programme committees will consist of about one third "persons taken from occupational life" in order to ensure that the education offered is geared to the demands of the occupational field in question.

The six existing universities will not be allowed to expand their student enrollment. Available resources in the decade ahead will be channelled to thirteen new cities.[10] It is far from clear, however, to what extent this will mean that traditional university education will be offered in more parts of the country than before. Initially, at least, the emphasis is on expanding vocational schools and training in single courses within the new common framework.

This scheme is supported by a number of arguments. It will result in a coherent and uniform organization within which all higher education can be "treated as a unity with regard to quantitative planning, the location of facilities, and the development of new educational programs." By integrating universities into the same framework as vocational institutions, the irrational differences in prestige value of various kinds of higher education may be overcome.

These institutions should have greater authority to act on their own

[9] A summary of the report is available in English, *Higher Education: Proposals by the Swedish 1968 Educational Commission* (Stockholm: Allmanna forlaget, 1973).
[10] In a few of these cities "university branches" for undergraduate education had been established in the 1960's.

than universities have today. But this is conceivable only if "the local de-cision-making organization is anchored in society at large." It is an old-fashioned conservative view, according to a statement by the prime minister, to keep universities like separate republics, isolated from society at large, and run by professors, when in fact universities are financed by taxpayers.

The critics reply, of course, that surely the state controls universities quite closely even with the present system. For government appointees to have a major role in running universities would be a deadly threat to academic freedom, and thus to an important part of the democratic system. In the long run, it is in the best interests of the whole society to grant universities a maximum of independence; it is argued that they are not exclusively vocational institutions, but have a wider cultural and polit-ical function in society. It is pointed out that the commission did not even touch upon the problem of guaranteeing the integrity of academic teaching and research in the face of pressure from the government or major interest groups, which would surely interfere, once they have been let inside.

This, however, is a kind of critique which simply does not carry much weight in the Swedish political context. The prestige of the universities in society is not high, for reasons which the preceding pages should have made clear. The main interest organizations, on the other hand, are the holy cows of Swedish establishment politics, powerful, prestigious, and increasingly represented on the boards of administrative agencies.[11] Furthermore, there is a tradition of Government intervention in areas which in most other countries would be regarded as extremely sensitive. Thus since the late 1960's public funds are used for subsidies to newspapers and political parties in order to prevent press monopolies and reduce the influence of wealthy interest groups. These reforms met with dire warnings, and of course they remain potentially formidable instruments for abuse of governmental power. But in effect they have been very fairly implemented, and today few would deny that they have contributed to a healthier democratic system. In short, the fears may be perfectly legitimate in principle and with regard to most political systems in today's world; but they seem far-fetched with regard to Sweden, where real abuse would hardly be conceivable without prior major changes in the working of the system.

Such considerations may explain why there is far from a unanimous opinion among university teachers on this issue. Many of them feel that the kind of "representatives of public interest" which are likely to be appointed will not really engage in improper interference. They will rather serve the universities well by representing academic interests with more political weight than professors can muster. Will they in fact provide political legitimacy for a university autonomy as managed by the faculty?

---

11 For a discussion on corporativist trends in Swedish politics and their effect on universities and students see Olof Ruin, "Participatory Democracy and Corporativism: The Case of Sweden," Scandinavian Political Studies, IX, 1974, p. 141 ff.

Furthermore, the public representatives can be relied upon to oppose another eruption of student activism, and do so effectively by virtue of their greater democratic legitimacy and their influence with the political establishment. Incidentally, the proposed reform would reduce present student power to the extent that departments are stripped of some of their functions; the proposed new structures will reserve far less than half the votes for students. Thus professors have to decide whom to fear most, students or public representatives. When Marxist students joint forces with conservative professors in the fight for university autonomy, the two allied camps obviously entertain different ideas as to which party would ultimately gain the upper hand if they had their way.

However, the debate over the Commission report has not really focussed on the issue of university autonomy in relation to students and Government. Nor has the occasion been used to analyze the extent of autonomy in the past and assess whether such autonomy has proved to favor, or rather to impede, "progress" in university development. It is of course legitimate to ask if universities are capable of reforming themselves on their own initiative. This may be a particularly pertinent question when the tradition is a low-keyed one of modest resources as allocated by central authorities, rather than one of rich universities operating under competition.

In any case, the only modification with regard to autonomy which seems to enjoy substantial political support is to have some of the representatives of "public interest" appointed by local or regional authorities instead of by Government—a change prompted by regional ambition rather than by concern for academic freedom.

The main thrust of the critique has concerned more practical aspects of the reform. It is maintained that the proposed decentralization of higher education will either result in a number of mini-universities, covering only a few areas of knowledge and giving very limited choice to students, or else pose a serious threat to the existing universities, which have felt the strains of declining enrollment and could not stand further bloodletting. In both cases, however, the quality of the education offered will leave much to be desired, as the Commission recommends no research facilities at the new sites. There is also some doubt as to the relevance of an essentially administrative reform, when a number of obvious flaws in university education ought to be the main priority.

V

An attempt to sum up would be premature. The play is not quite over. The commission report was full of loopholes and elliptic or contradictory statements which would cause the real character of the proposed system to depend on implementation. The minister of education has had the report reviewed by a group of members of parliament from the four main political parties. They have proposed some modifications or clarifications, and there may be further changes in the government bill or by the final parliament vote. But, though we must end with this note of uncertainty, it is worth nothing that the Commission report and the debate which followed still have much to say about the state of university autonomy in Sweden.

Epilogue: Reflections on a Worn-out Model

Charles Frankel

THE SIGNIFICANCE OF THE CHAPTER in the history of higher education which began more than ten years ago at Berkeley is still a matter of dispute, but of one thing there can be little question: it has left the higher educational community in a state of passivity, its imagination focused not on the problems of possibilities of the future, but on the unpleasantnesses of the recent past. In the public memory, the shouting and the fires have been put away as essentially evanescent phenomena, temporary in their causes and effects. In the minds of most university teachers and administrators, however, something very like a civil war has taken place, and they are living through its aftermath.

Is the analogy with civil war inflated? To be sure. The tendency to grandiosity was a not inconsiderable element in making the uproars of the past decade as loud as they were. The campus revolution was not honest-to-god. It was a charade, a protected piece of theater, a game. But there are games people play from which they never recover. The game played in colleges and universities during the last ten years was a passionate game, one into which people threw themselves entirely and in which they thought their basic principles and honor were involved, a game from which they emerged exhausted and exposed, having revealed themselves to others and, worst of all, to themselves. It is not surprising, after this experience, that the academic world is obsessed with its traumas, and not in a mood to come actively or even intellectually to grips with its problems.

The present "calm," indeed, is better than the violence that preceeded it, but that is about all that can be said in its favor. To begin with, it is less than universal. Toronto, Berlin, and Oxford, to take some not inconspicuous institutions, are still places where violent disruptions take place. They occur, too, in the United States. The calm, where it exists, is in the main the calm of numbness. Small sit-ins or brief ones are commonplace occurrences. Militant students can still keep people they do not like from speaking on their campuses. University presidents are verbally abused in public in ways unimaginable before the Berkeley uprising. People simply do not see the point of making an issue of such matters. That such a situation can be described as a return to "normal" suggests what the last ten years have done to university standards.

But perhaps the more important story is being told in developments that do not catch the public eye and hardly catch, it would seem, even the eye of the academic world. Consider the following phenomena: grade inflation; the progressive elimination of foreign language requirements from the curricula; the steady dilution even of mild distribution requirements; the regularity with which curricular reforms turn out to involve simply less reading and writing; the living conditions in dormitories, from which universities have almost entirely withdrawn their supervisory authority although they continue to pay the bills; the doubletalk about quotas that are not quotas and apartheid that is not apartheid.

One may approve or disapprove of one or another of these developments. Not one, however, has been the product of a serious discussion of fundamentals; not one has been the product of a faculty initiative. They are decisions of expediency, made not out of conviction but out of dispiritedness. They betoken an indisposition to exercise authority and to lead, an absence of confidence, of will, of thought, a depth of demoralization which, more than any other single matter, endangers the health and autonomy of higher education. Not even the lack of money is as serious. The professoriate, the permanent citizenry of universities, faces its future with its sense of community in tatters and its principles in disarray.

There could hardly be a worse time for it to choose to rest on its scars. For future issues are likely to have as profound an effect on colleges and universities as those through which we have just lived.

The issues that lie ahead, in their net thrust and direction, have to do, I believe, with the mounting inadequacy of the standard model of higher education that we have inherited. It is the model of the four-year college, sheltering people between the ages of seventeen and twenty-two, and joined to a university network designed to provide advanced training to a more limited number of people. According to the model, the faculties of such institutions, both college and university, are composed of scholar-teachers, most of whom are engaged in significant research. These facilities exercise sole de facto authority over the issuance of certificates and degrees, and over the selection of their professional colleagues.

In the British and American traditions, this institution has always been thought to have (particularly at its undergraduate level) a moral and civic function probably even more important than its intellectual one. "Piety," "virtue," were the words that used to be used to describe what colleges should teach. Now that the clergy has lost its authority to fill these words with a content that everyone will accept, we use more elastic ones like "leadership," "social concern," "democratic" or "humanistic" values, or, most stretchable of all, "socialization." The moral and civil function, however, has remained fundamental, and it has been connected with two others —the effort, through the college, to guide the student to that field in which he can combine the best use of his talents and the greatest service to society, and the effort to introduce the student to the world of learning in such a way that he sees it not simply as the plaything of scholars but as a vocation in the service of God or Man. This conception of the moral and civic purpose of higher education, and its role in expanding individual opportunity, has principally been behind the American effort to open the colleges to as many qualified people as possible, and to take the word "qualified" as standing for character and motivation, and not simply, or even mainly, for intellectual promise.

The classic model of higher education, however, has been a hybrid since the time approximately a century ago, that the continental model of the graduate school, devoted to the intensive advancement of scholarship and the learned professions, was superimposed on the Anglo-Saxon model of the undergraduate college. Neither the graduate training of undergraduate teachers nor the prestige and promotion systems in which they work habituate them to see themselves as counselors or tutors in the virtues. The increasing specialization and sophistication of the fields of learning, and the more uncompromising demands for precise skills made by the economy, provide other strong reasons why higher education at all levels has been forced to attach more importance to sheer intellectual performance. Actual practice has been a compromise between these two functions (not to speak of others), and the model of a good higher education has also been a compromise, as suggested by phrases like "the well-rounded man," descriptive of its putative goal. Nor do I say this to complain. Any educational model not the work of zealots will recognize the diversity of human interests to be served, and will need to strike some balance among them.

Finally, because it has been perceived to have a transcendent moral as well as intellectual purpose, which external intrusions can damage, the model university has possessed a quasi-feudal status. Like a manorial estate or a town with a charter of established privileges, it has had a hierarchical status system, parental and governmental responsibilities towards its members, its own codes of conduct, and its own not inconsiderable sanctions to aid in their enforcement. Moreover, even when it has been entirely tax-supported, it has enjoyed, within broad limits, autonomy from the government and the courts.

This, of course, is a *model.* The majority of American institutions officially accredited as schools of postsecondary instruction were not more than faint approximations of it even before 1964. Nevertheless, what I have described has been, I think, the effective *norm.* The pressure was on institutions to try to live up to it: if they differed from it, they were felt to be, and felt themselves to be, less than full-fledged members of the higher educational world. In the fifties and early sixties, for example, a long procession of two-year teachers' colleges was converted into four-year liberal arts colleges in deference to this conception of the normal and desirable.

Is this model adequate? To recover the power of self-direction, it seems to me, the higher educational community has to ask itself, deliberately and in the context of a sustained and controlled discussion and debate, what parts of this model can and should be preserved, what parts discarded, and what parts supplemented by quite different ideas of the normal and desirable.

I shall have to be brief, almost telegraphic, in suggesting my own beginning thoughts about these questions.

The Late-Adolescent School

The notion that the predominant norm for higher education should be the college and university for students seventeen to twenty-five must almost certainly go by the board. A college education is no longer a rare commodity. For many middle- and upper-class students it has been converted from a prerogative into a duty, somewhere in between unintelligible, boring, and onerous. The signs grow that many are looking for alternatives to it. Moreover, for a long time, our higher educational institutions have had more married students, older students, and students working full time on the outside than the traditional model has supposed. Most of these people, however, have been in municipal institutions and community colleges that rate, in the traditional perspective, as not-quite-really colleges. In this way the ratings within our educational system have given implicit endorsement to prevailing forms of social and economic stratification.

The inherited norm seems to me bad both for the universities and for equality of opportunity. Why should the institutions with greatest access to distinguished scholarship and advanced research facilities be so largely restricted to students in the years seventeen to twenty-five, a considerable number of whom have only the vaguest idea of why they are where they are? The rearrangement of scholarship programs, living arrangements, and curricula to provide, say, one third of the places in residential universities to people of twenty-five, thirty, or older might represent a more efficient and economical use of expensive resources, a fairer distribution of educational opportunity, and a stabilizing and energizing change in the composition of student bodies.

The effects of the traditional model are visible, and their desirability challengeable. In seeking greater equality of opportunity, the policy of the colleges has been to seek to offer hitherto disadvantaged seventeen-year-olds an opportunity to participate in that idyll of youth which, in imagination, the colleges have offered to middle- and upper-class young people. But the chance to choose people who have held jobs and demonstrated, by their performance and the efforts they have made to continue their education, that they have the requisite equipment and motivation, offers a surer way of finding the right people, and strikes at a central reason for the maldistribution of educational achievement. The burden that poverty and deprivation puts on the individual is that he usually takes longer to discover his opportunities and abilities. The chance to reenter the educational system at an older age is thus of particular value to the disadvantaged.

The Norm of Uninterrupted Schooling

Closely connected to the traditional notion of colleges and universities as the preserves of the young is the idea that ideally an education ought not to be interrupted. The departures from this ideal increase: the undergraduate leave of absence; the year between college and graduate or professional school; the periods of retraining required by industry; the return of married women to school and the job market when their children are grown.

But the change in the norm of uninterrupted schooling is called for, I suspect, by more than such trends. A generation ago colleges were populated mainly by students in two categories: the children of the privileged, who knew they were making the friends and learning the manners appropriate to people of station; and the upwardly mobile, jealous for position and eager not to throw their opportunities away. For both groups the parental disciplines of the classic college were more than bearable. They knew why they were going to school, knew that they had to go through this mill to be considered as having arrived at adulthood, and found their status as people at a halfway station both intelligible and agreeable.

This inner reserve from which the authority of the college as a communal political entity was largely drawn is now depleted. The greater affluence and changed social standards of our present society have brought to the colleges a large number of students who do not regard themselves as the children of a privileged elite (although many of them are), but who are not on the way up either. They do not expect to improve on their father's position, and many would hope not to have to live as he has. For such students, a college education of the old style can seem like a sustained period of hanging in the void. They see themselves as being in college only because of parental and social pressure. Only those with active intellectual interests are likely to know why they are where they are, and these often find themselves frustrated by the diversions, distractions, and flimflam of an institution in which they are a minority. Combined with the possibility of easy reentry into universities at later ages, a policy of allowing young people to leave, removing from them the pressure of the normal expectation that they stay, should help create university populations with many fewer conscripts. We would do well to replace the norm of uninterrupted schooling by the norm of permanent and recurrent education, joined to the provision of jobs and training experiences for the age group seventeen to twenty-five.

The Civic Function of Higher Education

One reason for the special status of the "normal" liberal arts college is that it was traditionally thought to be the major, and almost the only, purveyor of secular moral instruction beyond the high school. But this thought has long since been bypassed by events. For better or worse, mass circulation magazines, particularly those aimed at the richer 50 percent of the population which has had an education beyond the secondary level, exercise a powerful influence in this realm. They are, in the French expression, "*l'école parallèle.*" Equally to the point, and perhaps more encouraging, are developments in public television and the public program activities of agencies like the National Endowment for the Humanities and the National Endowment for the Arts, which can, if sustained and enlarged, serve major educational roles. The community college and adult education have also removed the monopoly of the liberal arts college.

Still to be fully exploited for the purposes of civic education are the graduate and professional schools, although I believe the latter are less to be faulted than the former. It is odd to announce, at the undergraduate level, the glories of the humanities and the liberation to be gained from the study of the pure sciences, and then, at the graduate level, to give next to no attention to the larger social, human, and even intellectual significance of the specialized subjects studied. The notion that "general education" is an undergraduate concern, and that a graduate school is professional, not liberal, is one of the expressions of the inherited hybrid model of higher educations—Anglo-Saxon at the base, continental at the top.

"Elitist" and "Democratic" Higher Education

The distribution of the function of civic education more generously throughout the higher educational system makes possible another adjustment—the unapologetic concentration by some colleges and universities on training that 10 to 15 percent of the population equipped to make intellectual contributions to the arts, sciences, and learned professions. The present drift is relentlessly towards homogenization and destruction of the most precious of all the characteristics of American higher education, its diversity. One reason for this drift is the dominance of the single model of the proper higher educational institution. It rapidly becomes an all-purpose model, making all distinctions fuzzy.

The inevitable question is whether the American public, with its egalitarian perspective, will be prepared to accept a postsecondary educational system in which clear distinctions exist between different kinds of institution. The partial answer is that it has been doing so for a long time. Another part of the answer may be that an educational system offering a broader range of alternatives, operating under an ampler notion of the normal and desirable, and less exclusively designed for the young, would be a more democratic system, more usable by those hitherto shut out.

After all, the problem of numbers is probably lessening. The issue for the future is not to meet the steadily growing demand from one age group for an education basically conceived after one model. The figure of 50 percent, which represents the approximate present proportion of youth enrolled in institutions of postsecondary education, may well be the high-water mark. The problem for the future is to find the right 50 percent, and to provide the ways and means for sorting them out and directing them to the school best suited for them.

The Teachers

In this setting the continued idolatry of the Ph.D. and the image of the teacher as also a productive research worker make for profound trouble. The members of teaching staffs of postsecondary institutions number, I believe, over 400,000. It is a transparent pretense that most of them are, or should be, engaged in significant research. It is merely an invitation to them, indeed, to look down on themselves when they perform their central task as teachers. Indeed, even in the most noted institutions the quality and importance of research are spotty. Is teaching less important, less intellectually demanding, less an art to be mastered or an achievement to be admired and rewarded?

Moreover, the coming of mass higher education, together with the confrontationist spirit of the decade since Berkeley, has altered the traditions of informal self-government within faculties. Although professors live within inherited traditions that are consensual and deferential, giving a central place to the individual's quality of work, the pressures for unionization mount, as do the centralizing and standardizing tendencies turned loose by the courts and legislatures. If the autonomy and tone of the higher educational system as a whole are to be kept, there must probably be a group of institutions from which collective bargaining remains excluded.

Higher Educational Autonomy

The classic model of higher education bids fair to become increasingly inapplicable in one respect in which it is indispensable that it be preserved. This is the assignment of autonomy to institutions of advanced learning. Colleges and universities are being pulled steadily into the central legal system. Their decisions are being made for them by the courts, legislatures, and bureaucracies. This is only in part because they are all more dependent on public funds. It is also a consequence of the fact that, thanks in good part to the decade of Berkeley, the internal governance of universities has been conceded to be a proper field for close external supervision. The cries of oppression have been heard; that scourge of injustice, the Nixon administration, has come to the rescue. Universities receive less money than they used to from the federal government but, in recompense, they receive more paternal guidance and protection from sin.

The issue is the universities' basic ordering of their long-term obligations. Whatever the higher educational system's capacity or incapacity substantially to correct major social injustices by its own direct efforts alone, surely part of its mission is not to perpetuate injustices in its own domain. But the remedies adopted must be proportionate to the wrongs to be cured and consistent with the universities' other obligations. In relation to racial and sexual discrimination, to come to particulars, the question must be asked whether public outcry, changed attitudes, and heightened sensitivity to the issues of people within the higher educational community will not in most circumstances be sufficient to set things right, without adding the tender ministrations of government bureaucracies.

Practices like the HEW guidelines, which require university officials to explain their behavior to suspicious functionaries and to work under presumptions of guilt, are nevertheless justified, it is said on their behalf, by their purposes. After all, they seek to root out racial and sexual discrimination, not Communists. But even in the name of the best of causes, should we be prepared to establish the habit in government of reading universities' files, and giving its advice-with-sanctions in regard to the selection of students and faculty? The cost can be university autonomy, and that autonomy is the indispensable prerequisite for the authority of the university and the performance of its unique role in a free society.

The questions shrugged off while blunderbuss methods of achieving social purposes have been used are extraordinary. Do we think it a good idea to domesticate, in universities, the habit of obedient conformity to political and bureaucratic pressures? What will universities be like after a generation of this sort of thing? And what assurance do we have that a future government will not use this power of inspection and punishment conceded to it to promote causes for which the members of universities will have less sympathy? The free speech revolt, the war protests, the Movement were not animated by trust of governmental authority. What they have accomplished is the strengthening of the power of the most conservative government in fifty years to send its inspectors into universities.

It is an accomplishment within higher educational institutions which goes hand in hand with the growth of the bloc system of governance and the adversary system of administration and justice. The vetoes have been multiplied, the power to decide and act reduced. No doubt the older model of a university, framed to stand *in loco parentis* for adolescent students, needs considerable modification; but the model of a university in which teachers and students are organized into blocs and treated as though they were competing social classes is not an improvement. It is laughable in itself and runs at cross-purposes to the effort to make teaching and learning a cooperative process.

I believe that restoration of more informal and consensual procedures of academic consultation and governance is indispensable to the reactivation of effective university self-government. In the larger political community it makes sense to provide elaborate procedures to insure that individuals are able to protect themselves against exploitation, deception, and oppression by others, particularly the powerful. But the presumption that teaching and studying ought to be carried on with the fear of *homo lupus* always present has never characterized civilized educational practice. It is merely the ritualistic one, written into the formal rules and procedures—which does not prevent it from blocking the processes of self-government.

These reflections bring us back to the circumambient issues with which we began—the higher educational community's present state of mind and morale and, more broadly, the recipient culture within which the discussion and conduct of higher education goes on. In the years since Berkeley we have had the chance to see some of that culture's special and disturbing faults. To the extent that they persist, the outlook is dim for a reasoned solution of many of the problems which confront colleges and universities.

When I think back to the campus troubles, what rises to the center of my mind is the sense they gave one of being caught inside something with a momentum of its own. One's colleagues, one's students seemed all to be reading from script's prepared in advance. One's university went to its fate as though hypnotized, sleepwalking over the precipice. Even now, at some years' remove, the impression that events followed a set path is fortified, not weakened. The degree to which the stories that unfolded on different campuses were similar is remarkable. A Platonic idea of a campus revolution migrated from institution to institution, at each place issuing its commands and finding its obedient soldiers. Even differences in national educational traditions only slightly affected the relentless unoriginality of behavior. The slogans, alternatives, factionalisms, and compromises rehearsed at Berkeley and Columbia were rehearsed as well at Florence, Copenhagen, and Amsterdam.

What was it that gave events this headless momentum and common direction? I think it was the environing culture of higher education—the eyes that interpreted what was happening, the ears that heard the words, the mouths that formed the responses. The common culture took what was happening, read its own prepared meaning into it, and gave the play back to the actors to take their cues. "All of us," wrote Raymond Aron about his experiences in Paris in 1968, "played a role in that period. I begin with myself, I freely say so, I played Tocqueville, which is not without a touch of the ridiculous, but others played Saint-Just, Robespierre or Lenin, which, all things considered, was even more ridiculous." [1] Perhaps people in Paris were somewhat more aware whom they were impersonating than were people in America but, if so, that is the principal difference.

The press is part, but only part, of the process by which events are kneaded into their stereotypes. The journalists come to a campus in trouble, listen to both sides, which is their job, give a hearing, and, with it, significance and legitimacy to groups that have been obscure before, and thus change the balance of power and authority. More, they particularize the stories, telling their who, what, when, and where, all in the singular, and encouraging the misapprehension that what is taking place is an event local in its causes and manageable if local reforms are made. Worst of all, however, they are in a hurry, they must make their deadlines, they are only human, and there is nothing like an ideology à la mode to help put a story together and give it a meaning. So the press and the media line up the disputants in the university: conservatives versus progressives, old versus young, powerful versus helpless, selfish versus idealistic. What can each man do but play his part?

Moreover, the ideology fades into the ideology that has spread into most of the empty spaces in the contemporary academic mind. Words have ritualistic uses. "Change," "innovation," "experimentation" are treated as automatically eulogistic terms. In this context all ambiguities in political nomenclature disappear as well. "Liberal" means, quite simply, the espousal of the new and therefore the better. "Radical" means the same thing, but with more impatience or perhaps more sincerity. "Conservative," by contrast, means hankering after the old and the worse—an attitude, needless to say, which is inexplicable in an intelligent man unless he is selfish and protecting his privileges. Once this vocabulary is sprinkled like powder over all issues, some stirring gymnastics are possible. One remains a liberal though one would deny the right to free speech to those with whom one disagrees; or one is labeled conservative because one does not think curricula

---

[1] Raymond Aron, *La révolution introuvable: reflexions sur les événements de mai* (Paris: Fayard, 1968), p. 33.

should be redesigned to introduce the insights of the encounter movement. No issue is examined on the merits. Each is pegged into the timetable of history.

And history, of course, is like a well-trained regiment that moves in a straight line across a field. This presumption, too, colors the meaning of ideas and events. Thus, if one opposes racial discrimination, one ought also to oppose discrimination of rights and functions between young and old or students and teachers. If one is of the opinion that redistribution of income is the wave of the future, one ought also to favor fewer classroom hours and more field trips, for that too is the wave of the future. The basic paradox, said a writer in *Le Monde*, describing the Venice meeting of the International Council on the Future of the University, is that so many of these scholars are liberals in politics and conservatives in education. Whether the conservatism amounted to more than a desire to preserve liberal principles of free speech and independent inquiry the author did not say. History will not put up with two-facedness.

The protection and reform of higher education will thus require something more than only specific programs. It will require a professoriate more concentrated on its common tasks and obligations, more ironically self-aware of what it has contributed to its own troubles, and better able to protect itself against its own vulgarisms. It is with this overarching objective in mind —the attainment of a new sense of shared purpose, the definition of the common principles of intellectual integrity and professional discipline around which the universities of the future ought to be built—that the International Council on the Future of the University was formed. There is a need for thought, specific and substantive, about the shape that higher education should take in a world that is going to be radically different from that in which universities in the old model emerged. But there is a need, even more, to demonstrate that, whatever the forces of "History," whatever the pressures to political factionalism, there are men and women in universities who do not make up their minds about what is true by asking which faction will be served. These are the people without whom universities and science and scholarship lose all claim to having any special authority.

The council exists to sustain them, to help them to find one another, and to make it possible for them to take counsel together across the borders about the future of institutions of higher learning. Some will be politically conservative, others will wish very radical changes in society. Some will believe that universities must help in bringing about such changes. Others will think that universities should be sheltered from such demands. There is a place for all of them in the council, as there should be a place for all of them in any free university. The sine qua non is that they believe that universities have a supreme commitment to seek an independent nonpolitical truth and to govern themselves accordingly.

Notes on Contributors

ALEXANDER M. BICKEL, before his death, had a distinguished career as a constitutional lawyer. A graduate of City College of New York, he attended Harvard Law School, subsequently serving as clerk to Justice Felix Frankfurter on the U.S. Supreme Court. A professor of law at Yale Law School, much of his scholarship, including *The Supreme Court and the Idea of Progress*, lent him the reputation of being a legal conservative. A critic of the Warren court, in politics he was a liberal Democrat. His thoughts, speeches, and writings were addressed to some of the foremost issues of his day and resounded with profound impact at the highest levels of the government whose constitution he interpreted so impressively.

MOGENS BLEGVAD has been professor of philosophy at the University of Copenhagen since 1964. He was librarian at the Royal Library from 1949 to 1960 and lectured at the Danish School of Librarianship from 1960 to 1964. He has been chairman of the editorial board of the Danish Yearbook of Philosophy since 1964, and was president of the Society for Philosophy from 1960 to 1970. He has been a Fellow of the Royal Danish Academy of Arts and Sciences since 1973.

FRANÇOIS BOURRICAUD is professor of sociology in the Faculty of Letters of the University of Paris, and formerly professor at the University of Nanterre (1966–1968). He served as special consultant in the cabinet of A. Peyrefitte in 1968 on problems of French higher education. His published works include *Eléments pour une sociologie de l'action, Esquisse d'une theorie de l'autorité*, and *Pouvoir et société dans le Pérou contemporain*.

ZELMAN COWEN, an Australian jurist and legal scholar, is currently vice-chancellor of the University of Queensland. A Rhodes scholar (1940), he was a Fellow of Oriel College, Oxford, and served as professor of public law and dean of the Faculty of Law at the University of Melbourne between 1951 and 1966. His publications include *Essays on the Law of Evidence* (1956), *Federal Jurisdiction in Australia* (1959), *Sir John Latham and Other Papers* (1965), and *The Private Man* (A. B. C. Boyer Lectures, 1969).

HANS DAALDER is a Dutch political scientist specializing in Dutch and British politics, comparative political development, Marxism and imperialism, and legislative behavior. Receiving his doctorate from the University of Amsterdam, he has been professor of political science at Leiden University since 1963.

291

RALF DAHRENDORF, German sociologist and prominent member of the Free Democratic party, is now director of the London School of Economics. Formerly professor of sociology at the universities of Hamburg, Tübingen, and Constance, he served between 1970 and 1974 as member of the Commission of the European Community. His many publications include *Class and Class Conflict in Industrial Society* (1957) and *Essays in the Theory of Society* (1968).

SØREN EGEROD has been professor of East Asian languages at the University of Copenhagen since 1958. He is also director of the Scandinavian Institute of Asian Studies and former dean of the Faculty of Letters of the University of Copenhagen. He has been a visiting professor at Columbia University and the University of Michigan. He is currently president of the board of Danish chapter of the PEN Club. He was knighted by the King of Denmark in 1966.

CHARLES FRANKEL, chairman of the Board of Trustees of the International Council on the Future of the University, is Old Dominion Professor of Philosophy and Public Affairs at Columbia University. A graduate of Columbia College, he received his Ph.D. from Columbia in 1946. His many public activities include service as Assistant Secretary of State for Educational and Cultural Affairs (1965–1967) and current chairmanship of the Commission on the Quality, Cost, and Financing of Education in the State of New York. Among his books are *The Faith of Reason* (1948), *The Democratic Prospect* (1962), *The Neglected Aspect of Foreign Affairs* (1966), and *The Pleasures of Philosophy* (1971).

CHARLES HANLY is professor of philosophy at the University of Toronto. A member of the Canadian Psychoanalytic Society, he has a private practice in psychoanalysis. His publications in the field of education and public policy include *Who Pays? University Financing in Ontario and Mental Health in Ontario*. He served for four years as executive vice-chairman of the Ontario Confederation of University Faculty Associations, and currently he is an elected faculty member of the Governing Council of the University of Toronto, serving as chairman of the Planning and Resources Committee.

STEEN LETH JEPPESEN has been professor of economics at the Danish School of Public Administration since 1974. He was a lecturer in economics at the University of Copenhagen from 1967 to 1969 and a senior lecturer in the Institute of Social Sciences at the same university from 1969 to 1974. He is currently a member of the Danish Government's Central Board of Education.

ICHIRO KATO is professor of law at the University of Tokyo. Born in 1922 in Tokyo, he graduated from the University of Tokyo in 1943 and served on the faculty since 1948. He was president of the University of Tokyo between 1969 and 1973.

SEYMOUR MARTIN LIPSET, professor of government and social relations at Harvard University since 1966, received his doctorate from Columbia University and subsequently was professor of sociology and director of the Institute of International Studies at the University of California in Berkeley. He has served as a member of the Board of Foreign Scholarships of the Department of State. His publications include *Agrarian Socialism* (1950), *Political Man* (1960), and *The First New Nation* (1963). He is the author and editor of many studies dealing with students, student politics, and universities, including *Students in Revolt* (1969).

RICHARD LÖWENTHAL is professor of international relations at the Free University of Berlin. Trained at the universities of Berlin and Heidelberg in the 1920s, he left Germany as a political exile in 1935, working as a journalist in France and England. A student of Soviet and Communist affairs, he has been associated with St. Anthony's College, Oxford, and the Russian Research Center at Harvard. He has been actively involved in German and international discussion of university reform and student unrest, and is one of three cochairmen of the *Bund Freiheit der Wissenschaft*, an organization of German scholars concerned with the protection of higher learning. His publications include *Ernst Reuter: Eine politische Biographie* (coauthored with Willy Brandt, 1957), *World Communism: The Disintegration of a Secular Faith* (1966), and *Hochschule fur die Demokratie* (1971).

JAMES MCAULEY is professor of English at the University of Tasmania. Educated at Fort Street High School and Sydney University, he was the founding editor of *Quadrant* magazine and since 1963 its coeditor. He is also vice-president of the Australian Association for Cultural Freedom and chairman of Peace with Freedom, a body concerned with political problems in the field of education. His publications include (poetry) *Under Aldebaran* (1956), *A Vision of Ceremony* (1956), *Captain Quiros* (1965), and *Collected Poems* (1971); (prose) *The End of Modernity* (1959), and *The Grammar of the Real* (in preparation with Oxford University Press). He has twice served as chairman of the Professorial Board of the University of Tasmania, with periods as acting vice-chancellor.

DONALD MACRAE has been professor of sociology at the London School of Economics since 1961. He has been visiting professor at the University of California (1959) and a Fellow at the Center for Advanced Studies in the Behavioral Sciences, Stanford (1967). He was editor of the *British Journal of Sociology* from its inception until 1965. His published works include *Sociology and Society* (1960).

BERNICE MARTIN has lectured in sociology at Bedford College, University of London, for twelve years. She has studied the process of educational policy-making in England and is currently engaged in a sociological analysis of progressive ideologies. Among her publications is "Progressive Education versus the Working Class," which appeared in *Critical Quarterly*, Winter 1971.

DAVID MARTIN is professor of sociology at the London School of Economics. Much of his published work has concerned the relationship between religious and secular spheres of human experience. His books include *Pacifism: A Historical and Sociological Study* (1965), *A Sociology of English Religion* (1967), and *Tracts Against the Times* (1973). He is a regular contributor to the *Times Literary Supplement, Encounter,* and the *New Statesman.*

THOMAS NIPPERDEY has been professor of modern and contemporary history at the University of Munich since 1972. Before that he taught at the Free University of Berlin for four years. A founder of the *Bund Freiheit der Wissenschaft,* he currently is one of its three cochairmen. His publications include *Die Organisation der Deutschen Parteien vor 1918* (1961). Professor Nipperdey is a member of the Social Democratic party.

PAUL SEABURY is professor of political science at the University of California in Berkeley. He received his Ph.D. from Columbia University in 1953. A former chairman of the national executive committee of Americans for Democratic Action, he has served as member and vice-chairman of the Board of Foreign Scholarships. He is vice-chairman of University Centers for Rational Alternatives, an organization of scholars concerned with the quality of higher education. His published works include *The Wilhelmstrasse: A Study of German Diplomacy under the Nazi Regime* (1954), *Power, Freedom, and Diplomacy* (1963), *The Rise and Decline of the Cold War* (1967), and *The Foreign Policy of the United States* (1973). He is currently serving on the foreign policy task force of the Democratic National Committee.

EDWARD SHILS, the editor of *Minerva,* is professor of social thought and sociology at the University of Chicago. He is serving concurrently as Fellow of Peterhouse, Cambridge, and is honorary professor in the Department of Anthropology at University College, Cambridge. Formerly a reader in sociology at the London School of Economics, and Fellow of Kings College, Cambridge, Professor Shils is the author of many works in intellectual history and sociology, including *The Torment of Secrecy* (1956); *The Intellectual between Tradition and Modernity: The Indian Liberation* (1961); *Towards a General Theory of Action* (1951) (with Talcott Parsons); and *The Intellectuals and the Powers* (1972).

KRISTER WAHLBÄCK is associate professor of international politics at the Swedish Council for Social Science Research. He has taught in the political science department of the Univeresity of Stockholm since 1965. His dissertation on Finnish-Swedish relations, 1937–1940, was published in 1964. His later publications include books and articles on Swedish foreign policy and Finnish and French politics. He spent 1974 as Senior Fulbright Scholar at Harvard, Berkeley, and Johns Hopkins School of Advanced International Studies in Washington, D.C.

INDEX

Index